Brian Fleming Research & Learning Library
Ministry of Education
Ministry of Training, Colleges & Universities
900 Bay St. 13th Floor, Mowat Block
Toronto, ON M7A 1L2

Guiding Change
in
Special
Education

This book is dedicated to Ms. Jane Hauser, U.S. Office of Special Education Programs, and to our many EMSTAC Linking Agents—trailblazers all.

Guiding Change in Special Education

How to Help Schools With New Ideas and Practices

Ronald G. Havelock
James L. Hamilton

Foreword by Maurice McInerney

CORWIN PRESS
A Sage Publications Company
Thousand Oaks, California

Copyright © 2004 by Corwin Press.

All rights reserved. When forms and sample documents are included, their use is authorized only by educators, local school sites, and/or noncommercial entities who have purchased the book. Except for that usage, no part of this book may be reproduced or utilized in any form or by any means, electronic or mechanical, including photocopying, recording, or by any information storage and retrieval system, without permission in writing from the publisher.

The development of this book was supported in part by a contract from the Office of Special Education Programs, U.S. Department of Education. Opinions expressed herein do not necessarily reflect those of the U.S. Department of Education or offices within it.

For information:

Corwin Press
A Sage Publications Company
2455 Teller Road
Thousand Oaks, California 91320
www.corwinpress.com

Sage Publications Ltd.
6 Bonhill Street
London EC2A 4PU
United Kingdom

Sage Publications India Pvt. Ltd.
B-42, Panchsheel Enclave
Post Box 4109
New Delhi 110 017 India

Printed in the United States of America

Library of Congress Cataloging-in-Publication Data

Havelock, Ronald G.
 Guiding change in special education: How to help schools with new ideas and practices/prepared by Ronald G. Havelock, James L. Hamilton.
   p. cm.
 Includes bibliographical references and index.
 ISBN 0-7619-3964-4 (cloth)—ISBN 0-7619-3965-2 (pbk.)
  1. Special education—United States. 2. School improvement programs—United States. I. Hamilton, James L. (James Lee) II. Title.
 LC3981.H38 2004
 371.9´0973—dc22

                 2003016582

03 04 05 06 10 9 8 7 6 5 4 3 2 1

Acquisitions Editor:	Robert D. Clouse
Editorial Assistant:	Jingle Vea
Production Editor:	Melanie Birdsall
Copy Editor:	Ruth Saavedra
Typesetter:	C&M Digitals (P) Ltd.
Proofreader:	Cheryl Rivard
Indexer:	Julie Grayson
Cover Designer:	Michael Dubowe
Graphic Designer:	Lisa Miller

Contents

Foreword	xiii
Maurice McInerney	
Acknowledgments	xvii
About the Authors	xix
Introduction	xxi
Case Study	CS 1
Stage 1. Care: Establishing the Need for Action	1
Someone Must Care Enough to Make It All Worthwhile	2
A Three-Step Model of Change: Unfreeze-Move-Refreeze	3
Unfreezing: Often the First Task of a Linking Agent	4
Moving: Only Possible if There Is Openness to Change	4
Refreezing: Making Sure That What Comes In Stays In	4
How School Systems Show (and Don't Show) That They Are in Trouble	5
When Everything Seems Fine	6
When Concerns Are All Over the Lot	7
When Concerns Are Not What They Seem	7
When Concerns Are Very Intense	8
Inside Versus Outside Forces	10
Inside Forces	10
Unforeseen Inside Events	11
Outside Forces	12
Linking Agent as Connector and Orchestrator of Forces	15
Whose Responsibility? The Value Issues in Helping	15
Care: Summary	17
Stage 2. Relate: Building a Relationship	19
Build a Good Relationship With the People You Are Trying to Help	20
Relating to the Primary Group	21
Diagram Your School or School District as a Social Network	23

Linker Configurations	26
The General Education Teacher as Linker	26
The Special Education Teacher as Linker	27
School Counselor as Linker	28
The School Principal as Linker	29
Special Linker Role at the District Level	29
Linkers at Other Levels, Other Places	30
University-Based Linkers	31
With Whom Should the Linker Work?	34
Relating to the Larger Social Environment	34
What Is Your Relationship at the Very Beginning?	36
Inside or Outside?	39
Managing Initial Encounters	41
The Ideal Relationship	43
Danger Signals	45
How to Size Up Your Relationship	47
Final Word on Relationship Building	47
Relate: Summary	48
Stage 3. Examine: Understanding the Problem	**49**
Turn Cares Into Problems You Can Solve	50
Making a Good Diagnosis	52
The Entry Phase	52
Do a Quick Take	52
Reach an Initial Conclusion	52
Perform a Quick Fix	53
Separate the Problem From the Solution	53
The Data Collection Phase	53
Lay Out Your Taxonomy	53
Think System	54
Assemble the Data	54
The Analytic Phase	54
Rate the Data and Prioritize the Real Problems	55
Respect the Obvious	55
Beware of the Obvious	55
Identify the Opportunities	56
Collaborate on the Diagnostic Process	56
Adopt a Linking Posture	56
Search for Underlying Causes	57
Rethink and Rework the Diagnosis as You Go Forward	57
Making a Diagnostic Inventory	58
A Definition of the Domain	58
Classification and Identification of Students for Special Education Services	60
Case Management	60
Equalization of Opportunity	61
Access to the General Education Curriculum	62
Special Education Infrastructure	63

Systemic Analysis: Understanding the System	63
Exercise in System Analysis	64
A Data Collection Process	66
Low-Profile Approaches to Collecting Diagnostic Data	66
High-Profile Approaches: Acquiring Systematic Diagnostic Information	69
A Set of Rating Dimensions	71
Rating Dimensions (for Any Area)	71
Creating a Diagnostic Matrix/Checklist That Points to Solutions	72
Integrating Diagnosis With the Other Stages	72
Some Pitfalls in Diagnostic Analysis	72
Examine: Summary	74

Stage 4. Acquire: Seeking and Finding Relevant Resources — 77

The Money Theory of Change	78
Educational Systems as Economic Entities	79
What Is Wrong With the Money Theory?	80
Hard Money, Soft Money	80
Innovating on Hard Money	81
Innovating on Soft Money: How New Money Is Supposed to Change Things	81
Pump Priming: How Soft Money Is Supposed to Work	82
The Linker's Role With Respect to Money	85
The People Theory of Change	86
Good People to Run the Project	87
Modelers of the Change and the Process of Change	92
People as Experts and Expert Information Services	92
Acquiring and Using Experts Wisely	95
What's Wrong With the People Theory?	95
Search the Internet for People Resources	96
The Knowledge Theory of Change	97
A Knowledge Acquisition Strategy	98
How to Build a Better Awareness of the Resource Universe	100
Homing In on a Specific Problem and Solution	101
Acquiring Materials (= Packaged Knowledge)	104
Comparing Alternative Materials	105
Using Electronic Resources	106
Building a Permanent Capacity for Resource Acquisition	111
Helping a System Learn More About Resources and Resource Retrieval	111
Acquire: Summary	112

Stage 5. Try: Moving From Knowledge to Action — 115

Giving a Fair Trial to a Well-Considered Solution	116
Choose	118

Assemble and Order the Relevant Findings	119
Derive Implications From the Research Knowledge Base	120
Generate a Range of Solution Ideas	120
Pretrial Feasibility Testing: Comparing and Selecting the Best	123
Degree of Benefit Promised	123
Validity and Reliability of the Promise	124
Comparability of Need	124
Comparability of Setting	124
Resources Required	124
Resistance Factors	124
Compatibility With Past and Present Innovations	124
Diffusibility	125
Doability	126
Showability	126
Adapt	126
Respect the Developers and Minimize Redevelopment	127
Repackage and Relabel	128
Plan the Implementation	128
Importance of a Written Plan	128
Importance of a Shared Plan	129
Importance of a Flexible Plan	129
Components of a Good Plan	129
Accepting Risk	131
Overcoming Inertia	132
Training	132
Timing	132
Accepting Stumbles	133
Recognizing and Managing Resistance	133
Protecting the Trial and the Integrity of the Test	133
Connecting the Trial to the Outside: Publicity	133
Evaluate	134
What Is the Process?	134
How Can You Evaluate Process?	135
Preserve Documentation	135
Keep a Diary	135
Use the Written Plan	136
What Are the Outcomes?	136
Program-Specific Outcomes	136
General Outcomes—Positive	137
General Outcomes—Null	137
General Outcomes—Negative	137
Can You Measure Outcomes?	138
Standardized Tests of Knowledge, Reasoning, and Performance	138

Ad Hoc Tests	138
Assumptive Outcome Assessment	138
Extension, Copying, and Diffusion as Inferred Positive Outcomes	139
Cautions on Evaluation	139
Using the Results	139
Sharing With Your Team	140
Package the Findings	140
Share Results With a Larger Sphere of System Stakeholders	140
Try: Summary	140

Stage 6. Extend: Gaining Deeper and Wider Acceptance — 143

Issues About Adoption and Diffusion	144
Solidifying Adoption at the Trial Site (Keeping Going)	144
Expanding Change at the Trial Site (Going Deeper)	144
Extending the Trial to Proximate Sites (Follow-On Adoption)	145
Extending Adoption to the Larger System (Diffusion I)	145
Going Wider: Strategies and Tactics (Diffusion II)	145
Solidifying Adoption at the Trial Site (Keeping Going)	145
Learning From the First Trial	147
Committing to a Second Round	147
Staying Flexible	148
Recycling the Major Steps of the Trial Stage as the Linker Backs Off	148
Internalizing	148
Improving Chances for Continuation	148
Expanding Change at the Trial Site	150
Readapt the Innovation	150
Shift Gears	151
Change Your Implementation Strategy	152
Adding More Innovative Features to the Core	152
Adding More Adopters at the Trial Site	152
Moving Toward More Systemic and Fundamental Improvements	152
Extending the Trial to Proximate Sites (Follow-On Adoption)	153
How Individuals Accept Change and Adopt Innovations	154
Matching Change Agent Activities to Adoption Steps	156

Using the First Trial to Launch Wider Diffusion and Greater Impact	158
Extending Adoption to the Larger System	159
How Groups Accept Change and Innovation	160
How the Linker Can Gain Group Acceptance	161
Variations of the Adoption Curve	164
Competition, Coexistence, and Market Dominance	165
Characteristics of Winners in the Innovation Marketplace	166
Adopters Who Do Not Fit the Pattern	166
The Interaction of Development and Diffusion	167
Going Wider: Strategies and Tactics (The Second Stage of Diffusion)	167
Written and Oral Presentations	168
Video and Film	168
Demonstrations	168
Person-to-Person Contacts	168
Group Discussion	169
Conferences, Workshops, and Training Events	169
The New World of Electronic Media	171
Orchestrating a Multimedia Program	171
Extend: Summary	171
Stage 7. Renew: Encouraging Ongoing Change	**173**
How Do Systems Absorb Changes?	175
Improve the Process	176
Retrospection	176
Redesign of the Process	176
More Inclusive Outreach	177
Keep the Change Fresh	178
Bring In New Blood	178
Respond to Changes in the Local Environment	179
Be Open to Redefining the Social Unit to Whom You Are Linking	179
Be Open to Redefining the Nature of the Concern	179
Be on the Alert for New Resources and Knowledge Sources	179
Be Ready to Reshape and Repackage the Innovation	180
Create a Self-Renewal Capacity	180
A Positive Attitude Toward Innovation	181
A Change Function Internal to the Host System	181
Inclination to Seek External Resources	181
A Positive View of the Future	182
From Item Change to System Change	182
What Are System Changes?	182
Taking On the Most Fundamental Concerns of a System	184
Redoing the Organizational Chart	184

Redoing Budgets	185
Changing the Rules	186
Installing the Change Function	187
Regenerating the Authority and Acquiring Long-Term Legitimacy	187
Recommitting the Resources	188
Solidifying New Roles	189
Reconfiguring and Integrating	190
Orchestrating the Process	191
Terminating and Moving On	192
When Do You Begin to Disengage?	192
How Do You Disengage?	192
Renew: Summary	193
Summary and Synthesis	**195**
References	**211**
Index	**217**

Foreword
Our Goal

Improving Special Education

Improved education is a shared goal of families and educators alike. We all want our children to be well educated. We also want our public schools to change instructional practices that are ineffective. Our shared goal is to improve current practice and deliver more effective educational programs and services in states and localities across the country.

This goal is especially strong for those of us responsible for educating children with disabilities. We have witnessed a sea change in the practice of special education over the past 30 years. In 1970, U.S. schools educated only one in five children with disabilities, and many states had laws that isolated certain students, including children with mental retardation or emotional disturbance or children who were blind or deaf. However, successive reauthorizations of the Individuals with Disabilities Education Act (IDEA), beginning with the passage of the Education for All Handicapped Children's Act (Public Law 94–142) in 1975 and continuing through the 1997 Amendments to IDEA (Public Law 105–17), changed the national landscape. At the start of the new millennium, almost six million American children with physical, sensory, cognitive, or emotional disabilities had access to a free appropriate public education.

Equality of access to education, however, is not enough. Children with disabilities need effective programs and services. Educational services for children with disabilities must be determined on an individual basis, according to the unique needs of the child, and must be provided in the least restrictive environment. Moreover, the focus of their instruction must be on teaching and learning approaches that should be individualized and should allow access to the general education curriculum in ways that support learning and high achievement for all.

Building on 30 years of progress in special education, we still need to deliver more effective instruction and to improve programs and services for all children, including children with disabilities and their nondisabled classmates. *Guiding Change in Special Education* explains how educators can guide and sustain improvements in the practice of special education.

Federal Support for Change in Special Education

The Office of Special Education Programs (OSEP) in the U.S. Department of Education shares the concerns of families and educators in supporting continued improvement in special education. OSEP's investments have led to the development of a national infrastructure for practice improvement. This national network plays a significant role in identifying, implementing, evaluating, and disseminating information about effective instructional practices.

Many practices employed by our nation's best teachers originate in OSEP-sponsored research. Across the country, OSEP researchers are working with teachers, therapists, and other practitioners to discover new ways to provide special education and related services. Through these collaborations, we are finding new ways to diagnose and assess special needs, new ways to deliver special programs and services, new ways to facilitate learning, and new ways to organize instruction and curriculum to enhance the educational experience for all children.

Many streams of innovative OSEP-sponsored research, sustained over 30 years, represent a tremendous potential resource for today's practitioners. But there is a special challenge: How do we best use this collective knowledge resource to improve practice at all levels? Various OSEP investments in training and technical assistance are helping practitioners meet this challenge. For example, OSEP sponsors more than 40 national centers and clearinghouses that operate under the banner of the Special Education Technical Assistance and Dissemination Network. This network provides ongoing training and technical assistance so that practitioners responsible for educating children with disabilities can employ research-validated practices with confidence.

From 1997 to 2002, the American Institutes for Research's Elementary and Middle Schools Technical Assistance Center (EMSTAC) was an active member of OSEP's Technical Assistance and Dissemination Network. EMSTAC's charge was to establish a comprehensive resource for technical assistance in schools that can be used on a national level. EMSTAC partnered with school districts in more than 20 states to help improve the local delivery of special education for elementary and middle school students with disabilities.

Wise action for change requires a great deal of sorting out of information. Thus, EMSTAC helped local practitioners sort out their own needs and then helped them sort through the array of research-validated practices to find those most relevant to their own unique needs and circumstances. EMSTAC also helped practitioners determine which alternative practices work best and which are most likely to be acceptable and practical. In short, EMSTAC provided *human links* connecting local service providers to research along with a complex and remote nationwide network of training and technical assistance.

Who Should Read This Book?

Guiding Change is written for anyone who wants to improve special education—any aspect of the special education environment; changes of any scope, large or small; and any content from social organization to curriculum to technology. Consider the possibility that you might be in one or more of the following situations.

- You are a leader or a member of a team that has been asked to implement a new program.
- You are a special education teacher who is concerned about how to improve services to children with special needs in your school. You would like to make a real difference and are willing and ready to invest some extra energy and time in that effort.
- You are a supervisor or a senior staff member in an intermediate school district or service center with responsibility for special education programs. A major part of your job is implementing laws, regulations, and mandates from the state or the federal government.
- You are the parent of a child with special needs and have a personal interest in improving special education service delivery in your child's school.
- You are in the middle of a project that is meant to bring about a particular kind of change, but you are running into some problems. It is not working out as planned and hoped for, either because there is resistance or because the expected outcomes are not being realized.

In each of these cases, you are cast in the role of a change agent. In some cases, you are concerned only with a particular group of children or a classroom. In other cases, the focus of your concern is a particular school or school district. Nevertheless, in all situations, you are truly a change agent and can benefit from a solid understanding of the process of change. In each case, you also hope that your efforts will lead to real and lasting improvements in the way services are delivered to children with special needs.

Guiding Change will not tell you what specific changes you should make. It does not advocate a particular change content, but it does advocate a process that optimizes participation, problem solving, and the intelligent use of the knowledge and experience of others.

Guiding Change as an Instructional Tool

Instructors in graduate-level and inservice courses should also find *Guiding Change* a useful introduction to the realities of school-level reform. The narrative history of an actual change effort is intended to provide the reader with the feel of being a linker in the field.

A Special Note to Graduate Students

Planned change projects make ideal thesis topics. They can be designed as action research case studies, but with some special advantages: (1) They may actually do some good; (2) they will teach you a lot about the change process, helping organize your experience in a coherent and memorable form; and (3) they should allow you to collect data and report on your experiences in a focused way that can serve as a dissertation. You can try to validate change theory and add to the knowledge of change process along the way. Many persons seeking advanced degrees have returned to the university from responsible positions in education or business. They have had experiences as progenitors, observers, or perhaps victims of other people's change efforts. A careful review of *Guiding Change* should provide many opportunities to match real-life experiences against the theory and wisdom of others as reflected herein.

Guiding Change in Special Education is an invitation for you to play a vital role in translating research into improved special education practice. Reading this book will get you started on learning about the change process and how to support meaningful, sustained innovation. Armed with this knowledge, regardless of your formal role in the larger system, you can provide hands-on assistance to local practitioners, helping them connect in a meaningful way to the world of research and development in special education.

Maurice McInerney, PhD
Managing Director
American Institutes for Research
Washington, D.C.

Acknowledgments

We would like to thank some of the people who helped us in the preparation of this book. First, we thank several colleagues at the American Institutes for Research: Dr. Maurice McInerney for his tireless assistance and encouragement in all stages of the work; Ms. Kristin Ruedel, who compiled the many special education examples found in the text; and Dr. Judy Shanley, Dr. Darren Woodruff, Dr. Don Dailey, Dr. Eric Mesmer, and many other coworkers who helped make the Elementary and Middle Schools Technical Assistance Center a successful demonstration of the change process. Second, we extend our thanks to Mr. Robb Clouse and his colleagues at Corwin Press for assistance and helpful comments on the manuscript. Finally, we offer a heartfelt thank-you to Ms. Val Llewellyn, our first linking agent, for her contribution to the text and for sticking with us as we learned how to guide change in local school districts.

Corwin Press gratefully acknowledges the contributions of the following individuals:

Maurice McInerney
Managing Director
American Institutes for Research
Washington, DC

Kristin Reedy
Director
Northeast Regional Resource Center
WestEd
Williston, VT

Joyce Anderson Downing
Assistant Professor, SPED
Central Missouri State University
Warrensburg, MO

Candice Hollingsead
Associate Professor
School of Education
Andrews University
Berrien Springs, MI

Isabel den Heyer
Educational Consultant
St. Francis Xavier University
Antigonish, Nova Scotia
Canada

Pamela Harwood
Professor, Department Head
Special Education Department
Armstrong Atlantic State
   University
Savannah, GA

About the Authors

Ronald G. Havelock is an internationally recognized authority on knowledge utilization. As professor and research scientist at the University of Michigan and later at the American University in Washington, D.C., he has directed studies of knowledge use, technology transfer, and the planning of change in many fields. His 1969 book, *Planning for Innovation Through the Dissemination and Utilization of Knowledge,* is widely regarded as a landmark work on that subject. Subsequent books include *A Guide to Innovation in Education* (1970), *Training for Change Agents,* with Mary C. Havelock (1973), *The Change Agent's Guide to Innovation* (1973; 2nd edition, with S. Zlotolow [1995]), and *Solving Educational Problems, The Theory and Reality of Innovation in Developing Countries,* with A. Michael Huberman (1978). His broad range of work includes studies of research use in advanced technology, education, and medicine. During the 1990s he served as an advisor to the American Association for the Advancement of Science on their long-term project to improve science education. For the past five years he has designed training materials and provided strategic advice to the American Institutes of Research, Washington, D.C., on programs to assist schools nationwide in the adoption of new programs in special education. He is currently preparing a book on the nature of human progress, summarizing what he has learned over a 40-year career studying how scientific knowledge has evolved and how it has impacted society.

Dr. James Hamilton is currently a managing director at the American Institutes for Research (AIR). He is Principal Investigator of the ACCESS Center, which provides technical assistance to states and school districts to help students with disabilities gain access to the general education curriculum. Previously, he was Project Director of the Elementary and Middle Schools Technical Assistance Center, which developed and evaluated a technical assistance model aimed at improving outcomes for students with disabilities in elementary and middle schools.

Before joining AIR, Dr. Hamilton held various positions, over a 20-year period, at the Office of Special Education Programs (OSEP) in the U.S. Department of Education. While at OSEP, he worked in the areas of research, leadership personnel training, early childhood, technical assistance, and dissemination. He held several OSEP positions, including Director of the Division of Educational Services, Chief of the Early Childhood Branch, Chief of the Leadership Personnel Branch, and Chief of the Research Projects Branch. During his tenure in the Department of Education, Dr. Hamilton was a member (and chair for a year) of the Joint Dissemination Review Panel and the Program Effectiveness Panel.

Prior to serving in the U.S. Department of Education, Dr. Hamilton was a classroom teacher, a senior research associate at the Research Institute for Educational Problems, and the coordinator of two graduate programs at Lesley University. He received his Ph.D. from the University of Missouri in 1972.

His primary interests include special education policy, early childhood, and identification and dissemination of effective practices.

Introduction

Education in general and special education in particular have needs and problems that often seem limitless. Fortunately, large numbers of talented and passionate people are dedicated to finding ways to fill these needs and solve these problems. In short, they are trying to change the educational system and improve the educational opportunities for all children. They are change agents.

Anyone who tries to bring about change is a change agent. Even though they all have the same general goal, change agents use different approaches. However, an effective change agent has special skills and knowledge from which others can benefit. Most change agents are content experts: doctors, lawyers, engineers, scientists, and, of course, teachers at all levels. Another common type of change agent is the advocate. These people want to help others and have some idea of what the problems are and what changes will lead to improvement. However, because advocates believe they already know what the real problems are and what the real solutions should be, they are inclined to push hard to get their ideas accepted by explaining, persuading, and training. This straightforward maximum effort strategy sometimes works, but more often it does not. Instead of inspiring people, it repels them. Instead of overcoming opposition, it builds resistance. Change agents who adopt the advocacy role are often unsuccessful.

Over many years, other types of change agent roles have proved to be more effective in many situations. Prominent among these is the role of process consultant or process helper. This role derives from the tradition of nondirective counseling developed by Carl Rogers (1951), among others. The process consultant does not provide solutions but nurtures a social process in which the system in need examines itself and solves its own problems through collaborative interaction.

Process change agents are a rarer breed; they are people who have the special understanding and skill to make real change happen. Many of these process change agents are also content experts, but over the past three decades, a new class of helpers has arisen who are primarily experts on the process rather than the content of change. These process change agents fall along a continuum from advocates tied to specific content areas at one end to counselors and therapeutic consultants with no ties to content at the other.

The linkage approach, which is offered in *Guiding Change,* presents yet another way of promoting the change process. A successful change requires many parts and many players. It requires a good social process among key players, a full understanding of needs, a serious search for appropriate solution ideas, and a pulling together of resources of various kinds. To move this process along, you need change agents with a special mix of skills. They should know how to bring people together to work on problems and solutions in a way that connects those in need to a larger world of solution ideas and resources. Connection is the core idea behind this role. Thus, we call this person a linking agent or a linker. *Guiding Change* defines what a linker is and explains how you can become one, regardless of where in the educational system you are working.

The linker can work across the process continuum, sometimes organizing a group to work as a change team, sometimes helping define needs, sometimes searching for new ideas and solutions, and sometimes helping implement the change on which the group has decided to work. Process versus content: what is the right mix for an effective change agent overall? There is no right answer to this question because sometimes a system needs a strong infusion of new content, new ideas, new technologies, and so forth. At other times, a system may be awash in new material but not have a clue what to do with it. An effective linker is ready to help with the process and make multiple connections to the universe of content resources, balancing inputs with what seems to be right for the user at a particular time and in a particular circumstance.

The Promise: New Knowledge, New Resources, New Structures

As we begin a new millennium, we see unmistakable signs of new hope and new energy focused on the problems of education in general and special education in particular. The body of useful educational knowledge has been steadily increasing in size and quality over the past 40 years. It is now becoming more accessible to users at all levels and in all locations, thanks to the Internet and other advances in communications technology. Spread before us is a vast menu of innovative offerings, model schools, model curricula, and model practices, not to mention a growing abundance of packaged products and programs.

Several things are special about special education. The first is the nature of the students who are within our purview. They have needs that other students do not have. These special needs are extremely diverse in nature and degree. To meet these needs, our society has assembled a corps of highly skilled, highly dedicated teachers. Special education has also become a magnet for technological innovation. Thanks to advancing technology, we are increasingly able to create new options and open new doors at every level. Another special advantage is the strong advocacy of highly concerned and highly motivated parents. Thanks in large part to them, but also to the equal opportunity values of the larger society, special education attracts extra resources from local, state, and federal sources out of proportion to the numbers of students involved. Partly as a result of this favorable political attention, special educators have been able to create an infrastructure and knowledge resource base that mirrors education in general but is in some ways stronger.

Given these potential advantages, the evolution of a new role of linker makes special sense in special education. Many of the pieces of the educational change puzzle are on the table. We now need people at different levels of the system who can show how the pieces fit together.

Knowledge Base Boxes: What Are They?

A massive literature of research, theory, and observation has accumulated about all the topics covered in *Guiding Change*. Because this book is intended primarily as a manual for practitioners and is based on a complex synthesis of different approaches melded into a coherent strategic orientation, it is neither possible nor appropriate to cite chapter and verse for every proposition made. However, for those who would like to see some of the research and documentation that underlie our major premises, we have provided a series of knowledge base boxes to illustrate some of this background and to point to other references for deeper exploration of many issues. This format allows a full reading of the text without interrupting the conceptual flow.

Knowledge Base

Why Focus on Change Process in Special Education?

Public Law 105–17, the Individuals with Disabilities Education Act (IDEA) Amendments of 1997, was the most significant change in the IDEA since its original 1975 enactment as Public Law 94–142. It mandates much stronger links between special and general education and insists on a much expanded effort toward inclusion, among other changes. The law also sharpens the links between IDEA-funded research, IDEA-funded technical assistance and dissemination, local educational practice, and student outcomes (e.g., Section 685), requiring the Secretary of Education to provide technical assistance to help local districts carry out local capacity-building and improvement projects (Section 685).

These changes were timely: Although special education research has produced an impressive knowledge base of principles of effective practice, these principles are rarely reflected in practice (Malouf & Schiller, 1995; U.S. Department of Education, 1995). Although increasing numbers of students with disabilities are being served in general education environments, neither they nor their teachers receive the support needed to improve learning outcomes (Wagner, Blackorby, Cameto, Hebbeler, & Newman, 1993). Complicating this picture is the potential for general education reform to increase the marginalization of students with disabilities while providing opportunities for them (Skirtic, 1991; McLaughlin & Warren, 1992; Cook, Gerber, & Semmel, 1997). In simplest terms, there is a tremendous gap between accumulated knowledge and practice.

This gap is even greater for special education (Carnine, 1997; Malouf & Schiller, 1995; U.S. Department of Education, 1995). More and more educators are being asked to include students with disabilities in their classrooms when they have neither the training nor the motivation to serve them, which breeds attitudes that often produce negative learning outcomes (Goodlad, 1984; McDermott, 1993; Talbert & McLaughlin, 1994; Pellegrini & Horvat, 1995).

In 1997, the U.S. Department of Education took a step toward bridging the gap by sponsoring a Center to Identify and Meet Technical Assistance Needs of Elementary and Middle Schools. The primary mission of this center was to develop a new type of knowledge-linking change agent, trained to provide better linkage between the knowledge base and special educators at the local level. It targeted practice improvements related to serving children with disabilities. *Guiding Change* grew out of that successful project (Hamilton et al., 2002).

Understanding Change as a Process

Change has both a content and a process. The content is what you want to achieve; the process is how you get there. The content of a particular reform initiative may concern the inclusion of children with special needs in the general education classroom or the implementation of a new reading program to assist children with learning disabilities in reading comprehension. That is what you want to accomplish.

To get there, you will have to understand the program in depth and the particulars of the setting in which it will be introduced. You will have to understand what the current level of need is and what the teachers, both regular and special, now think about these issues. You will have to bring people together, probably across levels, perhaps including the school principal and district-level specialists. You may also need to research many outside sources to find alternative program models. All these activities fall in the category of process and they all can be directed or managed by a linker.

What *Guiding Change* Is Designed to Do

Guiding Change in Special Education is designed to define the LINKER as a new role for reform-minded special educators, illustrate how PROBLEMS in special education can be framed for solution, allow a better understanding of the SOCIAL SETTING in which the reform happens, provide an expanded view of RESOURCES for change and how to gain access to them, and guide change teams toward workable PLANS for choosing and implementing a reform.

A Case to Ponder

Mrs. Byron has a problem. An experienced and respected second-grade teacher, she is confronted with an unruly boy, Jay, who grabs, hits, and yells. Jay is not a bad student and works in a nondisruptive manner when his teacher provides direct instruction, but when students are divided into tables of four and eight, he loses control. His asocial behavior is accentuated by the consequent disapproval and isolation from his fellow students. In spite of her long experience teaching kindergarten through fourth grade and her generally easy command of progressive classroom practices, Mrs. Byron does not know what to do.

Reaching Out for Help

Mrs. Byron takes the problem to the school principal, Dr. Elaine Rogers, who sees the problem in the context of a rise in behavioral referrals and a still wider context of violence in schools across the state as reported in the media. She also has an image to uphold a rating of her school as "exemplary" on "educational improvement." She is puzzled that this experienced teacher has come to her with such a problem; it contradicts her theory that classroom management is primarily a problem for inexperienced first-year teachers. With the situation unresolved, Mrs. Byron makes repeated but unsuccessful attempts to reach Jay's parents by phone. She then turns for help to Ms. Sue Peters, the school counselor.

A First Response

Ms. Peters takes direct action, summoning Jay's reluctant parents to a meeting at the school, some distance from their farm in this rural district. The parents deny knowledge of any behavioral problems with Jay but give a number of details of his home life and his relationship with an older brother. This information is gained at the cost of resentment from Jay's father, who now blames the school for the problem and asserts that he will not cooperate further.

An Innovative Solution Idea

Ms. Peters and Mrs. Byron confer on what to do next. An indirect solution is proposed by Ms. Peters, an innovative program called cooperative discipline (CD), which had been featured in a presentation at a recent teacher conference. CD was designed as a schoolwide program requiring heavy parental involvement and student participation in setting goals and deciding on appropriate behaviors. Ms. Peters had previously discussed the program with a receptive Dr. Rogers. Now, teaming up with Mrs. Byron, she sets out to test the possibility of a schoolwide implementation of CD. She organizes a meeting with eight teachers, including Mrs. Byron, all of whom had been exposed to CD at the teacher conference and most of whom have experienced classroom behavioral disruptions. Four of the eight buy into the idea of CD implementation; four decline, claiming a lack of time and retaining a perception that the program requires too much commitment and disrupts established classroom routines.

Trial Implementation

Ms. Peters invests substantial energy in preparing social-skills classroom guidance lessons, a sample classroom meeting, and a series of "Stop and Think" posters for prominent display in all classrooms as reminders of the new patterns. The involved teachers send letters to all their parents, inviting them to a special meeting to discuss the cooperative discipline technique. The meeting is well attended, although Jay's parents are absent. The parents generally respond positively to the CD plans, but the discussion also feeds anxieties about media reports of school violence. Dr. Rogers reassures the parents that full precautions are taken at this school. The parents agree to cooperate with the start-up of the CD program and to meet again in 5 weeks.

Early Success

For 5 weeks, the CD program seems to evolve very smoothly. Ms. Peters and Dr. Rogers independently keep tabs on early results, and both observe that fewer classroom disruptions and fewer disciplinary referrals occur. The innovative program seems to be working, and the principal is happy about it.

A Regressive Moment

In week 5, prior to the second parent meeting, Jay gets into a fight as he leaves the school bus. His disruptiveness carries over into the classroom, forcing Mrs. Byron to give him private attention to restore a temporary equilibrium. During the noon recess, under the watchful eye of Mrs. Byron and two other teachers, the socially isolated Jay acts out again, disrupting games and receiving another heavy dose of teasing and taunting. Jay takes the law into his own hands, stabbing another student hard in the arm with a pencil. No serious physical harm is done, but Jay is sent home with a 3-day suspension. His parents hear his side of the story and probably feel some of his pain.

Shut Down

The second CD meeting with parents occurs 3 days later, with Jay's parents in attendance. The school playground incident takes center stage. A shouting match ensues between Jay's father and the father of the stabbed boy. The principal, Dr. Rogers, and the CD program come under attack. Immediately after the meeting and without further consultation with anyone, Dr. Rogers unilaterally decides to abandon the CD program and informs the stunned Ms. Peters.

What Happened?

This is a sad story, a story about good people with good intentions who seem to make a good effort in a good cause. Why did they fail? What can we learn? Three major elements of the story stand out: concerns, people, and processes.

Concerns

This story is energized throughout by a host of strongly felt and often conflicting concerns. We start with Jay, frustrated, angry, isolated, teased, and tormented by his peers. He is, at this moment, a special child because he needs special attention and he gets it: from his peers, his teacher, his principal, and the school counselor; from his parents; and ultimately from the whole school. But none is the kind of attention that he really wants.

In addition is the general concern for behavioral disruption. The teachers feel it directly and they pass it on to the principal. The principal is also concerned about her reputation, both as an innovator and as the person to whom parents look to maintain control and protect their children. The whole community is concerned about school violence, which is frequently reported in the news media.

People

Each of the many people in the story is in his or her own way a problem solver. They form a complex network of social relationships. Some are strong. Some are weak. Some are hierarchical, some are collegial, and some are parental and familial. Sometimes these people act in concert as if they were one problem solver, but more often they go their separate ways or act as if they could. The parents' domain is the family and the household. The teachers' domain is the classroom.

Process

The narrative breaks into phases, but there is no overall model or process of change at work. Underneath it all, however, many models of change are at work, models of people trying to solve problems, trying to do the right thing, trying to keep things under control, and trying to do some new things that will make the system work better as a whole.

Basic Ideas and Definitions in the Change Discourse

We are all systems, just as we are all within systems. The term *system*, as used in *Guiding Change*, refers to any group of people who act together for common purposes. All the people involved in special education constitute a system, as do those who work only in a particular locality, school district, school, or classroom. The system includes those who are being served as students with special needs as well as those who serve them.

In *Guiding Change*, we will always talk about positive change, change that improves the circumstances of some system. With positive change, benefits strongly outweigh costs and can be sustained over a long time. *Guiding Change* also takes the view that systems should be deeply involved in changing themselves, taking command of their own change process while reaching out wisely and selectively for the help of others. Change should be system self-improvement.

A helping instinct lies deep within all of us. We count on this in the change process, both in ourselves and in others. This instinct is more highly developed in some people than in others, and a good change agent, like a doctor or a teacher, has to have a lot of it. We always need people who really care to provide the requisite energy to initiate a change process and to keep it going through to implementation.

> The helping instinct is strong in teacher Byron and even stronger in counselor Peters, who reaches out to parents. Ms. Peters is someone who always makes an extra helping effort.

In contemplating your own role in the change process, consider whether you are entering the scene as an insider or an outsider. Many users of *Guiding Change* will identify themselves as members of the system being helped, which is sometimes called the client system, whereas others may see themselves as outsiders who enter the system to provide help and intend to move on to help other systems. *Guiding Change* is written for both insiders and outsiders. Its major principles work equally well for both, but the difference in perspective is important. Sometimes the linking agent moves across the line from insider to outsider and back again as the change process moves along.

The Cycle of Change

All living systems maintain themselves in a state of quasi-equilibrium, coming apart and coming together again in endless cycles. Thus, the cycle is a fundamental notion in understanding all life processes, including the change process. All change activities move in cycles. People and social organizations require various sorts of problem solving to survive in a changing world. The underlying cycle of all such problem-solving activity involves a need and the response to that need. When the response fails to satisfy the need, the cycle repeats itself. The needy person or system tries again with the same response or a different response until the need is satisfied in some way.

Much of what passes as problem solving is reflexive, as epitomized in the expression, "Don't just stand there! Do something!" However, for any problem that is complex, enduring, and difficult, a one-step reflexive response is a poor guide to sensible action. The real key to effective problem solving is to get beyond simple one-step or two-step modes of thought and action by adding reasoning steps to the cycle. Rational action involves taking extra steps before a final action—stopping to think, stopping to explore, and stopping to plan.

Guiding Change Through a Seven-Stage Cycle

Guiding Change sets forth the notion that effective problem solving requires a series of stages, starting with a definition of the need and the problem and moving on to a concerted search for solution ideas and relevant resources. Using this knowledge, a linking agent can help the members of the client system sort through the assembled ideas and resources to find the combination that makes the most sense and has the best fit to the problem at hand. To complete the cycle, the preferred solution idea is put into action through a coherent plan to give the best chance of success. At each stage, the plan involves as many members of the system as possible.

The seven stages in the problem-solving cycle are summarized by seven verbs: care, relate, examine, acquire, try, extend, and renew. The initial letters of these words spell the acronym CREATER. They are depicted in Figure 1 as a circle surrounding another circle, symbolizing the completion of one process and suggesting the induction of another. Each stage represents a cluster of issues and actions that are important in understanding and guiding a change process. Although they are presented as a sequence, each stage is relevant throughout a change project. They build on one another and depend on one another and connect to one another in many ways, even though they are also conceptually distinct.

Care

Problem solving always starts with the recognition that something is wrong, that a situation requires change. This is Stage 1: Care, the rock-bottom prerequisite for a change activity. The level of caring is the energizer. It is not rational. It is what people feel more than what they think, but it is nevertheless the required beginning point for any rational process. Chapter S-1 of *Guiding*

Figure 1 The Core Concept Bundle: Seven Ideas in a Circle

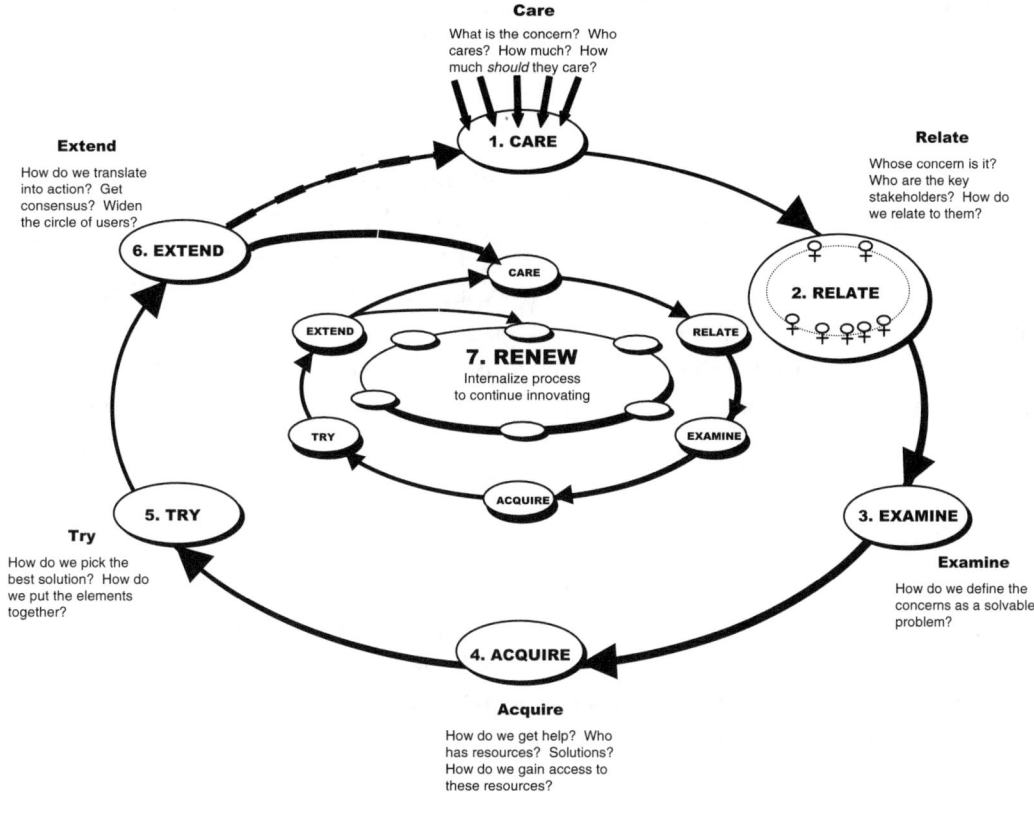

Change is devoted to the issue of caring: Who cares? How much do they care? How much *should* they care? It also considers the possibility that too much caring, too high a level of anxiety about getting something done, can actually get in the way of a positive change process.

Relate

Change never occurs in a social vacuum: There are always people to consider, different people with different needs but related to one another in complex ways. Thus, a crucial consideration is how to relate to the system as a complex social entity. Successful change agents are not merely technical experts; they are people movers. The psychological and social aspects of the change effort must always be kept front and center. The relationships of the change agent to the system and of the system to itself must always be nurtured. As the process unfolds over time and through successive problem-solving stages, the linker must return again and again to ask whether relationships are still holding and whether the system as a whole has enough integration to support the change effort.

A key to building relationships is creating a change team, a cluster of collaborators who work with the linker to sustain the effort and cement relationships to the larger system. As the change team defines the problem and reaches out for solutions, participation and involvement must continue as widely as possible. This sense of participation must be maintained at each stage so that the final solution will be "owned" by those who are affected by it.

Examine

When we consider needs, we must distinguish between caring and understanding. The examine stage is about the latter. In medical parlance, it is the diagnostic phase, the stage at which different needs and symptoms are sorted out and prioritized. Systems often need expert help with examining and defining what their real needs are, given a base of concern and a social will to do something about that concern. Examine is also a social process that requires some kind of consensus on what the problems are and in what order they should be taken up.

Acquire

Guiding Change departs from other conceptions of change agency by emphasizing the search for and acquisition of resources—and not just financial resources. Resources come in many forms: people, program ideas, research findings, and model projects that have been tried elsewhere, near or far. The rise of the Internet has given new life, meaning, and richness to this search.

Try

Every new change effort should be designed first as a trial, an open experiment that allows innovators to take on new behaviors without undue risk and allows others to watch and begin to model their own changes on the basis of their observation of the demonstration. The trial begins with a participative process of using the assembled resources at hand to choose and shape the change. It goes on to develop and then implement a plan.

Extend

Once a successful or partially successful trial has been completed, the next step is to extend the acceptance and adoption of the new program throughout the system. Here marketing and salesmanship come into play. The change team should include opinion leaders as well as innovators, and the process should take account of the interest level and questions that might concern later adopters.

Renew

The last stage is not so much a step as a restart. Once we have demonstrated a successful change process, how do we instill the motivation and the understandings to create a continuing process within the system? How do we sustain commitment? How do we keep the change process fresh and relevant? This is the true meaning of renewal.

> ## Knowledge Base
>
> *Why a Stepwise Model of Problem Solving and Why These Steps?*
>
> That problem-solving cycles are inherent and ubiquitous in animal and human behavior has been universally accepted by biologists for more than a century. All psychological research on learning processes, despite wide differences in methods and outlook, accepts some sort of need-stimulus-response-need reduction cycle as basic. Original credit for applying these ideas in the realm of social behavior is hard to assign, but special mention should go to gestalt psychologist Kurt Lewin (1951). He empirically demonstrated many of his field-theory concepts, including unfreezing-moving-refreezing and the importance of information gatekeepers, through a series of ingenious small-group experiments in the early 1940s.
>
> The specific formulation of stages in *Guiding Change* dates to Havelock (1970). He started with a model derived from Lippitt, a student of Lewin (Lippitt, Watson, & Westley, 1958). Havelock sought preliminary validation of the model by soliciting detailed critiques of a draft document from a sample of 115 educators from across the United States. He used their responses to shape the final product. Many others developed similar formulations in subsequent years. For example, Kotter (1996), focusing on leadership for change in business organizations, proposes "eight steps to transforming your organization": (1) establishing a sense of urgency, (2) forming a powerful guiding coalition, (3) creating a vision, (4) communicating the vision, (5) empowering others to act on the vision, (6) planning for and creating short-term wins, (7) consolidating improvements and producing still more change, and (8) institutionalizing new approaches. Kotter and Cohen (2002) have since bolstered the model with empirical studies of how it worked in more than 100 business organizations.
>
> Fullan, a leading synthesizer of educational research on change and innovation (1982, 2001b), notes "a recent remarkable convergence of theories, knowledge bases, ideas, and strategies" around five components of effective leadership: moral purpose, understanding change, relationship building, knowledge creation and sharing, and coherence making (2001a, p. 3). The correspondence between his five elements and the seven CREATER stages proposed here is obvious and will be referred to again as knowledge boxes are presented for successive stages. Fullan also references Kotter but characterizes his approach as top-down. Fullan, it should be added, is ambivalent about using stage models and giving advice on strategies, noting that "change cannot be managed. It can be understood and perhaps led, but it cannot be controlled" (2001a, p. 33).

Where Do Change Agents Fit in a Change Process?

Regardless of their formal job titles and official positions, people can adopt four primary roles as change agents: catalyst, solution giver, process helper, and people-resource linker.

> **Four Ways to Be a Change Agent**
>
> - Catalyst
> - Solution giver
> - Process helper
> - People-resource linker

The Change Agent as Catalyst

Some people play a useful role in the change process by prodding and pressuring the system to be less complacent and to start working on its serious problems. In education today, this role is often taken by students, concerned parents, or school board members. They do not necessarily have the answers, but they make their concerns loudly known. They upset the status quo. Because they energize the process without necessarily providing the best solutions, we call them catalysts.

The Change Agent as Solution Giver

Many people who want to bring about change have definite ideas about what the change should be. They have solutions and they want others to adopt those solutions. Sometimes their commitment to their solution gets in the way of understanding the real problem or understanding resistance to the solution they advocate. By emphasizing process and not content, *Guiding Change* does not give solutions, but it should be useful to solution givers who want to become more effective. Committed innovation advocates can play a constructive role in the change process, making people aware of new ideas and stirring up interest in the possibilities of change. Being an effective solution giver involves more than simply having a solution. It means knowing how the solution relates to people's needs and concerns. Change agents must be prepared to adapt themselves and their innovations to satisfy those concerns.

The Change Agent as Process Helper

The process helper assists the system primarily through building relationships and helping members of a system define problems for themselves in their own terms. It is a complicated role that is not always understood or appreciated by those who are committed to a particular course of action. The process helper is always saying, "Wait a minute; isn't there some other aspect we should consider?" or "Aren't there some other people who should be involved in this?"

The Change Agent as People-Resource Linker

Effective problem solving requires making all kinds of new connections. Some of these are people-to-people connections within the school. Some are connections between members of the system and outsiders: experts, state and local officials, researchers, teachers, and other experienced innovators in other school districts. Mental connections also have to be made between problems

---

> When counselor Peters turned to the cooperative discipline program, she locked onto one solution, advocating, persuading, and doing much of the detailed implementation work herself. We know that several teachers rejected the program from the outset, but Peters elected to move ahead anyway. She could have looked for alternatives that would have satisfied the legitimate concerns of these teachers about disrupted routines and the level of effort required. She could also have worked more with the teachers to adapt and perhaps downsize the innovative program. This overcommitment to a single approach put her in a painful and vulnerable position when things went awry.

> Ms. Peters started out as a process helper, listening to teachers and parents, forming working groups, and coordinating with the principal. As it turned out, however, she had not done enough to bring either key parents or the principal into the process.

and solutions, needs and resources. Because making connections is such a crucial aspect of the change process, a central role can be played by the linker, who specializes in making these connections. The linker brings others together both within the system and between the system and the outside. The linker also connects people to resources and helps them make the mental connections between needs and potential solutions. The linker should also understand processes and help in every phase of problem solving, sometimes as a catalyst or a solution giver and always as a process helper.

Knowledge Base

Why Do We Need Change Agents?

Research studies consistently suggest that although knowledge use is always local (McLaughlin, 1990; Fullan & Miles, 1992), it requires well-developed materials and external linkages and supports (Louis, Kell, Dentler, Corwin, & Herriott, 1984). Findings from multisite studies of school change indicate that successful change efforts benefit from support from outsiders who provide pragmatic, comprehensive, and ongoing linkages between researchers and practitioners (Louis & Rosenblum, 1981; Sashkin & Egermeier, 1993; Turnbull, 1981).

Cox and Havelock (1982) found that linking agents in various guises played a key role in successful innovation in a large nationwide study of federal efforts to improve educational practice. Likewise, Huberman and Miles (1984), in perhaps the most intensive and sophisticated study of the innovation process ever undertaken, looked at 12 projects in 12 dispersed field sites. They found that sustained assistance at every stage was essential for success, and especially important in later stages, "substantially increasing the levels of commitment and practice mastery" (p. 273). Several research studies have stressed the value of high-quality, ongoing human assistance at all points in the change process: problem identification, problem solving, implementation, and institutionalization (Crandall & Loucks, 1983; Hall & Hord, 1987; Louis & Miles, 1990).

Kim Grose (in Rust & Freidus, 2001) describes her recent success in developing a cadre of outside change facilitators, starting from a pool of volunteers who had no prior substantive experience in education but were chosen "for their commitment to children, a track record of leadership and involvement in their communities and strong communication and interpersonal skills." These Partners in School Innovation went on to provide substantial support for innovation in seven San Francisco Bay Area schools.

Why Linking Agents in Particular?

Empirical support for the importance of the change agent as knowledge linker was first reported by Sieber and colleagues (1972), who studied a pilot program to train and install linkers in state education agencies in three states. They concluded that the role was successful but too expensive a model to be supportable as a permanent, nationwide element.

Most recently, the value of such a role in special education has been fully demonstrated by Hamilton and colleagues (2002, pp. 1–8) in a project that recruited, trained, and deployed linkers in 58 local education agencies in 28 states.

> **A Case to Ponder: What Role Did Ms. Peters Really Play?**
>
> Much of the time, Ms. Peters seemed to play the role of a linker, sometimes to good effect, sometimes not. As the school counselor, she had the freedom to act and to relate to different members of the system. Whereas Mrs. Byron could not manage any contact with Jay's parents, Ms. Peters could call them into the school for a meeting. Ms. Peters also attended the teacher conference and, as a result, better understood the connection between the problems of the school and what the cooperative discipline program offered. She connected with teachers on several levels, reaching out to explain the program, providing model lessons, modeling some of the new behaviors required, and preparing posters. In doing all these things, she exemplified the role of linking agent.

The C-R-E-A-T-E-R Process Checklist

Take a few minutes to think about your school setting as it relates to each of the seven stages. Try to formulate a tentative answer to each of the following questions.

C *Care.* Is the system actively concerned about improvement?

R *Relate.* Do cooperative relationships exist among key players within the system which allow a sustained change effort?

E *Examine.* Has the system clearly defined its needs as solvable problems?

A *Acquire.* Has the system made a real effort to find alternative solutions?

T *Try.* Has the system made a commitment to try out new approaches?

E *Extend.* Has the system tried to spread the change effort to a wider circle of users?

R *Renew.* Has the system taken steps to ensure the survival of changes made and to develop an internal process to continue innovating?

Successful change ultimately requires positive answers to all these questions. At the beginning, the minimum requirement is a partial yes to Stages 1 and 2. Some members of the system must care about making changes, and some sort of network of relations must be in place to support a new effort. That network must obviously be one to which the linker can connect directly.

Case Study

Early Literacy Program Travels to a Rural Atlantic School District

Special Education Linking Agent in Action

A narrative history reported by Linking Agent C. Val Llewellyn with editorial comments on the process by Ronald G. Havelock

Theory Meets Reality

In the late 1990s, the Office of Special Education Programs in the U.S. Department of Education began supporting the Elementary and Middle Schools Technical Assistance Center (EMSTAC). It was a 5-year project with a mission of providing technical assistance to personnel working in the field of special education throughout the country. EMSTAC employs technical assistance liaisons (outside linkers) who support and train linking agents (inside linkers), who are local personnel working in the school system.

The following narrative is the story of a district-based linking agent. It is a good example of the change model in action. Although it does not follow the seven-stage CREATER change model step-by-step, we can see the underlying scaffolding of the seven stages throughout the narrative in what was done or not done to move the change effort along. And *effort* is the right word. This narrative gives us a picture of the continuing flow of changes, with their many streams and crosscurrents, that is happening in this school district. Any new initiative entering this stream must compete with those that have come before and those that are ongoing.

The Setting

Hilldale County lies in the mountains of western Atlantic. The school population has declined over the past 10 years to only 11,200 students. Of those, 1,738 are identified as needing special education services. The economics of the region have declined with the student population. About 47% of the students qualify for free or reduced-price lunch.

(Stage 1: Care)

Innovative History: General Education

Although Hilldale County schools have practiced site-based management for the past 6 years, the superintendent has implemented several countywide school initiatives. One is character education; another is implementing changes related to the seven correlates of effective schools, namely, (1) a safe and orderly environment, (2) a climate of high expectations for success, (3) shared instructional leadership, (4) a clear and focused mission, (5) the opportunity to learn and time on task, (6) frequent monitoring of student progress, and (7) authentic school-family-community partnerships.

Innovative History: Special Education

The County Special Education Department has a good history of change initiatives. For example, it has supported the training of personnel in nonviolent crisis intervention and conflict resolution. Inclusion training has been an integral part of staff development for special educators for at least 7 years. Because of the need to prepare special needs students for participation in state testing, such as the Atlantic School Performance Program and the upcoming Atlantic High School Assessments, the Department of Special Education also encourages special educators to participate in general education content area training. Additionally, the department has launched an effort to integrate special needs students into general education science and social studies classes with special education support. At the secondary level, this integration effort will be expanded to include an increasing number of major content areas.

This is not a district that rests on its laurels. There is good evidence from past history that district personnel care about making improvements. They have made a serious and continuing effort to provide a better educational environment by addressing a broad array of issues, including those that concern special education. They want to improve for their children.

(Stage 2: Relate)

First Connections: Establishing a Linking Agent Role and Selecting a Site

Seven years ago, the Hilldale County Special Education Department became involved with the Atlantic Coalition for Inclusive Education (ACIE) and took part in ACIE's statewide change initiative, the Least Restrictive Environment/Neighborhood Inclusion Project. ACIE, in turn, was contacted by EMSTAC, which had developed this inside-outside linker concept to improve the flow of new research knowledge into special education. Now EMSTAC was looking for counties in Atlantic that were open to innovation, and the ACIE nominated Hilldale County.

EMSTAC sent a proposal to the supervisor of special education in that county, asking whether she would be interested in participating in a technical assistance project. The supervisor responded favorably. Three representatives from EMSTAC visited the county. They met with the supervisor and with a person who, at that time, was serving part-time as a special education facilitator and part-time as a staff development specialist. EMSTAC proposed creating a new special educator role, that of a linking agent. EMSTAC wanted someone who could be released from other duties to learn how to fill this new role, which would specialize in introducing classroom and system change to support special education goals.

The district special education staff began a search for the right person to fill the role. The first person considered was Steve, the former assistant supervisor of special education who had returned to a classroom job in a step-down move toward retirement. Steve, who was intelligent, articulate, and well respected throughout the county, seemed to be the perfect choice. However, he was not interested in a new position with the district and EMSTAC. Several recent retirees were solicited with no success. It was proving difficult to arouse interest in a new position outside the mainstream of established educator roles. Ultimately, the special education facilitator and staff development specialist asked to be considered and was accepted.

Linking Agent Qualifications. The selected linking agent had taught both general education and special education in three schools (elementary and middle) and had worked in many schools in the county as a special education facilitator. She had also participated in numerous workshops and training programs through which she had developed positive relationships with many teachers, assistants, and administrators. She believed that she had established credibility and had skills that would be beneficial in facilitating innovations. Her supervisor and EMSTAC agreed that she was a good choice for the position.

Selecting the Initial Target Sites. The schools in the south end of Hilldale were already involved in two special education initiatives: an inclusion project and a professional development school project through the local university. Therefore, the Department of Special Education decided to concentrate on the other side of town (all of the schools in the county are in one town), which had three elementary schools and a middle school, and to begin the project in the three elementary schools: Cider Hill, Parkside, and North Slope.

(Stage 3: Examine)

First Round of Establishing the Need for Change

The linking agent provided the principals of the three elementary schools with information about the proposed project and asked them to meet with their staffs to identify the primary concerns of each individual school. The linking agent suggested that Hilldale County's School Improvement Team and its subteams, Climate, Achievement, and Partnership Teams, should be consulted about the findings. Because these teams met regularly in each school and monthly with teams from other schools and comprised both general education and special education teachers, administrators, support personnel, parents, and community members, the linking agent felt that their input was key to determining the perceived needs within each building.

Three members of EMSTAC visited the four selected schools in the district. Together with the linking agent, they visited each building to meet with the principal and to get a sense of whether the schools had shared needs. The principal of Cider Hill Elementary School canceled her meeting, telling the linking agent that she would "go along with" what the other principals wanted to do.

The principal of North Slope School, Catherine Stone, was the only one who expressed a real interest in the new project. North Slope was also the only school that had clearly defined its needs. Thus, it became the obvious choice as the first target of concentrated assistance. North Slope is a city school with a population of about 365 students, of whom 62% qualify for free or reduced-price lunch. Eight percent of the school population has been identified as requiring special education services. This number is unusually low because teachers at North Slope work diligently with all students and refer only those with significant needs for special services.

Catherine Stone met with the School Improvement Team (SIT) and the School Achievement Team (SAT). Together they determined that they would like to improve the reading instruction available to the special education population. They believed that the reading instruction offered in the special education classes should resemble that offered in the general classrooms.

General education teachers were using many different approaches to teach reading, including a great variety of materials, such as basal readers, trade books, literature books, expository text, newspapers, library books, and magazines. They also were using a variety of teaching and learning strategies, including graphic organizers, directed reading thinking activity (DRTA), guided reading, shared reading, sustained silent reading, literature discussion groups, whole-language instruction, phonemic awareness, and thematic units. Students were participating in whole-group instruction, small-group instruction, cooperative groups, individual instruction, peer reading, cross-grade reading, and individual oral reading. The school was involved with the Atlantic Reading Network and was concentrating on creating developmentally appropriate groupings for reading instruction.

The situation in special education stood out in sharp contrast to this innovative stew: The special education teacher was concentrating solely on basal readers and workbooks. Distressingly, test scores on the Atlantic School Performance Assessment Program (ASPAP), which were low for the school as a whole, were particularly poor among students receiving special education services.

(Stage 2: Relate)

A New Change Team Takes Shape: The Insider and the Outsider

As part of its support strategy, EMSTAC assigned a technical assistance (TA) liaison to work with the local linking agent. This TA liaison began frequent contacts with the linking agent to provide encouragement and a variety of technical supports to move the project forward. Prior to his work at EMSTAC, the TA liaison had been a school psychologist and had conducted needs assessments to help groups narrow and define their "true" needs. He was familiar with various research projects and had access to information about them. Thus, the linking agent initially depended heavily on the TA liaison because of his abundant skills, contacts, and knowledge.

(Stage 4: Acquire)

The Technical Assistance Liaison Gets to Work

The TA liaison began a search for information on reading programs for students with learning disabilities. To help in the search process, he requested information about the district's overall plans for school improvement, demographic information, and information about current or previous change efforts. He also inquired about the county's special education service delivery model, eligibility guidelines, and similar information. After the TA liaison received the information, he expressed an interest in making a site visit to Hilldale County to meet with teachers and visit classrooms. He sent the linking agent a questionnaire to complete prior to his visit. The questionnaire dealt with several topics: (1) area(s) of concern, (2) current curriculum and instructional strategies, and (3) the technical assistance environment (e.g., the willingness of teachers to participate in training, the time available for training). The questionnaire was completed by school personnel and returned by the linking agent. Thus, the TA liaison (or outside linker) was already fairly well informed on some key issues before he met with the linking agent, general and special education teachers, and with the principal, Catherine Stone.

On the basis of the information sent to him, the TA liaison presented three possible interventions that he thought might be appropriate for North Slope's use: Peer Assisted Learning Strategies (PALS) (Lynn and Doug Fuchs, Vanderbilt University), Collaborative Strategic Reading (Sharon Vaughn, University of Texas), and the Early Literacy Project (ELP) (Carol Sue Englert, Michigan State University). He left summaries of each approach for the teachers and Principal Stone to read and think about. Principal Stone then divided the teachers into study groups, and each group examined a different intervention.

(Stage 5: Try)

Initial Response to a Good Effort: Rejection

After a few days, the teachers reported back to Principal Stone and the linking agent that they did not like any of the approaches! The one they liked best was the ELP, but they turned it down because the TA liaison's summary indicated that it required a change in the entire language arts curriculum. They had already been working on making changes and did not want to completely revamp what they had. This was very discouraging news for the TA liaison and the local linking agent.

Finding the Match

That night, the linking agent careful reviewed the ELP and compared it with North Slope's current initiatives. She found that North Slope had already made many of the changes suggested by the ELP. Thus, there seemed to be a good potential match between North Slope and the ELP. The school would not have to undertake a major revamping to introduce the ELP innovations. The next day, she met with Principal Stone, and together they went over the ELP curriculum, point by point. The principal also saw a good match and recognized that the school had already implemented many of the changes in curriculum, thereby reducing the stress that would come with incorporating the other innovative features of the ELP. She met with her teachers and shared this new insight. The staff then agreed that the ELP was an intervention they could seriously consider.

(Stage 5: Try)

Planning the Intervention

The linking agent contacted the TA liaison and shared the good news. The planning for bringing an expert ELP training consultant to Hilldale County could now begin. The TA liaison, the linking agent, and the principal discussed providing training on the first available staff development date to keep the momentum going. They decided that both general education and special education teachers should participate in the training. As the principal put it, "With the new assessment and with our resource kids already struggling with the rigors of ASPAP, I think we are probably going to have to include them in more and more classroom activities. That's another selling point for all teachers."

Clearing Bureaucratic Hurdles

January 22 was already a designated professional development day on the school calendar. By the end of November, Principal Stone had written a letter to the assistant superintendent of curriculum and instruction and to the school board, asking that North Slope be allowed to dismiss students 3 hours early on January 21. This would allow the consultant to meet with the staff in the afternoon of the twenty-first and the morning of the twenty-second. Teachers could then use the afternoon of the twenty-second to process and plan. The principal and the linking agent met with the assistant superintendent and presented their case personally. He approved and passed the proposal on to the board, which gave final approval on December 22.

(Stage 2: Relate)

Establishing External Linkages

The TA liaison made contact with Carol Sue Englert, an ELP researcher at Michigan State University. She was not available to work with North Slope but recommended a core searcher, Troy Mariage. When Troy's interest was established, the TA liaison introduced the linking agent and they began an interaction.

Troy shared information about his project sites in Michigan, and the linking agent gave him information about North Slope. Troy suggested that it could be beneficial for a few teachers from North Slope to visit some of the schools in Michigan where he was working so that they could see firsthand how the interventions worked.

(Stage 4: Acquire)

Organizing a Field Trip

After trying and failing to get commitments from any teachers to go to Michigan, Principal Stone and the linking agent decided to visit the schools in Michigan prior to the inservice meeting. Troy suggested that they visit two sites in Lansing and one in Bangor, where he was working in a school very similar to North Slope. Principal Stone e-mailed the linking agent in reference to the upcoming trip and training: "I do so hope this is something good! I will die if it turns out to be something we already do or something everyone hates. I think it is so hard to come up with something because we have already been forced to make so many changes due to ASPAP." She and the linking agent made plans to be in Michigan from January 10 to January 12. Plans for Troy's visit to Hilldale County were also finalized, and travel arrangements were confirmed.

In January, Michigan had one of its biggest storms in 20 years. Principal Stone and the linking agent worried that their trip would be canceled, but Troy encouraged them to come. They arrived in Lansing, Michigan, in 20 inches of snow and subzero windchill temperatures. They were able to visit three schools in Lansing and to see classrooms where ELP strategies were being used successfully. However, the snow did make them cancel the visit to Bangor, which Troy had identified as the closest match to their own situation. Nevertheless, they were very excited by what they observed at the demonstration sites and were enthusiastic about returning to North Slope to share what they had seen. They were particularly impressed with the written language aspects of the ELP.

(Stage 5: Try)

Shaping the Message

Principal Stone then made an administrative decision to ask Troy to concentrate his presentation on the writing strategies from the ELP. She wanted him to spend minimal time on the reading strategies, mostly reinforcing with teachers that what they were already doing was appropriate and beneficial to students and focusing the majority of his presentation on the excellent writing strategies of the ELP program.

On January 14 and 15, school was canceled because of snow. Principal Stone called the linking agent at home on the morning of the fifteenth to tell her that the superintendent had decided to change the morning of January 22 to instructional time; the afternoon would remain professional development time. The principal was distraught. How could teachers have enough time with the ELP consultant when the morning of the second day was being taken away? She and the linking agent discussed several options:

- Option 1: Ask the school board to approve closing North Slope for the entire day on January 22.
  Problem: There was not enough time to get the approval.
- Option 2: Arrange for substitutes to cover all classes for that morning.
  Problem: Not enough substitute teachers were available to cover all classes.
  Problem: Principal Stone was not comfortable having all classes covered by subs.
- Option 3: Use resource and Title I teachers to cover classes so that at least one teacher from each grade could attend throughout the day. Teachers could rotate in and out of the training as their planning time allowed. The principal felt that this was the most feasible option.

The next day, Principal Stone began arranging coverage for teachers so that at least one teacher from each grade could attend the training on January 22.

(Stage 2: Relate)

Expanding the Circle of Participation

Special education teachers from the other two elementary schools that had been selected for the project were invited to attend the training. Two teachers from Parkside and five from Cider Hill were able to attend. Two teachers from another school, who had heard about the inservice training, contacted the linking agent because they thought it would be beneficial for their classrooms as well. They were granted permission to attend.

The linking agent and the expert consultant, Troy, continued to exchange information electronically and by phone almost up to the day he arrived. Troy asked about the Atlantic State Content Standards and planned his presentation to coincide with Atlantic's learning goals. He sent his handout, which the linking agent copied for all those attending.

The linking agent picked up Troy at the regional airport, and the two arrived at North Slope by 11 A.M. Troy was able to visit classrooms and meet some of the teachers prior to the training event. The TA liaison arrived shortly thereafter. The linking agent had arranged for a catered lunch for all the participants, which gave Troy the opportunity to interact informally with more of the teachers. The change team (Principal Stone, the linking agent, and the TA liaison) jointly decided that if either the TA liaison or the linking agent were to introduce Troy as the expert, it might appear too much like an "outsider" show. Therefore, Principal Stone formally initiated the proceedings and introduced Troy to the group, giving reassurance that this would be a resource of real relevance to their situation.

Troy shared his research and school-based experiences for 3 hours that afternoon and concentrated mainly on writing interventions. Using charts and samples of actual student work, he described Morning Message and POWER (an acronym for organizing writing—plan, organize, write, edit, and rewrite) as two efficacious methods for teaching children to write. Teachers were noticeably impressed with the samples of student work.

Because students were in the building the next morning, arranging for training space was more difficult. The Learning Assistance Program (in-school suspension) room was the only space available. Although a nice size for a classroom, it was small for a presentation. The logistics of putting charts where everyone could see and finding room for seating were a challenge and not resolved to anyone's satisfaction. Coffee and doughnuts were provided while Troy struggled to arrange his materials satisfactorily. Troy continued his discussion of the writing strategies, then moved on to reading strategies. Teachers were interested in the reading strategies and found some of what he was saying to be new and innovative, but they also felt that much of it was old hat.

Planning for Implementation

That afternoon, during the professional development time when students were not in the building, the teachers worked in groups to plan how to implement the strategies that Troy had shared with them. It became clear very quickly that they were most interested in concentrating on the writing strategies. Principal Stone and the linking agent offered to model Morning Message in classrooms for teachers. By the end of the day, two teachers had asked for a date when that could be done.

(Stage 5: Try)

Teachers completed evaluations after the workshop. Generally they indicated that the information presented was relevant. They believed that the interventions were feasible and could be successful. That evening, the linking agent and her husband took Troy and the TA liaison to dinner. The consensus of the group was that the training had gone well, despite the difficulties and roadblocks. Troy was enthusiastic about working with North Slope because he believed that the school was already doing many positive things with students and could easily implement the ELP strategies. The TA liaison also felt that the teachers had been very receptive.

(Stage 2: Relate)

Strengthening External and Internal Linkages

The next morning, Principal Stone met with the TA liaison, the linking agent, and Troy. She asked Troy to return in June for additional training with the teachers. She wanted to give her teachers time to digest what they had heard, experiment in their classrooms, and then meet again with Troy to expand and refine the strategies. The group encouraged her to ask teachers how they felt about having Troy return to conduct a follow-up training session. The next day, the linking agent drove Troy back to the airport with a tentative agreement for his return in June.

The linking agent followed up the presentation with letters to the teachers, thanking them for their participation and offering support in their efforts to implement the ELP. She also informed them of the possibility that Troy would return in June for a follow-up training session and requested feedback about this idea. She wrote a thank-you note to Troy and sent copies of the inservice evaluation to the TA liaison.

(Stage 5: Try)

In-Class Demonstration and Implementation

The linking agent bought binders and plastic sleeves to prepare for modeling Morning Message (MM) in classrooms. In MM, one student acts as an author and dictates a story to the teacher. The other students edit, sentence by sentence, as the author tells his or her story. Each completed and edited story is typed. One copy of the story is given to the author to take home and share. Another copy is placed in a binder in the classroom for students to read during free time. The linking agent hoped that the binder would be an incentive to teachers to continue doing MM after the initial demonstration.

Within 5 days of the training, the linking agent demonstrated MM in a classroom of third- and fourth-grade students with learning disabilities. The students and the teacher participated enthusiastically. The linking agent typed the story and designed a cover page for the book on the computer. The next day, when she presented a copy of the story to the student and the book to the class, the teacher was already in the middle of doing MM. The children were very excited and wanted to read their story to her. The linking agent also e-mailed a copy of the story to the TA liaison.

(Stage 6: Extend)

The Spreading Process

Vickie, Hilldale County's Teacher of the Year and a teacher at Cider Hill School, had attended the training. She called the linking agent to request to be included in the June training. She expressed enthusiasm about implementing the presented strategies and asked whether the linking agent could model an MM lesson in her classroom. The next day, another teacher from Cider Hill who had heard the linking agent was to demonstrate the new intervention requested a demonstration in her classroom as well. The linking agent readily agreed to all requests and prepared to model the lesson once again.

Principal Stone and the linking agent then demonstrated MM to a first-grade classroom at North Slope. The children were enthusiastic, but the teacher, a veteran of many years, did not seem receptive, even though she had initiated the demonstration. The linking agent sensed that the issue was as much a power struggle between the teacher and the principal as it was resistance to change. The teacher commented in private to the linking agent that she had hoped it would be only the linking agent modeling the lesson.

Spread to Special Education Populations. Later that week, the linking agent traveled to Cider Hill School to help implement MM in yet another setting. This classroom consisted of seven 5- and 6-year-old students with mild mental retardation and only basic language skills. The speech therapist, who had heard that this strategy might improve oral language as well as written language skills, asked to sit in on the lesson. The school principal also attended.

At first, the selected children were hesitant to participate. One student was finally coaxed into telling his story, but the other children could not be coaxed into editing. Eventually, the teacher said, "Boys and girls, I know that we have learned that it is not nice to criticize someone and make them feel bad. However, this is different. We are not criticizing what Jamie is saying. We are helping him say it better. So please help." The children then began offering suggestions to the author, and the lesson proceeded smoothly.

The teacher apologized for the slow start to the lesson and explained that she had worked very hard on teaching her students to be considerate of one another's feelings. Nevertheless, she thought that they had understood the difference today and was looking forward to doing MM regularly in her classroom.

After the lesson, the speech therapist was excited about the potential effects of using MM and asked whether she could bring several students from the deaf education class to the next classroom demonstration. The linking agent thought this was a great idea and agreed.

The next demonstration lesson of MM was conducted in a classroom of a dozen 9-year-old and 10-year-old students with mild mental retardation, including one student who was mildly autistic. The speech therapist also brought two 10-year-old students with profound hearing impairments. The language delays among this group were much more apparent than they had been with the younger class, but with the assistance of the group, the author was able to dictate a paragraph and the group worked to edit the story. At first, the students with hearing impairments were hesitant to participate, but with the encouragement of the therapist, they became the most helpful editors.

After these two demonstrations, the linking agent met with the principal of Cider Hill School. She stated that she would like MM modeled for her general education teachers. Dates and times were established for the linking agent to return. However, the principal did not confer with her teachers prior to making this commitment for them. Perhaps as a consequence, only one teacher at this subsequent meeting showed any interest. The other attending teachers sat in the back of the classroom and checked student papers. In fact, some teachers simply walked out!

More External Linkage and Feedback. The linking agent e-mailed Troy about the excitement and enthusiasm of the speech therapist. Troy said that the speech and language community in general had shown interest in ELP. He said that they were curious about how techniques such as MM and POWER "give students a language to talk about text." The linking agent shared this new insight into the use of MM with Principal Stone and the speech therapist.

The TA liaison also contacted Troy and arranged for a conference call with the linking agent and Principal Stone. Topics discussed included the experiences of the principal and the linking agent in modeling MM. Troy suggested ways to expand the use of MM and provided information on the procedures for evaluating the project. Finally, they discussed the possibility of having teachers ask Troy questions and discuss issues related to MM with him via the Internet. They also discussed a tentative date in June for Troy to return and conduct the follow-up presentation.

A teacher from John Humbird School contacted the linking agent. She was part of the SIT, which was interested in improving writing scores. She asked the linking agent to make a presentation at the next faculty meeting. The linking agent suggested that the two of them meet first to clarify whether ELP might fit the needs of the school, so a meeting was coordinated with both the teacher and the principal. After the program was explicitly explained, the principal decided that it did not meet the criteria for their writing program.

During February and March, the momentum to implement the ELP strategies slowed. Countywide testing and snow days took precedence over everything else. State testing was looming only a few months ahead, and teachers felt pressure to use every available moment for time-tested methods to prepare students. New initiatives were unproven in their minds. Precious time could not be wasted in this way.

Planning Continues

Principal Stone, Troy, the TA liaison, and the linking agent confirmed dates for Troy to return in June. The plan was for him to concentrate on MM and to explain how to expand it to individual writing through the use of POWER. After much discussion with the teachers, Principal Stone decided that North Slope would concentrate on and commit to the writing strategies offered by ELP and would continue to use their current reading strategies. She was also considering implementing a model of full inclusion for the next school year. Thus, all students would have access to the strength in the general education reading program.

Solidifying Implementation

In April, the linking agent was invited to observe a kindergarten class at North Slope where MM was being used daily as part of the morning opening exercises. The experienced kindergarten teacher gave an enthusiastic report: "I have seen tremendous gains in language skills! Since we started using Morning Message, the kids have learned how to ask questions, a concept I have had trouble teaching in the past." She expressed an interest in becoming the county "Morning Message expert" and coordinating teacher; she would be willing to do workshops with other teachers or to model lessons.

While at the school, the linking agent checked in with the special education resource teacher. She noted that with weekly use of MM, she was seeing an improvement in the length of paragraphs. She was also becoming aware of patterns in her students' writing and using this information to develop lessons to expand the students' writing repertoire. She stated, "Morning Message is a beneficial program, and the students have learned a lot about the editing and revising process."

In the meantime, Principal Stone contacted the linking agent with a "slight problem." Through the Accelerated Schools project in another school, Principal Stone had inherited a part-time consultant who was expected to conduct professional development activities and inservice programs with the teachers in the building. The consultant, Sue, had been a classroom teacher in the county and was considered skilled in teaching language arts. She had looked at the ELP material and did not believe that the writing strategies were compatible with her approaches to teaching writing. Principal Stone sought the linking agent's help in resolving this conflict. Because the linking agent and Sue had a Tae-Bo class together, they had already had several informal conversations about school, strategies for teaching reading and writing, and the MM initiative. The linking agent decided it was time to set up a formal meeting to systematically discuss and resolve the differences. Considering Sue's reputation of expertise in the area of language arts, the linking agent was nervous that the North Slope school and community might decide to withdraw from the project if a compromise could not be reached. The next time that Sue was scheduled to be at North Slope, the linking agent arranged to be there also. The two met and discussed all ELP material together, systematically addressing each of Sue's concerns. By the end of the session, Sue felt that she could work within the framework of the ELP strategies, expanding on them and introducing compatible materials. (As it turned out, Sue spent little time at North Slope that year, and was assigned to a different school building the following year.)

In April, Hilldale County received wonderful news. Principal Stone was honored as National Distinguished Principal from the State of Atlantic. She was recognized for her leadership and her tireless efforts to improve the quality of education at North Slope School.

Planning for Troy's return to Hilldale County consumed a good deal of time in May. The TA liaison confirmed Troy's travel arrangements, and the linking agent coordinated lodging arrangements and sent invitations to the teachers at Parkside and Cider Hill Schools who had attended last year's workshop. Principal Stone planned an agenda.

(Stage 5: Try)

More Evaluation Data

As part of the evaluation of the year's activities, a representative from EMSTAC visited North Slope School and interviewed approximately 80% of the teachers, using EMSTAC-developed questions. The interview revealed that teachers in the early grades had been regularly using MM, whereas the teachers in grades 2 and 3 had implemented the other ELP reading and writing strategy, POWER. The teachers using the strategies reported that they had seen some improvement in student learning and felt comfortable recommending the strategies to others.

(Stage 6: Extend)

Training Event 2

When Troy returned to work with the teachers in June, he was greeted warmly. He began his workshop by encouraging teachers to talk about their experiences with working with the ELP strategies. He then concentrated on the use and extensions of MM. He spent the second day expanding on the use of POWER in independent writing. Teachers felt that they gained much more from the second exposure to the ELP materials because they had had time to digest and think about the original presentation.

Principal Stone arranged for her teachers to have a third day to plan and prepare materials for implementing the strategies. The teachers worked on lesson plans. They made POWER mobiles for their classrooms. Most importantly, they shared their experiences with working with the interventions. A new impetus for implementing the strategies in the general education classroom was confirmed: North Slope was implementing a model of full inclusion in the 1999–2000 school year. All students with special needs would be instructed in the general education classroom, and teachers would have to learn how to accommodate and instruct students with learning disabilities and limited cognitive abilities.

At the first faculty meeting in September, the linking agent addressed the North Slope staff and thanked them for participating in the summer training. She offered to serve as a support person and to facilitate communications with Troy as questions arose throughout the year. She also offered to be available to model MM lessons as needed. Within a few days, the linking agent received several requests to demonstrate MM in various classrooms. Each time she entered the building, someone else approached her about coming to his or her classroom. Teachers in grades 3, 4, and 5 were most eager to learn how to facilitate an MM lesson.

(Stage 5: Try)

Second-Year Evaluation

Principal Stone, the coordinating teacher from North Slope, and the linking agent met and developed a plan to evaluate the project for the 1999–2000 school year. The plan called for collecting and scoring writing samples at the beginning and the end of the year for comparison purposes. They also planned to compare this year's Comprehensive Test of Basic Skills (CTBS) and ASPAP scores with scores from the previous year. The plan fully described the collection of survey data from teachers about their use of the ELP strategies. The linking agent sent a copy of the plan to the TA liaison and received positive feedback.

The linking agent conducted the teacher survey in October. She called it the Two-Minute Survey and offered small incentives, such as Post-Its, markers, and colored pens, for completing it. Of the 25 teachers, 17 responded. Twelve indicated that they were using ELP strategies at least once a week. Three others indicated that they were employing the strategies at least once a month. Others indicated that they would begin using the strategies later in the year.

(Stage 6: Extend)

Extending and Reshaping the Innovation

As more and more teachers began using MM as part of their language arts instruction, the linking agent met with them and discussed ways to expand and modify the process to meet the needs of each classroom. Teachers continued to call on the linking agent to model lessons and requested follow-up observations with her as they facilitated MM. Eventually, the teachers began to feel more comfortable with the process and began experimenting with various approaches.

The linking agent began publishing a newsletter that was sent to all special education teachers, support personnel, principals, and supervisors in the county, and board of education members. In the first issue, she featured a story on MM in which she described step-by-step how to facilitate the lesson.

Principal Stone and the linking agent discussed sending interested teachers to Michigan to visit school sites that were successfully implementing MM. They believed that a visit would increase the enthusiasm that was developing. They agreed to send two teachers, and Principal Stone asked interested teachers to fill out an application and describe why they should be chosen for the trip. In the meantime, the linking agent sought approval for the trip from the assistant superintendent and contacted Troy to determine the best date for the visit. Mid-December was the date that Troy felt would work best for him.

What should have been an easy task became difficult. After much effort, three teachers were found with enough interest to make the trip to Lansing, Michigan. Travel plans became complicated when one teacher refused to fly. Hence, a 14-hour train trip was arranged. Numerous phone calls between the linking agent, Principal Stone, Troy, and the three teachers about dates for the visit ensued. Schedules kept changing. Finally, they all agreed on a February date, 3 months later than originally planned.

By this time, Principal Stone had rethought their mission and told the teachers she would like them to develop a summer workshop on the basis of what they learned in Michigan and their experiences this year. The linking agent spoke to the three teachers about planning and conducting the summer workshop. The teachers agreed, and a date in June was chosen for the workshop. They were to present two sessions: one designed for kindergarten to second-grade teachers and another for third- to fifth-grade teachers. In both workshops, the teachers with ELP experience would instruct their peers in MM and POWER with the hope of spreading the ELP strategies throughout the county. Principal Stone also planned to have the trio present their impressions and insights from the trip at a faculty meeting. She was hopeful that more of her staff would thereby become involved and that test scores in the spring would reflect growth in students' writing skills.

Strengthening the Evaluation Platform

At the same time the trip was being arranged, the coordinating teacher from North Slope was gathering writing samples from the teachers. She had explained the scoring process, and the linking agent had offered each teacher a monetary reimbursement for the time spent on scoring the writing samples. Nevertheless, teachers indicated that they did not want to take the time to score the writing; as a result, samples were not collected. The linking agent met with Principal Stone and told her that she was willing to score the samples if the teachers would compile the paragraphs. The TA liaison also volunteered the services of the EMSTAC staff to help score whatever writing samples could be elicited. Finally an edict from Principal Stone resulted in the submission of the paragraphs. Writing samples from grades 2 through 5 were scored by the linking agent with help from EMSTAC. This information was returned to the teachers with a comparative database and graphs of class performance in the various assessed areas.

Reflecting on the experience of 2 years of change effort, the linking agent noted the continued enthusiasm of the staff at North Slope despite understandable feelings of being overwhelmed by new interventions and the associated time requirements. She has seen a willingness in the teachers to implement many of the ELP writing strategies.

Principal Stone and the teachers were pleased when they received the results of the CTBS testing. This standardized test is administered in grades 2, 4, and 5 in Hilldale County. Scores indicated a growth of 16.5 percentile points for those students tested in the second grade and then again in the fourth grade. A growth of 9.2 percentile points was shown in 1 year by those tested in the fourth grade and then again in the fifth grade.

(Stage 6: Extend)

Extending Diffusion in Earnest

The following May, at the International Reading Conference in Indianapolis, the North Slope staff made a presentation on balanced literacy, which included the elements from the ELP (MM and POWER) that they had incorporated in the schoolwide program. A standing-room-only crowd exhausted their supply of 160 handouts and left two pages of requests for more information about the program. Attendees were especially impressed that this program could be implemented in a school setting of such limited resources as those available in Hilldale. Boosted by the response from personnel from other school districts and reinforced by observing the positive results of their own efforts, the teachers renewed their enthusiasm and resolved to continue the program into another year.

In June, three teachers with ELP experience presented two half-day workshops to 31 county elementary school teachers. Typical comments included "The ideas were creative and helpful!" "I think Morning Message will help my students with editing skills," and "North Slope is on the right track!"

When school started in August, many more teachers were eager to implement the ELP and to include all the components of their balanced literacy program. All grade levels were using the ELP strategies with modifications appropriate to students' ability levels. The linking agent sent a survey to all teachers asking about the frequency of conducting MM in their classrooms and their feelings about the strategies.

Every teacher who responded to the survey indicated that she saw an improvement in students' writing skills. They added such comments as "I think this is an effective strategy, which helps to introduce many language components"; "I loved using POWER and Morning Message last year. The children enjoyed building the notebook with all the Morning Messages inside for them to read"; and "Have seen a marked improvement in students' approach to writing since these strategies over a year ago. I see more confidence in them and myself. I will continue to use them."

The linking agent again asked for writing samples to use as a baseline to determine the success of the interventions. This time, Principal Stone decided to encourage teachers toward further commitment by requiring them to score their own samples. She enlisted the linking agent in the task of training teachers in scoring techniques.

At the Atlantic Coalition for Inclusive Education Conference, Principal Stone and two North Slope teachers gave another presentation on the Balanced Literacy Model. They emphasized the value of MM and POWER when instructing students with learning disabilities and students at high risk. At this conference, North Slope School was honored as being one of the top five inclusion schools in the state.

In October, Principal Stone made a presentation of the Balanced Literacy Model to the Hilldale County Board of Education. One board member pressed her with many questions, including one about how teachers assess students' progress. Principal Stone was pleased to be able to report that her teachers were being trained in how to score writing samples and, therefore, would be able to use those data in the assessment process.

On October 13, the scoring training session was held. The linking agent facilitated the training, but teachers took an active part in designing the rubric for scoring. Although the teachers realized that the scoring would be time-consuming, they quickly saw the numerous benefits of scoring their own students' work. They recognized that this involvement would enable them to better determine individual strengths and weaknesses and thus prepare lesson plans that more appropriately addressed the individual needs of all students.

Principal Stone gave teachers a half day to work at scoring the writing. The plan was for teachers to score all writing samples by the end of October and to submit these data to the linking agent for comparison and evaluation purposes. On the day of the training, two teachers from North Slope, Beth and Stephanie, presented an overview of MM and POWER at the John Humbird School, at the request of the school principal. Unfortunately, the teachers there were rude and talked in small groups during their presentation. Beth and Stephanie returned to North Slope feeling disappointed.

CTBS scores were again compared with those of the previous year, and substantial growth was seen in the students' writing scores. ASPAP scores will be released in December and comparisons will be made at that time. The staff at North Slope is eagerly waiting to see whether those results also reflect growth in skills.

A number of linkages developed out of the linking agent's activities in Hilldale. Five persons worked as part of a change agent team: the linking agent; the principal at North Slope; the coordinating teacher at North Slope; and two people external to the school district, the TA liaison and the trainer affiliated with the ELP, Troy. (See Figure 2.6 on page 32.)

For the remaining portion of the case study, use the circles to indicate which part of the change process (Care, Relate, Examine, Acquire, Try, Extend, or Renew) you think the linking agent is experiencing. After reading through the various chapters in this book, revisit this portion of the case study and revisit your thinking about the change process and the stages of change.

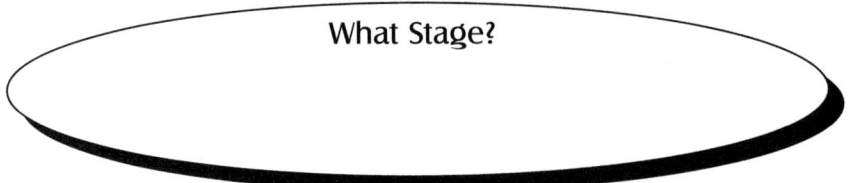

At the beginning of the 1999–2000 school year, the linking agent began contacting middle school principals and attending secondary council meetings to get a sense of perceived needs at the middle school level. In addition, she reviewed the needs assessment completed by special education teachers at the middle school. They had identified improving reading skills as the primary concern at the middle school level.

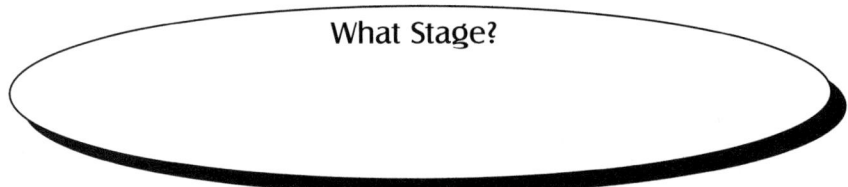

Acquiring Fresh Resources for a New Trial

The linking agent reviewed current research and talked with colleagues and with the TA liaison. As a result of this search process, the Strategic Instruction Model (SIM) emerged as an appropriate, relevant, and research-based intervention for students at the middle school level. The linking agent made direct contact with the developer, Dr. Don Deshler at the University of Kansas. She talked to him about local demographics and needs within her school system. Dr. Deshler sent additional materials about the program and gave her a list of trainers in her geographic region. She contacted a trainer at Johns Hopkins University, who was enthusiastic about doing a workshop in her geographic area and supplied her with numerous details about the intervention.

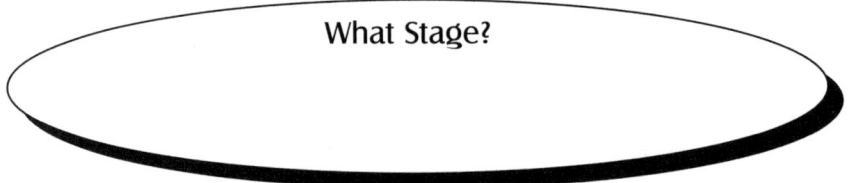

The linking agent contacted individual administrators, gave them copies of print material about the program, and scheduled a meeting during which they could ask questions and assess whether this intervention would meet their needs. Information about the intervention and specific strategies for teaching students with disabilities was also sent to all middle and high school special education teachers. Further, teachers received a survey that asked them to prioritize a number of strategies they thought would best meet the needs of their students. The linking agent developed these surveys on the basis of SIM information she gleaned from the University of Kansas Center for Research on Learning Web site. The site briefly described the various strategies within the intervention. The two strategies that consistently received the highest priority were word identification and paraphrasing.

Building a New Sense of Caring and Choosing a Solution

Meeting as a group in January, the supervisors were enthusiastic about giving students the skills that would help them become more successful in content area classes. They chose word identification and paraphrasing as the strategies they wanted special education teachers trained in first and chose concept mastery and concept anchoring for the general education teachers.

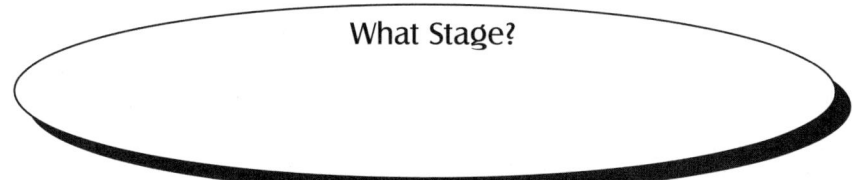

The administrator of a grant that provides transitioning services to students also attended the January meeting. She felt that her grant money could justifiably help pay for training in these strategies and thus expand the pool of high school teachers qualified in these strategies. In March, the linking agent received another encouraging call, this time to tell her that the Atlantic State Improvement Grant (ASIG) money for the Western Atlantic region could be used for SIM training for elementary school teachers. Now teachers at all grade levels could be trained in the same intervention! Elementary teachers were paid from the ASIG money, middle school teachers from EMSTAC, and high school teachers from the transitioning grant.

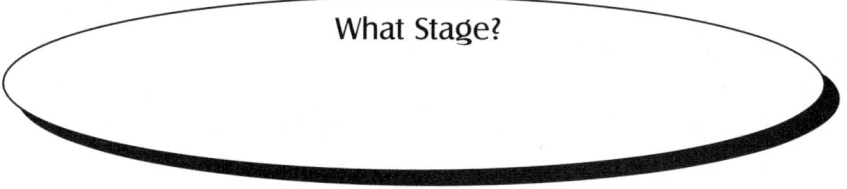

Training for the SIM Model

The linking agent presented all information about the intervention and the strategies to the principals in the secondary council and asked them to encourage teachers to attend the summer training. One middle school principal was very interested and asked for additional information. He was applying for a large grant to improve reading instruction in his school and expressed a desire to add SIM as one of the strategies that would be used.

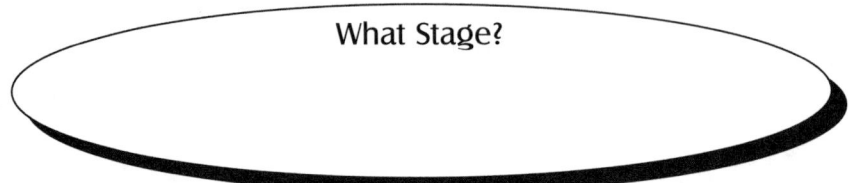

The linking agent composed a memo explaining the SIM model and gave workshop information such as dates, times, and places. The special education supervisors signed the memo and sent it to all teachers. The response from elementary teachers was immediate, and their session filled quickly. In contrast, the response from middle and high school teachers was sparse, but by May, after the linking agent asked the supervisors to encourage their teachers to enroll in the training workshop, the teachers agreed to enroll.

SIM training occurred in early August. Teachers were paid not only for the duration of the training but also for an additional half day to plan how they would implement the interventions. At the training were 19 special education teachers and 20 general education teachers. Many expressed enthusiasm and said that they would definitely incorporate SIM into their teaching plans. Many others indicated that they felt they would not have the time or energy to use the new strategies.

Following Up and Acquiring More Resources

Realizing the need to support the change effort, the linking agent planned to send out a memo right after the training. As soon as school started, the letter would follow up with all teachers who had attended to identify who was not implementing the new strategies and why. Having acquired a catalog of materials that supported the SIM paraphrasing strategy, she also planned to provide additional materials to any teacher willing to try the strategies. As was the case with MM at the elementary level, she planned to offer to provide demonstration lessons to help teachers implement the strategies.

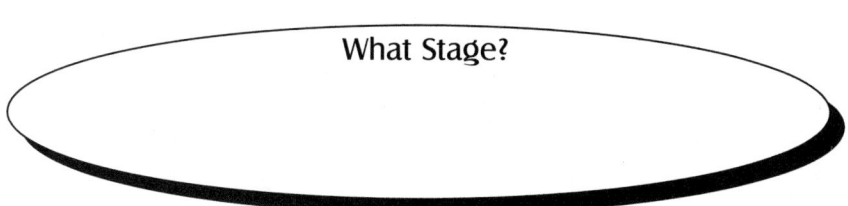

A Budget Crisis. Unfortunately, this plan could not be realized in a timely manner because of financial difficulties in the school system. At the end of the previous school year, the district was operating with a projected deficit of between $1.5 and $3.5 million. The county needed financial relief from the state, which resulted in a state-ordered audit to determine areas where savings could be realized. Among other cost-cutting measures, the board of education ordered the closing of two schools and the reconfiguration of five others. This audit overlapped the time of the SIM training and consumed the time and energy of everyone in the central office for 3 full weeks. Auditors requested data, interviewed personnel, and examined records. As a central office employee, the linking agent was involved in this process, which left her with no time to work with teachers on implementing the SIM strategies.

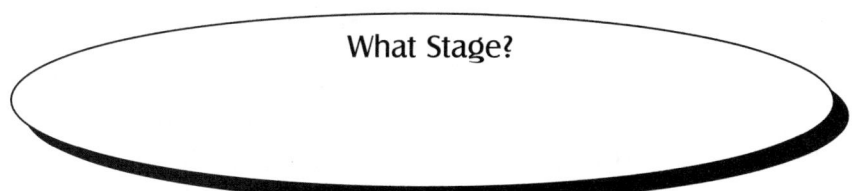

A Weakened Response. When the planned memo was finally distributed to the training participants, only 7 of the 19 teachers responded. Of those teachers, only 3 said that they would instruct their students in SIM during the school year. To address this barrier, the linking agent planned to contact individual teachers to pinpoint the cause of what she felt was a low adoption rate and a lack of interest and to offer support to those who were trying to implement SIM.

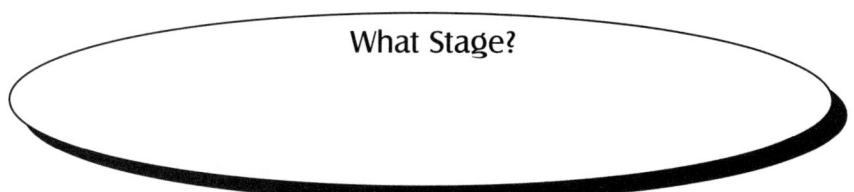

A Linker Derailed by Conflicting Role Demands. Again, demands of the system interfered with the linking agent's ability to fulfill her linker responsibilities. The state was offering a $675,000 grant to counties to establish comprehensive, multiagency preschool centers. Because the system is small, employees often wear many hats. The linking agent was assigned to help write the application, which was due by the middle of October. The linking agent is currently assigned as a special education facilitator for elementary programs for emotionally disturbed students; she is the coordinator of two grants she has cowritten over the past three years; she serves as a trainer in several topic areas; and she is staff development specialist–linking agent. Because this particular grant was so large and considered so important as an early intervention tool, it was assigned top priority.

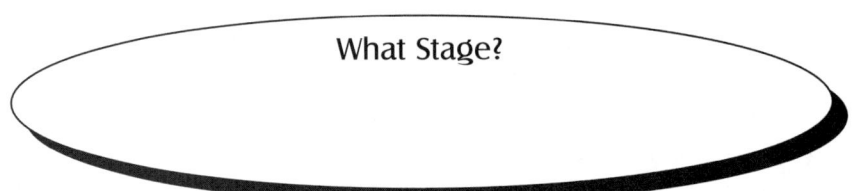

Back on Track but Frustrations Ensue. Once the application was finished and delivered, the linking agent was finally able to begin contacting teachers. She also called Harry, the middle school principal who had said that he was including SIM in his reading grant. Only two of the teachers in Harry's school had indicated a commitment to the project, and the linking agent was soliciting his support in getting more teachers actively involved. She was shocked when he informed her that his committee had decided not to include SIM in the grant proposal. He further stated that his teachers had developed a good reading improvement plan on their own and did not feel that their plan needed the SIM component. He would not interfere with those who wanted to use SIM, but he would not encourage others to participate.

The linking agent was stunned. She had counted on Harry's support and had no previous indication that he had not incorporated SIM in his proposal. Somewhat daunted but not defeated, she contacted the principal at the other large middle school, who said that his school was using one of the SIM's components, accelerated reader. The teachers were generally pleased with the results, and one of his special education teachers, Linda, was enthusiastic about using the SIM strategies. The principal supported her decision but felt that it was up to each teacher to decide how to teach reading.

The linking agent met with Linda, who explained that she was working in general education sixth-grade classrooms with students with disabilities in an inclusive model. She had seen the value of the SIM strategies at the time of the training and had begun teaching them as soon as school started. She reported definite improvement in student skills and requested more materials so that she could move on to the next strategy. The linking agent assured Linda that she would order the materials immediately and asked Linda whether she would be willing to write an article for the special education newsletter about the process and the successes she had already seen.

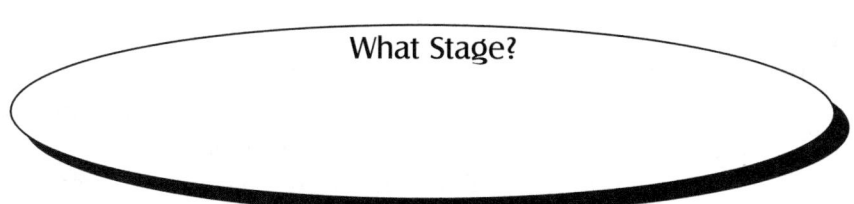

Effort to Extend Awareness and Interest in SIM. The linking agent produced a newsletter for the opening of school, which described the workshops that had occurred during the summer and highlighted the SIM workshop. She gave it to the director of special education and pupil services to approve and to write an opening letter. Many weeks passed without either a cover letter or an approval. The linking agent revised the newsletter and inserted another article in the space previously reserved for the opening letter. More weeks went by as she awaited administrative clearance.

The linking agent also made contact with the other two teachers who had indicated a commitment to teaching SIM and suggested that they talk with Linda and discuss strategies and materials. They enthusiastically agreed to a meeting for the three teachers to plan together and share ideas and experiences. Unfortunately, this meeting was delayed when the linking agent was needed to work again on the application for the state grant.

Process Notes and Lessons Learned From the Hilldale Case Study

The case study illustrates the bumpy road of the change process. Successes are followed by setbacks. Progress stalls when resistance grows. The Hilldale case study clearly shows that the change process in real life is not smoothly linear. It also demonstrates a number of important principles about the process.

Resistance to Change Is Palpable and Ubiquitous

Resistance is a natural reaction to change. In general, people feel comfortable with habits and routines because they know what to expect. Tampering with these behaviors and routines can cause stress, discomfort, and fear. Similarly, in schools and classrooms, the roles and responsibilities that people have (e.g., teacher, principal) have been around for about 1,000 years. The field of special education is no exception. We can sense that roles and lines of responsibility are well established and are not often crossed; procedures are in place and are rarely modified. When the system is presented with an opportunity to set up a new role of a linking agent, few are interested because of this ubiquitous fear of change and the natural reaction to continue with habits and routines that are comfortable. It takes a special person to facilitate the process of change within a school system.

Change Takes Place in Spite of Resistance

Although people are generally resistant to change, to remain successful, systems cannot be impervious to change. School systems must be able to respond intelligently to pressures, to new research and developments, to societal evolution; they must absorb what is new and enhancing. In fact, change is inevitable, and some room for change is always present. Generally, though, educational change exists primarily within a rather narrow spectrum, only when people in the system perceive that something is seriously wrong with the system as it stands and thus have a sense of urgency to fix the problem. This did not seem to be the case in Hilldale County. In this environment, it was difficult to encourage personnel in the school district to get motivated and united around a particular concern for a new initiative because no crisis highlighted the need. There was, however, some pressure resulting from low test scores on the ASPAP, which did encourage many teachers to unite and work together. The main point is that major change will take place only when the level of caring about a problem or a situation reaches a certain threshold. It remains unclear whether that threshold was reached in Hilldale County.

Building Relationships Is Key to Successful Innovation

A main job of the linking agent is to link people: creating connections between people, strengthening existing connections, getting people together in meetings and training sessions, and so on. To succeed in this role, a person must be good at developing social and professional relations and proactive in building new relationships with individuals both within the school system and outside the system. The case study illustrates at least four important points about relationships.

- Building relationships is a never-ending process. The linking agent needs not only to reach out to more and more people but also to continually mend, shore up, and strengthen already established relationships.
- Successful innovation requires teamwork by a solid team representing a mix of skills and leadership attributes. It must include someone with administrative clout, someone with opinion leadership among colleagues, someone with experience in the setting or similar settings, and someone with substantive expertise.
- Good relations must be built and maintained among all key school personnel: special education teachers, regular education teachers, administrators, and central staff.
- It is important to build good relations with people who are external to the district to build personnel, informational, financial, and material resources. In this case study, the linking agent (inside linker) benefited from the relationship between the TA liaison (outside linker), EMSTAC, and Troy (the external consultant for the ELP).

Examination of Needs Should Be Systemic

The process of examining needs should encompass not just the needs of one specially targeted group but the needs and concerns of the majority within the system. In this case, the majority certainly included both general and special education teachers. By conducting a sound needs assessment that acknowledges the needs and concerns of all key personnel in the school system, the change agent is likely to reduce potential resistance at later stages. Further, anything new has the potential to be disruptive. The classroom is a system unto itself with its own equilibrium, not to be undone without substantial reason. Anything new will require extra time and effort, but through a commitment to the concern, school personnel will be willing to modify existing school schedules to accommodate the new intervention.

Innovations Require Downsizing and Building Back Up

Resistance reshapes and distorts the change process in many ways. One phenomenon is downsizing. This is the process of reshaping, repackaging, and many times reducing the scope of change that an intervention will effect in an attempt to make it more acceptable to more teachers and more compatible with existing classroom practice. This process is seen in Hilldale in the decision to implement only the writing strategies of the ELP. By reshaping the program and making amendments to fit a specific situation and particular circumstance, the change agent is able to mold the program to individual needs. The intervention can then be accepted into the system because it does not compete with or contradict other innovations already in the stream. The ELP program became acceptable only after it was shown that the ELP had many features similar to what was already being done and that the writing strategies adopted did not interfere with the progressive work the teachers had been implementing previously in reading.

The Change Process Does Not Run Smoothly and Swiftly

This case study highlights many instances in which progress was slower than anticipated. Many steps had to be repeated and new people had to be brought on board. The linking agent seemed perpetually consumed with local relationship building and maintenance issues as well as logistics and new behavior modeling, which left little time for searching for knowledge and experts. Fortunately, in this case, the linking agent was working with the TA liaison, who was able to assist her in numerous ways and provide support as needed.

Demonstration Is Important

Seeing is believing. Both doability and effectiveness have to be demonstrated in a believable way, which usually requires a site visit to a place where the intervention is successfully being practiced. It is important that this site be comparable to the sites in the locations to which it is being transferred. After the linking agent and Principal Stone saw the ELP intervention in practice, they were able to envision the effectiveness of the program in their own setting. Similarly, through the model lessons that the linking agent performed in the classrooms throughout the district, individual teachers were able to experience the effectiveness of the program.

The Effects Spread

Perhaps the most exciting and hopeful segment of this true case narrative pertains to the diffusion that occurred after teachers were able to observe and give tentative tryouts to certain aspects of the ELP, most notably the Morning Message. A successful demonstration can lead to the rapid spread of an intervention if the linking agent has laid the groundwork: strong connections among the linking agent, teachers and principals in different schools, and the central office. The danger of early resistance by a majority of teachers is that the linking agent could be left with an unrepresentative subset of highly motivated and highly change-oriented teachers. If these teachers do not have much opinion leadership among their colleagues, the innovation will not spread beyond their classrooms. However, in the Hilldale case, diffusion did take place in some directions. We can see the spillover of the innovation from special to general education classrooms and from students with one kind of disability to another. We can begin to see how a well-designed and coordinated innovation, led by a team with a mission to improve the reading and writing opportunities for children with special needs, can have a strong impact on general education instruction.

The Innovation Is Extended and Strengthened in Place

By the second and third year of implementing an intervention, people are more and more comfortable with the changes they have instituted and begin to add back in more elements from the original package. The initial adoption of a single component, such as the Morning Message, is a wedge to open the door for the ELP program as a whole and for a more comprehensive and far-reaching change in classroom practice.

The Innovation Extends to Other Places and Other Levels

The linking agent's successful experience with the ELP in one school encouraged her to extend the innovation to other schools and to make presentations to the principal and teachers, using the ELP strategies from her North Slope School experience. The initial trial site was transformed into a demonstrator site for the entire district and became the focus of a diffusion effort that will have significant impact.

The Linking Agent Learns a Process

As she now moves on to work with middle school populations, the linking agent has worked through the steps of the process of change, which she can now apply to new settings and other interventions. Likewise, we expect that the principal at North Slope will start using her newly developed change teams to look at other ways to improve her school.

As we proceed through the full cycle of stages in a change project in subsequent chapters, we will return again and again to this real-life case and others.

Stage 1

Care

Establishing the Need for Action

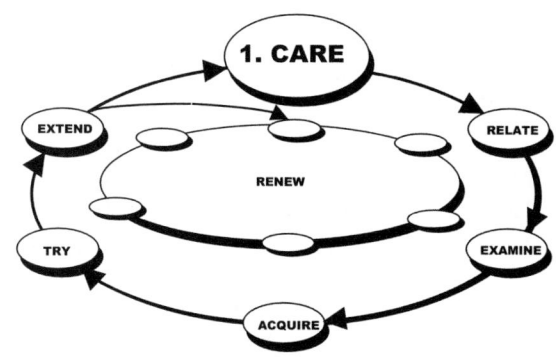

ORGANIZER QUESTIONS

- What motivational set is needed to initiate a change process?
- What initially makes a social system move toward change and why is this necessary?
- What types of change agents are most important to begin a change?
- What are the major forces for change in special education, inside and outside?
- What are the downsides of too much caring?

Change begins with a problem or a need that somebody really cares about, a recognition that something is wrong, that something requires change. This recognition must be accompanied by a sense of urgency, a feeling that action must be taken either now or soon. Social systems like schools or school districts do not automatically welcome such impulses to action. Stability is a hard-won and tenaciously held attribute. Thus, the people who really care and are willing to voice their concerns serve the valuable function of unfreezing the status quo, upsetting the stability, and forcing the powers that be to confront issues they might prefer to ignore. Therefore, this chapter is devoted to the caring aspect of the change process. Who cares? How much do they care? How can they most effectively express their caring so that the system is unfrozen, then moved, and then restabilized in a new configuration that deals with their concerns in a better way? It also considers the possibility that too much caring, too high a level of anxiety about getting something done, can actually get in the way of a positive change process. Caring is not the same thing as understanding. Those who care the most may not be the best people to define what the real dimensions of the problem are or to work on solutions. The delicate task of the linking agent is to find and empower the people who care the most so that they can fill the helpful role of catalysts for change while introducing other players and other resources to work on the other aspects of the overall process.

Someone Must Care Enough to Make It All Worthwhile

The first stage of the CREATER model is Care because change begins with a care or a concern, a feeling that something is wrong and that something should be done to correct that wrong. Caring provides the necessary energy to get things going, to overcome the inertia that inevitably presents itself in the face of change. Where is this concern located? Who has it? How strongly is it felt? Is this concern the right starting point or an appropriate rallying cry to action?

Special Education Linking Agents in Action

In the case study about the Hilldale County schools, which have a history of implementing strong change initiatives, it is clear that a great deal of care lay behind the push toward change.

This is not a district that rests on its laurels. There is good evidence from past history that district personnel care about making improvements. They have made a serious and continuing effort to provide a better educational environment by addressing a broad array of issues, including those that concern special education. They want to improve for their children.

It's important to start with a rough conception of the school system, which contains the group of people (special educators, other school system personnel, parents, students) who have a common concern. In what sense are they a "group"? To what extent are they even aware that they have a shared concern? Are they capable of achieving enough

> consensus to drive joint action toward a solution? If they do have a shared concern, can an outside linking agent be useful to them? And if so, what type of skills would make that linking agent most useful to the school system?
>
> *The only principal who expressed a real interest in the new project was Catherine Stone at North Slope School, which was also the only school that had clearly defined its needs. She met with the School Improvement Team (SIT) and the School Achievement Team (SAT). Together they determined that they would like to improve the reading instruction available to the special education population. They felt that the reading instruction offered in the special education classes should resemble that offered in the general education classrooms.*

A concrete concern, such as North Slope School's need to improve reading instruction for special education students, provides a focus for the energy of caring. When you sense a concern, you must direct yourself to the question of whose concern it is and how you interact with those people. The next step is to identify the real problem underlying the concern, which will help focus the search for solutions and for a strategy that will put the solutions into practice. When you have identified an appropriate solution, tried it out, and found it to be effective, you will then want to extend its application to solve the problem for the school, or school system, as a whole.

The change process is cyclical. The seventh stage, Renew, leads back to the first stage, Care. Have you successfully altered the conditions that got you started in the change process in the first place? To find out, you start at the beginning again by asking, What is the concern now? This question should lead you into a whole new cycle of relating, examining, acquiring, trying, and extending.

As you progress through these stages, you must continue to identify what the real need is, whose need it is, and what level of concern is driving that need. As you complete each cycle, you should reflect on your process and build your capacity to solve problems and make a school system that continually improves itself. This is the meaning of the seventh step, Renew.

A Three-Step Model of Change: Unfreeze-Move-Refreeze

School systems are required to absorb new inputs from the outside daily, but they generally do so in a highly controlled manner that does not disrupt the existing infrastructure. Barriers to outside influence and cohesive ties within the school system are necessary for stability, but these same barriers and ties hinder change coming from either within or outside the system. Internal rigidities and commitments inside the system prevent reorganization, innovation, and growth. Strong barriers protect the school system from unwanted external intrusions but also inhibit the entry of new people, new resources, and new ideas. The model described below, unfreeze-move-refreeze, posited by the social psychologist Kurt Lewin (1951), explains how social systems change. These three steps also apply to school systems, which are a kind of social system.

Unfreezing: Often the First Task of a Linking Agent

Lewin proposed that the initial posture of most social systems encountering change is "frozen." Therefore, the initial change task is to unfreeze the system, to create an environment in which ties are at least temporarily loosened and protective barriers are made temporarily permeable. We could also call this "system openness."

Moving: Only Possible if There Is Openness to Change

"Moving" is the introduction of the change and its initial acceptance. The more permeable the barriers are, the more rapidly and easily new elements are able to enter. Permeable barriers allow advanced and sophisticated school systems to retain a great deal of internal stability while still welcoming many types of innovations.

Refreezing: Making Sure That What Comes In Stays In

"Refreezing" is the system's return to a new equilibrium in which the change is incorporated. Changes may be tolerated for a time but then rejected when, for instance, members of the system are forced by circumstance to decide what is really important (e.g., when budget trimming is required). Thus, the greatest challenge is to gain a level of acceptance for the innovation that is strong enough to survive this closing-up process.

Lewin's three-step model of change is simple and corresponds to the CREATER model. Lewin's step of unfreezing helps explain the importance of Care, the first CREATER stage. Care is the level of concern for a problem. Care unfreezes a school system and starts the change process, along with open relationships (linkages) that allow the flow of new ideas into and through the school system. The moving part of Lewin's model relates to the later stages of Acquiring, Trying, and Extending. It is during these three stages that the school system selects an intervention, implements the initiative in an initial pilot site, reevaluates effectiveness, makes adjustments to the project, and extends to include additional sites. Finally, Lewin's refreezing step can be related to the Renew stage of the CREATER model. Renew is the acceptance of the intervention by the school system as a regular part of the school program, which allows the intervention to become institutionalized.

Special Education Linking Agents in Action

North Slope School *Unfreeze*

- Teachers told the principal they did not like any of the reading approaches selected as possibilities.

- The Early Literacy Project (ELP) was the best, they thought, but it would require a change in the entire language arts curriculum.
- The linking agent and the principal went over the ELP curriculum point by point and concluded that North Slope had already made a lot of the changes suggested in the ELP. Therefore, they could focus on incorporating the program's other innovative features without a lot of stress.
- The staff then agreed that the ELP was an intervention they could consider seriously.

North Slope School *Move*

- Troy concentrated mainly on writing interventions. Using charts and samples of actual student work, he described Morning Message (MM) and POWER (an acronym for a way to organize writing: plan, organize, write, edit, and rewrite).
- Teachers were impressed with the samples of student work that he provided.
- Within 5 days of the training, the linking agent demonstrated MM in a special education class. The students and the teacher participated enthusiastically.
- The next day, the linking agent returned to the class with a copy of the story. When she got there, the teacher was already in the middle of doing MM with her class! The kids were very excited and wanted to read their story to her.

North Slope School *Refreeze*

- All grade levels were now using the ELP strategies with modifications appropriate to students' ability levels.
- In late September, the principal and two North Slope teachers gave another presentation on the Balanced Literacy Model, emphasizing the value of MM and POWER when instructing students who are learning disabled and at high risk.
- At this conference, North Slope School was honored as being one of the top five inclusion schools in the state.

How School Systems Show (and Don't Show) That They Are in Trouble

As the linking agent enters the scene, different school systems may show widely differing caring postures. For example, they may profess that everything is fine: There is no need for change. At the opposite extreme, a system may appear to be so completely absorbed with a particular concern that its members have no time for you. People are capable of expressing, and also of

> **The Four Types of Caring Postures**
>
> - When everything seems fine
> - When concerns are all over the lot
> - When concerns are not what they seem
> - When concerns are very intense

hiding, their concerns in a baffling number of ways. Like a good psychotherapist, the linking agent needs to listen with the third ear. What members of a school system say may not really be what they mean and may even be a cover for something else. Let us take four types of caring postures and consider what they might really signify: when everything seems fine, when concerns are all over the lot, when concerns are not what they seem, and when concerns are very intense.

When Everything Seems Fine

Is there such a thing as a school system without concerns or without the need for change? Perhaps in theory, but not in practice. All human systems are unfulfilled, incomplete, or lacking in some ways. Yet, ironically, the systems that are most able and willing to change are probably in the best shape. These systems can adapt to changing circumstances, grow, and take on new missions. Therefore, if a school system presents itself as having no concerns that require a significant change effort, what is really going on? At least four explanations are possible (if we dismiss perfection): The school system is frozen; its members are not yet engaged; the key concerns have not reached the boiling point; or its members are not willing to tell you what is going on.

The System Is Frozen

Having achieved a certain level of equilibrium and integration, members of a school system may not wish to go further at this time—to rock the boat—particularly if the state of integration has been recently achieved. At the opposite extreme, some school systems may have existed at one level of integration for so long that even the thought of change is perceived as a threat to the system's stability. In either case, the system needs to be unfrozen before any serious change effort can be implemented.

Personnel Are Not Yet Engaged

We often make the mistake of assuming that people hear what they are told and see what they are looking at. Very often, especially on first encounters, what appears to be hearing, seeing, understanding, or agreeing is merely the polite or ritualistic posturing of people who are not really attending to your message. Linking agents may be angry and frustrated when they try to proceed with what they thought was an agreed-on plan of action only to find that their work is unsupported, contradicted, and undermined by the very people they thought were on their side. No doubt deceit is involved in some of these cases, but you should first consider the much simpler theory that genuine engagement never did exist. The other parties simply were not attending to what you were saying. The antidote to this problem is effective initial communication and active solicitation of feedback. If you can get your listener to repeat your message back to you, there is a good chance that it got through.

Trouble Is Bubbling Just Under the Surface

Think of concerns in terms of threshold. Below a certain level of intensity, these concerns remain unarticulated—we might say unconscious. Then something happens to bring them to the surface: something breaks, someone dies, or someone quits. Many vital concerns can lie just beneath the surface for years until some catalytic event comes along and brings them to serious attention. Of course, you can be that catalytic event (linking agent as catalyst).

> **Convey Your Caring to Your Colleagues: An EMSTAC Linking Agent Comments on *Care*:**
>
> There were many times when I grew frustrated and simply wanted to give up. It is important to persist in motivating yourself and the district that you are working with as things go slowly or new roadblocks are encountered.
>
> —EMSTAC linking agent

System Is Not Leveling With Outsiders

When linking agents from outside the school system enter the scene, people may not share concerns with them, particularly if they are thought to be a threat, of inferior status, from an alien work culture, or unable or unlikely to understand and respond appropriately. These perceptions are aspects of the definition of "outsider" that linking agents from outside the system must overcome before they can obtain real insights into how the system works. If you think this may be your situation, then your first task as an outside linking agent is to work on building relationships (Stage 2: Relate). After you have done this relationship work, return to a consideration of what the school system's concerns are.

When Concerns Are All Over the Lot

In some school systems, a linking agent may face an overwhelming number of diverse concerns expressed by different members of the system. This multitude of concerns may reflect a nonsystem—a dysfunctional school system with weak internal linkages, a lack of integration, and a lack of perceived common purpose. If, however, system members' concerns are somewhat coherent but tend to line up as polarities or as irreconcilable needs and conflicts, the linking agent may be confronting two strong subsystems that must be reconciled before positive change can occur. In either instance, the first task of the linking agent is to start building bridges, making the first change project a system-building exercise.

When Concerns Are Not What They Seem

It is possible that members of a school system may signal one concern to the linking agent although they really want help with another. It is important for the linking agent who is invited into a situation first to listen carefully to the manifest concern and second to consider that it might not be the real concern. Members of the school system may not be able to articulate their real concerns for a variety of reasons. One might be defensiveness or embarrassment. Another might simply be an inability to articulate what is really bothering them. Asking for outside help, for instance, on the disproportional representation of minorities in special education, might be the manifest request when the underlying problem is racial tension. Linking agents should always enter situations with an open mind but be prepared to view the presented concern skeptically. They should look for any signs that contradict the priority claim of this concern and independently develop their own list of concerns to see whether they match the official one.

When Concerns Are Very Intense

Sometimes the concern may be so intense that it interferes with constructive problem solving. The high anxiety level may lead to paralysis or counterproductive, quick-fix solutions. Further, focusing excessively on one issue may blur perception of other concerns—the school system will not get the big picture, may miss other important concerns that might yield more easily to problem solving, or may fail to perceive underlying problems that need to be addressed.

An intense focus on a concern may also diminish an appreciation for the need to apply deliberate, rational, and collaborative processes. The sense in the school system that action is needed immediately can forestall the diagnosis of problems, the search for resources, and the consideration of alternative solutions. In effect, all the change processes that are described in *Guiding Change* are rendered useless. Thus, the linking agent may need to develop strategies to calm the intense pressure for solutions and buy time to create space for reflection and for viewing the school system's concerns.

Knowledge Base

The Care Stage

In his most recent writings, Fullan (2001a, 2001b) describes moral purpose as the appropriate starting point for thinking about change and exerting leadership on its behalf: "The moral purpose of schools is to make a difference in the lives of students" (2001b, p. 16). This concept is close in meaning to Stage 1: Care as used here. Slogans such as "leave no child behind" articulate broad societal goals for what we really care about. The goal of ensuring that children with disabilities have "access to a free appropriate public education" as mandated by the Education for All Handicapped Children Act of 1975 is another example of a Stage 1: Care statement expressed as a broad societal goal.

Gene Hall (1974) originated the Concerns-Based Adoption Model (CBAM). Hall's focus was the concerns that teachers had when they were required to adopt innovations passed down from on high. To understand the real change process on the ground, we must pay attention to the real concerns of teachers. They know what the real problems are, and they know what additional problems are going to arise when they try something new. Huberman and Miles (1984) used the same model to contrast the motives of administrators and teachers. This contrast has a loud resonance in special education, where mandates, or pressure from above, are passed down to regular classroom and special education teachers. Hall has continued to pursue studies based on his CBAM model for more than 30 years (Hall & Hord, 2001).

Fullan (2001b, pp. 30–31) observes that all real change involves loss, anxiety, and struggle, regardless of where the initiative comes from—top down, bottom up, or from the side. Because the real meaning behind any change is usually obscure at early stages, stakeholder response is shrouded in ambivalence. Hence it is vitally important to share the care among all those affected. Fullan quotes Marris (1975): A (planned) change "cannot be assimilated unless its *meaning* is shared."

In their zeal to advance a cause, change agents may rush ahead on the assumption that everybody has bought in to the obvious need, but many real Stage 1: Care issues can remain hidden. Fullan warns, "Be wary of superficial acceptance of adoption decisions" (2001b, p. 195). Argyris (2000, pp. 202–203) also warns of the dangers of false consensus. Later on you can expect silent doubters to "drag their feet in implementation or work actively to subvert implementation."

When concerns are all over the lot, a lack of care focus can also be a problem. Hatch (2000) (cited by Fullan, p. 22 ff.) reports on 57 California and Texas school districts surveyed from 1992 to 1995. The typical urban district was found to have 11 major change initiatives going on simultaneously. The result: "frustration and anger at the school level."

Deal and Peterson (1999) describe "toxic school cultures" in which key opinion leaders become "negaholics," pessimistic storytellers who create a hostile environment for any proposed change. Clearly, in such environments, the real Care issue and the first responsibility of any change agent is not how to implement this or that innovation but how to change the school culture.

Deal and Peterson (1999, p. 87) also note that a school leader can sometimes personify the Care issue by becoming a visionary who mobilizes the community by articulating "a deeply value-focused picture of the future for the school." In the presence of such a leader, the special educator change agent has the added mission of making sure that children with special needs are included in that picture.

In the special education linking agent study (Hamilton et al., 2002) where 32 separate change projects were initiated and tracked as they progressed through the seven stages, those projects driven by local school initiatives moved much further into implementation than projects responding to district or state mandates. Stage 1: Care must have a local origin or a strong local meaning in Fullan's terms.

Improving Behavior in Denville: Alternative Approaches to Discipline

The Elementary and Middle Schools Technical Assistance Center (EMSTAC) has been working with Denville for 3 years to implement positive schoolwide discipline practices. Through the diligent efforts of a school-based linking agent and support at the district level, EMSTAC works with both an elementary and a middle school.

School staff received training in teaching social skills lessons and are in various stages of incorporating the social skills curriculum into their regular teaching routines. In the middle school, social skills lessons are video-recorded and then played on the closed-circuit television network. The lessons are used as a tool to expose all the children in the building to expected positive behaviors and alternative ways of solving problems. At the elementary level, the social skills initiative is just getting off the ground, with further training and support activities expected. EMSTAC's work in Denville has been exciting and has provided the linking agent with opportunities to network, facilitate staff development activities, and support colleagues in her school building.

Figure 1.1 Sum of Forces External and Internal

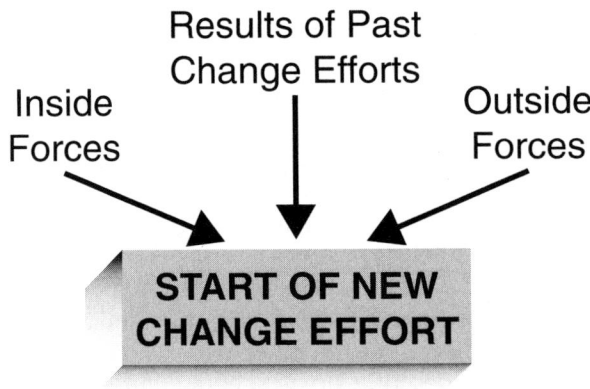

Inside Versus Outside Forces

The level of caring required to push a school system into new action is a product of many forces, and the way these forces sum up will vary greatly from time to time and situation to situation. Most of these forces are either internal or external, that is, they come either from inside the system or from outside of it.

Many of these forces may conflict with one another. Some inside forces, for example, may be pushing the school system toward an equilibrium in which students receiving special education services are taught in self-contained classrooms and thus are isolated from their general education peers. Other forces could be pushing for increased inclusion of all students in the general educational classroom. Further, outside pressures, such as state and federal mandates, may be pushing for changes that require students with special needs to have access to the general curriculum in the least restrictive environment. Note that one strand of forces in Figure 1.1 comes from the continuing cycle of problem solving on some issues within a school system. As one cycle of innovative problem solving concludes, successfully or not, it inevitably changes the needs of the system, thereby contributing to the new mix of forces that will impel the next round of action.

Inside Forces

Within a school system, a number of influences, pressures, and circumstances can often be identified as inside forces impelling change in special education. Five categories are listed here as examples: pressure from the families of students, level of concern shown by particular parent and student advocates, level of concern shown by particular teachers or administrators, consensus level of concern among educators inside a school system, and unforeseen inside events.

Pressure From the Families of Students

Families of children with special needs have been instrumental in advocating for enhanced services and educational opportunities for their children at national, state, and local levels. Through their efforts and the work of other advocates, Public Law 94–142 (the Education for All Handicapped Children Act) was developed, which requires a free appropriate public education for each child with a disability in every state and locality across the country. Families and parents continue to put pressure on federal, state, and local governments, in addition to local school districts, to improve results for their children with special needs.

Level of Concern Shown by Particular Parent and Student Advocates

Somewhat apart from the pressures cited above are the articulated needs of particular parents and their children, often crystallized around a particular incident.

Level of Concern Shown by Particular Teachers or Administrators

> **What Problems Do Inside Linking Agents Face?**
>
> A common hindrance has been the lack of synchronization between the support and interest of the school-level staff (principal, teachers) and the central office (superintendent, special education director, special education staff). In districts where the inside linking agents are school-based, they sometimes do not have the full support of the special education director, the superintendent, or even their own principal. In this situation, it may be difficult to achieve buy-in across an entire school or school district. Without support from the principal, interventions can die on the vine because the school is unwilling to act on the central office's mandate.
>
> —EMSTAC linking agent

It is very common for change to be initiated by one person, often a teacher or an administrator who has become frustrated with the way things are done in his or her school system. This person could already be a linking agent or could decide to become a linking agent. In any case, such a person is definitely a self-designated linking agent, initially of the catalyst variety.

Consensus Level of Concern Among Educators Inside a School System

It is also possible that a level of concern is shared by a number of educators inside a school system. General and special educators may share common concerns about how to help all students do well on state assessments or how to address the high incidence of violence in their schools.

Unforeseen Inside Events

Life holds many surprises, even inside smoothly operating school systems. A key person may leave. A school that has just instituted inclusive classrooms may have veteran teachers who are hostile to the idea of having students with disabilities in their classes. Their resistance to implementing an inclusive model of education could be because they lack knowledge about how to teach children with disabilities or do not want to participate in team-teaching in their

> **Thoughts of an Outside Linking Agent**
>
> The meetings with inside linking agents were primarily designed for the insiders to do the talking, and for the outside linkers to do the listening, to help them think through their problems and to help problem-solve with them. These meetings are intended to remind them of their roles as change agents, to celebrate their progress, to share their problems, and to solve problems as a group among their fellow linking agents. Because these meetings are informal and discussion-oriented, the inside linking agents lead the course of the discussion and the meetings, while we outside linking agents listen and guide discussions.
>
> —EMSTAC linking agent

classroom or simply do not want to disturb their classroom routines. In fact, there could be numerous reasons for resistance. It is important for a linking agent to build relationships with all key school personnel to gain a solid understanding about the causes of resistance in order to reduce their effects. Any of these events may change the mix of forces leading to a new round of problem solving.

Outside Forces

"Outside" covers a lot of terrain. Unwanted influence is typically seen as coming from outside and hence as somehow being illegitimate. Here we define outside as being outside the official bounds that enclose the administration, teachers, students, and the parents of those students. Outside describes forces that are working to effect change in a school system although they are not a part of it. The local outside is the sum of all the influences coming from people and groups in the geographic area covered by the school system; the larger outside includes the state, the nation, and the world at large. Many potential forces emanate from all these areas. Here is a short list.

The Local Outside

It is commonly asserted that education is a local matter and that local schools should be locally controlled. However, this belief has rarely meant autonomy for teachers or administrators. Rather, it indicates that control should rest in the hands of local government officials and elected representatives, such as school boards. The insiders of a school system, those who experience the daily challenges and successes of the school and the students, often perceive such influences as coming from outside. Outside influences can help create great positive change as long as they recognize the needs as expressed from the inside.

> **What Do Outside Linking Agents Do?**
>
> Provide contacts and networking with other linking agents.
>
> I work with the linking agents to coordinate all training events.
>
> I call linking agents and other district partners, e-mail linking agents in order to ask for updates and communicate about the progress the districts are making.
>
> I think that my primary task is to keep things moving forward.
>
> —EMSTAC linking agents

Local Community: Churches, Businesses, Voluntary Organizations, Media. The importance of nongovernmental groups varies greatly from one community to another. Numerous local not-for-profit organizations have the mission of improving opportunities for children with special needs. Further, companies, both local and national, have become increasingly invested in contributing to social activities, particularly to education. Often in a small rural town, the business leaders and their families exert enormous influence and can be excellent resources in the process of initiating change. In communities with high church attendance, especially where one religion dominates, members of the clergy exert such influence. Anyone who has power in the community may have a tremendous influence on schools and school boards.

Federal Laws and Mandates

Numerous pieces of key early federal legislation supported improved programs and services for individuals with special needs. By 1968, the federal government had supported training for more than 30,000 special education teachers and related specialists and the education for children with disabilities in preschools and in elementary, secondary, and state-operated schools across the country. These laws laid the foundation for Public Law 94–142 more than 25 years ago. The four purposes of the law articulated a compelling national mission to improve access to education for children with disabilities. The reauthorization of Public Law 94–142 (the Individuals with Disabilities Education Act [IDEA]) in 1997 articulated a new challenge to improve results for children with special needs and their families. Further, through IDEA-Part D programs, a significant amount of research has been federally funded to improve the identification, implementation, evaluation, and dissemination of information about effective programs and practices. IDEA-Part D programs provide an infrastructure of practice improvement that supports the national goal of educating infants, toddlers, children, and youth with disabilities and their families.

> **What Skills Do Outside Linking Agents Need?**
>
> Taking a real interest in their needs and concerns and circumstances and exhibiting this interest through good listening skills.
>
> —EMSTAC linking agent

An effective linking agent will need a fairly detailed knowledge of the various special education laws and funding opportunities and should know how to obtain additional information. Further, many states have implemented mandates that complement and enhance the federal law, IDEA. Therefore, understanding the state laws and funding opportunities is very important to linking agents who work with personnel in special education and for children with disabilities for a variety of reasons. Although linking agents do not want to be viewed as enforcers, they do want to be regarded as enablers who help their school systems find the most beneficial and cost-effective paths to full compliance. In the unhappy circumstance that linking agents are not accepted in such a role, they can use the teeth of the law as an opening wedge for change, but in taking on this catalyst role, linking agents may compromise their ability to act as honest brokers and connectors to other outside resources.

National Advocates and Advocacy Groups

Advocacy groups working toward enhancing educational opportunities for children with special needs and equality of opportunity for adults with special needs cut across religious, racial, social, and economic boundaries and exert influence far greater than their numbers would suggest. Special education linking agents are at an advantage because they have such allies.

Popular Culture and Mass Media

All school-related activity survives despite a flood of influences from popular culture, most of which are conveyed by the mass media in a relentless and constant stream of messages about who we are, what we should look like, what we should possess, and how we should behave. Highest on the list is television, which pours its diverse commercial and entertainment content into nearly every household in the country at the rate of three to six hours per day. Growing influences are computers and the Internet, with its vast, readily accessible resources. These influences are neither uniformly negative nor uniformly positive, but they are omnipresent.

Effective teachers are good at tracking these influences just enough so that they can use those that are most positive to illustrate their own teaching content. Linking agents need to do the same but at a different level, tuning in to the aspects of popular culture that teachers and others whom they hope to influence most attend to. EMSTAC, for example, harnessed the popularity and versatility of the Internet by providing linking agent training on its website, www.emstac.org. Using the Internet to provide this training greatly increased the number of potential linking agents that EMSTAC could reach and train. It also provided many resources collected especially for EMSTAC linking agents, who could chat with each other online about their various change initiatives; read up on areas of change, such as social skills or reading programs; and connect to a wide variety of linked pages and special education resources.

New Technologies

Linking agents should be informed about and alert to the potential of new technologies. They should always be ready to support their appropriate introduction (as will be discussed under Stage 4: Acquire), but it is important that they not overestimate such new technologies as a force for change.

Unforeseen Outside Events

The many other outside influences that may become an important part of the Care mix are hard to predict. Some may be helpful; others may not. For example, a severe economic downturn on a local, regional, or national scale always puts pressure on local tax rolls—and education takes a hit. The administration of President Eisenhower in the 1950s paid no attention to education until a Soviet-launched

---

> **What Do Outside Linking Agents Do?**
>
> We have coordinated and conducted periodic "checkpoint" meetings that have served at least two purposes: (1) provided an opportunity for inside linking agents to share their progress and roadblocks they have experienced in their attempts to bring research-based practices into classrooms; and (2) provided a forum for inside and outside linking agents to problem-solve and consult among and with each other. We also communicate regularly with an intermediate-level linking agent within the county district, arranging and coordinating meetings with her, and learning about how the local school districts are doing.
>
> —EMSTAC linking agent

satellite, Sputnik, appeared, plain for all to see as it streaked across the night sky. After that, the federal role in education increased sharply. With the Cold War long over, we cannot expect another Sputnik to shock the country out of complacency, but lesser events can still move us, such as an unusually close national election in which education emerged as a consensus reform target.

Linking Agent as Connector and Orchestrator of Forces

Some linking agents will choose to be catalysts, jumping to the front of the battle as advocates for improvement in special education, but they do not have to become catalysts to be useful in the initial stages of a change process. The first question should always be, *Does this school system care enough to initiate a serious change effort?* If the answer to that question is definitely yes, it may be appropriate to continue with the process, starting with Stage 2: Relate. If, however, you are somewhat uncertain about the level of shared concern about the issue you intend to work on, you should first review the array of potential forces, both internal and external, that might become involved (as partially identified in this chapter) and, second, ask what you might do to strengthen or redirect any of these forces. Are there potentially caring influential forces, either inside or outside, that might be alerted? Is there an appropriate awareness and consideration of the special education laws and rules that might be violated? Does the local newspaper know what is going on? Linking agents have a number of ways to bring out the concern that a school system should have without directly being the advocate for that concern.

Whose Responsibility? The Value Issues in Helping

The word *change* can be a very hot button indeed. If you are the self-appointed linking agent and I am the one you are planning to change, I am not likely to welcome you with open arms. Who has the right to change anyone, after all? As the heroic farmer of an old western movie might have said, "That railroad ain't comin' through my land." Thus, it is important for us to clarify early on some value issues that swirl around the change process. When is change just obstruction and disruption of a school system that works? When is it just interference and meddling? More ominous, when is change subversion or manipulation? Can you ever justify serious intervention in other people's lives, however good your intentions may be by your own lights? This kind of question can be answered meaningfully only within the context of your personal values.

One way to avoid such a values question is to ask whether anyone has the linking agent "license." If you are called in by legitimate representatives of a school system to provide help of some kind, paid or voluntary, you have a kind of moral cover. You are not a self-serving independent operator; on the contrary, you are doing their bidding and you have their permission. By following the CREATER model, a linking agent works collaboratively with a school system toward improvement objectives that the system can see and value. However, such stipulations do not protect you from moral challenges on a number of grounds. It can be argued that both people and entities such as school systems have a fundamental right to privacy to work out their own problems in their own ways. This problem is as old as the helping professions themselves. Indeed, the stricture of the ancient Hippocratic oath is applicable: *primum non nocere,* or above all, do no harm.

Yet, can you ever guarantee that you will do no harm, that you will leave the school system in at least as good a condition as you found it? Definitely not. After all, you are trying to make significant changes in ongoing, living systems. You are interfering with linkages and arrangements that may have been in place for ages. When you open up a new room, how do you know that you are not tearing down a bearing wall, threatening the collapse of the entire structure? There is inherent risk in what linking agents do, and you should be aware of it. You should strive always both to minimize the risk and to provide the system in which you are working with enough information about your intervention so that it can give informed consent.

One of the trickiest moral dilemmas concerns your school system's initial expectations. You are invited in because school personnel think you will do one kind of thing for them, but inevitably, if you are a good linking agent, you will seek to do more and different things than they may expect, things they may appreciate only after they have experienced them. If you are brought in by one member of the system to *serve his or her needs,* is it legitimate to reach out in an attempt to serve other members with other needs? As a linking agent, you will have to resolve these questions for yourself in your own way. *Guiding Change* should help you sort out these issues, but it will not resolve them for you.

Defining your role as that of a linking agent is also helpful in providing cover for many of the value issues of planned change, and it is partly for that reason that this concept is promoted here. As a linking agent, you can view your primary task as connecting people with each other, people with resources, people with knowledge, inside people with outside people, needs with solutions, and solutions with appropriate applications. It is really your job to make the connections and then back out of the way, leaving the members of the school system as the primary doers and the ones who should and will take responsibility for what happens.

Do's and Don'ts of CARE

Westville, a school district in a suburb not far from a major city, was shifting from site-based management of curriculum to a common-core curriculum of best practices.

Do

In choosing potential solutions to improve reading outcomes for special education students, the two linking agents in Westville emphasized helping all students benefit from the new initiatives instead of dividing the resources between special education and general education.

Don't

Because the linking agents first worked only with personnel at a high level to determine the focus of the change effort, teachers at the school level were not involved during the Care stage. When teachers were finally pulled in during the Relate stage, they were not supportive of the new reading initiative, which they felt was no better than the approaches already in place. Not including *all* important personnel at the Care stage can cause problems in the later stages.

Care: Summary

System change can be viewed as three steps: unfreezing, moving, and refreezing. Care is about unfreezing, getting the system to start moving toward serious change. Schools and school systems can show that they are in trouble in various ways, but often they do not want to show it at all. Complacency and manifest calm can be a cover for a host of serious problems. Sometimes it is the job of the linking agent to be a catalyst, upsetting the status quo by raising troubling questions and lending support to activists within the system. The parents of children with special needs often play this role.

The care stimulus can come from various levels within the system, and it can also come from outside—from the local community, from state and federal mandates, and from advocacy groups that work regionally and nationally for people with various disabilities. New technologies can also act in a catalytic way by opening up new possibilities. The linking agent's special role is to ensure that these various forces and voices for change are coordinated and orchestrated so that they can be heard by the system and can unfreeze the system so that movement is possible.

To get started, the linking agent should always address these Care questions:

- Is the system you are working with or about to work with sufficiently concerned and motivated to begin a change process to improve special education?
- Are particular persons or groups acting as catalysts, showing active concern, or agitating to improve special education in your setting?
- If the school system's level of concern is insufficient, are there ways to raise the level of concern that promote movement toward positive change?
- Does the school system require more unfreezing before any change effort can proceed? What is the best way to bring about this unfreezing, and who should do it?
- What is your own level of concern as a change agent in this situation?
- Does your level of concern and your type of concern match well with the concerns of the catalysts you identified above?
- Does your concern match well with others in the setting, such as the major stakeholders and decision makers?
- Is your level of concern enough to keep you motivated to proceed into a serious change effort with this system?
- What is the primary concern directly voiced by the school system leadership with which you will be working?
- How well does this voiced concern match the concerns and priorities set forth in federal and state legislative mandates for special education?
- How well does this voiced concern match the concerns of local special education catalysts?
- Are competing concerns present within this school system that might interfere with this change effort? If so, can you develop a strategy to contain them?

Stage 2

Relate

Building a Relationship

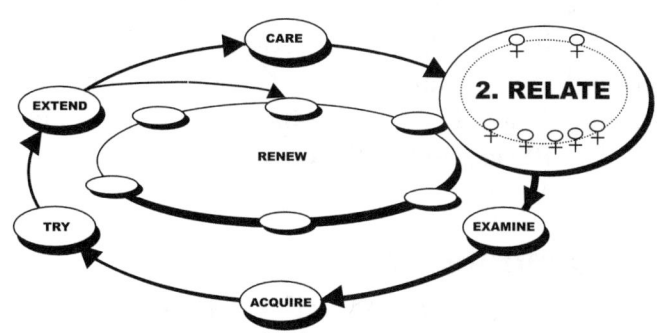

ORGANIZER QUESTIONS

- What is the contract and how should it develop over time?
- What are the four major linking agent tasks for Stage 2: Relate?
- What are the pros and cons of being an insider and an outsider?
- What is the best way to build a change team?
- What are the ideal features of a social group that is working toward change?

From first contact to last good-bye, you as the linking agent have to think about the people you are relating to and how they are relating to one another. To be fully effective, you have four Relate tasks: to understand the social system and how it works, to understand the relationship between yourself and that social system, to do whatever you can to improve how members of the social system work with one another, and to improve your own relationship with the system and its key members.

The social environment for any change activity in a school context is a complex entity. There are levels upon levels—a formal hierarchy and informal networks. There are the general education system and the special education system, together yet apart, united in overall goals and yet inevitably divided in priorities. As the process unfolds through each successive problem-solving stage, the linking agent must return again and again to ask whether relationships are still holding and whether the system as a whole has enough integration to support the change effort.

A key to maintaining relationships while continuing the momentum toward change is the nurturing of a change team, a cluster of collaborators who work with the linking agent and cement relationships to the larger system. Participation and involvement must continue as widely as possible as new practices are demonstrated and implemented. The sense of participation at each stage ensures that decisions about changes will be "owned" by those who are affected by them.

In spite of a linking agent's best efforts, some system configurations may be so inhospitable that it is advisable to bide time or move on to more promising venues. Signs of these relatively rare circumstances include a long history of unresponsiveness to change, near total isolation and powerlessness of the people who need and favor change, signs of major system pathology or incapacity, and total failure of key system members to respond to the linking agent's well-conceived and well-executed initial encounters.

Build a Good Relationship With the People You Are Trying to Help

A strong, creative relationship can carry a change program through the most difficult obstacles. Your relationship with a prospective school or school system must be carefully planned and thought through if you are going to succeed with a project. This chapter offers some specific criteria to help you as a linking agent assess your relationship with a school or school system. If you know where you stand with the school personnel and you know how they see you, you will be in a good position to adapt and enhance this relationship as the change effort progresses.

Guiding Change uses the terms *school personnel, school district,* and *school system* to refer to the group of people the linker is trying to help. This entity will vary in size and complexity. It might be as small as a single individual or as large and diffuse as a community. If personnel in the system (teachers, school-based administrators, and districtwide administrators) seem to have common goals and are trying to work together to achieve those goals, the linker is working for the school district rather than for a specific school or individual teachers within a school. Sometimes it will not be entirely clear at the beginning just who will take part in the change initiative. You may find that you cannot work effectively with one group unless, at the same time, you are working with relevant others. This network of relations can get pretty complicated and unmanageable. Therefore, it is important at the outset to define who should be involved. This boils down to two basic questions:

- What group are you going to work with *directly*?
- What *other groups* are connected to the group with which you are directly working?

Relating to the Primary Group

Once you identify the primary group with whom you plan to work, your first task is to learn as much as you can about the group, its members, and its larger social context.

What Are the Norms of the Group?

Boundary signs of various kinds define the groups you will be working with. These signs separate those who are *members* from those who are *outside*. Some boundaries are physical and obvious—like the wall and the barbed wire fence—but most boundaries are less visible. Members of any social group share many common beliefs, values, and rules of behavior. These shared ideas are the norms of the group. They delineate "us" from "them."

The linker should become familiar with the key norms that characterize a prospective school system or subgroup. Know how sharply the norms are defined and how strictly they are adhered to. Although these shared beliefs and behaviors are seldom unique, the members may view them as so. Social systems maintain group identity partly through the mechanism of *local pride*, which identifies what "we" have as special, as high status, as most important, and as most relevant. This belief that "we are unique" can be a major stumbling block, hindering an awareness of a need for change.

In the special case of schools, traditional norms protect the integrity of the classroom and assign the teacher as the governor of the classroom and classroom procedure. Classes begin and end at certain times. Students do not come and go while a class is in session, and so forth. Obviously, then, innovation must be largely about breaking old norms and establishing new ones. For example, the concept of team-teaching has recently become popular among both general education and special education teachers, even though this practice breaks traditional norms for both the teachers and the students in their classes.

> **A Case to Ponder**
>
> When a student disrupts the class, as Jay did in our case, the student is breaking norms. When Ms. Peters came in to model certain behaviors for the teacher, she also was breaking norms.

Who Are the Members of the Group?

Knowing with whom you are working—and with whom you must establish a productive relationship—is essential to your success as a linking agent.

The Leaders. To establish a satisfactory relationship, an understanding of the formal leadership structure is also important. Some systems are only loosely structured, whereas others have a strict chain of command. The more clearly defined and structured the leadership pattern is, the more critical it is to establish solid relationships with the leaders.

Schools and school districts have a clear command structure. The principal is in charge of the school but reports to the superintendent, who, in turn, reports to the school board. This hierarchy remains true even when the principal or the superintendent holds to a strongly democratic and participatory management style. In the Jay—cooperative discipline case, the principal was clearly in charge from beginning to end and, in turn, felt an obligation to the parents to run a smooth operation. Her inadequate involvement in and commitment to the innovation proved fatal.

> **A Case to Ponder**
>
> In the Jay—cooperative discipline case, it is not obvious who the influentials or opinion leaders really are. The teacher, Mrs. Byron, has some seniority and is well liked, but is she really influential with her peers? Ms. Peters, the counselor, is a good organizer but is unable to persuade a number of the teachers to go along with the new program.

The Influentials. In addition to the formal chains of command, many informal channels and leadership structures exist. As a linking agent, you should get to know the informal leaders, the influentials, the people to whom others turn for new ideas. All social systems contain such opinion leaders, the respected friends and colleagues who set the standard for the group even though they may not have formal status as leaders or supervisors.

The Gatekeepers. The linking agent may also find that certain individuals hold key strategic positions with respect to the flow of new ideas and information. Such gatekeepers play a central role in innovation and they may be distinct from the formal leadership and the opinion leadership discussed above. The librarian, the guidance counselor, and the assistant principal may hold little formal power or informal influence, but they may still be in key positions because they control channels of information on certain topics. The "boss's secretary" is probably the most famous example of the gatekeeper in this sense.

> **A Case to Ponder**
>
> In the Jay—cooperative discipline case, the principal is clearly a gatekeeper. Things do not happen in this school without her assent. But the counselor is a kind of information gatekeeper. She is the only one who fully understands the cooperative discipline program.

Other Key Stakeholders. Many people inside the system and many others peripheral to the system may have a serious stake in what happens. In a school context, the students and their parents are certainly stakeholders. In some cases, their involvement and participation will be important; in other cases, they will not. The school board, as the designated representative of the community, is another obvious stakeholder in many innovations, particularly when the change initiative affects a whole school, many schools, or the entire school district.

Diagram Your School or School District as a Social Network

Take a look at Figure 2.1, which suggests a school as a possible group with which a linking agent will work. This group has two or more key subgroups and a variety of connections, weak and strong. This figure shows the linking agent's first approach to a new system or school. The most accessible point initially might be the office of the principal or it might be a teacher or a group of teachers. For special education linkers, the first contact point might be the director of special education at the district administrative level.

An important consideration will be the degree of internal integration and the real center of power with regard to the type of innovation you have in mind. Is this center the principal and administrative staff, or is it the teachers? Regardless of which it is, the linker will also need to know whether these two potential sources of power are well connected to each other, in harmony or in conflict, and fully in charge of the system as a whole.

A potential linking agent can arise from anywhere in the system or can come from outside. Figure 2.1 suggests the complexity of any change configuration but also shows the many opportunities for influence and action. In many states, intermediate district offices also provide special services. Every state has its own special education office within the state department of education. Each of these represents a specific kind of power and influence base so that your strategic thinking will have to be governed by what your power base is, where it is, how visible it is, and how strong it is.

Draw a diagram to represent the school or school system with which you will be working. First draw the primary group, the people you really want to help directly and the ones who will be doing the most changing. Next, draw in the other people to whom this primary group must relate in bringing about this change—those who must cooperate, approve, provide extra resources, give time and attention. Then sketch in the main people or groups that these people need to attend to. As you identify these three system layers, try to identify opinion leaders and gatekeepers on your diagram. Then show where you are with respect to this system and to whom you are connected. When you have finished, look at your diagram and ask yourself these questions:

> **A Case to Ponder**
>
> In the Jay–cooperative discipline case, parents were obviously important stakeholders who were purposefully involved, but their commitment and involvement in the end proved inadequate.

> **A Case to Ponder**
>
> The Jay–cooperative discipline case study described at least three people who took on change agent roles of one kind or another: the general education teacher, the counselor, and the principal. But there could have been others as well. Someone from the district office could have been involved. Also involved could have been a person representing the "cooperative discipline" program. It could have been someone from a local university or community college.

Figure 2.1 The Linking Agent and the Primary Client System

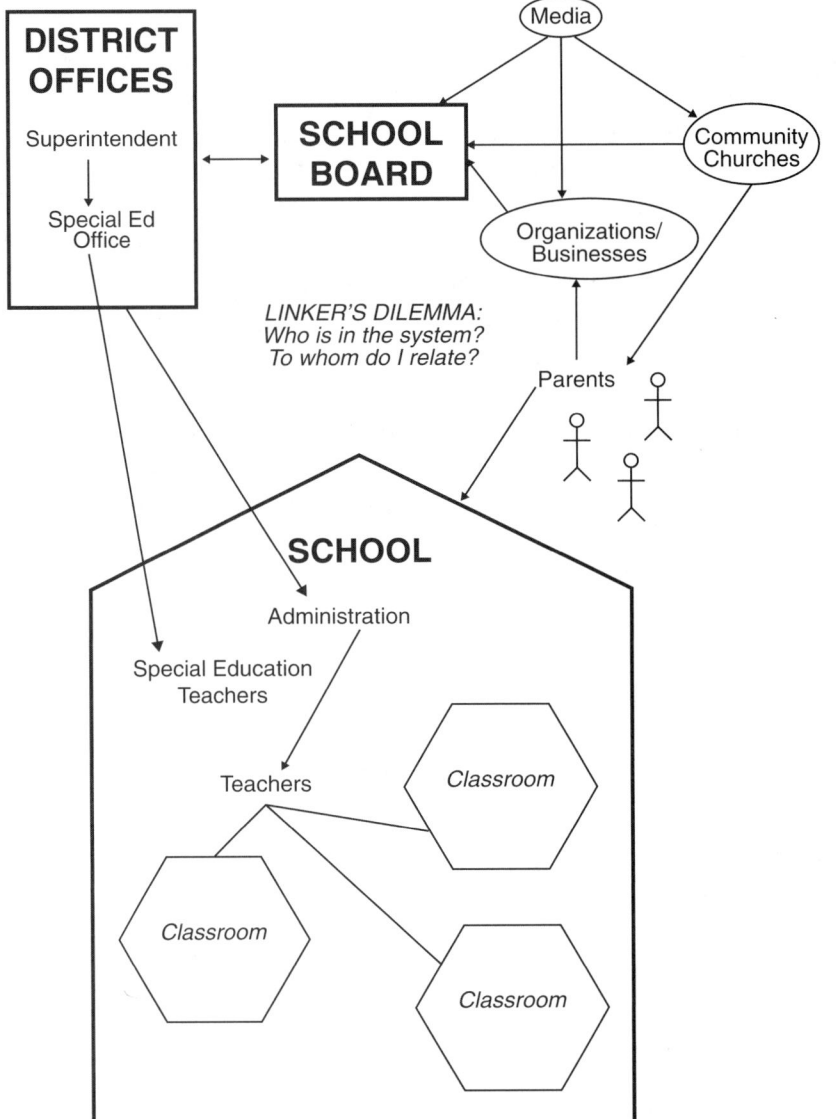

- Am I connected to people who can really change this system? *If not,* are there specific ways I can begin to make these connections?
- Are the internal connections among subgroups strong enough to support effective communication and commitment to a change process? *If not,* are there ways I can start to help build these connections?
- Are the barriers to outside influence permeable enough so that new ideas can get a fair hearing? *If not,* are there ways to break down these barriers or make them more permeable?

	The Primary School Setting	The School District	The Larger System (including community, parents, and state department of education)
How well connected am I?	IF NOT, HOW? _____	IF NOT, HOW? _____	IF NOT, HOW? _____
How well are they connected to each other?	IF NOT, HOW? _____	IF NOT, HOW? _____	IF NOT, HOW? _____
How open are they to new ideas?	IF NOT, HOW? _____	IF NOT, HOW? _____	IF NOT, HOW? _____

Knowledge Base

Stage 2: Relate

Every scholar who has studied change will attest to the dual requirements: understanding the social system and making a vigorous effort to connect to it at many levels, regardless of the change agent's point of entry. Fullan, for example (2001b, p. 191), estimates that "effective consultancy is 25 percent having good products and 75 percent helping to develop local conditions."

In their survey of 41 United Nations–sponsored innovative teacher-training projects from all parts of the developing world, Havelock and Huberman (1978) found that poor coordination and connection with political leaders, opposition from key groups, and poor social relations within the project were major barriers to success.

Many other research studies document the correlation between the good management of Relate factors and success. For example, Harris, Eiseman, Harris, Crandall, and Doyle (1979); Huberman and Crandall (1983); and Goldenberg and Gallimore (1991) note the importance of addressing the local context. Kennedy (1991) and Osher and Kane (1993) highlight the importance of a high level of end-user participation in the problem-solving process. Berman and McLaughlin (1975), Kane and Kocher (1980), Fullan (1982), and Little (1982) all cite the need to gain support from gatekeepers and to provide for ownership by the participants. These are all aspects of building good relationships and developing a good understanding of the user as a system.

In the special education linking agent study (Hamilton et al., 2002), the importance of relationships was a dominant finding. The initial recruitment of linkers was greatly facilitated by personal connections between the national project and the special educators in the cooperating districts. Later, the successful pursuit of change projects was highly correlated with the extent of collaboration among key players as well as support from school principals and district leadership.

Figure 2.2   Teacher as Linker: The In-School Change Team

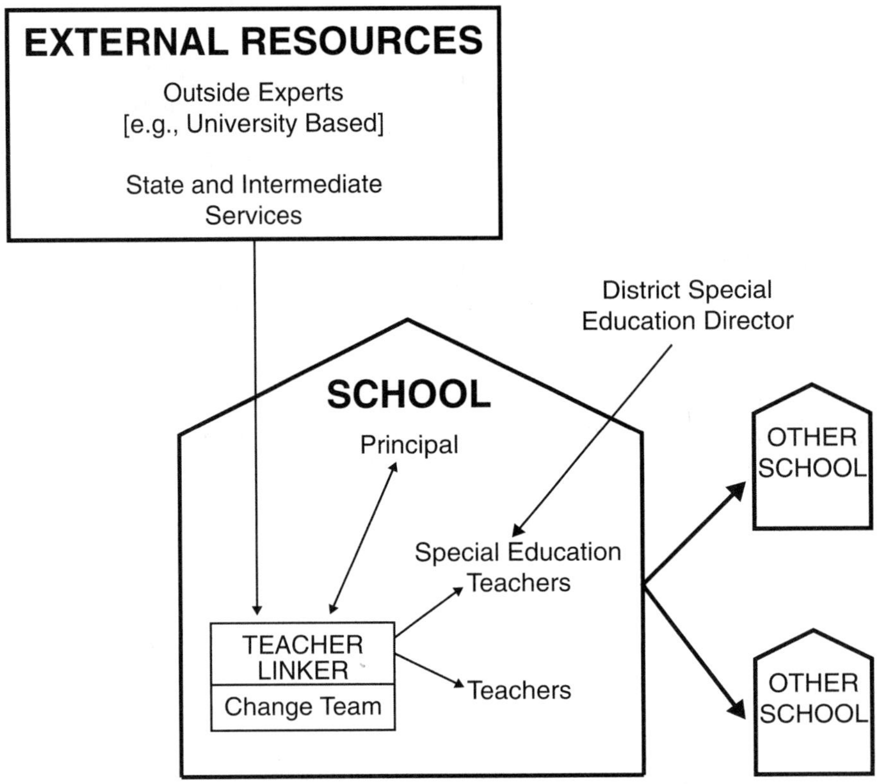

```
┌─────────────────────────┐
│   EXTERNAL RESOURCES    │
│     Outside Experts     │
│  [e.g., University Based]│
│                         │
│  State and Intermediate │
│        Services         │
└───────────┬─────────────┘
            │          District Special
            │          Education Director
            ▼
     ┌──────────────────────────┐
     │         SCHOOL           │
     │        Principal         │         ┌─────────┐
     │                          │         │ OTHER   │
     │          ↑               │         │ SCHOOL  │
     │                          │         └─────────┘
     │              Special Education
     │                ↘Teachers
     │  ┌─────────┐                       ┌─────────┐
     │  │ TEACHER │                       │ OTHER   │
     │  │ LINKER  │──→Teachers            │ SCHOOL  │
     │  │Change Team│                     └─────────┘
     │  └─────────┘
     └──────────────────────────┘
```

Linker Configurations

In some fields, it may be possible to designate linkers or other kinds of change agents as belonging to a particular organization with a particular status and role designation, filling a designated organizational slot, representing a budget line item, and having particular educational and experiential qualifications. However, such professionalized role designations are a rarity in both general education and special education. Anybody can choose to be a linker or a change agent just by deciding that that is what he or she wants to do. If these linkers are fortunate, some (e.g., staff developers, area coordinators) will be in positions that give them a good deal of freedom of movement and decision and command of significant resources.

Guiding Change makes no such assumptions. It allows you to go forth and become a change agent from wherever you are, provided that you have the energy and will to do so. Nevertheless, how you proceed and how you shape your role will depend greatly on where you start from and how you wish to define yourself. This section suggests a few possible linker configurations and highlights the pros and cons of each.

The General Education Teacher as Linker

The teacher as linker has some very special advantages (Figure 2.2). First, if the primary innovators are supposed to be the teachers, then a fellow teacher has perhaps the most credibility as a model and as a colleague. Second, the teacher is located in the classroom and has maximum contact with individual students for whom the change initiative is usually designed to create the largest impact. Third, the well-trained and experienced teacher probably has the strongest sense of what is needed and what is possible within the constraints of a particular school, within a classroom in that school, and possibly for the individual student members of that classroom.

These advantages need to be weighed against some distinct disadvantages. First, the average teacher already has substantial responsibilities and time commitments just to keep the system running the way it is. Does he or she have the necessary excess capital in time and energy to invest in substantial new undertakings? Second, the teacher normally does not operate from a position of formal authority within the school or the district. The normal domain of the teacher is just one classroom, not many, and not even one whole school. This lack of formal authority means that the teacher will have additional challenges in sustaining innovations once they are adopted. He or she will have to depend solely on his or her own opinion leadership, ability to teach and demonstrate to colleagues the effectiveness of the new intervention, and ability to convince higher-ups that the innovation is worth saving and maintaining over the long haul.

Given these relationship issues, certain relating tasks emerge for the teacher as linker:

- Evaluate and try to establish your own status as an opinion leader.
- Connect to the principal and keep connected.
- Build an in-school change team that includes
    - Significant numbers of fellow teachers, some with opinion leadership, and perhaps the principal, and
    - Other school staff, especially counselors and special education teachers if the change contemplated is related to special education.
- Build skills in your team members as you build your own so that you can spread the load.
- Capture full involvement with full participation.
- Connect to an experienced outsider who can connect you to the larger resource world (such as a person who works to facilitate or directly provides technical assistance).

The Special Education Teacher as Linker

Special education teachers share many insider advantages with general classroom teachers (Figure 2.3). They have the same background of education and experience and may be recruited from the ranks of classroom teaching. To be effective linkers, however, they need to retain their connections to other teachers and to not be seen as too specialized to be relevant to other teachers' concerns. They also need to retain the feel of the classroom and fully empathize with the teachers who have to manage that environment day in and day out.

If they can manage to retain this level of connection and insider status, special education teachers may have special advantages. At personal and

Figure 2.3 Special Education Teacher or School Counselor as Linker

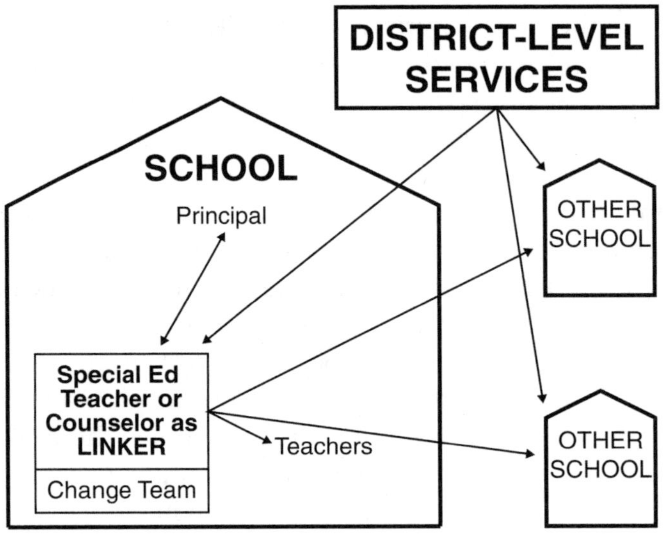

professional levels, they are more knowledgeable about individual students and their needs, particularly students who receive special education services. They have more advanced training in certain areas and are better connected in a variety of ways. They have responsibilities that often cut across classrooms, grades, and teachers—even across schools. Special education teachers are likely to have worked in a variety of school settings over the years. They also have reporting responsibilities and hence connections to school district personnel. Because their role expectations are more varied and because they cut across the responsibilities of general education teachers, they are in a good position to observe the need for and to initiate change. Most important, in many cases, they have ongoing consultation and coteaching responsibilities with general education teachers that give them legitimate access to many classrooms through their efforts to provide individualized services and support for inclusion-based strategies.

School Counselor as Linker

What is true for special education teachers is also somewhat true for counselors. Counselors may have a better grasp than anyone else of what is going on with particular children, including their relations to siblings and parents as shown in the Jay—cooperative discipline case study. Counselors may also have more flexibility in their work schedules and hence more potential to free up time for special projects than does the average general education or special education teacher. They also are likely to have more connections to networks beyond the school, but these networks are specialized to their profession and may not be helpful or relevant when it comes to issues of curriculum and classroom management. The functions of special education and school counseling clearly overlap, and many counselors may also be former classroom teachers. However, counselors clearly do not have the same insider advantages. They will need to work harder at building the insider networks required for successful change.

The chief advantage of a school counselor as a potential linker lies in the degree of flexibility that this role allows in terms of the counselor's ability both to manage his or her own time and to have access to all the other main actors in the school environment, including parents, teachers, and the school principal. This flexibility of access also extends beyond the school to the district level and to a world of expertise and professional association that extends way beyond the locality. This advantage is well illustrated by Ms. Peters in the Jay—cooperative discipline case example. She was well connected to other teachers and made sure that the principal was kept informed. She also had an enormous amount of extra energy to invest in developing materials, preparing special classes, arranging meetings, and acquiring the necessary knowledge resources from outside the system. The principal reason given by noncooperating teachers was lack of time to invest in the project.

The School Principal as Linker

There are some good reasons for considering the school principal as a potential linker and general change agent. Over the past 25 years, many studies have looked at principals as instructional leaders, just as many studies have compared more and less effective schools (e.g., Berman & McLaughlin, 1977; Fink & Resnick, 1999 [cited in Fullan, 2001a]; Hall & Hord, 1987, 2001). The principal obviously has more clout than anybody else in the school. Many principals have been classroom teachers and therefore both understand problems at the classroom level and have some degree of credibility with teachers on that account.

Combining a linking agent role with an authority role can lead to real problems, however. Linkers should be seen as honest brokers of knowledge and new ideas, not as people who are there to tell others what to do. It is difficult for most people in positions of authority to convey this sense of nonthreatening collegiality and unforced helping, even when they have the best of intentions.

There is no question that people in positions of power need to be involved in the change process from beginning to end. They are there to legitimize what is happening; to provide protection from premature interference; and to provide necessary material resources including release time, travel authorization, funds for materials, and extra personnel. They can be good catalysts for change and sometimes have useful ideas about what should be done.

Special Linker Role at the District Level

The district office is a natural choice for a linking agent's home base. The district bureaucracy should have room for specialists in innovation, and the office of special education is an appropriate location. Figure 2.4 suggests a possible arrangement.

There is a certain logic to placing major responsibilities for change at the district level. First of all is the possibility of having widespread effects, perhaps involving many schools. The power to effect change and access financial resources exists here in greater degree than in other levels of the school system. District-level personnel are also likely to have more varied backgrounds, more connections to outside experts, and more contacts with state and federal agencies.

Figure 2.4 Model of a District-Level Linker and Change Team

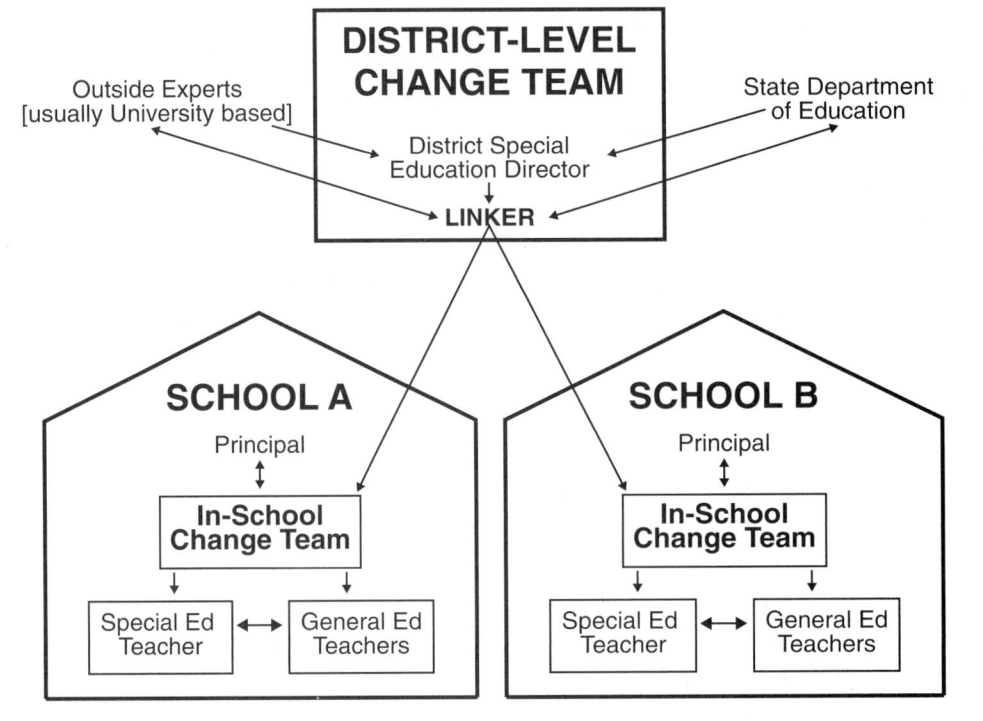

A specially designated linker at the district level is in a good position to relate directly with specific schools and school principals on the one hand and with more remote sources of knowledge and power on the other. Such a person should be able to develop day-to-day relationships with individual teachers in two or more schools and be an active organizer and member of change teams in each school. The linker should also be part of the larger district-level change team that includes principals from each participating school as well as teacher representatives. This is only one among many possible configurations. The point is to take advantage of the unique possibilities allowed by each setting and to create a viable intradistrict change network, given the realities of the context.

One reality of great importance is the attitude of both the superintendent and the school board toward innovation. For example, a district that is constantly beset by budget crises and that emphasizes minimizing school taxes would be a poor environment for welcoming a new role with a somewhat loosely defined responsibility. In some cases, special funding through state or federal grants may be the only way to introduce the new role. In these cases, you, as the linker, will have to prove your value to the local authorities before the funds run out so that they can make room in their world and in the line items of their world for the new role.

Linkers at Other Levels, Other Places

The school district is not the only place where change agents of various types, and specifically linking agents, can operate successfully. Figure 2.5

Figure 2.5 Linker Located Outside School Districts

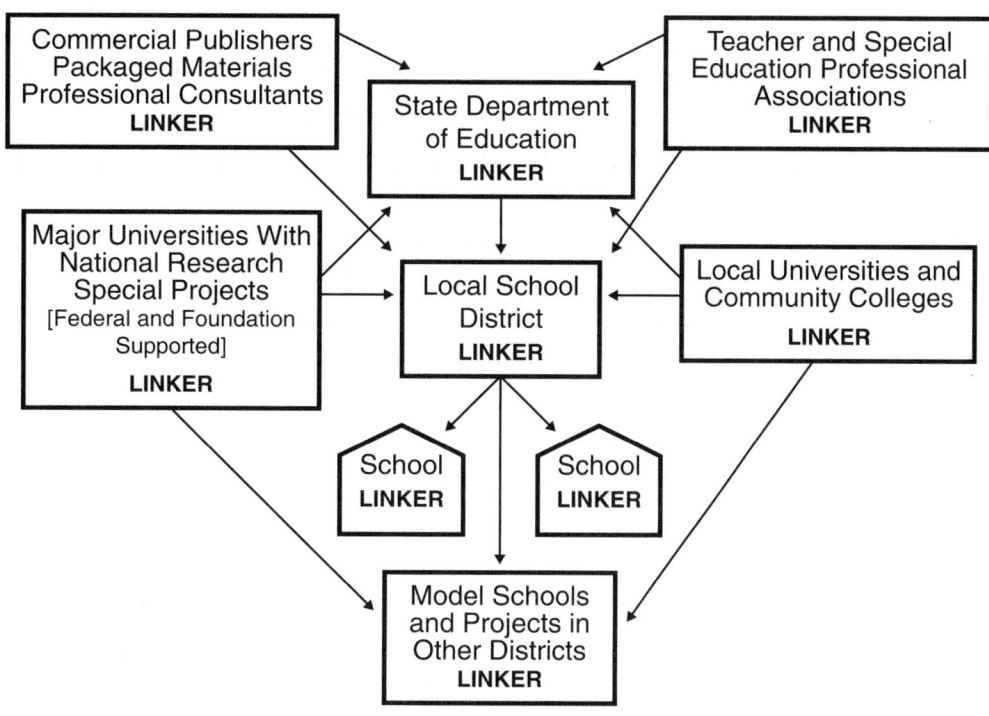

suggests several places where change agent roles have been successfully positioned. In the 1970s and 1980s, the U.S. Department of Education sponsored a National Diffusion Network (NDN) to promote innovation at the local level. The NDN supported two types of change agents who worked in coordination. The first was the developer-demonstrator (DD), typically a person or a group who had developed a successful program as judged by a national panel of experts. Often these model projects were developed in a local school district by creative teachers. DDs were given additional funds to package their programs for nationwide distribution, including training and some hands-on implementation help for adopting districts. The other role was the state facilitator, who was usually affiliated with the state's department of education. This person or group was responsible for building in-state awareness and coordinating the DDs.

Figure 2.5 suggests many types of outside linkers who can play useful and sometimes critical roles in every stage of the change process. In the Hilldale case study, a key role was played by a federally funded project, which supplied a technical assistance liaison in addition to training and financial support for a linker inside the school district. Many states have intermediate school districts or intrastate technical assistance networks to provide similar support mechanisms. Usually these services include specialists to support special education initiatives (Figure 2.6).

University-Based Linkers

Universities should be involved in educational change for a number of good reasons. Most educators receive their training through universities, and

Figure 2.6 The Linker Configuration in the Hilldale County Adoption of ELP

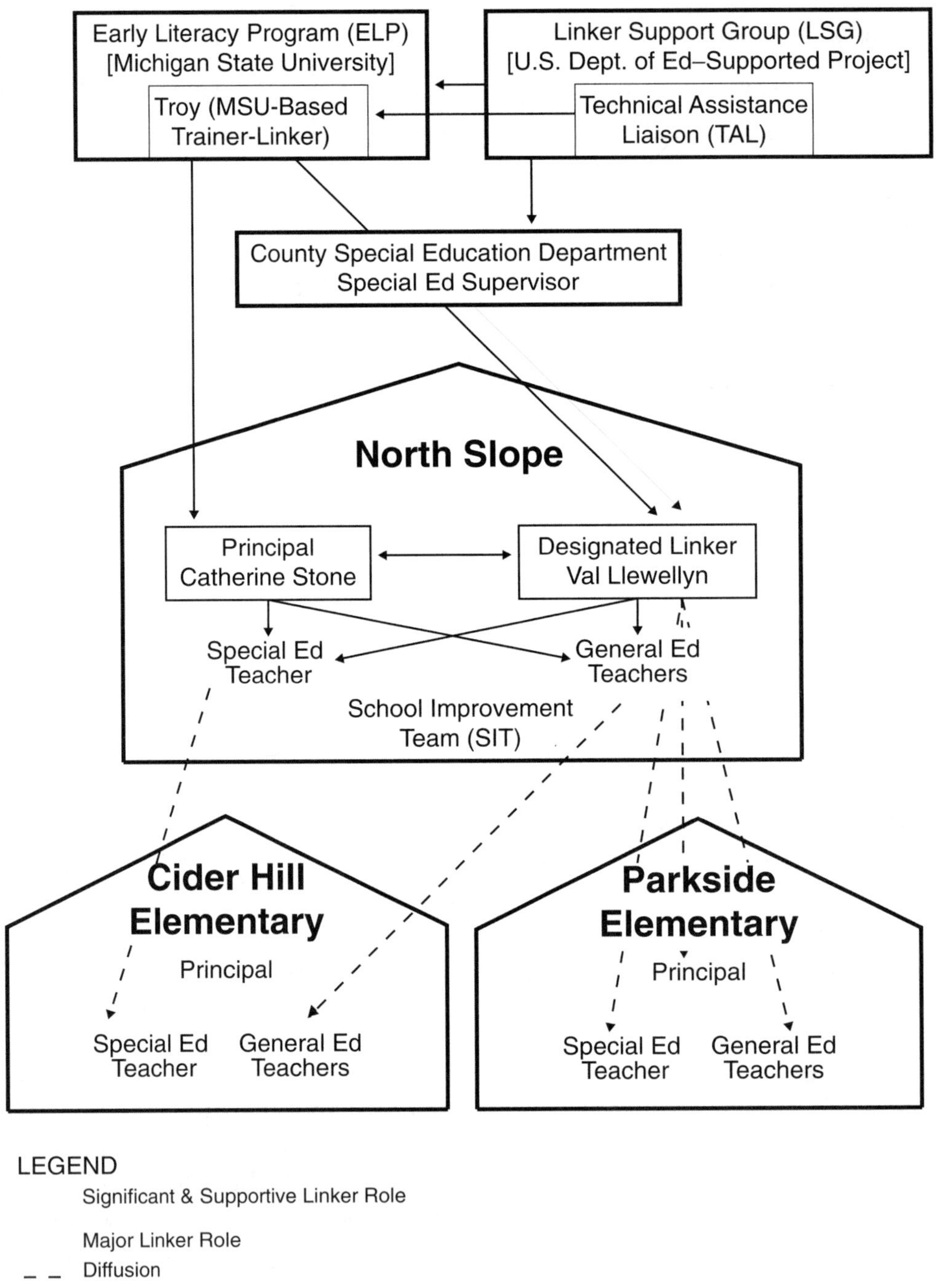

```
┌─────────────────────────────┐  ┌─────────────────────────────────┐
│ Early Literacy Program (ELP)│←→│ Linker Support Group (LSG)      │
│ [Michigan State University] │  │ [U.S. Dept. of Ed–Supported     │
│                             │  │  Project]                       │
│ ┌─────────────────────┐     │  │ ┌─────────────────────────────┐ │
│ │ Troy (MSU-Based     │←────┼──┼─│ Technical Assistance        │ │
│ │ Trainer-Linker)     │     │  │ │ Liaison (TAL)               │ │
│ └─────────────────────┘     │  │ └─────────────────────────────┘ │
└─────────────────────────────┘  └─────────────────────────────────┘
```

```
          ┌──────────────────────────────────────┐
          │ County Special Education Department  │
          │ Special Ed Supervisor                │
          └──────────────────────────────────────┘
```

North Slope

```
┌─────────────────┐  ←→  ┌─────────────────┐
│ Principal       │       │ Designated Linker│
│ Catherine Stone │       │ Val Llewellyn   │
└─────────────────┘       └─────────────────┘
       ↓   ↘          ↙           ↓
   Special Ed  ←→   General Ed
   Teacher           Teachers

        School Improvement
        Team (SIT)
```

Cider Hill Elementary

Principal

Special Ed Teacher   General Ed Teachers

Parkside Elementary

Principal

Special Ed Teacher   General Ed Teachers

LEGEND

——— Significant & Supportive Linker Role

—— Major Linker Role

– – Diffusion

---

some maintain connections to former professors throughout their careers. Universities are also the loci of much of the expert knowledge that a society has. Much research is carried on in universities, and many texts are written by university professors. Often the cutting edge of educational research is found in the pilot schools that are affiliated with universities, and most universities have active extension and continuing education programs. Thus, there is a certain logic to establishing linkers at universities as part of the university system.

This practice is exactly what happens in agriculture. In the Cooperative Extension Service, the designated state university plays a central role, supporting both the extension specialists and the county agents and maintaining an agricultural experiment station, which carries on all types of research relevant to the agricultural needs of the state. Many states have analogous arrangements for education, but they are typically not as formalized and they vary a great deal from state to state. However, many teacher training programs at state universities work closely with area public schools and provide educational extension services. State universities are not alone in providing outreach; many private and church-affiliated colleges also provide extension programs and services of all types.

The downside of a university-based linker system is that there is no lasting commitment to any particular school system. University teaching and research always take priority over service. Thus, university-based linking activity often comes within the framework of research projects whose primary objective is the discovery of new knowledge, not the provision of direct service. The typical university-managed, school-based research project is a trade-off: School personnel surrender their time and agree to disrupt their normal classroom routines for research purposes in exchange for some free help, new ideas, and a chance to try out new practices. School personnel sometimes can feel exploited if they do not see the benefit to the school and may not even understand the purpose of the project. Further, when the research is done, there is typically no follow-up and certainly no ongoing support for whatever changes might have been made.

Special Education Linking Agents in Action

Consider again the case study in Hilldale County and, specifically, the introduction of the Early Literacy Project into a few schools in the district. The narrative reveals not just one but four linkers who played important roles at different times. The designated linking agent volunteered for the project and committed time to the project from the beginning to the end. Her primary role was as a coordinator, handling the complicated logistics and running the gauntlet of bureaucratic approvals. For a while, she was the project, the one person investing significant time in it and fully identified with it.

Next in importance was the principal of the lead school. She too volunteered on behalf of her school, when other principals held back. Much of the initiative for the project rested with her. She traveled with the linking agent to the demonstration site in Michigan, got fully engaged in the substance, and followed through with strong support for and participation in the training events. A school principal can be an instructional leader and a catalytic change agent, and this fact is on display here.

The outside change agent, defined in the linker program as the technical assistance liaison (TA liaison) also played a critical role. He made several

> site visits and was frequently on the phone with the linking agent, providing guidance and support in various forms. When it came time to search for alternative innovations, the TA liaison did the searching and then prepared summaries of each approach so that their value and relevance could be compared. The TA liaison was also essential in finding and gaining initial access to the developers at Michigan State University.
>
> Finally, credit should be granted to the host at Michigan, who coordinated visits to the demonstration site, then visited Hilldale to provide training and to give on-site demonstrations. He was the substantive expert on the scene and the linker to other expert resources.

With Whom Should the Linker Work?

As linking agent, you may not have much choice in selecting the first members of a change team, but as you become more aware of who is who in the system and as the choice of new members is more in your hands, you should follow some important guidelines.

> **Important Abilities for a Change Team**
>
> - Opinion leadership
> - Formal authority
> - Affiliation with key factions or vested interests
> - Public relations ability

Above all, pick team members who have some degree of opinion leadership among those you hope to influence, people who are respected as peers. Second, make sure that one or more team members have some formal authority within the system, either as a principal or as an administrative leader in a relevant area. Third, try to select people who represent key factions or vested interests, such as teachers' unions or parent groups. Finally, try to include someone who has good public relations skills, such as the ability to relate to large and diverse audiences as a persuasive speaker or writer, and someone who can provide an articulate defense of what you are doing should the need arise (Figure 2.7).

By keeping in mind these major characteristics, you can identify the people in the school district or school who can effectively aid the change efforts. With such people working on your side, you will have a good chance of influencing larger and larger networks of potential users. In choosing this change team, however, you should not forget another consideration, which in some ways is more important than those already mentioned: compatibility with you. If you and your team members cannot work together effectively as friends and colleagues, your project will be in trouble.

Relating to the Larger Social Environment

Relating to insiders is important but will not be sufficient to bring about real and sustainable change. No group of human beings is completely isolated from the influence of outsiders. All systems and organizations exist within a context of other systems of which they are a part and on which they depend. Therefore,

Figure 2.7 Relating to the Larger Community

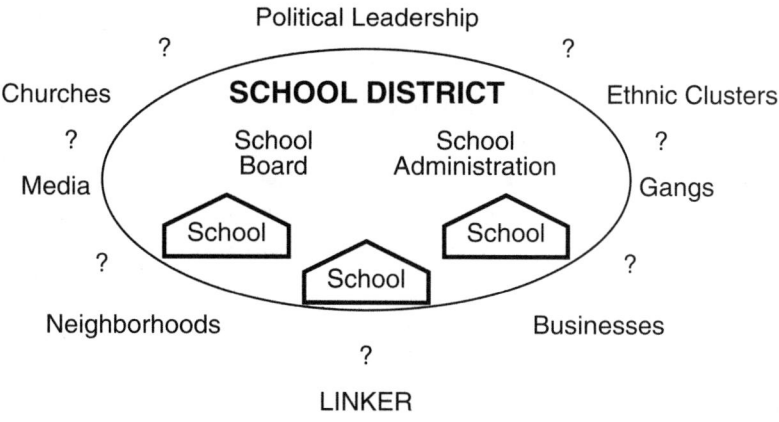

the linker must consider not only the characteristics of the particular school or environment but also the nature of the community, the larger social system of which the school is a part.

What Are the Important Elements of the Larger Social Environment?

If you are new to the system, just beginning your relationship, you must learn the answers to three questions about this larger system with some degree of specificity:

- Who are the most powerful and influential people in the community?
- How do they usually react to innovation (e.g., conservatively or progressively)?
- How can they be approached and influenced to endorse the change effort?

Who Are the Influentials in the Community? If you are able to review the history of the community, you will usually be struck by the strong influence of certain groups—pressure groups, key individuals, and key institutions—over what has gone on in the school district over the years. For example, you may find that the school board has a great deal of power, that the superintendent or one of her assistants is particularly important, or that certain progressive or conservative pressure groups have major influence either in fostering innovation or in inhibiting or disrupting it. Outside pressure from such sources can lead to increased conflict within the school or it can create an atmosphere of rigidity and complacency. You must be sensitive to the likely effects of these different outside pressures on school personnel, for you will need to quickly assess the relative potency of various forces while you are developing the relationship.

What Is the Community Leadership Like? Certainly, the linking agent will want to take a good look at the formal and informal leadership of the community. To what extent is this leadership cohesive? Does it work as a harmonious system or is it factional and strife-ridden or is it merely diffuse and weak? Are any of the leaders or influentials the parents or advocates of children in special education?

It is also important to know how to approach the leadership. Can an outside linking agent safely make contact directly, or should you work through inside representatives as emissaries? If the leadership is factional, are all factions approachable? Further, must specific kinds of conventions and rituals be observed when dealing with the leaders of each faction?

How Much Effort Should You Devote to Outside Forces?

The effort you expend in identifying and dealing with these outside social forces will vary greatly from case to case. Sometimes, only a casual accounting of these external forces will be necessary. Nevertheless, the testimony of countless change agents suggests that these outside forces are almost invariably underrated in the early stages of a project (e.g., Fullan [2001b] cites an array of factors that affect the initiation of a change and those that affect implementation and continuation). The social forces that can affect change within the environment in which you find yourself are complex. Different forces will dominate in different contexts. Their relative importance will vary depending on the particular need area or concern on which you have chosen to work. Some of these groups will have viewpoints and concerns of their own relevant to this change topic or to change in general. Others may be irrelevant, and a few may be sleeping giants you will want to keep asleep.

List the outside forces and groups that are relevant to your situation. Think about how they overlap and interrelate. Then ask yourself these questions:

- How strong are the links between the schools and the community as a whole?
- Where does the real power that affects the schools lie? Who is really in charge?
- Are there community factions that toss school-related issues back and forth?
- Is there community consensus on certain school-related issues or special education–related issues?

What Is Your Relationship at the Very Beginning?

A new change project seldom represents a completely new beginning. Here, as in most of the affairs of life, the past is prologue. The success of a school's past encounters with change and with change agents will greatly color the success of its future relations with you. When starting out on a new project, you are likely to be in one of four situations:

- Having no prior relationship with the system—the blank slate
- Reestablishing a formerly good relationship

- Reestablishing an uncertain or ambiguous relationship
- Redefining an existing ongoing relationship

Each situation has special advantages and disadvantages.

Having No Prior Relationship—The Blank Slate

A good relationship is a complex and delicate bridge, very difficult and expensive to build and very important to maintain. You can really appreciate this fact only when starting completely new. In a new relationship, nothing can be taken for granted. You must be acutely aware of norms and values, leadership, influence patterns, and so forth, while maintaining an image of complete trust and serene confidence. The number of concerns which will tax your energy and absorb your attention is greatly multiplied.

A completely new relationship is beset by a host of uncertainties and unknown quantities. The linking agent is faced with the task of acquiring information from every available source while making crucial decisions about the project. Such decisions will inevitably be based on partial and distorted knowledge, which may make or break the project. It is a delicate task.

But a brand-new relationship also has many benefits. First of all, the new change agent, especially a linking agent, is not initially identified with any special internal faction. Thus, you may have a chance to become and to remain an objective observer as well as a friend and helper. Second, a linker may derive special benefits from initial guest status. If you are a complete newcomer, even potential enemies will probably be polite and will not try to shout you down or shove you out without a fair hearing; you may be granted a honeymoon period during which you are relatively free from critical scrutiny and harsh judgments. If you sense that most of the teachers in your target school start out with an open-minded attitude, you should take full advantage of the opportunity to assure all factions of your own open-mindedness and eagerness to be a friend and helper to all. A new face may suggest that new things are truly possible, whereas an old face with new ideas may be seen merely as an old face with old ideas.

Reestablishing a Good Relationship

If the teachers, administrators, and school personnel already know you and value your past service, you have a strong base on which to build a new change project. Such an advantageous starting point should not be taken for granted, however. The cautious linking agent might ask the following questions in preparing for a new project:

- Does the client still view that former relationship as positive?
- Do aspects of the relationship need improvement?
- Have any intervening events muddied the waters (e.g., change of leadership, changed fiscal climate)?
- Could the nature of the prior relationship lead the school system to any erroneous expectations (e.g., Were you seen as a change agent before?)?

By preparing to deal with such potential snags, you can ensure that your relationship will continue to grow from a solid base.

Reestablishing an Uncertain Relationship

It is difficult, but not impossible, to make a fresh start with teachers and school personnel with whom your prior relationship was not fully adequate. In such a situation, it is mandatory to create a positive atmosphere and confidence in the new you. Teachers must come to believe that the prospects for success are now much better. You can evaluate the probabilities for success by answering the following questions:

> **Signs That a New Start Will Be Successful**
>
> - A major change in the leadership of the school district
> - A change in the political climate
> - A change in the fiscal climate
> - An improvement in your own status
> - Public recognition of the importance of your new role

- Have you adequately analyzed the problems in the prior relationship?
- Has anything been done in the interim to correct these problems?
- Have you attempted to build a new image of yourself as a change agent, instilling new expectations about your role?
- What, if anything, has happened in the interim that would alter the prospects of success—either positively or negatively?

If the previous encounter was, in fact, a failure, it would be unwise to begin all over again before the problems in that relationship are patched up and new expectations are instilled. Even then you should have evidence that a new start will be successful despite past experience.

Redefining an Existing Ongoing Relationship

In assuming the role of linking agent, you are moving out of a prior role with which the school system has identified you. This is almost always true of the change agent who emerges from the school district itself, for example, the teacher or administrator who becomes director of a new project or program. Special suspicions and resentments can build among peers if it is perceived that

- You are gaining power over others, especially your peers,
- You receive special recognition (perhaps undeservedly in the eyes of peers),
- You garner resources that others either do not have or believe they have equal claim to, or
- You get relief from other (perhaps onerous) duties to perform your new role.

Modifying or redefining an existing relationship may require a good deal of diplomatic skill and sensitivity to human relations. The linking agent has to be especially aware of the perceptions of all the key persons and interest groups who may be affected by the change—outsiders as well. To properly reconstitute your image, you may have to consider doing each of the following:

- Inform key persons that you have assumed a new role.
- Solicit from key persons recognition that your role has changed.
- Become comfortable in the new role so that you will not slip back into your old role behavior if, for example, your associates start making demands of you to perform in your old role. The need for training and practice in the skills of relating is nowhere more apparent than in the situation that requires you to modify an existing relationship.

Inside or Outside?

Although such distinctions are not always clear, change agents have long debated the relative advantages of beginning as an insider or an outsider. Consider the pros and cons of each position.

The Inside Linking Agent

The inside linking agent has the following advantages:

- *You know the system.* The insider knows where the power lies and where the strategic leverage points are and is better able to identify the gatekeepers, opinion leaders, and innovators than a newcomer could.

- *You speak the language, literally and figuratively.* The insider knows the special ways members discuss and refer to things and has the accent, the tone, and the style.

- *You understand the norms (the commonly held beliefs, attitudes, behaviors).* The insider, at least in part, probably follows and believes many of them.

- *You identify with the system's needs and aspirations.* The insider agent's cares are the system's cares. Thus, you have a personal incentive for helping.

- *You are a familiar figure, a known quantity.* Most of what the insider linking agent does is understandable and predictable as "member" behavior; therefore, you do not pose the threat of "the new" and "the unfamiliar."

The insider also has these disadvantages.

- *You may lack perspective.* The insider may not be able to see the school district as a whole because of your particular place and perspective within the system.

- *You may not have the special knowledge or skill relevant to the innovation.* The insider may not have had enough outside training or experience to be a true expert.

- *You may not have an adequate power base (unless you are at the top, as some are).* The insider's plans may be thwarted or distorted by superiors or competing peers.

- *You may have to live down the past.* As an insider, you may have to live down your own past failures or jealous residue from past successes.

- *You may not have the necessary independence of movement.* The obligations of membership may severely limit the time and energy that you can invest in the new role.

- *You usually face the difficult task of redefining ongoing relationships with the other members of the system.* In assuming the new role, the linking agent must be able to change the expectations of associates about their appropriate role and behavior, which can be difficult.

The Outside Linking Agent

The outsider has these advantages:

- *You start fresh.* In many cases, the outsider is not burdened by negative stereotypes.

- *You are in a position to have perspective.* The outsider can look at the school district objectively and thus may see problems that the insider would not see.

- *You are able to identify needs and opportunities.* The outsider can see things that insiders are unable to perceive. Moreover, insiders often have a special axe to grind. They tend to see this or that problem as most pressing because it is the problem that impinges on them most directly. You, in contrast, can look at the problems of all members collectively and make a more objective diagnosis. (Outsiders are not always objective, of course. Often, indeed, they are heavily invested in the adoption of particular innovations and, consequently, stress certain needs. Nevertheless, the outsider is in the position to be objective about diagnosis.)

- *You are independent of the power structure in the local system.* The outsider always has the option of pulling out if and when such action is deemed necessary. The outsider is not compelled to identify with any particular faction and is not forever threatened or inhibited by superior authorities.

- *You are in a position to bring in something genuinely new.* An outsider is more likely to have had the opportunity to gain expertise beyond what the school or district already possesses.

The outsider also has these disadvantages:

- *You are a stranger and therefore represent a potential threat.* What the outsider will do is unknown and unpredictable; it might cause discomfort, conflict, or some sort of disturbance to the natural order of things.

- *You may lack insider knowledge.* The outsider may not understand the system and its language, norms, or values, especially those that are deeply held but unspoken.

- *You may not care enough.* The outsider may not be able to identify adequately with the needs of the client. Their pain is not your pain, so you may seem to be indifferent to the needs that locals feel most acutely. Even if this is not true, it may be the perception.

- *You may get trapped unwittingly in internal strife.* The outsider may be seen as belonging to one side or the other.

The Inside-Outside Team

To capitalize on the advantages and avoid the problems of both insider and outsider agents, many experienced change agents suggest that the best solution is a change agent team in which both insiders and outsiders work together (e.g., Huberman & Miles, 1984; Grose, 2001; Hall & Hord, 2001). Thus, the insider who is initiating a change effort would do well to enlist someone from the outside to work as a collaborator. Such an outside person could provide an expert legitimacy for the insider's efforts in addition to contributing real expertise. This outsider could provide an objective perspective on the world in which the inside change agent is working. The outside expert could also give moral support to the insider whose efforts to do what is right for the system are being received by colleagues with something less than enthusiasm.

Conversely, the outsider who initiates change would do well to enlist the inside support of a member who both understands the school district and is familiar with the change process. Preferably, this insider would be someone with reasonable security and status within the system, as a leader, an influential, or a gatekeeper. The selection of members for the inside-outside team should maximize the strengths of both positions in the service of innovation.

Depending on resources, change teams can bring in members and advisors to serve a number of different functions: special content expertise, legitimacy with one or another faction, skills in group process or change process. Change agents and change teams may themselves find it desirable to involve outside process consultants.

Managing Initial Encounters

A relationship builds on the first encounter. What happens in the first contacts between you and members of the school district—how they see you and how they feel about you initially—will determine whether you will be able to proceed to any other stage of problem solving. In a sense, you are a package that the school is going to buy. Most people want to look over the package and read the label first. The first contacts are used by both parties to size each other up and take a quick first reading. Therefore, you must plan and prepare for these encounters with special care. Four considerations are paramount: friendliness, familiarity, rewardingness, and responsiveness.

Friendliness

Any change agent, even a linking agent, is an intruder. As with any intruder, those intruded upon will ask themselves, "Does this person mean us well or ill?" The question may seem absurd to you as the linker; after all, you know that you are a nice and trustworthy person. To those whom you are planning to help, however, the answer is not obvious unless they start with a high trust for strangers. Nevertheless, the initial criteria for friendliness are usually not hard to meet: a smile, a firm handshake, a straight look in the eye, a warm greeting as you make a firm mental note of the name of the person so that you can use it later. It also helps to make some positive and sincere comment of recognition, such as noting a special attribute or accomplishment of the school, the place, or the person you are greeting. Most of these suggestions are matters of etiquette, but they are not trivial, especially at the first encounter.

Familiarity

As a person who has deliberately chosen a new role, you are different. Yet as someone who knows and cares about a range of issues in special education and education in general, you also have much in common with the people you want to help. Therefore, you should try to be a familiar object in ways that are incidental to your mission. Dress, outward appearance, speech, and bearing should not be out of the ordinary. It also may help to identify some common interests that are far removed from any change project, such as sports, entertainment, or politics (that is, if you are likely to be on the same side of an issue). Jokes or humorous comments, which are likely to be shared, are especially effective in draining any tension from the situation. Small talk, even about the weather, helps make you a familiar object in initial encounters.

Rewardingness

The linking agent should find the earliest opportunity to do something for the school that will be perceived as helpful or useful. The point of such an act is not just the help itself, but the idea that is planted that "this person can be helpful." Usually this token reward can be just a useful piece of knowledge relevant to a problem that the school is concerned about. It might be a book or a pamphlet or perhaps a useful lead to a person or a technique that your contact has not thought of.

Responsiveness

A good linker should always be a good listener, especially at the beginning of a relationship. Most importantly, you should show that you are a good listener by nodding if you understand, by asking for clarifications when you do not, and by indicating verbally and nonverbally that you are interested and care about what your local contacts are saying. Show that you share their feelings and that you want to be helpful in whatever way you can. One specific way in which the linker can indicate responsiveness without commitment to solutions is by repeating back what you think the other person has said but in different words. This gives that other person a chance to hear your version of his or her thoughts and allows him or her to correct misunderstandings through reiteration. It further shows that you are really trying to listen.

This echoing type of response communication is a special skill. It should be learned and practiced by all change agents, especially linkers, until it comes naturally. It is especially important when the school district is about to make a major commitment of time, money, personnel, or effort; when you need to get across a rather complicated set of ideas; when you suspect that school personnel are having a hard time hearing your message for whatever reason; or when you and the school or school district seem to be in conflict over a key issue.

These first steps in relating to a potential knowledge user or participant in the change process fit in the category of good politics or good public relations. They should not be taken as the substance of change agentry but only as preliminary, though necessary, niceties. As soon as possible, you should start moving toward a serious dialogue on areas of need. This dialogue might be seen as a series of problem-solving cycles that start with something small and manageable that your contact group sees as manifestly urgent. Successful problem solving at this micro level cements the relationship and builds the trust necessary to move to issues that are more serious, systemic, and controversial.

The Ideal Relationship

Good relationships have no formula, and each has its own unique dimensions, but the best have several common features. Nine attributes make an ideal base for a change-supporting relationship: reciprocity, openness, realistic expectations, expectation of reward, structure, equal power, minimum threat, confrontation of differences, and involvement of all relevant parties. Use these nine points as a checklist and a yardstick to assess your relationship with a prospective user of your services. Do not just do it once; look at this list again as you progress through the change project and ask yourself whether you are continuing to relate well to key stakeholders, improving on weak areas, and making the relationship ever stronger.

Reciprocity

The relationship should be one in which both parties are able to give and take. To the extent that there is transfer of information, there should be transfer both ways, from linker to school personnel and from school personnel to linker. This reciprocity increases the mutual appreciation of the problem and makes the diagnosis more accurate. One-way relationships breed dependency and inhibit the initiative of the school system to help itself.

Openness

Openness to new ideas is fundamental to innovation. Both the linker and the key stakeholders in the school or school system should be ready to receive new inputs from each other. Several dimensions to openness should be considered: openness to receive new ideas, active eagerness to seek out new ideas, willingness to share new ideas with others, openness to listen to the problems and ideas of others, openness to give authentic feedback to each other, and an active desire for self-renewal.

Realistic Expectations

All too often, a change agent is viewed as some sort of miracle worker. Some linking agents even encourage such a perception. Thus, assumptions may be made that enormous benefits will come from the innovation. At later stages of the change process, these unrealistic expectations may return to haunt the project, giving undue disillusionment and discouragement to school personnel and change agent alike. An important rule of change agentry that applies especially to linkers is to set reasonably realistic expectations from the outset. Do not oversell yourself or the innovation. You are a linker, not a messiah.

Expectations of Reward

Do not, however, set expectations too low. It is equally important to give teachers and administrators in the school some reason for optimism and a picture of how much better things will be if the innovation is successful. The linking agent must be seen as providing a valuable resource, something that will solve problems and address areas of need. Sometimes it may be necessary to start out the relationship by providing some token of a future reward. Demonstrations or pilot programs serve this purpose by highlighting what can be done without committing the entire system to major involvement in time and expense. School personnel need some tangible evidence that you are a helpful person. If you can provide even the smallest bit of such evidence, you will nurture the belief that the relationship will be rewarding in the long run as well as in the short run.

Structure

Successful relationships must have some structural basis—some definition of roles, working procedures, the flow and integration of tasks and responsibilities, and expected outcomes. The question of how much structure is advisable and at what stages will always be present. Judging and assessing how much structure is needed lie at the heart of skilled change agentry. Some definition of the situation and the understandings between the parties is always desirable, but it is also important to be somewhat open-ended. Leave room for changing the relationship as you go along, expanding it in some areas and perhaps contracting it in others. The formalization of structure as an explicit contract is sometimes advisable, particularly where the linking agent sees certain aspects of the relationship as problematic, such as a lack of commitment by the leadership. Such contracts should probably be open-ended and reciprocal. That is, they should specify a sequence of points in the process at which the project could be terminated or redefined by mutual consent.

Equal Power

It is difficult to build a successful relationship between parties of grossly unequal power. This is perhaps the overriding consideration when you are including an outside agent in a change agent team. When the power of the two parties is equivalent, power itself no longer plays the controlling role in bringing about change, and its distorting effects on the process are minimized. An unequal distribution of power may bring about the appearance of change when the weaker partner offers compliance without the commitment necessary for lasting change. A linking agent has some advantage over the other types of change agents in this regard because the linker offers only the power of knowledge and the prospect of connection to other resources.

Minimum Threat

The very idea of change is threatening to most of us, particularly when it is presented by an outsider who is billed as a change agent. Most people like their world pretty much the way it is, warts and all, and they look on changes first as potential disturbances before they see them as potential benefits. It is extremely important that the change agent do everything possible to minimize the perception of threat. Again, the linking agent is likely to pose minimum threat, whereas the catalyst or the solution-giver types of change agents often appear to be threatening.

Confrontation of Differences

The linking agent, teachers, administrators, and other key stakeholders should have the ability to talk out their differences. They need to be frank with one another about critical matters that disturb them about their relationship. Suspicion of hidden motives should be discussed, and fears of exploitation should be brought out into the open. A relationship that tolerates the honest confrontation of differences may be stormy at times, but it will also be healthy and strong when the going gets tough.

Involvement of All Relevant Parties

As noted earlier, the linking agent must relate not only to teachers and administrators in the school but also to the people in the community who are most directly influential in the school system. In school settings, these entities are usually the school board and perhaps the local chamber of commerce, the local newspapers, and the churches. It is important to involve these other relevant parties to a degree, but it is not easy to decide what degree is appropriate. Those others whom you have initially identified as highly potent with respect to the focus of your change effort should at least know that you are there, know why you are there, and to some degree approve of your being there.

Few relationships between system and change agent will live up to all these criteria. You must usually settle for less than the ideal. Nevertheless, keep these nine points in mind as you make the best of what you have. Know where you are weak and how you can improve as the opportunity arises.

Danger Signals

The change relationship can be an exciting and rewarding experience, but at times, it can degenerate into a stagnant exercise that produces frustration and disappointment. Sometimes, you may feel that you have to go ahead with a project regardless of an unpromising relationship, but at other times, it may be really important for you to question whether to start at all. The following circumstances should tip you off to the existence of a bad relationship and a probable failure of your change effort.

- *A long history of unresponsiveness to change.* If teachers and administrators in the school and district are persistently indifferent and show no interest either in changing themselves or in accepting innovations of any sort, there is probably little point in spending much energy trying to help them. Interest, of course, is hard to measure, and you should not assume that the first try will be greeted with enthusiasm. Nevertheless, even though you may view your linking and other change agent talents as unique and your ability to bring about change as impressive, study the past history of the prospective system in dealing with similar change efforts. If the system has persistently responded with indifference or rejection, it is probably a signal that the system is a poor bet for future efforts.

- *Your sponsor within the school district wants to use you as a pawn.* Sometimes school personnel will be eager to seek outside agents only to serve their special purposes in an internal power struggle. The linking agent should be wary of this common type of exploitation.

- *Your local contacts within the system are already committed to a particular position.* Sometimes school personnel use the support of an outside change agent only to help prove a point or to affirm a position to which they are already committed. Such circumstances give little opportunity for genuine reciprocity and genuine innovation.

- *Your local contacts are powerless in their own house.* Sometimes the contact person in the school system eagerly invites a change agent into the system and is open to new ideas and wholeheartedly committed to cooperation but has no real power to effect change in others. Some systems, for example, will be completely dominated by a remote and inaccessible leadership that is fundamentally hostile to change. The leaders may allow a certain degree of latitude to the membership to "play games," but they firmly resist serious and lasting change. This pattern is frequently found in bureaucratic business organizations controlled by conservative boards of directors or in school districts controlled ultimately by conservative school boards.

- *The system shows many signs of pathology or major incapacity.* Linkers should learn to recognize in a school or school district certain signs of pathology that will make a continuing relationship difficult or impossible. Among such signs are excessive rigidity or obsessive concern with particular kinds of issues and an excessive tendency to externalize conflicts and to see issues in rigidly black-and-white terms. The system may also suffer from some sort of incapacity, such as an inability to effectively assemble resources when needed, to communicate clearly, to assemble key members for important meetings, and to provide financial and administrative backup for inside members of the change team. Regrettably, such signs of incapacity may reveal themselves only long after the project is under way. However, the appearance of a large number of such signs in very early stages may be a signal that your efforts will be wasted. No single sign necessarily indicates a "no go" situation. Indeed, various signs of pathology and incapacity may be singled out by the linker as targets for change effort.

- *Key local stakeholders respond negatively to your well-managed initial encounter.* The initial encounter is partly a test of the school district and partly a test of the change agent. If you have presented yourself as friendly, familiar, rewarding, and responsive but are greeted with hostility or indifference, your ability to succeed may be in doubt. However, you should be very cautious in drawing such a conclusion. Sometimes a tough exterior is simply one of the school's norms in dealing with initial encounters. It is important to assess the true feelings of the school and the school district, which may be at variance with outward appearances.

How to Size Up Your Relationship

This chapter has identified the major elements that go into a good change relationship involving a linker on the one hand and a school-based user system on the other. Most readers of *Guiding Change* will already be committed to various types of change-oriented relationships that exhibit varying degrees of stability and promise. To make maximum use of the material presented here, such readers should ask themselves five questions to size up the present relationship and give clues on how to make improvements.

- Have you managed to build an inside-outside team? This team is probably the most important building block of effective linking.
- Have you worked out a strategy for initial encounters? Does this strategy include adequate quantities of friendliness, familiarity, reward, and responsiveness?
- Can you identify in your situation the nine features of the ideal relationship? Can you rate where you stand on each of these nine dimensions? Are there specific things you can do to improve your ratings on any of these?
- Do you suspect that any of the danger signals apply? If yes, can you mitigate their effects? If too many apply to your situation, can you exit gracefully?
- Are you doing all that you can to protect and maintain your relationships with all key system stakeholders? Maintenance is far easier and far less expensive than rebuilding.

Final Word on Relationship Building

This chapter has introduced the essential features that make up successful relationships between a linking agent and a school system. It should be understood that this is a continuous process. Relationship building is vitally important for all other stages in this model, starting with Care and proceeding through

Renew. A good relationship continues to build as it goes along. It will be strengthened by a successful collaborative effort in defining needs, acquiring resources, selecting and installing the innovation, and extending it beyond the trial site. It will also depend on your relationship-building skills and on how adequately you can define and redefine your role as the change process moves forward.

Relate: Summary

As the linking agent begins to work with a system, an implicit contract defines the scope of work and the people to whom the linker will relate in carrying out the work. As relations become more involved and commitments more intense, the nature of that contract expands and clarifies. The linker must first be able to identify who makes up the system: the major interest groups and what they value, the key players, the stakeholders, and the relations among them. Beyond the immediate school setting, the linker must understand an array of forces and actors in the larger social environment.

A variety of linker-system configurations are possible, each with advantages and disadvantages. Most linkers are set in one system, but knowing the others will help you form a change team. The most effective team balances insider and outsider elements. In relating to any and all system stakeholders, you should try to hold a posture of friendliness, familiarity, rewardingness, and responsiveness, always observing and listening for the concerns of others while trying to establish openness to new ideas. The ideal group atmosphere to encourage collaborative system self-improvement has at least nine features: reciprocity, openness, realistic expectations, reward expectations, structure, equal power, minimum threat, confrontation of differences, and the involvement of all relevant parties. You, as the linking agent, can take actions to enhance each of these aspects.

Stage 3

Examine

Understanding the Problem

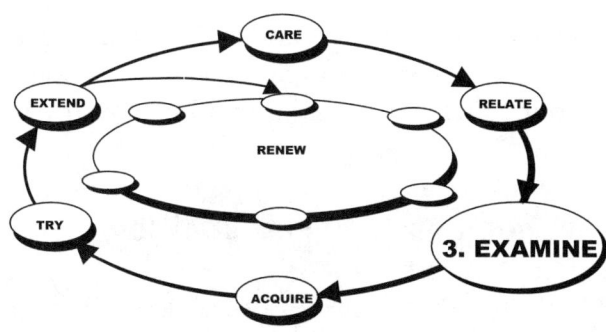

ORGANIZER QUESTIONS

- How does Stage 3: Examine differ from Stage 1: Care in a change process?
- What are the three phases of a diagnostic examination of the change setting?
- What are the major domain concerns of general educators and special educators?
- What is systemic analysis? What questions qualify as systemic?
- What are examples of low-profile and high-profile data collection approaches?
- What are some pitfalls to be avoided in the Examine stage of the change process?

In addition to, and in contrast with, caring about the need for change in a situation, the linking agent should undertake a deliberate stage of examining what the nature of the problem really is and framing the problem in terms that suggest possible solutions. Stage 3: Examine is the true analytic and diagnostic phase. Different concerns and symptoms need to be clearly defined and then sorted in terms of priority and amenability to solution. Systems often need expert help with examining and defining what their real needs are, given a base of concern and a social will to do something about that concern. This stage is also a social process that requires achieving a significant level of consensus on what the real problems are and in what order they should be taken up. Inevitably, it requires special educators to collaborate with general educators and with the larger system

Turn Cares Into Problems You Can Solve

You began to understand the problem at a gut level in Stage 1: Care. You have expressed a concern, a feeling strong enough to become a call for action. That concern led you to establish a relationship with a school system in need (Stage 2: Relate). You got to know more about the school system and made connections with different levels of personnel that allowed you and the members of the school system to begin addressing your concern. You are returning now to the concern in a somewhat different way. It is important at this point to step back and view the concern in perspective: to look at it in much more detail, to examine what lies behind the need for change, and to view it in relation to other needs and concerns that the school system might have. You are making sure that the implementation of your concern is necessary and that your concern is a need.

> ### Special Education Linking Agents in Action
>
> It was by examining the needs of the different teams in her school that Catherine Stone, the principal of North Slope School, found that a disparity existed between the reading instruction available to general education students and that available to students in special education.
>
> > General education teachers were using many different approaches to teach reading, including a great variety of materials such as basal readers, trade books, literature books, expository text, newspapers, library books, and magazines. They also were using a variety of teaching and learning strategies, including graphic organizers, directed reading thinking activity (DRTA), guided reading, shared reading, sustained silent reading, literature discussion groups, whole-language instruction, phonemic awareness, and thematic units. Students were participating in whole-group instruction, small-group instruction, cooperative groups, individual instruction, peer reading, cross-grade reading, and individual oral reading. The school was involved with the Atlantic Reading Network and was concentrating on creating developmentally appropriate groupings for reading instruction.
> >
> > The situation in special education stood out in sharp contrast to this innovative stew: The special education teacher was concentrating solely on using basal readers and workbooks. Distressingly, test scores on the Atlantic School Performance Assessment Program

> (ASPAP), which were low for the school as a whole, were particularly poor among students receiving special education services.
>
> Through this examination of needs, it became clear to the principal that improving reading instruction for special education students was, indeed, a need—a necessary concern.

Taking the time to examine needs can be difficult when the concern seems to be urgent. You are under a lot of pressure to get on with it, to grasp at obvious solutions. However, if you do not take the time to determine what the *real* need is and how it relates to the current state of the school system, your change efforts are, in the long run, likely to be misdirected and disappointing. For this reason, you and the school personnel who are involved should take a careful look at the concern in the context of the school or the school system—to examine. You should systematically attempt to understand the concern in more detail and depth, in relation to other needs, and in relation to the school system as a whole—whether that system comprises all the schools in a school district or, as in the case of North Slope School, an individual school building. For brevity's sake, throughout this chapter the term *school system* refers to the entity with which you, the linking agent, are working, regardless of whether that entity is a school district, several school districts, several schools, or an individual school.

An appropriate analogy is a medical diagnosis, which involves describing a patient's problem through the essential details of symptoms, history, and possible causes. The school or school system is the "patient." Diagnosis begins with the obvious, the school system's "pain"—its concern or need, as stated in Stage 1: Care. As you begin to work through the diagnosis, you help the members of the school system to articulate that need: to describe the type of pain, to pinpoint its location, and to recall its origin. When the diagnosis is complete, the original concern identified in Stage 1: Care should have been transformed into a defined problem stated in a way that allows you, as a linking agent, to work toward a solution.

Knowledge Base

Why a Separate Examine Stage Is Needed

Datnow and Stringfield (2000) conducted in 300 schools an intensive longitudinal study of 16 innovations intended to benefit students considered to be at risk. They found that sustainable innovations were most likely to derive from a finite set of widely shared goals. In *Guiding Change* terms, they had to move from global Stage 1: Care issues to Stage 3: Examine. They had to look at their circumstances in detail to arrive at a more specific consensus on what problems they should work on. Another sustainability requirement was a critical process of inquiry about what needed to change and why before the selection of a specific intervention.

(Continued)

> A good case in point is provided by Gross and colleagues (1971). They studied a program to redefine teacher roles so that they could deal better with the motivations of children in low socioeconomic groups. The poor definition and ambiguity of these worthy change goals led to frustration and tension among teachers and ultimately to program failure.
>
> Deal and Peterson (1999, p. 86) observe that "every school is a repository of unconscious sentiments and expectations that carry the code of the collective dream—the high ground to which they aspire." It is the job of the Examine stage not only to capture and articulate this dream but also to translate it into specifics that invite constructive problem solving.
>
> Several other authors, supported by many research studies, have emphasized that an effective change strategy must address individual, cultural, and structural barriers to improving practice (Sarason, 1982; McLaughlin & Talbert, 1992; Tyack & Cuban, 1995).

Making a Good Diagnosis

A good diagnosis requires three phases: entry, data collection, and analysis. Each phase has several steps.

The Entry Phase

- The quick take
- The initial conclusions
- The quick fix
- Separation of the problem from the solution

The Entry Phase

The entry phase has four steps: the quick take, the initial conclusions, the quick fix, and separation of the problem from the solution.

Do a Quick Take

A good doctor listens carefully to what a patient is saying. What type of pain is it? Where is it located? When did it start? How long has it lasted? How intensely is it felt? How does it compare with other pains the patient has had? What has the patient done about it, if anything, before seeking medical assistance? These questions must be asked immediately. They represent the first take on the problem, against which the doctor then matches his or her medical training and experience

Reach an Initial Conclusion

The doctor's medical training and knowledge, the resources the doctor uses to make the initial assessment of the patient, come mostly from experience with other patients but also from textbooks, manuals, research papers, and lectures and demonstrations—some from long ago. For a medical doctor, 95 percent of all situations fit into a few major categories ("OK, this is a case of X and I have seen a thousand X's in my time."). For a linking agent working with a school district, the situation is likely to be far more complex. You are dealing with a sprawling social entity rather than with an individual, and each entity has its crucial differences.

Perform a Quick Fix

If it is immediately clear that the patient's pain fits into one of the major categories identified by the doctor, there may be an easy fix—a medicine or a quick surgical maneuver that can ease the pain and deal adequately with the underlying condition. The doctor with such a case thinks, "If it is an X, then I do Y." All professional helpers like quick fixes. They save time, thought, and resources, and they reduce the anxiety that comes with doubt. True quick fixes also make the patient happy. Thus, if a true quick fix is available, they usually go for it.

Some quick fixes are also possible in education. A child with a mild visual impairment is moved to the front of the classroom; a child with a moderate hearing impairment is fitted with a hearing aid. A child with delayed reading or a behavior problem is given special attention in a resource room. Quick fixes like these apply to particular children in particular situations. The linking agent, however, should be targeting problems of a larger scope, especially those that are systemic and probably require long-term solutions.

Separate the Problem From the Solution

Assuming that you do not have a quick fix, you now want to examine the problem from several angles. You know that you are expected to be helpful, but it is important at this point to resist the temptation to heap potential solutions on the personnel in the school system. There is a further temptation to lean heavily on your own experience and expertise with specific solutions. Remember the old expression, to a hammer, every solution is a nail. Keep your ideas for solutions at bay until you have reached a satisfactory definition of the problem at hand. In other words, just stand there, don't do something!

The Data Collection Phase

The data collection phase has three steps: lay out your taxonomy, think system, and assemble the data.

Lay Out Your Taxonomy

Every established field has a semantic structure that orders the things that people are concerned about. As people's experience grows and they become more educated in a given area, the vocabulary and word structure they use when referring to that area become more differentiated. As people share these word structures, consensus about their meaning grows. *Guiding Change* is, itself, a proposed taxonomy, a verbal classification system for dealing with the change process. As you begin to apply new concepts to your particular change process, you will start using a new set of words and word structures to think about what you do, making your thinking about change both more sensible and more comprehensive. An effective diagnosis starts with a review of the concerns that you, the linking agent, and other linkers—including school system personnel—bring to the table.

> **The Data Collection Phase**
> - Lay out your taxonomy: What is your classification system?
> - Think system
> - Assemble the data.

Think System

The school district you are working with is a system, a set of elements that are supposed to work together to achieve some common goal. Social systems are like people in a lot of ways. The elements of social systems have structure, cohesiveness, and interdependence that are analogous to the organic unity and purposefulness of individual organisms. Like an individual, a system has goals and a structure for achieving those goals. Two overarching diagnostic questions are, What are the system's goals? and How effectively is the system working to achieve them? Subsidiary questions relate to the adequacy of the system's goals and the degree of internal understanding and consensus regarding these goals. An organic systems model also gives you a set of coherent and convenient categories for analysis, starting with the big three: input, throughput, and output.

Assemble the Data

It has long been common practice in education circles to perform periodic needs assessments to lay the groundwork for new initiatives. However, instead of guiding future decisions, the needs assessment can sometimes degenerate into a laundry list that merely serves as bureaucratic justification for what is already planned. Thus, it is important to clearly articulate to key members of the school system the purpose of the needs assessment process, but checking off every item on an elaborate taxonomy would make a fearful list, too long to comprehend and too exhausting to complete. Planning a successful needs assessment requires working with your team to build an inventory of the salient diagnostic facts pertaining to your situation while remaining aware of the larger context and of other problems that still need a resolution.

With a good understanding of the most urgent areas of need in your school system, you are ready to collect appropriate data. Start with what is already available, of course. Existing needs assessments can be useful if they are well conceived and fit your taxonomy. Then go to your key informants (for a definition, see "Low-Profile Approaches to Collecting Diagnostic Data"). A number of suggestions on how to do this are presented later in the chapter.

The Analytic Phase

- Rate the data and prioritize the real problems.
- Respect the obvious.
- Beware of the obvious.
- Identify the opportunities.
- Collaborate on the diagnostic process.
- Adopt a linking posture.
- Search for underlying causes.
- Rethink and rework the diagnosis as you go forward.

The Analytic Phase

Eight steps make up the analytic phase: rate the data and prioritize the real problems, respect the obvious, beware of the obvious, identify the opportunities, collaborate on the diagnostic process, adopt a linking posture, search for underlying causes, and rethink and rework the diagnosis as you go forward.

Rate the Data and Prioritize the Real Problems

Once you have a list, you have to decide on priorities and connections between the items on the list. Ask these three questions to narrow down your priorities:

- What needs seem to be most urgent (i.e., pressing right now)?
- What needs are the most important or fundamental in the long run?
- On what areas can you have a real impact with the available resources and knowledge?

Respect the Obvious

If the school system approaches you with problem A, start with the assumption that the real problem is A or something related in some way to A. Respect the problem as stated by the system while you clarify and expand your understanding of what the real problem is. The danger is that linking agents will see the problem primarily in terms of their own expertise—what they think they have the competence and knowledge to provide. The good linker can start by focusing on what the school system personnel are saying because the linker is not bound to one solution pathway. The first step is to survey the surface symptoms by interviewing key persons, meeting with a focus group of representative members, or even simply by talking with the change team. Surface symptoms represent the topmost layer of a problem, what the physician calls the patient's complaint. It is the initial concern that led the system to seek help.

Beware of the Obvious

Perhaps the next most important thing to remember about diagnosis is to beware of the obvious. Initially, the most obvious problem will be the Stage 1 concern, the need that the members of a system say they feel. However, most problems have several layers. After posting the list of concerns produced by the members of a school system, you should ask them what other things are wrong: Do they see other indications that the school system has not been functioning as well as it could? If the problem originally stated was "disproportional representation of minorities in special education," you may want to ask whether there is also evidence of poverty, racial conflict among students, and so forth. These problems should be recorded and compared with the school system's list of problems to see whether they reveal any common patterns. When you have assembled all these surface symptoms, you may want to probe further to get at some of the less obvious factors that lie beneath them. Here you might look for certain attitudes and beliefs on the part of students, parents, teachers, or administrators that led to those symptoms. You may also find features of the learning climate or structure that breed such surface symptoms. These second-level elements should also be identified.

Identify the Opportunities

The linking agent should avoid focusing exclusively on what is wrong with the system. You should also identify opportunities, the system's areas of strength and areas of greatest potential for change. Sound psychological and practical reasons support this posture. Psychologically, an accent on the positive makes the members of a system feel less defensive and more hopeful that change can be beneficial. From a practical point of view, the overall diagnostic picture becomes much clearer when strong points as well as weaknesses are noted. Members of the system see that they can begin their change effort by using their capacities and capitalizing on their areas of greatest potential.

Strengths and weaknesses can be identified at various levels. Some things that appear to be problems on the surface may, in reality, indicate an underlying strength. For example, veteran general education teachers may not want students with special needs in their classrooms because they are afraid that they will not get enough support to meet these students' needs and those of the general education students (a surface problem). However, the inclusion of students with special needs in general education settings could lead to greater cohesion in the classroom (a potential underlying strength) as general education students and students with special needs mingle and get to know each other (a potential underlying strength) and as students with special needs are presented with opportunities formerly unavailable to them (a potential underlying strength). The linking agent should take special note of the school system's history of coping with problems. Sometimes a school or a community that seems hopelessly disorganized and strife-torn will reveal surprising resiliency and competence in coping with difficulties in certain areas at certain times. These areas and times should be noted and recorded in the diagnosis.

Collaborate on the Diagnostic Process

Involve school system personnel at every stage (Stage 2: Relate), but especially in defining the problem. As a linking agent, you should work collaboratively so that personnel share your perception of problems and needs. You should provide guidance while personnel make their own examination of the situation. This way, their findings will be acceptable to them by virtue of being their own. Use your relationships with school personnel to build a consensus on what the problems really are. In the process of moving toward consensus, you will also improve and strengthen these relationships. The one is a vehicle for the other. Thus, Stage 3: Examine grows out of Stage 2: Relate. A strong and collaborative Stage 3 diagnostic process also enhances and reaffirms Stage 1: Care. As system personnel identify problem areas, they will probably learn that they need to be concerned about more issues than they had at first realized. Their understanding of the priorities among these issues will build a more reality-based level of concern.

Adopt a Linking Posture

Playing the role of linker enhances the diagnostic process. Think of your diagnostic strategy as an ongoing social process in which you reach out to various members of the system to tap their perceptions of what is going on and what needs improvement. Internal analysis is not the only way to define opportunities for change. Sometimes a comparison to another system gives the members ideas about what they need and what they can do. For example, information about an innovation that has been successful elsewhere will often lead to an awareness of a need, which fosters the motivation to create change. Outside innovations sometimes suggest inside opportunities—in this sense, they create needs. Further, outside systems that are successful and innovative also provide a yardstick against which school system personnel may measure their own performance. Reaching out to experts and experienced observers of various types in other organizations can help with the diagnostic process. These outsiders can help the system personnel make judgments about the problems and needs that underlie surface symptoms. They can also provide perspective on the relative importance of different signs, thereby helping you view this particular school system against national or regional trends and levels of performance.

Search for Underlying Causes

At a still deeper level, you may wish to interpret the evidence and infer underlying causes. Surface symptoms, such as the reluctance of a general education teacher to have a child with serious emotional disturbance in his or her classroom, could be related to the teacher's fear of being unable to meet that child's unfamiliar (to the teacher) needs. Such "depth" interpretations may be valid and valuable in some circumstances, but linking agents should base their judgments on two criteria:

- Does the interpretation match an objective analysis of available evidence?
- Does it help us understand what sort of solution we should be looking for?

On the one hand, sometimes an analysis of underlying causes may suggest solutions that are not apparent at a superficial level. On the other hand, deep causal interpretations are sometimes irrelevant to the search for solutions and can delay constructive work. As a linking agent, you must be constructive and practical. You can choose to work on any level of a problem, keeping in mind that the problem has other levels and that working on these levels might also lead to successful problem solving. Regardless of which level you choose, you should be sensitive to the self-perceptions of school system personnel as well as to their willingness and ability to define the problem on the same level that you have defined it.

Rethink and Rework the Diagnosis as You Go Forward

It is a mistake to believe that the diagnostic process is ever finished. Even when you have thoroughly identified and prioritized needs in full collaboration with key members of the school system, you should remain sensitive to the possibility of emerging needs and changing priorities. Your work with a school system on a particular solution may reveal strengths, weaknesses, or concerns that did not show up in your first diagnostic evaluation. The appearance of new people on the scene continually changes the social dynamics. Their priorities may be different from those that you have identified. Your task is then to absorb their concerns, bring them up to speed on your concerns, or both.

> **Special Education Linking Agents in Action**
>
> The technical assistance (TA) liaison began a search for information on reading programs for students with learning disabilities. To help in the search process, he requested information about the district's overall plans for school improvement, demographic information, and information about current or previous change efforts. He also inquired about the county's special education service delivery model, eligibility guidelines, and so on. After the TA liaison had received the information, he expressed an interest in making a site visit to Hilldale County to meet with teachers and visit classrooms. He sent the linking agent a questionnaire to complete prior to his visit. The questionnaire dealt with several topics: areas of concern, current curriculum and instructional strategies, and the TA environment (willingness of teachers to participate in training, the time available for training, etc.). The questionnaire was completed by school personnel and returned by the linking agent prior to his visit.

Making a Diagnostic Inventory

> **Features of a Good Diagnosis**
>
> - A definition of the domain
> - A data collection process
> - A set of rating dimensions

There is no such thing as a complete diagnosis of a system's needs. All such efforts are necessarily incomplete, tentative, and cursory. However, every diagnosis should include at least these three features: a definition of the domain, including major relevant categories; a data collection process; and a set of rating dimensions. And like a doctor who is examining a patient before deciding on a diagnosis, the linking agent can best evaluate the strengths and challenges of a school system by asking a lot of questions.

A Definition of the Domain

For general educators, major issues can be divided roughly into three categories: the *content* of education, educative *processes*, and educational *systems*.

Education Content Issues

- What do we want our children to learn? Are we teaching those things?
- Are we changing what we teach to keep up with the changing culture?

- Are we teaching content that reflects state and local standards and assessments?
- Are we training for the current job market and the job market of the future?
- Do the content areas being taught adequately reflect the existing knowledge base? Do they reflect the latest research or thinking? Science? Conventional wisdom? The latest cultural products and trends?
- Are things being taught that should not be (e.g., prejudice, sex, violence, bad habits)?

Educative Process Issues

- Are students really being educated? Is content being learned as well as taught?
- Are classroom time and school-year time adequate?
- Are students learning in the right way (e.g., Are they learning how to solve problems?)?
- Is the classroom environment conducive to learning? Is it safe? Nondisruptive? Open? Welcoming?

Educational System Concerns

- Students
  - Are they prepared for school?
  - Are their needs for assistance being addressed?
  - Are their rights properly served?
- Teachers
  - Are there enough? Are they adequately prepared? Are they open to change?
  - Are they adequately supported and rewarded? Are they effectively linked to one another as a social network?
- Principals and administrators
  - Do they understand their role in the educative process?
  - Are they change-oriented? Do they relate adequately to teachers?
- Other school personnel: Is there an adequate mix of roles (counselors, librarians, aides, etc.) to support learning?
- Parents and members of the community: Are they adequately involved in the schools?
- Schools
  - Are the structures open to change? Are they adequately staffed? Adequately equipped?
  - Are their buildings and building layouts optimal for learning?
  - Are they equipped with the appropriate materials and technologies?
  - Do members of the school function collaboratively? Do they work in teams?

- Classrooms
    - Are there the right number of students? Teachers?
    - Are there enough books? Supportive technologies? Adequate space?
    - Are there linkages between teachers and students? Among teachers? Among students?

- School districts (same questions as for schools plus these)
    - Are there adequate resources for change?
    - Is there flexibility of structure to allow new ways of working between schools?
    - Is there acceptance and support for change in the community?
    - Is there adequate linkage to state, regional, and federal resources?

- Nonformal education (television, radio, movies, popular music, print press, sports, work culture, peer cultures, churches, membership groups)
    - What are the effects of each of these on attitudes and behavior involving sex, violence, smoking, drugs, and alcohol?
    - What are their effects on the political system, technology, and science?

For special educators, most of the big issues and challenges fall into five categories: classification and identification, case management, equalization of opportunity, access to the general education curriculum, and creation of infrastructure for special education.

Classification and Identification of Students for Special Education Services

> **What Skills Do Outside Linking Agents Need During the Examine Stage?**
>
> Don't let others rush you to solutions—conduct a thorough examination of your school or school district's needs. They all seem to want to jump into the selection of an intervention rather than research and think about a direction more strategically.
>
> —EMSTAC linking agent

- Are the screening and appraisal processes and the categorization of disabilities for special education accurate and effective? For example, are overrepresentation of minorities in special education and misidentification of reading-delayed students as mentally retarded non- or low-incidence issues? Where they are issues, are they being addressed?

- Do schools have effective prereferral systems that provide adequate and appropriate interventions and, when necessary, referrals that lead to evaluations? Are parents appropriately involved in the process?

Case Management

- Is Public Law 94–142 (including its 1997 reauthorization, the Individuals with Disabilities Education Act [IDEA]) upheld?

- Is a free appropriate public education (FAPE), the right of every child with a disability in the United States, actually available?

- Are students with disabilities educated in the least restrictive environment, within a continuum of alternative placements such as regular classes, resource room classes, self-contained classes, day and residential special schools, home instruction, hospital instruction, and institutional instruction?

- Are criteria established to determine resource room placement?

- Are special education and related services available (e.g., speech therapy, psychological services, physical and occupational therapy, social work services and transportation, training in daily living skills, adapted physical education)?

- Are students eligible for special education receiving appropriate individualized education programs (IEPs)?

- Are these IEPs appropriately prepared, maintained, and reevaluated?

- Are IEPs appropriately used to evaluate and promote progress?

- Are assistive technology and augmentative communication devices appropriately available to increase, maintain, or improve the functional capabilities of students with disabilities? Do they enhance communication, support access to learning opportunities, support mastery of both basic skills (decoding, reading, and writing) and complex material (enhancing reading comprehension, developing active learning skills), and make assessment and evaluation more manageable?

- Is training in the effective use of assistive technology easily available to parents, teachers, and students?

- Are criteria established to determine when and to what extent students with disabilities are integrated with their peers in their home school and have access to the general education curriculum?

Equalization of Opportunity

- Is there compliance with Public Law 94–142 and its 1997 reauthorization, IDEA, in the provision of special education services (e.g., wheelchair-accessible schools and classrooms for students ages 3 through 21 who have a wide range of disabilities)?

- Is appropriate and adequate extra support provided at school and in the classroom for students with disabilities (e.g., appropriately trained and supervised paraprofessionals, aides, and assistants)?

- Are appropriate state-of-the-art assistive technology and augmentative communication devices available?

- Are there high expectations and challenging standards and curriculum for all children?

- Are prereferral services appropriately carried out?

- Are IEPs provided, maintained, and reevaluated?

- Is there meaningful participation of all children in all aspects of the school?

- Is there good leadership and organizational vitality in the school and community and collaborative relationships among special and general education school personnel?

- Are parents, students, teachers, and schools making the effort to work as a team?

- Are the rates of attendance of secondary school, graduation from secondary school, and enrollment in postsecondary programs of students with disabilities improving?

- Is there improvement in postschool job placement services to ensure that higher numbers of students with disabilities enter the workforce?

Access to the General Education Curriculum

- Do students with disabilities have the opportunity to receive a FAPE, to access the general education curriculum, and to be integrated to the extent appropriate with their peers in general education?

- Is there teaming between general education and special education teachers?

- Is there coteaching between general education and special education teachers?

- Is there training for general education teachers in special education issues in general and in those particular issues or disability areas relevant to their particular classroom situations?

- Are teachers adequately prepared in appropriate skills?

- Do teachers know how to use appropriate accommodations to address student disabilities?

- Are students with disabilities attending their home schools whenever possible?

- Are students with disabilities being educated in the least restrictive environment possible?

- Are students with disabilities receiving the appropriate range of special education and related services?

- Are general education teachers providing adequate prereferral interventions?

- Are students with disabilities included in state- and districtwide assessments?

Special Education Infrastructure

- Is the school district creating and supporting a social infrastructure within special education that is parallel to general education?

- Does this infrastructure facilitate the points above?

Knowledge Base

What the Examination Should Look At

The special needs of various student populations are well understood by special educators and require no further elaboration here. Second-order needs are those of the educators themselves as they begin to contemplate innovative changes.

One of many dangers in needs assessment is trivialization. McLaughlin (1990) observes that change efforts cannot be rated as successful unless they address matters of sufficient complexity to pique interest and are seen to promise meaningful changes. Numerous authors have documented the importance of various barrier or resistance factors that should be a part of this examination. Here is a sampling:

- Lack of incentives for change, such as not seeing a need for change or believing that the change is not worth the expenditures of effort and resources (Sieber, 1981; Louis, Kell, Dentler, Corwin, & Herriott, 1984; Little, 1993).
- Structural barriers, such as school social structure (e.g., isolated teachers), staffing ratios, and work schedules (Miles, 1981; Huberman, 1983; Corwin & Dentler, 1984; Ball, 1995).
- Cultural barriers, such as collective beliefs about students and learning (Sarason, 1982; McLaughlin & Talbert, 1992; Talbert & McLaughlin, 1994; Tyack & Cuban, 1995).
- Individual attitudes, such as the fear of change and the fear of inability to master new ways of doing things (Showers, Joyce, & Bennett, 1987; Ball, 1995; Borko & Putnam, 1995; Hargreaves, 1996).

Systemic Analysis: Understanding the System

Society, the family, the school, and the classroom are examples of systems. Although the complexities of these systems can be and have been studied individually, they are actually intricately interwoven. Understanding the school system and classroom requires understanding the numerous external systems that affect the functioning of the system and the child within the system. Thus, the linking agent should try to see the school system as a number of people and groups who are interrelated and at least partly interdependent, trying to work together to achieve common goals. In education, as in most areas of endeavor, these goals are not clearly spelled out, but they are there, nevertheless. When members of the system sit down together to talk about their goals, they are usually able to arrive at a consensus on what their major goals are. This is a useful exercise that the linking agent can use as a first step in getting school system personnel to think clearly and diagnostically about their problems.

Once the goals have been clearly articulated, the kinds of activities that must be included and coordinated to make those goals realities can be defined. Members of the school system can start by looking at their system and ask themselves whether the system, as it exists, can really achieve these goals.

Exercise in System Analysis

> **Systemic Analysis Must Respond to These Questions**
>
> - What are the system's goals?
> - Is there an adequate structure for achieving these goals?
> - Is there openness in communications?
> - Are members rewarded for working toward stated goals?

The following five questions can form the core of a system analysis inventory. Place each question at the top of a sheet of paper. Below each question, list the related problems and opportunities that come to mind. Leave space to respond to the additional questions about each area listed below.

What Are the System's Goals?

- Have leaders and members openly discussed what the goals should be?
- Are the goals clear to both the leaders and the members?
- Is there a consensus on goals?
- Are members fully satisfied that the stated goals are adequate?
- Are goals flexible? Can they change as times and circumstances change?

Is There an Adequate Structure for Achieving These Goals?

- Is there an adequate division of labor?
- Do members have a clear understanding of what they are supposed to be doing in the system?
- Do the different roles fit together as a system for achieving goals?
- Are some elements missing that are needed to make the community work as a system?
- Are there weak elements (e.g., overloaded, underused, ineffective, irrelevant)?
- Are elements adequately coordinated?
- Is the structure flexible? Can it be changed to meet new conditions?

Is There Openness in Communication?

- Are major subgroups (teachers, administrators, parents, students) able to talk to one another? Can they express their feelings and exchange ideas freely?
- Are members open to new ideas from within? Do they actively seek such ideas?
- Are they open to new ideas from outside (e.g., universities, outside consultants and specialists, people from other systems that have similar problems or have found interesting solutions)? Do they actively seek these outside sources?
- Does the system have (or can it muster) the needed resources in people, time, money, materials, and facilities?

- Can the system train its own people?
- Can the system recruit new people needed for a successful change?

Does the System Reward Its Members for Working Toward Its Stated Goals?

- Are students rewarded for learning? For contributing to the learning process?
- Are the teachers rewarded for innovating? For working to improve the system?
- Are administrators rewarded for innovating? For being open to students and teachers?
- Are the rewards that people get reliable?
- Do the rewards that people get come soon enough to connect to their behavior?
- Are the rewards compatible with and supportive of the overall goals of the system?

With a list of questions such as these, you can make a diagnostic inventory that should help you and your school system throughout the change process. It is not important that your list include all these questions, but it is important that you make some effort to identify and record salient facts in each of these five general areas so that you have a profile of the system as a whole in addition to a list of specific problems. Only when you have such a profile will you be able to start making judgments about priorities for the change effort. Later, this inventory should also serve you and your school system as a baseline against which to measure progress.

Knowledge Base

Systemic Analysis

Among the many researchers who have attempted a systems analysis of educational environments, four can be singled out. The first two are Havelock and Huberman (1978), whose chapter "Social Systems and Innovation Systems" looks at the change activity itself as a smaller temporary system in interaction with the larger social system of the educational setting. Following an extensive analysis of system inputs and outputs, they conclude that "because innovations in most cases can be seen as new inputs to larger systems, the quality, structuring and extent of dialogue surrounding their introduction is of crucial importance" (p. 49).

A second good reference on systemic analysis is by Reigeluth and Garfinkle (1994), who lay out the elements of the system being changed and the assumptions about the nature of that system (its purpose, members, how it works, its governing constraints, and so forth). The intervening change agent must first question those assumptions to see whether they still hold true. They must look inside long enough and hard enough to understand its subsystems or stakeholders and how they relate to one another and to the larger whole. Effective planning for change also requires a serious look outside the system to see whether and how other systems, such as business or higher education, are connected to the local system. Such an understanding may cast current intentions in a new light, flagging certain issues and sometimes suggesting a redirection of effort.

A Data Collection Process

As you enter the scene, you want to put aside as many presuppositions and assumptions as possible. You are in a listening mode and everything is up for grabs: what the real need is, what the school system is, what can or should be done, even what your own role might be. It is very difficult to be this open about anything. Humans are orderly beings who crave definition and position. As a linking agent, you should restrain these tendencies at the outset. There will be plenty of time for them later.

How you approach data collection will depend largely on available resources and time, the extent of cooperation you can count on from the school system, and the level of urgency of the problem as perceived by school system personnel. You can therefore group specific data collection tactics into two groups, low profile and high profile. The low-profile approaches work best in an introductory phase, where limited time and limited resources are available for determining what the problem is. The high-profile approaches assume more familiarity with the system, more time, and more resources that can be set aside to examine the system's needs and the nature of the problem.

Low-Profile Approaches to Collecting Diagnostic Data

Here are four ways to begin an expanded search to determine where you are, who the school system is, what they need, and where you belong in their process: Use the problem vocalizer as your informant, use key informants within the system, hold group interviews, and observe.

Use the Problem Vocalizer

> **Low-Profile Approaches to Collecting Diagnostic Data**
>
> - Use the problem vocalizer as your informant.
> - Use key informants within the system.
> - Hold group interviews.
> - Observe.

The person who invites the linking agent into the school system usually has the most concern or the most acute sense of the problem. This person, the problem vocalizer, is necessarily your initial source for diagnostic information. Keeping in mind that this person may not have the clearest, most perceptive, or most objective view of the overall situation, you may still use him or her as an informant to obtain most of what you need to know. Above all, it is important that you make face-to-face contact with this individual, preferably at his or her place of work, residence, or both. It is also important that you have a chance for extended contact so that you can get to know each other (see Stage 1: Care) and so that this person can share his or her perceptions of the problem with you honestly and straightforwardly.

To get the most out of your informants, you should follow a three-step strategy:

- Listen
- Reflect
- Inquire

Listen. Begin by listening, allowing your informants to tell you as much as they want to tell you and as much as they think you need to know. If they are very experienced and adept at using consultative help, they may tell you all you need to know without any active inquiry from you.

Reflect. Once the initial contact persons have stated the situation to their satisfaction, tell them what you heard them say by restating, as accurately and concisely as you can, what you thought they were saying. When you are done, ask them whether that is what they meant to say. If you are really communicating, they will agree with your reflection of their statement; however, there may be points of misunderstanding or areas where there is a lack of clarity. By repeating the same statement-and-reflection process again and again, you and your informants will gradually move toward consensus.

Inquire. Finally, when you have consensus on your informants' stories, you may want to make further detailed inquiries or probes, especially to fill in gaps in your understanding.

Recording diagnostic information received from human sources (problem vocalizers, key informants, groups, etc.) can be tricky. Most interviewers prefer not to take extensive notes while the interview is in progress because this method interferes with their ability to listen, reflect, observe, and respond. If accuracy and comprehensiveness of the data are important, there is no substitute for the tape recorder, but if only highlights and overall impressions are needed, the simplest procedure is to record your summary of what was said immediately after the interview, either on paper or into a tape recorder. An open-ended form, like one you could generate from the diagnostic inventory described in Stage 2: Relate, would be useful. Do not record more information than you need.

Use Key Informants Within the System

It is usually important to acquire preliminary, baseline information from more than one source and, in a complex school system, from more than one level and more than one faction. The same general rules that apply to the person who vocalized the problem also apply to key informants, with one significant exception: You cannot assume that key informants will be eager to tell you their views of the problem because you, not they, initiated the contact. You need to establish your legitimacy and sincerity as a diagnostician and a consultant (see again Stage 1: Care). You may have to start by telling them why you are in the system in the first place and why you are asking them questions. For this purpose, face-to-face contact is vital. Once you have established yourself as a trustworthy individual who is sincerely trying to help, you can proceed through the listening-reflecting-inquiring sequence.

> **Special Education Linking Agents in Action**
>
> **The Linking Agent Extends Her Linking Efforts: Another Innovation at Another School Level**
>
> At the beginning of the 1999–2000 school year, the linking agent began contacting middle school principals and attending secondary council meetings to get a sense of perceived needs at the middle school level. In addition, she reviewed the needs assessment completed by special education teachers at the middle school. Improving reading skills had been identified as the primary concern at the middle school level just as it had been at North Slope School at the elementary school level. The linking agent contacted individual administrators, gave them printed material about the program, and scheduled a meeting during which they could ask questions and assess whether this intervention would meet their needs. Information about the intervention and specific strategies for teaching students with disabilities was also sent to all middle and high school special education teachers. Teachers also received a survey that asked them to prioritize a number of strategies they thought would best meet the needs of their students.

Hold Group Interviews

When time is short and it is essential to get a variety of perspectives, the linking agent may ask the school system spokesperson to bring together a representative group (e.g., principal, assistant principal, veteran and novice teachers, student leaders of different races). With the assembled group you can proceed through the same listening-reflecting-inquiring sequence, but there are important differences between interviewing a group and an individual. You should observe how the members of the group relate to one another; how much they defer to authority; and whether individuals are reticent about disagreeing, speaking up, or adding to the story being told by other members of the group. The interviewer should test the group members' willingness to open up about what they perceive the real issues to be. To do this, you need a good understanding of group dynamics and preferably some experience in human relations training. With such a background, you can derive a great deal of valuable diagnostic information not only from listening to what members of the group say but also from observing how they react to one another.

Observe

Using human resources in face-to-face interchange, as described in the three techniques above, provides verbal information, but it also has an important dividend: the chance to observe the people in the system—how they relate to you and to one another, how they act and react in response to a number of situations. It is sometimes valuable to make site visits without asking questions, solely for the sake of observing what is going on. Early on, you may conduct such visits without a clear idea of what you are looking for, but being a good observer, especially of anything as complex as a school or a classroom, requires training and experience as well as open eyes and ears. Be especially sensitive to how others see you and to whether they will accept your observer status. To be accepted, strangers generally need to provide a pretty good explanation for their actions.

Outsiders who have known the school system for a number of years can be a potential source of supplementary observations and information. The editor of the local newspaper is one favorite source, but other consultants who have worked with the school system can also provide valuable insights.

High-Profile Approaches: Acquiring Systematic Diagnostic Information

To narrow the search to a specific diagnosis, the linking agent may need to acquire more detailed information about the school system and about the specific problem under consideration. Ideally, you should systematically acquire this information in a form that allows quantitative comparison so that you know the dimension and importance of the problem relative to other problems in the same system and the same problem in other systems. In the taxonomic analysis above, you can find a number of conceptual models and a number of dimensions that you can apply when making a systematic diagnosis, but you will need to understand the actual mechanisms for acquiring information to put in these categories. Five such mechanisms are listed in increasing order of complexity and difficulty: observe and measure system outputs; organize a self-diagnostic workshop for the school system; use an outside diagnostic research team; create a collaborative, systematic diagnostic program; and set up continuous, quantitative diagnostic monitoring.

Observe and Measure System Outputs (Intended and Unintended)

Hard evidence that students have attained meaningful and measurable educational objectives is nearly impossible to obtain from our schools today. Although there is much pressure to move toward accountable systems, the availability of hard data is a long way off in almost all school environments. However, some telltale signs can suggest that things are not going well, such as high teacher turnover, high frequency of disciplinary actions, and high dropout rates.

Reliable signs on the positive side are fewer. College placements and national honors are likely to reflect neighborhood and parentage as much as schooling. But high attendance at PTA meetings, passage of school tax rates, and even high attendance at school sporting events may indicate a healthy community concern and support. Even the printed outputs of the system—newsletters,

> **High-Profile Approaches to Collecting Diagnostic Data**
>
> - Observe and measure system outputs.
> - Organize a self-diagnostic workshop for the school system.
> - Use an outside diagnostic research team.
> - Create a collaborative, systematic diagnostic program.
> - Set up continuous, quantitative diagnostic monitoring.

catalogs, yearbooks—may reveal a good deal about the range of courses and activities, the degree of participation, the orientation of the curriculum, and the diversity of student interests. Although *Guiding Change* is not a detailed guide to these varied sources for diagnostic information, various potential sources are available. As a linking agent, you should be flexible in your search for data that can be retrieved from existing and readily available records.

Organize a Self-Diagnostic Workshop for the School System

Linking agents with considerable skills in human relations, group work, or conference management may want to initiate a series of meetings throughout the school system. At these meetings, members representing all personnel levels (perhaps including students, parents, and community leaders in addition to teachers and administrators) can sit down together to assess the problems in their system. This procedure, known as a self-diagnostic workshop, is complex and risky, but it has two special advantages. First, it allows a genuine confrontation of existing problems and involvement in initiating change on the part of members at all levels. Second, if it is done well, a self-diagnostic workshop provides a detailed and accurate accounting of the prevailing situation. In other words, the diagnosis that results may be better than it would have been if fewer individuals representing fewer perspectives had taken part.

Use an Outside Diagnostic Research Team

If the system is very large and the problem is pervasive, and if considerable financial resources are available for diagnosis, the linking agent might well consider contracting with a university, a social research center, or a private consulting firm to administer survey instruments for a thorough, systematic, and scientific job of diagnosis or needs assessment. However, the underlying problem with such an approach will probably be its perceived relevance. In spite of mountains of data and tests of statistical significance, it may be hard to convince members of a school system that a diagnosis arrived at by a team of outside experts is really relevant and valid unless the school system itself collaborates in developing the measures and collecting the data.

Create a Collaborative, Systematic Diagnostic Program

Probably the most elaborate and elegant procedure for acquiring diagnostic information is a combination of the foregoing strategies: An inside-outside team organizes a program for system self-diagnosis using outside experts as trainers and instrument developers for the members of the school system. This strategy can have many variants and many components.

Set Up Continuous, Quantitative Diagnostic Monitoring

The most sophisticated type of diagnostic information is gathered by the school system for itself on a continual or periodic basis, using objective behavioral criteria that are recognized as legitimate and valid by both insiders (including students) and outside experts. Such a diagnostic capability would be the equivalent of the accountability that so many outside experts are now insisting schools must develop. To design and install such a monitoring system is a major change project in itself, requiring all the skills, artistry, and know-how that a linking agent can muster. However, a school system that has such a capability would already have come a long way toward genuine self-renewal.

Knowledge Base

How to Collect the Data

Deal and Peterson (1999) suggest that two important roles that a good school leader can assume are historian (understanding the social and normative past) and anthropological sleuth (analyzing and probing to uncover current norms, values, and beliefs). Both roles would support Stage 3: Examine.

Lee and Barnett (1994) propose reflective questioning as an effective nonthreatening tool for outside change agents to use (1) to establish relationships, (2) to retrieve important diagnostic data, and (3) to begin a self-examining motivational process inside the respondent, a first step toward change. Grose's *Partners in Innovation* (2001) deliberately adopted this approach, which was originally developed by Carl Rogers (1969) as a psychotherapeutic technique.

Deal and Peterson (1999), after describing a specific example of an outside consultant confronting a toxic culture, go on to explain how the consultancy evolved and eventually achieved some success. A key intermediate step was holding one-on-one interviews with key members of the toxic culture, which eventually became the key to unlocking resistance. The interviews had two good outcomes: (1) a better inside understanding of the elements of the culture (good data) and (2) the generation of a feeling among initially hostile stakeholders that someone was seriously listening to them.

A Set of Rating Dimensions

Whatever methods you employ and whatever categories you use, you will always have to make comparative judgment calls on a number of dimensions. The linking agent probably starts out by making these calls alone, but as the circle of cooperation in the Stage 3: Examine process grows, more and more people will be involved in sharing and reaching consensus on the rating dimensions and the ratings themselves. Appropriate rating dimensions are outlined below.

Rating Dimensions (for Any Area)

- *Centrality.* Is this a topic or an issue that is occupying the attention of the school system at this time? Is it the key issue right now? Is it a core issue?
- *Adequacy.* How well is the system dealing with this area at this time? Is it handled in an exemplary manner? Reasonably well with room for improvement? Barely adequately? With clear deficiencies?
- *System Motivation.* What is the current Stage 1: Care level in the system regarding this issue? Is there enough mental energy on the part of enough members to make serious changes here?

- *Resource Magnetism.* Is this a problem area with the potential to attract the necessary people, dollars, time, energy, calendar space, physical space, and so on?

Creating a Diagnostic Matrix/Checklist That Points to Solutions

Make your own list of the major concerns that relate to the school system that you want to help. Do your concerns match those of certain stakeholders? Are the concerns of different stakeholders compatible with one another? Can concerns be combined or worked on simultaneously? The first step is to narrow the range of concerns that can be called major. You don't necessarily start with the concern that is most important either for you personally or for the system. Here are some considerations in weighing your choices:

- Choose a problem area where an impact can be felt during your time of action.
- Choose a problem area that you can address with reasonable resources to match it.
- Choose a problem area large enough for impact to be appreciated.
- Choose a problem area that is meaningful to several members of the school system (Stage 1: Care).
- Choose a problem area that can be subjected to constructive analysis (Stage 3: Examine).
- Choose a problem area for which information (e.g., research knowledge) and other resources are applicable (Stage 4: Acquire).
- Choose a problem area to which a variety of solutions and innovations are applicable (Stage 5: Try).
- Choose a problem area in the hope that solutions will lead to other positive changes (multiplier effects) (Stage 6: Extend).
- Choose a problem area where a change will have good odds of surviving over the long term (Stage 7: Renew).

Integrating Diagnosis With the Other Stages

Stage 3: Examine can be thought of as a better-articulated and -differentiated version of Stage 1: Care. As you develop the specifics of what your needs are, you should continue to look back at your original concerns and ask whether these are the things you really care about and whether they are in the right priority. There is a danger of shifting priorities away from the things you really care about because other things are more doable.

Some Pitfalls in Diagnostic Analysis

Although the careful examination of the problem is an important step in the change process, it can also be a trap for the linking agent if it is not handled properly. You should be careful to avoid five patterns: too much focus on diagnosis, "study" as a pattern of avoidance, diagnostic analysis as destructive confrontation, imposition of a favorite diagnosis, and fire fighting.

Too Much Focus on Diagnosis

Sometimes linking agents can get stuck on diagnosis, using up most of their time and energy just in defining the problem. This is not only wasteful but may also have negative side effects. For example, school system personnel may begin to feel so overwhelmed by the number of problems coming to light that they cannot take constructive action. In some cases, they may feel overwhelmed by the hopelessness of their situation; in other cases, they may become defensive about the number or scope of the school system's problems and attempt to shelter themselves from the bad news, perhaps rejecting the linking agent in the process. The preceding section of *Guiding Change* suggested a systematic and comprehensive approach to diagnosis, but this does not mean that you must be exhaustive. On most questions you will have to be satisfied with sketchy and partial answers; your diagnosis may not get you an A in survey research, but that is not your purpose. The diagnosis should be just good enough to give you a general picture of the school system's situation.

> **Five Diagnostic Patterns to Avoid**
>
> - Too much focus on diagnosis: examining a problem to death
> - Study as a pattern of avoidance
> - Diagnosis as destructive confrontation
> - Imposition of a favorite diagnosis
> - Fire fighting

Study as a Pattern of Avoidance

Diagnostic studies can be used by a school system as a way to stall or put off needed changes. The call for further study is a familiar form of brush-off. Change-minded members of the school system may, therefore, be understandably restless and suspicious of prolonged diagnostic activity on the part of the linking agent. You should not only get to it but also get through it—and move on to the other steps in the change process.

Diagnosis as Destructive Confrontation

Your perception of serious defects and urgent problems may incline you to speak bluntly to the members of the school system. You may sometimes want to be frank and direct to unfreeze the school system, to shock its members into an awareness of their needs and the necessity of change. If you pursue such a strategy, you should understand the possible consequences. Above all, you should have a good estimate of how much your school system can take. The biggest danger is that a confrontation will destroy the relationship you have with your school system. If school personnel reject you completely because they cannot accept your drastic diagnosis, all your labors may be lost.

Even when you, as the linking agent, do not intend to be confrontational, you must be aware of the negative power of the information you are gathering.

It may make members of the school system feel stupid, childish, naive, or incompetent, which will not motivate them to change. Therefore, the form and timing of your diagnostic presentation are critical. Too much bad news revealed too suddenly is a circumstance to be avoided. As noted earlier, your diagnostic analysis should include positive as well as negative information and should be cast in a constructive form that makes it amenable to solutions and encourages the belief that solutions are possible.

However, if the members of the school system can accept confrontation, they may come to respect your honesty and may be moved to work more actively with you to bring about change. The decision to use or to avoid confrontation is a difficult one and illustrates the importance of assessing the basic strengths of the school system as well as its weaknesses.

Imposition of a Favorite Diagnosis

It is difficult for experts in one particular area to be truly objective in their diagnostic approach. Most people see their own specialty as the most important area. If your skills are in human relations training, for example, you will be more inclined to see a school system's problems as human relations problems; if your skills are in systems engineering, you may see the school system's problems in terms of planning, organization, and quality control; if you are a curriculum specialist, you will see problems primarily in terms of course content. Everyone has these professional blinders, which is natural and inevitable. However, even if you see yourself as a solution giver rather than a process helper, you are still a linking agent. Be aware of your limited perspective, and consciously strive to avoid imposing your favorite diagnosis on the people with whom you are working.

Fire Fighting

Finally, the linking agent should avoid falling into the opposite trap of attending only to the problems that the members of a school system see as immediate and important. Meaningful and lasting changes are more likely to come about if they are based on careful planning that stems from a well-rounded and reasonably comprehensive diagnosis. Many school systems may not appreciate this fact initially; they may see their problems as fires that have to be put out now, before anything else is done, and they may want to cast you in the role of firefighter. In some circumstances, you may have to accept such a role temporarily, if only to prove your usefulness. In the long run, however, fire fighting is a potential trap, as well as a waste of both your energy and the school system's resources, because it rarely precipitates real and lasting change.

Examine: Summary

As the linking agent enters the scene, the system usually has already diagnosed what the problem is that needs to be solved. However, the system must be asked to take a step back and look at the need situation more analytically. This

Examine stage can be further divided into three phases: entry, data collection, and analysis. It is important to make both data collection and analysis as collaborative and collective as possible. Together, the linker and school system personnel should identify opportunities and strengths as well as needs and deficits and open the door to reinterpreting and reworking the analysis as new data are unearthed and new stakeholders get involved. The result of this collaboration should not be a laundry list of needs. Rather, the results of a diagnostic examination should be framed as a systemic analysis that lays out system goals, rates the adequacy of existing structures to implement goals, and rates the openness and internal capacity to meet goals and the extent to which members are rewarded for achieving goals.

Approaches to data collection range from low cost, low profile to high cost, high profile. Among the former are using key informants, informal group interviewing, and observation; the latter might include measuring system outputs in quantitative terms or employing a professional diagnostic research team from outside. An extended diagnostic process can sometimes be counterproductive, however, leading to avoidance of action and sometimes to destructive confrontation or paralysis if the negatives seem to overwhelm the positives.

Stage 4

Acquire

Seeking and Finding Relevant Resources

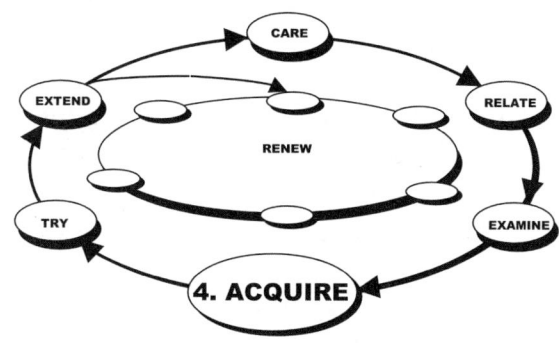

ORGANIZER QUESTIONS

- What are the four main types of resources that feed a change process?
- What is the money theory of change and why are both hard and soft money important?
- In what three ways can people serve as resources?
- What are the most important attributes to look for in staffing a change project?
- What are the different purposes to which knowledge resources apply?
- How can the Internet support all aspects of resource acquisition?

Guiding Change places special emphasis on strategies for acquiring resources of all kinds: financial, human, intellectual, and material. Of special importance are programs and practices that are based on sound research and whose effectiveness and staying power have been well demonstrated in diverse settings. Unfortunately, in spite of years of investment in trying to develop such products, they are few and far between. The reform-minded practitioner has to be creative and aggressive in acquiring what is available from existing sources, aided by the wise counsel of outside experts and observations of what is happening elsewhere, near and far. The wisdom from these diverse sources can be merged to prepare the most promising local application. The rise of the Internet has given new life, meaning, and richness to this search.

Decisions about how much time, money, and energy to devote to resource acquisition must be weighed against the goals to be achieved and the purpose for embarking on the process. When you, as the linking agent, are spending time, money, and energy on resource acquisition, you should always have a reasonably clear idea of why you are doing it, especially if your purpose is something other than maintaining awareness. If you are too broad and loose in defining your needs and in defining relevance, you will be swamped with information you cannot use. If you define your information needs too narrowly, however, you may overlook critical facts that are required to make problem solving and innovating effective and beneficial. In a knowledge universe that is expanding rapidly, linking agents and school systems need to develop the capacity to plug in and to home in on the contents of this universe whenever and wherever they need help.

Stage 4 of the CREATER model is Acquire. This chapter illustrates the great variety of resources that are useful or even essential to the success of a change effort. A linking agent is, above all, a conveyor of resources and a facilitator to the resource search and acquisition.

Linkers are different from other change agents in one main respect: They link to resources. A resource can come in the form of money, people, and knowledge, but it is probably the knowledge part that gets the least attention. Knowledge is too often underrated as an aspect of the change process, yet there is no project that cannot be made substantially more successful by applying information from the outside. The acquisition effort is almost always worthwhile, especially if you have a coherent strategy for getting connected. In this new networked world, it is becoming ever more essential and ever more easy to access the knowledge world.

The Money Theory of Change

When a question of resources arises, people usually think first and foremost of money. Money is the stand-in for all value in economic terms, and it can be viewed as the essential driver of all change in education or in any other aspect of life. According to the money theory, a system needs a certain amount of money to keep going the way it is. If the supply of money goes down, the level of functioning of the system must also go down: fewer inputs, less throughput, fewer outputs, or less of all three. If the money supply goes up, there is room for more inputs, more or different throughputs, and more outputs. According to the money theory, if new money is not available, there is no room for change in a positive direction; if money is reduced, the change will be in a negative direction.

There is much to be said for this simple money theory of change. It has long been observed that wealthy public school districts tend to be innovative and that the most innovative schools are private schools with large endowments. They have more money for new materials, more teachers, more and better teacher recruitment and training, stronger libraries, more and better computers, specialized teachers, specific programs to meet the individual needs of each child, assistive technology for children with special needs, and on and on.

Exemplifying the money theory is Paul Mort's Metropolitan Schools Study Council, a consortium that brought together relatively rich and relatively poor school districts, large and small (1953, 1964). According to Mort's theory, wealthier districts have a surplus financial capacity, something akin to discretionary personal income, which can be spent on luxuries, improvements, and incidentals. For a school district, this discretionary spending power might mean higher teacher salaries, an improved teacher-student ratio, a new gymnasium, a science center, a language lab, or a computer lab. Mort's study observed that wealthier districts with an innovative orientation would choose more innovative projects, changes in curriculum and teaching methods, team-teaching, new management structures, and special courses of one kind or another. Mort periodically brought the rich and poor, innovative and noninnovative districts together to generate an active exchange about what they were doing to improve their schools. Through this network-sharing mechanism, poorer districts could copy and adapt the most successful innovations developed by wealthier districts. Mort conducted extensive studies on the flow of innovations over many years and clearly demonstrated the validity of his theory. He showed that it was not just money that brought about the most innovation. It was money in some districts plus many innovative ideas from many places plus an active network for sharing ideas and experience across districts.

Educational Systems as Economic Entities

Education is a costly enterprise. For at least the past hundred years, the U.S. education system has been sustained by large fixed capital and labor expenditures, almost all with funds generated from local taxes. Most of these funds are earmarked for teachers' salaries, administrative costs, buildings, and maintenance, leaving almost nothing in Mort's innovative surplus account. Further, teachers and administrators are chronically underpaid compared with their equally educated and skilled counterparts in other fields. The vulnerability of the local tax base has meant poor economic leverage and chronic underfunding. All this is old news to most educators.

However, another story began to unfold in the 1960s, as the federal government took on a new role in education. It was a role circumscribed by the politics of the time, which restricted funding to assisting poorer districts, students with special needs, and research and development. Most significant, though, was the federal involvement with innovations, inspired in part by the research of Paul Mort and others. Since the 1960s, a significant amount of federal money has been available to support innovative projects undertaken at the school district level. By now there have been thousands of such projects, and many of them have been carefully documented and evaluated.

Special education, in particular, has benefited from federal funding for research, development, and innovation through continuing grants to school districts, universities, and independent entities. These funds have flowed in recognition of the high costs and great difficulties of implementing new federal mandates associated with the 1997 reauthorization of the Individuals with Disabilities Education Act (IDEA). Legislation supporting special education has represented a major challenge for the traditional system over the past three decades. Special programs, equal access, least restrictive environment, and other new requirements add enormous costs, and some of these costs have been met by earmarked federal aid.

> **Federal Funds Contribute to Research-Based Practices**
>
> IDEA-Part D programs play a significant role in identifying, implementing, evaluating, and disseminating information about effective practices.
>
> These programs provide an infrastructure of practice improvement that supports all other national expenditures used to educate infants, toddlers, children, and youth with disabilities and their families.

What Is Wrong With the Money Theory?

Money and access to financial resources can explain a lot about innovation, but they are not the whole story. Consider the following points:

- Changing the way people do things may cost no money and may even save money.
- People will often do things because they want to do them regardless of the money involved (e.g., to improve themselves, to feel better about what they do, to enjoy themselves).
- Conversely, when people do not want to do something or do not know how to do something, money by itself will not help. The further danger is that money that is made available will be used in ways not favorable to the change process.
- Many types of nonmonetary resources are there for the asking, at little or no financial cost, although there may be costs in terms of time and effort to gain access and to absorb their meaning.
- Infusions of money do not necessarily lead to innovation. Constant pressure on fixed budgets tempts administrators to redirect funds intended for innovative programs into supplements to their operating budgets. For example, a special program grant for a knowledge linker could be assigned to a staff person already engaged in other work by simply changing the role designation without materially changing the nature of the work.
- There is smart money and there is dumb money. Often, the amount of money is not crucial to success; rather, the way money is spent makes the real difference.

The following pages present a few tips on how to get and use money in a way that supports long-term, sustainable change.

Hard Money, Soft Money

Hard money and soft money: What's the difference? Hard money is always there to support the educational enterprise. Hard-money expenses include teacher salaries, administrative costs, and building maintenance. In contrast, soft money is one-time or time-limited money, which comes into the system at a particular time, perhaps through a special project or a grant; the source may be the federal government, local businesses, and nonprofit organizations, among others. Contributors often earmark soft money for a special purpose. It is here now, it is limited, and it usually must be spent within a limited time. Money to support innovative projects most often comes in this form, and thereby lies an inherent problem and a special challenge for all linking agents.

Innovating on Hard Money

All school budgets are subject to fluctuation. Because most school funding is local, it is also vulnerable to local conditions and local shifts in public opinion. In inflationary times, it is difficult to increase the school budget to keep pace with the cost of living; in hard times, it is difficult to even hold the line. Nevertheless, below a certain line, a school district cannot function sufficiently to provide the basics of grades 1–12 education. This line defines the low water mark of hard money. In the past three decades, states and the federal government have raised this line somewhat by providing reliable extra funds through grant programs for poor students and other students in special categories. Where teachers have successfully organized for collective bargaining, the union contract also represents a kind of hard-money standard because the district is legally bound to find funding to comply with the contract provisions.

In theory, there is no reason hard money cannot be used to reform education and to introduce innovations. School administrators have some discretion to use hard money as they see fit and appropriate to maintain standards and to run an effective system. Likewise, salaried teachers have some control over what they do in their own classrooms. Anyone who has discretion should be able to innovate. Indeed, the clarion call of fiscal conservatives is innovate to save money! Reinvent the school so that fewer administrators are needed; reinvent the classroom so that fewer teacher hours of instruction are required. It is possible, but it is also a tough edict to put on overworked and underpaid teachers and administrators.

> **Getting Buy-In: Administrator Support in Funding**
>
> Although encouraged to secure outside funding, the building administrator, motivated by the new interventions and addressing the needs of his students, told the linking agent, "If outside funding is not obtained, I [the director of special education] will pay for at least one school to receive training."

Innovating on Soft Money: How New Money Is Supposed to Change Things

Extra money or new money empowers people to buy things that they could not otherwise have or do things they could not otherwise do. It has been used in various ways to improve education. Six uses are most notable: (1) capital improvements; (2) new technologies and materials; (3) teacher training; (4) administrative and managerial innovation; (5) teacher incentives; and (6) instructional innovation.

> **Six Uses of Soft Money**
>
> 1. Teacher training
> 2. Administrative and managerial innovation
> 3. Teacher incentives
> 4. Instructional innovation

With soft money, the question of sustainability always arises. How will the money invested have long-term impact? For uses 1 and 2, the answer comes fairly easily. A new building is a permanent structure although it may require maintenance. New facilities and materials last until they wear out or become obsolete, at which time a new insertion of soft money will provide restoration and renewal. However, for uses 3, 4, 5, and 6, the question is not so easily answered. Will investments in training or innovation pay off in a way that will last beyond the funding period? If special incentives are provided this year and next, what about the year after that?

Pump Priming: How Soft Money Is Supposed to Work

The pump-priming philosophy of funding rests on the assumption that successful innovative practices will be adopted and attract hard money if they are convincingly effective in the home setting. Soft money is provided to demonstrate effectiveness, perhaps for one, two, or three years. When and if the demonstration is successful, the school district will adopt the new practice because its personnel are wise observers and judges who see the benefits to their system.

Pump priming is a favorite strategy for many donors because it holds out the hope of long-term improvement from short-term investment. In a nutshell, the concept is this: Put in a lot of money at the beginning to make things easy for everybody; release time, materials, incentives, new space, special training, site-visiting travel, expert consultants. The change effort is administratively isolated and protected from bureaucratic requirements. Teachers are given extra time, perhaps extra money, and extra freedom to engage in the new process. All parties know up front that all these special arrangements cannot be sustained in the long run, but they hope and expect that the change project will be successful. The project will then be a model that others can copy and that will be incorporated into the overall system, the school curricula, and the regular school budget. In other words, it will attract hard money.

Why Pump Priming Often Succeeds in the Short Run

Typically, a project begins with a proposal that shows the logic of the change, the research on which the change is based, citations of other places where the proposed change has already worked, a time line, a work flow plan, and a budget. Once the project is funded and the developers have done their homework and are realistic and reasonably diligent, there is a good likelihood that they will actually do what they proposed to do. The project will have the short-term impact that they predicted it would have. Many thousands of short-term projects—one, two, or three years long—have been funded in thousands of school districts across the country over the past 30 years, mostly with federal funds but often with state and private support as well. The pump has been primed over and over again all across the country.

Why Pump Priming Often Fails in the Long Run

Although pump priming seems to produce good results through the first cycle of effort, its impact typically fades or disappears in a disappointingly short time after the initial funding is discontinued. At least four factors account for this phenomenon: inflexibility of the hard-money budget, failure of the project in its own terms, failure to demonstrate, and failure to plan and gain commitment.

Inflexibility of the Hard-Money Budget. Hard money is the long-term money that the system depends on to keep going. It is carefully guarded and rarely modified. In many situations, a new soft-money project is tolerated as an add-on to the system, even as a relief to the system because it frees up one or two full-time employees for its duration. Yet the system often cannot and will not make way for the new project as a line item in the hard-money budget, no matter how good it is. Some districts are reluctant to take on new soft-money projects for the very reason that they raise expectations that long-term commitments will follow from a short-term proof of success when no such guarantee can be given.

Failure of the Project in Its Own Terms. Sometimes projects do not turn out the way they were supposed to, so they collapse of their own weight when time is up. Perhaps the selected project was poorly designed or poorly implemented. Maybe it simply did not accurately meet the needs of the school district. However, it is rarely the case that nothing is gained in the process. The very act of innovating may open up the system, and the individuals involved may take away some very good lessons.

> **Why Pump Priming Fails in the Long Run**
> - Inflexibility of the hard-money budget
> - Failure of the project in its own terms
> - Failure to demonstrate
> - Failure to plan and gain commitment

> **Demonstrate the Linking Agent's Value**
>
> Recognizing that the funds for the linking agent role were limited and the grant was expected to terminate soon, the linking agent spent time working directly with the director of special education to demonstrate the usefulness of the linking agent's position to county decision makers.
>
> "I feel that the director of special education already sees the value in the linking agent position, but this may not be enough to secure the position in times of financial trouble."

Failure to Demonstrate to the Right People in the Right Way. More often the failure is not in the project itself but in the effectiveness of the project as a demonstration to the powers that be. The management of an innovative project must arrange for many opportunities to demonstrate the project's effectiveness both to other teachers and to the administration and the people who control the hard money. Clearly, building relationships among all key stakeholders (Stage 2: Relate) is essential.

Failure to Plan and Gain Commitment for Insertion in the Hard-Money Budget. Soft-money projects sometimes are structured to operate entirely independently of the existing system. They make their own rules, hire their own staff, and evaluate what they are doing by their own standards. Such detachment and freedom have many advantages when people are trying something entirely new, but it is deadly when the time comes to move toward hard money. The project has no advocates. No one has any expectations of continuance. No one is prepared to take on the continuing responsibilities, so the innovation dies right there.

Smart Money Acquisition Strategies

Soft pump-priming money does not have to be wasted. When you have decided that new money is an essential ingredient to the success of your innovative effort, even recognizing the caveats discussed above, you have a variety of ways to proceed: Shape the need into a proposal, build awareness of money sources, match the need to known resource pools, parade the proposal, and involve the hard-money gatekeepers.

> **Five Actions That Lead to Positive Results**
>
> - Shape the need into a proposal.
> - Build awareness of money sources.
> - Match the need to known resource pools.
> - Parade the proposal.
> - Involve the hard money gatekeepers.

Shape the Need Into a Proposal and Attach Rough Dollar Figures. You need to start with a rough idea of what your start-up costs will be, especially for items that cannot be volunteered or acquired except by paying for them.

Build Awareness of Money Sources. Next, you need to make yourself and your change team aware of the many sources that can be tapped. If you work in a developed country, you probably enjoy a social environment that generally values education and gives special attention to special needs. This means that for special education, in particular, the list of potential donors for worthy special education projects is very long, depending on the type of need, the type of disability toward which the project is directed, and so forth. At the top of this list in the United States is the Office of Special Education Programs (OSEP) of the Department of Education. OSEP has sponsored many research and development projects based in universities, other educational institutions, and independent organizations such as the American Institutes for Research, which housed the linking agent program, EMSTAC, and has supported the preparation of *Guiding Change.* Numerous private, nonprofit, special interest groups at the local, regional, and national levels also have money to spend on children with special needs. Private funds tend to come in modest amounts, but they also tend to be much easier to acquire quickly with a minimum of red tape. They can be used more flexibly. Businesses, private philanthropists, churches, and civic organizations are all potential funding sources for worthy projects.

Match Need to Known Resource Pools. Identify which potential donors might be interested in your project as a whole or perhaps in different aspects of your project, such as special technologies you wish to acquire or special expertise you need to bring in.

Parade the Proposal Until Serendipity Strikes. You now need to try out your proposal with various potential sources, starting locally and working up, soliciting advice along the way about how to reshape the proposal and always asking who else might be interested in supporting it.

Involve the Hard-Money Gatekeepers. It is especially important to keep the administrative and budgetary leadership (the hard-money gatekeepers) involved in the solicitation process to encourage buy-in and to keep them aware of your possible long-term need for hard-money support and the desirability of eventually integrating the project into the larger ongoing system.

The Linker's Role With Respect to Money

The discussion above assumes that the linking agent is fully immersed in the money-raising process, but this is probably not the best way to view the linker's role. Rather, as with other aspects of the change process, the linker may work better as a facilitator of fundraising than as the lead actor. The linker could usefully perform at least six possible facilitator functions.

> **Facilitating the Process of Securing Additional Funding**
>
> To help the principal implement the new schoolwide reading intervention, the linking agent located possibilities for additional funding and provided guidance in how to write a proposal to obtain funding. The principal then worked through the application process, using the linking agent as a resource when necessary.
>
> "Without these funds, the school could not afford to implement the project," said the principal.

Help Sort Out the Money Issues. The linker may be able to help the school change team think through many of the issues involved in acquiring funds: hard versus soft money issues, the appropriate scale of a project in terms of financial constraints, and the amount of help that a project can gain with little or no new money.

Help Identify Financial Resources Outside the System. An effective linker should have a cognitive map indicating who the potential outside resource providers are and how to gain access to them. This map should include private as well as public sources, such as churches, civic groups, businesses, and philanthropies that might have an interest in funding a particular aspect of a project.

Help the Change Team Prepare to Acquire Such Resources. Linkers may feel that part of their role is to write proposals for funding new projects, but it is usually more appropriate for the school change team to undertake this function. This approach allows many participants to collaborate through coordination and facilitation by the linker.

Identify Potential Funding Sources Within the System. Part of the job of the linker is to expand the thinking process of innovators so that they will be more creative in their search for special funding within, as well as outside, the system.

Help Put Together Appropriate Funding Ponds. If you view funding sources as a series of streams that can be channeled in various directions, it is useful to think of any project as a pond into which these streams can flow. A large and complex project may require a large pond supplied by many streams. The linker can act as the flow manager, making sure that there is enough flow from different sources.

Help Guide the System to a Broader Conception of Resources. The linker should keep the school change team focused on all aspects of the change process, including the five P's: people, practices, programs, products, and print. The emphasis on money can be so strong that alternative resources are overlooked. Many of these resources are available for the asking. Costs can be shared; items can be borrowed; time can be volunteered; and time can also be invested as a legitimate part of the work that people are already doing for pay. Most of the important resources for change are not in the money category.

Search the Internet for Funding

The Internet is an ever-increasing source of useful information on every conceivable question, including thousands of items on special education. Some sites may want your money, but others encourage you to take their money. One useful starting point is the U.S. Department of Education's Office of Special Education and Rehabilitative Services site, www.ed.gov/offices/OSERS/index.html.

Go in and look around, but do not stop there. Any good web search engine will get you to sites representing private foundations, regional centers, state agencies, and local agencies, which offer help in specific categories. Many of these sites present in-depth information, such as the names and contact information of people who can help you apply for funding. Good linkers will make their colleagues aware of these Internet sources by sharing relevant Internet URLs, downloading, printing, and circulating information, initiating group discussions, and organizing proposal-writing teams. More will be said about Internet use later in this chapter.

The People Theory of Change

People can also be the primary resources for change. These people, of course, have special skills, ideas, and initiative. Innovators, like linkers, are special kinds of people. They seem to have more energy than the average person; perhaps they also have more ideas. Most innovators also have good connections inside and outside the local system. These connections feed them a constant stream of new ideas about what is wrong with the status quo, what would make it better, how things should work, and what specific steps are needed to make things work more effectively.

A person is a convenient walking package of ideas, skills, connections, and knowledge. This person package may display certain attributes, but what's inside the package may not correspond very well to the picture on the cover. Thus, the first challenge in implementing the people theory is finding out what value and resources the person can bring to your project. A quick reading, an interview, or a résumé may not be the best indicators of what a person has to offer. Therefore, implementing a people strategy requires either immense good fortune or a foolproof selection and recruitment process. To select the right people, you really need to think through what you want to do and what knowledge, attributes, and skills are required to get the job done.

Start using the people theory with yourself. You are, by definition and self-designation, already involved in the change process. You may, in fact, believe that you are uniquely equipped and situated to bring about the change on your own, either from your intimate knowledge of the system, your understanding of the change you want to initiate, or both. However, if you are serious about adopting the stance of a linker, it is unwise to assume such an all-encompassing responsibility. You need others to make the project work, to take a burden off your shoulders, to provide more extensive linkage than you have on your own, and to relate to more key stakeholders and individuals within the school system than you can on your own. Most important, you need an associate who will be able to carry on the work after you have moved on. This is what the linker is supposed to do—initiate a process, establish connections, see to it that a good change strategy is executed, and then move on to help others with other needs. Clearly, therefore, the linker needs partners who are involved in serious ways up to and including managing the process, providing ideational input and expertise, and seeing that things get done. For all this you need other people: good people to run the project, modelers of the change and the process of change, and people as experts and expert information sources.

> **Connecting to New Resources Through Communication**
>
> After effectively meeting the needs of one school, the linking agent addressed two new needs areas within the school system. She once again searched for new resources and initiated communications with new researchers and consultants to get the information necessary to address these new areas of need.

> **Key Players on the Change Team**
>
> - Good people to run the project
> - Modelers of the change and the process of change
> - People as experts and expert information sources

Good People to Run the Project

One key to successful reform is finding the right people to do the job. But how do you find these people? And what do you do if you can't find them? Recruitment can be a major issue and a major task. Here are some aspects to consider.

The Talent Pool. How large is the talent pool? Think of all the members of your own system as potential human resources for change—teachers, administrators, counselors, parents, community members, and even students. Anyone who is a part of the system has the potential to play some role in the change process. When you think about the total human talent pool, ask yourself whether you have thought broadly enough. Can the useful pool be enlarged?

The Standouts. Within the talent pool, certain persons will stand out as obvious choices, but there is reason to proceed cautiously with the most obvious. Each possibility can be viewed as an opportunity and each may be cause for concern. Table 4.1 lists a few examples.

Attributes of the Ideal Candidate. The general attributes of an ideal candidate should correspond to the steps in the CREATER-planned change cycle. Here is a list of possible attributes grouped roughly by stage.

- Stage 1: Care
    - Dedication to the cause
    - Ability to inspire others
    - Energy (all stages)
- Stage 2: Relate
    - Ability to relate to others
    - Friendliness and openness to others
    - Ability to work as a team member
    - Ability to take initiative and to lead others
    - Openness and willingness to change, to listen to others, to take negative feedback and use it constructively (all stages)
- Stage 3: Examine
    - Ability to sense and diagnose needs
    - Special knowledge of needs
- Stage 4: Acquire
    - Connectedness to people resources within the system, to people resources in other similar systems, to people resources in the larger world of special education or in educational research and development
    - Connectedness to and comfort with the new technologies of connections, such as the Internet and e-mail
    - Openness to new sources and information from new sources
    - Special knowledge, experience, or expertise in a given domain (Stage 5)
- Stage 4: Acquire
    - Ability to absorb new knowledge in different forms
    - Objectivity: ability to evaluate

People	Opportunities	Concerns
People who are assigned to you or given to you	It's great to have the recruitment issues settled before you begin. Maybe these people are just as good as anybody else.	You may need to look these gift horses in the mouth before taking them. Are they available to you simply because the superintendent couldn't find another place for them? Are they available because of past difficulty or because they were unacceptable recruits for other positions?
People you know your circle	You can get to them quickly and converse with them easily. You can explain what you are trying to do in ways that will be understood, and your probability of recruitment may be high.	They may not have the right connections to the larger system; they may duplicate your shortcomings as well as your assets.
People who come to you	Their initiative is promising; they appear to be committed to our cause, and they solve your recruitment problem quickly.	Do they have the requisite qualifications beyond motivation? Do they have other motives for coming to you, which might later detract from their usefulness?
People who are already known as innovators	They have already been through the mill. They have already experienced many of the problems associated with introducing something new.	Innovators are sometimes able to function because they are on the margin. They feel they can ignore accepted opinion and go their own way. As a result, they can also be marginalized by society and viewed as flakes or eccentrics. This will detract from their usefulness if your goal is to get the changes fully implemented by the system so they have lasting impact.
People who are known as opinion leaders	Respected senior members of the system who are popular with their peers are the best people to have on your team or leading your team if you expect to have major and lasting impact.	Opinion leaders tend to be initially cautious of innovations, especially major ones that might get disruptive. They can play hard to get. If they are conservative opinion leaders, they may also held you back or implement the ideas in a way that is too minimal to have much impact on the larger system, which should be your goal.
People who are known to have exceptional special skills	Many potential candidates will have special ackground and skills either working with a particular population or working with a particular kind of innovation. These specialists will greatly reduce your training costs and will allow you to avoid numerous errors along the way to implementation.	Specialists may be too focused on their particular approach to appreciate an innovative change that is outside their realm of experience. They may lack some of the social and process skills that successful innovators require

- Stage 5: Try

    - Experience, general and specific
    - Ability to organize and manage projects of various types

- Stage 6: Extend

    - Perseverance, the ability to stick with a project to its conclusion
    - Longer term perspective

- Stage 7: Renew

    - Holistic-systemic perspective, looking out for the good of the system as a whole
    - Process orientation, seeing change as a process that applies to many different change activities in an ongoing, integrated flow

A Recruitment Strategy. Define what you are looking for and develop your hiring criteria. Decide what traits successful innovators in general have and what traits this particular situation needs. Identify the attractive features of this job: having freedom, meeting a challenge, working creatively, doing good, doing something new, having an impact. Create an enticing image of the kind of person you are looking for, then cast your recruitment net as widely as is practical. Give candidates a chance to mentally explore the scene and the mission. Give yourself a chance to see them as they are and as they respond to the stimulus of your situation.

In choosing among candidates, consider these additional issues:

- *Can you afford to keep them?* If they seem ideal, are they likely to stick around long enough to make their involvement worthwhile? Or will they be tempted away by higher pay or some other enticement before your project has run its course?
- *Insiders versus outsiders.* Insiders know the ropes but may carry a lot of baggage; outsiders have a fresh perspective and add more to the pool of experience but may lack concern and connectedness.
- *Old-timers versus newcomers and experience versus baggage.* Will old-timers have sufficient openness to doing things in a new way? Will newcomers make too many mistakes?
- *Substantive specialists versus generalists.* It is nice to have some of both. The balance depends on the level of skill and knowledge the selected innovation requires. If you have not already fixed on the change you want, then the choice of a specialist in a given area will distort the choice of innovation. To a hammer, all solutions involve nails.
- *Innovators versus opinion leaders.* Some of both is great, but many leaders are naturally conservative and many innovators are naturally loners.
- *People like you versus people who complement you.* Recruiting people like yourself speeds communication and cooperation but does not add to the talent mix; a good team needs complementary knowledge and skills.

- *Are they replicable?* Do they possess a set of traits and skills that you could find in others or train in others? Being unique and uniquely qualified may create problems downstream when someone else has to take their place. A related question is a candidate's suitability to fill your role if the need should arise. Could one of these people take over your role if you left?

Questions a Change Team Candidate Might Want to Ask You. Candidates to participate in or manage the change team or conduct a change project will also come to you with their own set of questions, so it is probably a good idea to anticipate them.

- *Definitions.* The terms *linking agent* and *change agent* mean different things to different people. It is important that you and the candidates be on the same page. Do you really understand the mission of the linking agent and the distinction between the linker and other types of change agent? This has to be a dialogue; you explain; then they feed back to you what they heard; you try to modify and qualify their perceptions; they restate what it is they think they heard; you judge whether you and the candidates are on the same page.
- *Chances of success.* Candidates may differ greatly in their willingness to take risks. Bringing about change is always a somewhat risky business, so risk-aversive candidates are probably inappropriate. A solid knowledge of how other sites have implemented the innovation and what others have been doing, particularly in similar circumstances, is invaluable in bringing about a sense of security.
- *Their own abilities.* Self-confidence is always a desirable trait, but over-confidence may not be. People who are supremely confident in their abilities and understanding of the field may too easily slip into the solution-giver mold.
- *Freedom of action.* Candidates will want to know how much freedom they will have to organize the project, choose the solution, and manage their time. They may also want to know how much freedom they will have to change means and ends. There is also a happy medium here. Candidates who want

---

A Team Approach

Teaming is an important part of our school. We are a middle school, and we have been using the team approach for the school for about 10 years now. In special education, however, we have been teaming for about 15 years here. We have learned a great deal. One of the first things that is important to do is to be sure that everyone has the same ideas about what teaming is. There are those who have never been introduced into the world of collaborative, cooperative efforts. It is interesting that we teach cooperative learning to our students, but many of us are not so good at it ourselves. Over the years, two of us have been the consistent elements in the team, and other members of the team have come and gone. Of course, it is important to have people who are committed, and most of these folks were, but finding folks who were willing to stay and focus on the project were hard to find. We've had more stability over the past few years, but just this past year, we lost one member and have never been able to replace him with someone who was as committed and caring. A stable and caring team is absolutely necessary for the implementation of change.

to do everything their own special way may not be good listeners and, therefore, not good linkers. At the other end of the continuum, candidates who want everything specified in advance about what they should be doing when, where, and how may lack the flexibility required for the role.

- *Financial backing.* Candidates have a right to know what financial resources back up the effort. A certain amount of volunteerism is usually required to get anything going, but it can only go so far. It is fair to ask what funds are available to support materials, visitations, release time, partial salary, honoraria, attendance at training events, hired consultants, per diems, travel, and so on.
- *How long will it last?* It is important to place a projected effort into a time frame. That is why the initial effort should always be conceived as a trial that will last a term or a school year but always with the promise of an extension if it appears promising or successful. Likewise, the candidate must be able to make a commitment for the period of the trial with the possibility of continuing on into the longer implementation phase.
- *Who has the power to make a real commitment to them?* As a linking agent, you will rarely be in a position by yourself to make a full commitment. You may therefore need to clarify where you stand in the hierarchy and how strong and long is the commitment by your superiors to back you up.

Modelers of the Change and the Process of Change

A rather different way to think of people as the drivers of a change process is to find good models for what you are trying to accomplish. Good models serve two primary purposes:

- They provide a clear sense of what is to be done. Potential adopters need to get a holistic sense of what is being proposed. Observing someone else doing it in an actual classroom situation is the best way to learn.
- They provide a great feeling of comfort that the innovation can be done successfully with the people and resources at hand. Observing another person somewhat like yourself functioning in a normal classroom situation with children something like your own gives credible testimonial for the fact that

    a. It works.
    b. You can do it with your resources.
    c. It will have good or great outcomes.
    d. It can be made to last, become part of the system, and bring lasting benefits.

People as Experts and Expert Information Services

A great many of the innovations that are being adopted in the schools have been developed, sometimes at great cost over many years, by specialists, academic researchers, skilled developers, and highly talented and creative people. Although it is good to have these people around and to recruit them to help in your particular situation, problems can arise. Experts tend to be difficult to reach and to schedule. They also tend to be expensive, and their presence is fleeting; they are here today and gone tomorrow. Because of their rarity and their cost, their use needs to be carefully considered and planned for maximum value. You need to ask yourself in what areas you need the most outside expertise and help on things that you do not know yourself and cannot get others within the system to help with. The answer will vary with the situation and the change you have decided to work on.

Before you recruit an expert, consider first how you want to use an expert. Like you, an outside expert is by definition a change agent. Consider the different change-agent roles and ask yourself which role you need most to move your change project along: motivator and catalyst, process specialist, knowledge source, legitimizer, content-specific motivator–inspirational leader, role model and demonstrator, or process and outcome evaluator.

> **External Consultants Fulfill Different Roles**
>
> - Motivator and catalyst
> - Process specialist
> - Knowledge source
> - Legitimizer
> - Content-specific motivator–inspirational leader and catalyst
> - Role model and demonstrator
> - Process and outcome evaluator

Motivator and Catalyst. Some experts are great at stirring people out of a sense of complacency and getting them to be concerned and to think seriously about their problems and the need for change. If the system seems to be complacent and unwilling to start on a serious change effort, you may need this kind of outside expert, someone who advocates not for a particular solution but for the need to do something about the problem.

Process Specialist. Some experts are simply good at the change process. They are able to quickly grasp the situation in your system; the level of readiness for change; and the connectedness, motivation, and involvement level of the key players from the superintendent on down. They may be able to help you bring together some of these key players (Stage 2: Relate) and get them involved in a series of change steps (all stages).

Knowledge Source. Experts can be walking encyclopedias, sources of information on the innovation under consideration as well as on the change process and other possible innovations. A live information source on-site may be more valuable than a book, a set of materials, or an online source for certain kinds of information, particularly details about implementation that are not adequately covered elsewhere. There is the added advantage that the expert on-site can get a good idea of what your real needs are and what aspects of your situation are unique.

Legitimizer. Experts, particularly well-known ones, can be helpful in legitimizing a project to the leaders of your own system. The status of your expert may impress some key decision makers in your system, especially at higher levels. A university professor with a long publication record may impress some; a long history of practical experience as a teacher or an administrator of note may impress others. The corresponding danger is that these same experts may be seen as too lofty, too uniquely gifted to set an example for your people. They may also demand a high price and have limited availability because of their popularity.

Content-Specific Motivator–Inspirational Leader and Catalyst. Some experts are great at inspiring and motivating. They convey a sense that the prospective change is something really worth doing. If they are associated with the innovation under consideration, their belief in the value of their own invention is strong and their enthusiasm can be catching. They are not much different from the legitimizers in being expensive and hard to get, but they come with a reputation and experience in actually motivating and influencing people. It is important to take full advantage of their enthusiasm while reserving some judgment about their ability to view their own creation objectively.

Role Model and Demonstrator. It is often very important at the trial stage to bring in people who have actually performed the set of behaviors and successfully used the materials in a variety of other settings. Preferably, some of these settings correspond to yours in key characteristics. The demonstration needs to be as real as possible and should be followed by observations of practice runs of the same behaviors by your people. Experts who are also developers and exhibit a tremendous range of abilities may be good inspirational leaders, but they may not be good demonstrators if your people believe that their own skill levels are less than ideal.

Demonstration and role modeling are parts of a larger process that could be called training, but training is a broader concept involving all of the foregoing six roles. It also includes the ability to train the trainers, that is, to train one or more members of your own change team so that you do not depend on outsiders as new staff come on board.

Process and Outcome Evaluator. Finally, you should not forget the importance of outcomes and getting good data on what you are doing in a change project. Absorbing and using these data meaningfully as you go along are essential as feedback so that you can systematically improve what you are doing as you proceed from one annual cycle to the next. Process and outcome evaluations require a specific type of expertise that is associated with both testing and research. It comes in large supply in graduate schools of education but in rather short supply in schools. Wise use of experts for this purpose requires that the experts create and you adopt a workable system of observation, self-report, and outcome-data collection and analysis. This system should be both meaningful and minimally burdensome on your staff so that they will be encouraged to continue its use long after the experts have left the scene.

Acquiring and Using Experts Wisely

Because experts are usually expensive and relatively hard to get, it is important to think strategically before you enlist their help. Here are some tips.

- Do the most you can do first with resources and people you already have.
- Do the most you can do up front with information resources available online or locally. You will be better prepared, know what the right questions are, and know where your holes really are.
- Establish a clear need for the experts before you hire.
- Give the experts an opportunity to prepare in advance by sending them information on your system and what you perceive your needs are.
- Plan the experts' time on-site to maximize their value.
- Use your experts as connectors to knowledge (superlinkers). Think of experts as stars in a knowledge network. They are experts partly because they know and have access to a lot of people you don't know and don't yet have access to. They know many others who might bring valuable help to you either through their writings and materials or through their direct experience.
- Try to think through what the experts should be doing that will transfer easily to you or to your people. What will be left with you when the experts leave? Transferability is the key.
- Plan training events carefully to take full advantage of the experts' presence.
- Make sure that you have access to the experts after the training ends.

What's Wrong With the People Theory?

Although the value of people resources to advance a change process is undeniable, you should also be aware of certain drawbacks. First of all, it is dangerous to rely too heavily on particular people, either inside or outside the school system, to carry off a successful change effort. People come and go; the system remains. Mobility tends to be particularly prevalent among young, highly skilled, highly energetic people on whom you often depend (in fact, as you read this, you may recognize yourself). They are on the go both figuratively and literally, and that is a problem.

Innovative school superintendents tend to move up and out rather quickly, sometimes leaving their pet projects as orphans to be shunned by their successors who want to put their own stamp on things. The same is true as we go down the line and into the ranks of the teaching profession. Superstars with super skills are cherished resources and marvels to behold, but they may also be here today and gone tomorrow. For this reason, it is important to instill a sense of ownership among all the participants of the change and to build change teams that do not overly depend on the skills or charisma of one particular person.

We need the high-energy innovators as catalysts for change, but we should not let them carry the whole burden. Burnout happens, and an emphasis on particular people as the carriers of the process can lead there, especially if you are also relying on them to volunteer extra time without compensation. Some volunteerism is great, but relying on total volunteerism is folly. People can do a lot of little things within their personal sphere of action without money, but significant changes are going to require monetary resources at some point in the process.

People are walking repositories of knowledge, but they are not substitutes for knowledge. It is important to have resources that are local and easy to reach and that you can review repeatedly on demand. For this, nothing is better than a print resource on your desk. Increasingly, the personal desk library is being supplemented and enhanced with online resources. When using the latter, do not forget that printing the information allows you to carry what you have learned into the meeting room or the classroom to be a constant reference and an item to share.

Search the Internet for People Resources

For twenty-first-century change agents, no search for people resources will be adequate unless you spend some time online. Any expert with relevance to your needs and your project is going to be there somewhere. Using online resources will give you a chance to get some feel for who they are and who is most relevant. Enter your topic in a search engine and then narrow your search to sites that focus on your topic. The problem with the Internet—and it is a major problem—is that there is no quality control. The junk exists side-by-side with solid material, and you have to figure out which is which.

- Within the research realm, consider these attributes of quality:
  - Does the research appear in a refereed journal?
  - Is the research sponsored?
  - Do the researchers report outcomes in quantitative terms?
  - Are the researchers people you have heard of?
  - Was the research done at a respected institution?
  - Was the research done in ordinary school settings comparable to your own?
- Look for materials that seem relevant to your concern.
  - Are sample materials available at minimal cost or online?
  - Are the materials fully developed?
  - Are they tested with outcome data?
- Is expert advice or consultation offered online?
- Is training offered online? At a specific time or place? At your site?

Online resources are constantly expanding and becoming more sophisticated and user-friendly. Always keep yourself attuned to important changes.

The Knowledge Theory of Change

Knowledge is at the core of everything you do and includes all of your past experience and habits. Knowledge is also the documented record of what other systems do or have done, along with the results of their efforts. Knowledge is the full body of the collective understanding of the educative process, educational systems, cognitive and behavioral psychology, and the nature of individual differences. Most modern knowledge is stored in books and journals and, increasingly, in electronic storage media. Knowledge is also stored in the heads of innumerable experts who teach and train and write and advise. A fraction of this huge knowledge base is used in the educative process with varying degrees of creativity and effectiveness. Most of it is used routinely just to keep the system going, to maintain things the way they are. Yet within the knowledge corpus is also an enormous potential for change.

Resources come in many forms, but most can be classified as one of the five P's: people, practices, programs, products, and print (or electronic media convertible to print). Knowing when, where, and how to acquire them are essential linker skills. Before you can make intelligent choices, you and your change team should have a good understanding of what has been done before and what is available now. You should make a deliberate effort to acquire as much knowledge as possible, including

- The specific need and problem area you are focused on, with a premium on sound research
- Specific innovations and innovative practices that have been tried or are now being tried by others
- Whatever evaluative or observational data might exist on these innovations

---

Knowledge Base

Gap Between Research and Practice

The disconnect between research and practice applies across the board in education. Most researchers are driven by theoretical interests, publish their findings in academic journals, and focus their research on "why" questions or on the validation of propositional knowledge that is stripped of contextual data (Hood, 1975; Mishler, 1979; House, 1981; Fuhrman, 1992; Kauffman, Schiller, Birman, & Coutinho, 1993). The research-based literature thus does not "easily map on the ways teachers think" (Richardson, 1990, p. 15). Most practitioners are driven by the press of their daily work (Huberman, 1983; Turnbull, 1991), are concerned with "how" and "what" matters (Huberman, 1995), rely on intuitive and craft-validated resources (Huberman, 1983), and when they adopt changes, do so in their own way (Crandall & Loucks, 1983) and without waiting for hard evidence (Slavin, 1989; Engelmann, 1992; Carnine, 1995).

(Continued)

> This gap may be even greater when it comes to special education (Malouf & Schiller, 1995; U.S. Department of Education, 1995; Carnine, 1997). Many general educators who do not have much special education training, nonetheless teach special education students. Moreover, some general educators have negative attitudes toward or are uninterested in serving diverse students (including students with disabilities). These attitudes can produce negative learning outcomes for themselves (as adult learners in staff development activities) and their students (Goodlad, 1984; McDermott, 1993; Talbert & McLaughlin, 1994; Pellegrini & Horvat, 1995). In addition, special education research focuses on individuals' performance and variability, rather than on average group performance, whereas most schools and school districts focus on groups of children (Deno, 1989; Gersten, 1990; U.S. Department of Education, 1995).

A Knowledge Acquisition Strategy

Each potential change situation requires two kinds of search activities. The first is connected to defining the need, and the second is connected to finding the solution. They are not the same although they are often easily confused. The need search phase logically comes before the solution search phase, but in reality, they overlap. All too often, practitioners get wedded to a solution before they have thought through what they really need. Try to avoid that trap.

The Search on the Need Side: Wide to Narrow. Your search for knowledge resources starts with your point of entry into the situation, the initiating concern or catalyst that brought you to the point of trying to bring about change in this place at this time. Your search orientation at the outset should be expansive. You are learning about the environment that you are in, the levels of caring about different issues (Stage 1: Care), the numbers and types of people involved and their interrelationships (Stage 2: Relate), and how your emerging change team works as a system to identify the various needs of different stakeholders (Stage 3: Examine).

When you believe you have enough raw data about what is going on, you will want to shift gears, setting yourself on a path toward narrowing the alternative targets for change and the range of cares and concerns to be dealt with. In this first narrowing process, you will tentatively set a lot of things aside, not because they are unimportant, but because they cannot be reasonably accommodated in this first change effort. As you move toward defining the problem that you are really going to deal with in this first round, you will be engaged in a different sort of search, one that is far more directed. You will now have a number of key words that can increase the efficiency of your searches of libraries, databases, and information services. You will also have specific questions to put to various informants and key players, questions that will allow you to get underneath the surface of the problem.

The Search on the Solution Side: Narrow to Wide to Narrow Again. With the problem situation and goals well defined, you will shift gears again, expanding your search to take in the widest spectrum of solution ideas. The knowledge resource environment is so rich that you cannot possibly absorb all that is out there, so you will have to limit your search in various ways. What is the optimal strategy for a good search? Optimal problem solving requires that you begin by making sure you are adequately aware of potential solution ideas. Users with a broad span of resource awareness are rarely stopped by a problem, because they know where to home in on solutions. When they hear a problem stated, they say to themselves, "I remember reading (or hearing or seeing) something that pertains to that problem."

Once you are able to make that mental connection to a general class of solutions, you can start narrowing your search again, homing in on specific solutions, contacting the relevant people and organizations, retrieving the relevant research, acquiring the relevant materials, and so on. You are now assembling a limited array of possible choices and collecting the kind of information needed to decide which has the highest probability of payoff, which is the most practical in this situation, and which is the most suitable and acceptable to the school or the teacher or the system in its present circumstances.

The Close: Choosing One and Preparing for Implementation. Finally, you will need to make a decision cooperatively with the change team and with relevant stakeholders. In full dialogue, you and these others will have to choose one solution. Now the search will be specific to the chosen alternative and include gathering materials, preparing for training, and evaluating the outcomes of the first trial.

In summary, an ideal knowledge resources acquisition strategy has the following five stages:

1. Expand the awareness of knowledge sources relevant to the need and situation.

2. Narrow the focus to the one need area that is most relevant to this situation at this time.

3. Widen the search to include all the approaches that might be taken to deal with this need.

4. Narrow the focus to solutions that have the best fit and the best prospects.

5. Choose what looks best and acquire the specialized knowledge needed for implementation and evaluation.

Knowledge Base

The Importance of Linkage to High-Quality External Sources

Individuals incorporate new information through the lens of prior knowledge, and they make sense of new knowledge "in the context of their daily activities in everyday school and district life" (Fuhrman, 1992). Thus, knowledge use is always local (McLaughlin, 1990; Fullan & Miles, 1992). However, this use is enhanced tremendously by well-developed materials combined with external linkages and supports (Louis et al., 1984). Reporting on their strong database of 150 schools attempting improvements, Crandall and Loucks (1983) found that success was related to providing

(Continued)

> practical, high-quality materials, but this had to be combined with high local involvement and extensive change-agent contact. Carnine and Gersten (1985), Gersten and colleagues (1987), and Loucks-Horsley and Roody (1990) reached the same conclusions in studying programs designed to assist special needs students.
>
> Turnbull (1984) and Louis and Miles (1990) report that change was more successful when support was provided to address problems and access resources from the external environment. Multisite studies of school change have similarly found that success correlates with support from outsiders (linkers as defined here) who provide pragmatic, comprehensive, ongoing linkages between researchers and practitioners, but effective knowledge use was most likely to occur in settings where there was a willingness and a capacity to explore a wide range of alternative solutions (Louis & Rosenblum, 1981; Turnbull, 1981; Sashkin & Egermeier, 1993).

How to Build a Better Awareness of the Resource Universe

Awareness is the key to an intelligent overall acquisition strategy. You cannot be a universal expert. Rather, be a knowledge broker, a linker to outside resources. Maintain a generalist's perspective in relation to specific innovations. You should be a mile wide and an inch deep when it comes to specific facts. You should have broad awareness of the resource universe while retaining a capacity to zero in on detailed sources when the diagnosis fits. Here are a few pointers on how to build and maintain this generalist perspective.

Building First-Time Awareness. Professional educators will always know what is going on in their specialized field. From that formal background, they carry with them a general set of categories associated with names and books and sometimes places. If you are new to a field or if your training is outdated, you should build or rebuild your memory bank by reading one or two introductory texts on the subject or, if possible, by taking an introductory university course. An introductory text is a truly marvelous tool that is usually treated too casually or taken for granted. It is an organized and indexed summary and synthesis of knowledge, written to show how the various pieces of the knowledge domain go together and build on one another. Only in introductory courses and texts are we likely to find this kind of organized and comprehensive overview.

Maintaining Awareness. The most useful tools for maintaining awareness are newsletters and periodicals; personal acquaintances; and knowledge of information systems and services, including online sources.

> **Useful Tools for Maintaining Awareness**
>
> - Periodicals and mass media
> - A personal acquaintance network
> - The where, when, and how of information systems

Periodicals and Mass Media. Several interesting periodicals concisely cover a broad range of educational topics. By reading these periodicals, you can keep informed about what is new in the field, what is fully developed, and what is projected for the future. Periodicals also provide enough information to steer you to more specifics when you need them. Other mass media are also important for maintaining awareness, although they are usually not as reliable. Newspapers and, to a lesser extent, television should also be scanned for relevant items, but the coverage is likely to be sporadic and there is no good way to file such items for future reference.

A Personal Acquaintance Network. Maintaining personal contacts with a variety of knowledgeable people is very important. Many studies have shown that the best innovators in any field have numerous contacts and encounters with others outside their system—people who are different from themselves in background, role, perspective, skill, and knowledge. Maintaining a personal-contact network keeps you aware of new developments in a variety of fields and within easy reach of people who can provide detailed information when you need it. Certain activities are likely to build and maintain this interpersonal network:

- Attending professional meetings
- Visiting other locations (for whatever purpose)
- Phoning or e-mailing outsiders (for whatever purpose)
- Interacting with people in different roles and different systems
- Maintaining a habit of consulting insiders and colleagues

The Where, When, and How of Information Systems. Approaching an information system might be a forbidding prospect for the uninitiated, but it should not be. Most libraries, clearinghouses, document centers, data banks, and information services employ friendly, helpful people who can quickly steer new users in appropriate directions. For the change agent, the critical factor is being aware of what types of information services and centers are available for educators, where they are located, and how they can be contacted.

Homing In on a Specific Problem and Solution

As you and the change team begin to focus on the problem and have some notion of possible solutions, you should develop a strategy for homing in, acquiring the information and materials you will need. There are probably as many ways to home in as there are change agents, but the following strategy may contain elements you will want to adapt to your own needs: Get an overview from a comprehensive written source, contact at least one knowledgeable person who has had direct experience for an overview, observe the innovation in operation, obtain evaluative data, obtain the innovation on trial, and acquire a framework for evaluation after trial.

> **A Homing-In Strategy**
>
> - Get an overview from a comprehensive written source.
> - Contact at least one knowledgeable person who has had direct experience for an overview.
> - Observe the innovation in operation.
> - Obtain evaluative data.
> - Obtain the innovation on trial.
> - Acquire a framework for evaluation after trial.

Get an Overview From Written source. Even if you have a specific plan in mind, it is good policy to become generally knowledgeable about research, development, theory, and past practice in the area on which you have chosen to focus. This usually means reading a current textbook or a current scholarly review article in that domain. Many areas of educational reform have conflicting theories and competing innovations. To be on firm ground, you should have an overview of the field even if you are committed to one of these competing forces.

A scholarly review article, a book, or an encyclopedia entry should give you a feel for the scope of the topic, the work that has been done in various places at various times, the level of solid research understanding of the topic, and valuable leads to more detailed sources. However, such general review sources probably will *not* give you the range of innovations available, enough information to evaluate specific innovations, enough information to diagnose specific problems, or practical suggestions about what to do. These drawbacks can be remedied by referring to more popular books or articles and to knowledgeable human resources.

Contact at Least One Knowledgeable Person. Usually other people will have already done, successfully or unsuccessfully, what you are contemplating doing. You should talk to at least one of them, preferably in person, as part of your homing-in process. Such individuals will give valuable information for evaluation before trial. They will give you leads about relevance, workability, and problems, which promoters of an innovation are unlikely to divulge voluntarily. If you, as a change agent, find these contact people to be articulate and informed, consider them as potential on-site consultants and resources.

Observe the Innovation in Operation. If the innovation under consideration is available in a printed or packaged form that can be borrowed or sampled, you should obtain it. Complex innovations are available in multimedia kits and packages, which may give a more complete impression of how the innovation will really work when implemented. In addition, if the innovation is operating somewhere, you should go and look at it, asking yourself three key questions:

- Is it really *working* for them?
- Is it really *benefiting* them?
- Will it really *work for us*? (Are there differences between these classrooms or schools and our school system that might make the innovation unfeasible in our setting? Conversely, are there advantages to our setting that might make our experience with the innovation more positive than theirs?)

Obtain Evaluative Data. Even if you are really enthusiastic about an innovation after observing it, you should still try to find scientific evaluative data to check out your impressions before you or the team actually makes a commitment. Such data may or may not confirm what you have already concluded about the innovation and what its promoters claim. In looking for evaluative information, do not restrict yourself to one source if more are available. Too often, evaluations are partisan and partial, especially when made by the innovation's author or promoter. The more disinterested the evaluation is and the more the evaluator adheres to scientific rules of evidence, the more you can count on the results.

Evaluative data are often found in formal reports to the government; hence, they are available through Educational Resources Information Center (ERIC) or are reported in research journals. The language may be technical and the findings difficult for laypersons to interpret. If you cannot understand the data or the explanation or if the implications for practitioners are not clear, it may be worth your while to call the authors or evaluators for an informal chat. You will probably find that they have thought a great deal about practical implications and can offer their informed judgment in a clear and nontechnical way. You will probably gain more cooperation if you indicate that you have read their research.

If you find that no hard data are available to evaluate the innovative program you are considering, you should try to acquire soft data in the form of personal evaluations by at least two persons representing different perspectives (e.g., one who has tried it and one who has critically observed someone else try it).

Obtain the Innovation on Trial. If your pretrial evaluation data confirm your judgment to proceed, you should attempt to acquire the innovation or the necessary materials for an experimental trial and demonstration in your school system. This will usually involve direct contact and negotiation with the developers or suppliers. In asking for materials or other resources on a trial basis, make sure to inquire about the availability of written materials on the costs of installation and maintenance, performance specifications, claims about short-term and long-term benefits, supplementary materials required and provided (e.g., manuals), limiting conditions, guarantees of quality and reliability, and problems that might be encountered in terminating the innovation at a later date. You will probably not get many answers to these questions, but if you feel that the supplier is being evasive and you find you are getting *none* of your questions answered, it is probably a good clue that you should search elsewhere.

Acquire a Framework for Evaluating the Results of the Trial. Even before an actual trial effort takes place, the change team should commit to a plan or procedure for evaluating the trial and making a "go—no-go" decision. All too often, a so-called trial experiment results in permanent adoption simply because the clients have no plan for evaluating and, if necessary, rejecting what does not work; they accept it because it is there and for no better reason.

In establishing a framework for evaluation, your first information need is for criteria on which to base a judgment. See Stage 5: Try for some of the relevant criteria that fall under three headings: potential benefit, workability, and diffusibility. At the trial stage, you should collect your own data, judgments, and impressions about installation costs and problems and maintenance costs and problems. The criteria used in available evaluation reports on the same innovation in other settings will also provide ideas for criteria to be applied in your setting.

Of special value (and special rarity) are research evaluations, which may use the fulfillment of specific behavioral objectives as criteria. Because of the specificity and observability of the measures in such cases, you will have little trouble adapting them for your setting. Because of the current trend in educational research and evaluation toward more and more specificity and behavioral statements of objectives and outcomes, in future years we may look to the research literature for more meaningful guidance in designing posttrial evaluations.

If an innovation is expensive, complex, or unusually risky, you may want to acquire the services of an outside professional evaluator or evaluation team. As yet, few individuals who are really skilled in evaluation are available to school systems, but the numbers are growing and the need for them is recognized increasingly at all levels. Regional laboratories, resource centers, and state education departments are working on training programs for evaluators and quality assurance specialists to fill this function.

This proposed strategy for homing in intentionally accentuates the positive because most change agents and change teams do not try hard enough to reach out for available resources. However, you will not always succeed in getting the information you want. This fact should not stop you, however, because you can always turn to human resources, people with relevant experience and knowledge from which you can benefit. Moreover, as you will see in Stage 5: Try, it is also possible for the system to invent its own innovation to meet a specified need if it cannot find adequate outside resources.

Acquiring Materials (= Packaged Knowledge)

Most materials are derivatives of knowledge, so what applies to knowledge acquisition also applies to materials. However, a few additional points need to be made about materials. There is something to be said for making a separate category just for materials because it is often difficult to get a real feel for what the innovative practice is all about until its associated materials are in your hands, until you see what they really look like and begin to understand how your teachers and students will be likely to receive them.

It is generally more expensive to acquire materials than to acquire the knowledge on which they are based. The cost of knowledge is mostly the cost of the time spent trying to absorb information in written, oral, or audiovisual form. People who produce materials usually expect to be reimbursed for their production costs at the very least, not to mention their development costs and profit.

> **Four Levels of Material Development**
>
> - Good ideas
> - Prototypes
> - Validated models
> - Production models

Extent of Development of Materials. Materials that find their way into classrooms have diverse histories. As an effective linker, you need to keep a sharp eye out for the pedigree of the particular materials under consideration. Like other manufactured goods, educational materials go through a series of developmental stages before they become widely distributed. What you have in hand may be at an early, an intermediate, or a fully developed stage. Knowing the difference is important because it significantly affects how you should treat the material. Consider these four developmental levels from least to most developed: good ideas, prototypes, validated models, and production models.

Good Ideas. Someone has proposed what the materials should be like, leaving it up to you, the change team, or the teacher to turn these good ideas into concrete form. The advantage here lies in the maximum creativity that you are given. What you have to go on are a concept and guidelines or descriptions of what you are supposed to produce. Such guidelines might be vague or explicit, but in either case, you have to interpret them and create the actual materials locally.

Consider where the idea comes from. It should be a credible source. If it is a widely accepted theory, consider whether the theory actually fits your situation and also has a lot of empirical evidence to back it up. Perhaps the idea comes from someone's research reported in a journal you have read. The same questions apply. How good is the research? How strong are the findings? How relevant are they to your situation?

Prototypes. Prototype materials have been designed and put together elsewhere, probably in draft form. You may have borrowed or copied them from the developers with their permission; you may even be part of their experiment if they are academic researchers. However, you use these materials at your own risk. They come with no specific seal of approval or guarantee, even though they may be derived from sound research and established theory, and without a lot of guidelines on how they should be used. Like the good idea materials, they leave a lot of initiative in your hands. You can adapt, combine, reshape, and repackage prototype materials to suit local needs and conditions.

Validated Models. Prototypes that have gone through a testing and validation process are called validated models. Data back them up, so if used as directed with similar populations in similar circumstances, they should yield similar results. The downside is that they are not flexible. If you adapt them to fit your situation, they may not produce the same results. Another negative aspect may be poor production values. If the materials are derived from a research project, they may not have been reshaped and packaged for widespread use.

Production Models. In their most developed state, materials are not only validated but also prepared and packaged in ways that encourage easy access and widespread dissemination. They are called production models and look good in a way that will inspire user confidence. They now come with teacher guides, which may also have been through a testing process. The downside is likely to be cost. Putting together a production model is an expensive process. Publishers expect to recover their costs and make a profit, but if the materials save you time and effort and also lead to a better result, the cost will be worth it. For commercially produced materials, the linker should always continue to look critically at the validity and relevance of the research and testing on which these materials are based and at their appropriateness to level, setting, and type of special education needs of the students in your system.

Comparing Alternative Materials

As with the search process as a whole, it is important to have more than one set of materials from which to choose. You should have two or preferably three or more sets to compare on various dimensions, such as cost, difficulty of use, basis in valid outcomes, relevance to your identified needs, flexibility and adaptability of use, and amount of impact promised or hoped for.

Using Electronic Resources

> **Surfing the Web: Finding What You Need**
>
> Learning how to better access research and financial resources via the Internet has been a very helpful aspect of EMSTAC's technical assistance support.
>
> —EMSTAC linking agent

No resource guide for linkers and other change agents can be complete without a reference to the Internet. Every linking agent must have Internet access and be familiar and comfortable with its use. A new initiative or project should entail at least one extensive Web search, and probably several, to explore all the issues discussed above. The Web is an important potential source for all four types of resources: money, people, knowledge, and materials.

When and Where to Start. The Elementary and Middle Schools Technical Assistance Center (EMSTAC) designed a special Web site (www.EMSTAC.org) for linking agents from which they can gather specific information and connect with other linking agents across the country to learn, to build networks, and to share experiences.

The EMSTAC Web site offers a great number of resources for special educators in general and linking agents in particular:

> EMSTAC's mission, objectives, and activities guide our work with local school districts and are designed to develop a national comprehensive technical assistance approach that will improve outcomes for elementary and middle school students with disabilities. The strategies we use and our relationships with our partners facilitate our success in ensuring that teachers have access to research-based practices that are proven to enhance the success of students with disabilities.

- Contact information
- Information about the mission of EMSTAC
- A listing of the EMSTAC staff and their interests and areas of expertise
- Information about all linking agents across the country and the initiatives they were implementing
- A description of the role of a linking agent and the steps required to become involved in the project
- Resources on a variety of areas that school districts have previously identified as areas of need (e.g., disproportionality, study skills, English language development/ESL, reading instruction, autism)

Web Sites of the U.S. Department of Education. The largest national repository of information about all aspects of education resides with the federal government. Indeed, although its involvement in education is highly circumscribed, in the information arena the federal government has played a substantial role for the past 40 years, beginning with the National Defense Education Act of 1958, the first U.S. response to the shock of the Soviet Union's Sputnik, the 1957 launch of the world's first satellite. Special educators are fortunate to have one of the oldest and most developed information services at their disposal, dating from that time. The Educational

Resources Information Center (ERIC) is a massive repository for research in education, and one of its major centers has always been devoted to special education. Thanks to the Internet, this material is now easily accessible online. The Web site of the Office of Special Education and Rehabilitative Services (OSERS), http://www.ed. gov/offices/OSERS/index.html, is the main gateway to the online federal resources for special education. To carry out its functions, OSERS consists of three program-related components, each of which has its own Web site.

Office of Special Education Programs

OSEP (http://www.ed.gov/offices/OSERS/OSEP/index.html) has primary responsibility for administering programs and projects relating to the free appropriate public education of all children, youth, and adults with disabilities, from birth through age 21. The bulk of special education funds is administered by OSEP's Monitoring and State Improvement Programs division, which provides grants to states and territories to assist them in providing a free appropriate public education to all children with disabilities. The early intervention and preschool grant programs provide grants to each state for children with disabilities from birth through age 5.

Rehabilitation Services Administration (RSA)

The RSA (http://www.ed.gov/offices/OSERS/RSA/index.html) oversees programs that help individuals with physical or mental disabilities obtain employment through the provision of such supports as counseling, medical and psychological services, job training, and other individualized services. RSA's major formula grant program provides funds to state vocational rehabilitation agencies to provide employment-related services for individuals with disabilities, giving priority to individuals who are severely disabled.

National Institute on Disability and Rehabilitation Research (NIDRR)

The third component, the NIDRR (http://www.ed.gov/offices/OSERS/NIDRR/), provides leadership and support for a comprehensive program of research related to the rehabilitation of individuals with disabilities. All of its programmatic efforts are aimed at improving the lives of individuals with disabilities from birth through adulthood.

Using Internet Resources

The linking agent should take a balanced approach to using the Internet. The balance will vary greatly from one linker to another. Some will be inclined to use it as the primary search tool, whereas others will use it sparingly. Be careful at both ends of this continuum: Never rely on the Internet exclusively and never ignore the Internet entirely. What you do in between will depend on your level of comfort and experience with the Internet in your role as a change agent and in other spheres of your life and on the ease, convenience, and cost of access.

If your starting point is the Internet, make sure that you extend your search beyond electronic sources, both for backup and for a wider range of resources.

If your starting point is not the Internet, remember to include Web searches to broaden your perspective on what is available.

The amount of material available on the Internet can be overwhelming. As you begin a new project, think through how to set up your computer folder structure hierarchically to reflect both the nature of your project and your paper filing system. This will become your local and personalized library that is always at hand for easy reference. As you browse, remember to download interesting items onto your personal computer. Take time offline to review downloaded material, separating items into don't save, save, and save and print categories. You can then place the most important items in paper files or pop them into your briefcase. They will be available for you to review and share as the occasion arises.

Getting Others Involved

Internet searching and information retrieval is mostly a solitary activity, done by one person who sits at a terminal and makes a series of independent and solitary choices. In many ways, this is a good thing and the reason why the Internet works as well as it does. There is no censor, no mediator, no inhibitor, and no barrier between the user and this vast knowledge storehouse. You can go in and come out at any time, and you can stay in as long as you want. Unlike a library, the Internet never shuts its doors. You do not have to go anywhere to get anything. You do not have to get permission to read anything or copy anything for your own use. You do not have to sign out material, and you never have to return it when you are done.

These wonderful features make the Internet the ultimate individualized search tool. As a change agent, you should think of ways to use it in conjunction with the multilayered social action of a change project. If you have organized a change team, you should consult with its members, share information, and talk with them at each phase of a search. To get others involved, consider using the following tactics.

Presearch and Mid-Search Conferencing. Discuss with your group the kinds of topics and key words on which you should be searching. Relate these to assessed needs, perceived obstacles to change, solution ideas, and experts that various members may have heard of or have some interest in pursuing. These mini-conferences can take place at any stage and should be reconvened after one or more searches to review results and consider new directions that might be more fruitful.

Printing and Copying Standout Items. The Internet searcher should always be looking for items to download and print out not only for personal review offline but also for sharing with others, in one-on-one and group settings. Many valuable change team members will not have the time, experience, or inclination to get online to do their own searching. They will be grateful for your effort, and some may learn to follow your example and do some of their own searching because you have shown them the way and demonstrated its utility.

Sharing the Web Search Experience. In addition to displaying the search product, explain how you got it and how you navigated the Web. Encourage others to follow your example. If they do not yet have access, explain how to get it. Take advantage of any opportune moment for hands-on demonstration and practice with other members of your change team. Encourage school administrators to acquire up-to-date computers and high-speed Internet access lines.

Knowing When to Stop. The Internet is wonderful, and for many people it is very new. For knowledge searching in particular it is revolutionary: instantaneous and effortless access and more knowledge than you know what to do with, but that is the problem. You can spend all your time searching without thinking hard enough about what you will do with the information.

No signpost warns "that's enough!" or "keep going." The linking agent has to know when to stop. Your time is not free. The cost of not doing something else because you are preoccupied with one endeavor is what economists call opportunity cost. Web searching has an important and growing niche in the overall search process. As more and more knowledge becomes available online and as search engines become more efficient, more specialized, and more user-friendly, the Internet search process will expand accordingly. Nevertheless, this one activity should not be allowed to crowd out everything else.

Using Other Online Resources. Online services of all types should be used whenever appropriate as an adjunct and a supplement to real-time telephone and face-to-face communication. Use the Internet to connect to the various human resources and collaborators who are relevant to your project. Listservs and e-mail are effective forms of Internet communication. As you make personal contact with resource people, you should always ask them for their e-mail address and ask whether there are Web sites you should look up and listservs you should join.

EMSTAC and Linking Agents Use the Listserv to Share Information

A linking agent in Tennessee expressed her mixed feelings about the support provided by the listserv.

Pro: It is a helpful tool because through it, she discovered that some of the other school districts were dealing with issues similar to those in her district. The linking agent shared this information (additional resources, research, etc.) with her colleagues.

Con: The information provided was not always based on programs with a solid research base or specific solutions to problems. Instead, the linking agent sometimes felt that people were using the listserv as a forum to voice their concerns about problems at their schools.

Listservs. Nearly every topic in special education has a corresponding interest group. Today, where there is an interest group, there is also a listserv or an online chat room of some kind and probably more than one. Online groups are available for every type of disability, for every problem area, and for every type of innovation relevant to special education in general. You need to search out the groups that work in your area of interest. Monitor these groups and join their listservs where appropriate.

If you are not experienced or comfortable using online services, ask someone who is to help you establish your own listserv and chat room for your project. Most online services have special provisions for such groups, which can be set up as either closed private exchange groups or open groups that allow anyone to eavesdrop and join in. A closed group might best serve the needs of an emerging project. Closed or open, these mechanisms have several advantages over traditional modes of communication:

- They allow everyone to participate without interruption.
- They allow contributors to say as much or as little as they want or just to listen.
- They allow commentary from one person to another, which builds on specific prior comments.
- They provide a written record of all exchanges.
- They allow conferencing among a number of individuals, which can occur in real time by prior arrangement or in extended time to accommodate anyone's schedule.
- They provide a convenient method for arriving at and testing consensus within the group on any particular issue.

If you can develop a listserv for your project, make a habit of reading it daily; if you acknowledge and reinforce others who use it daily, gradually others will chime in. When you meet with project personnel individually or in a group, refer to the listserv and ask whether they use it: How useful is it? How can it be improved? This kind of mention will eventually lead to increased use. Embedding cross-references to Internet sites in listserv messages will also encourage your colleagues to use the Internet.

E-Mail. Use e-mail to supplement your communications whenever possible. As we progress through the first decade of the twenty-first century, more and more people will become accustomed to using the Internet as a routine aspect of daily living. As this happens, the relevance of online communications for all aspects of a change project will increase. As a special education linking agent, you should make an effort to connect everybody on your change team electronically. E-mail has many advantages over traditional one-on-one communications. First of all, it does not depend on timing and schedules. A message can be sent whenever the sender wants and received whenever the receiver chooses to go online. Among busy educators with complicated schedules, this is a tremendous advantage. Second, e-mail, like letter writing, forces writers to compose their thoughts and allows them to edit and rethink their thoughts before they are sent. You can be more precise, have a clearer idea of what you are saying, and retain an exact record of what you have written for future reference.

Building a Permanent Capacity for Resource Acquisition

Acquiring diagnostic information, maintaining awareness, and homing in are skills and procedures that all change agents should know and have, but they are also activities that the systems with which change agents work should learn to initiate on their own. Knowing how to acquire resources is a large part of building a self-renewal capacity (see Stage 6: Extend for more discussion of this concept). Above all, encourage your system to build and maintain a broad awareness of the outside world. This means establishing and maintaining meaningful human links with other school systems, universities, state education departments, regional laboratories, regional centers of various sorts, and the resource mechanisms set up by professional associations, foundations, and the U.S. Department of Education. These linkages are built and maintained through developing habits of visiting, being visited, phoning, reading, and generally being curious and open-minded about the larger social environment.

Extensive use of a variety of resources is not always a common practice among innovating educators. Frequently they show substantial resistance to resource retrieval as a result of their negative impressions about its helpfulness. In other words, they do not believe that there is anything in outside resource systems worth acquiring. The change agent can encourage these educators to become more familiar with the advantages of using outside resources.

Helping a System Learn More About Resources and Resource Retrieval

Provide a Supportive Atmosphere. Help members of the system retrieve resources. Get official recognition and legitimization of the need to use resources by giving people the time, money, and materials to carry out retrieval and acquisition operations.

Maintain Existing Interaction and Search Norms. It is always easier to get people to add on new behavior than to replace one kind of behavior with another. Some old habits of acquiring information are good habits. Your goal should be to support and supplement those good habits.

Seek Out and Use Creative Practitioners and In-House Experts. They may supplant the need for more difficult acquisition outside the system. Also, overlooking their contributions could create antagonism.

Generate Open but Realistic Expectations. Do not oversell or undersell the performance capabilities of the new information systems and services. Any resource should be approached with a realistic view of what it is capable of giving. People who depend too heavily on one resource for a total solution to their problems are bound to be disappointed. Each resource has its own special purposes. When combined, they can provide substantial impetus for the change process.

Assess the Impact of Past Experience. Find out whether the system has had previous experience with resource retrieval and how that experience has influenced the system's prevailing attitudes about retrieval. Experience may have made the system more sophisticated about innovations and resources, but it also may have led to some disillusionment about the difficulties inherent in translating innovation experiences from one setting to another. You may have to work hard initially to turn around such expectations by demonstrating successful resource acquisition and by expanding your colleagues' awareness of both resources and resource-acquiring strategies. Showing school personnel how the creative use of human resources can assist and simplify the retrieval, translation, and adaptation of print and product resources is an essential part of the process.

Acquire Resources. Demonstrate how acquiring resources can pay off by using illustrations from successful cases. Reinforce the message that it is possible to acquire useful information from "out there." Teach your coworkers how to structure resource acquisition so that they do not get lost in stacks of irrelevant or overtechnical print.

Localize Resources. Localize resources and resource system terminals wherever you can. The first law of information use is proximity. High-quality people, print, and product resources should be made available locally wherever possible. The telephone is a significant tool in resource acquisition because it makes almost all people resources proximate. The Internet goes a giant step further by making all knowledge resources proximate.

Acquire: Summary

The core function of the linker is to connect the system that is seeking change with the resources it needs to carry out the change. Such resources break down into three general categories: money, people, and knowledge. The money theory of change posits that a certain amount of surplus capital must be made available to a system before it can innovate, something like the discretionary spending in a family budget. Up to the trial stage, financial resources tend to be soft, that is, temporary, tentative, and pulled from this discretionary budget. The ultimate desired status of a change is to get on hard money, which means becoming part of the routine annual budget. The linker can help on the money front by sorting out the issues, identifying possible sources, and helping put together a funding pond.

The linker can view people as resources for change in three ways. The first is to have people on the change team who have various strengths—especially dedication and the ability to inspire others. A second is to use people as demonstrators or role models so that others can see that a new way of doing things is possible and can observe what behaviors are involved in doing it. Yet a third way that people can serve is as expert consultants, either on specific content areas or on aspects of the change process itself.

Knowledge resources are arrayed in the five Ps: people, practices, programs, print material, and products. All are potentially relevant at different stages, and the linker should maintain a broad awareness of how they can be retrieved to support a change. As in other stages, the linker should encourage a collective knowledge acquisition strategy, one that taps into the local social network, material on the Internet and in libraries, regional and state networks and clearinghouses, and the extensive federal information and research network that supports special education. The linker then can home in on solutions once a need has been fully framed as a problem to be solved.

Throughout the resource acquisition process, the modern-day linker must make continual and extensive use of the Internet while keeping track of other channels and budgeting time to different channels in reasonable balance. Whatever resource linking actions are taken should also be demonstrated to and shared with others so that a permanent resource acquisition capacity is built within the system.

Stage 5

Try

Moving From Knowledge to Action

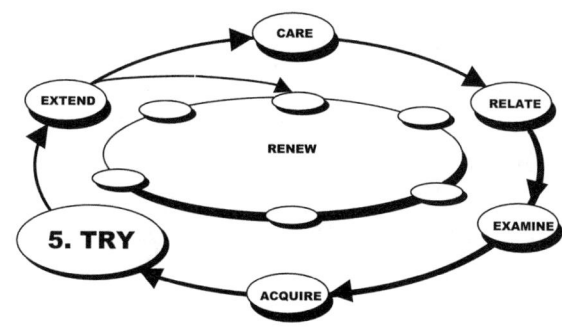

ORGANIZER QUESTIONS

- What five steps constitute Stage 5: Try?
- What considerations should you take in choosing a set of activities for trial?
- What elements should be included in the written plan for a trial?
- What are some concerns and issues to look for as a plan is implemented?
- What is process evaluation? Why is it important? How do we measure it?
- What outcomes of a trial should be measured? What are alternative ways of measuring them?
- How should process and outcome evaluations of a trial be used?

A good understanding of the problem at hand, preliminary approval from above, enough funding for starting up, a balanced and motivated change team, and a lot of new ideas and models of good practice: All these elements set the stage for choosing an innovation and giving it a good trial. That is what

Stage 5: Try is all about. Every new change effort should be designed first as a trial, an open experiment that allows innovators to take on new behaviors without undue risk and allows others to watch and begin to model their own changes on the basis of their observation of the demonstration.

The trial begins with a participative process of choosing and shaping the change that uses the assembled resources now at hand. It goes on to developing a plan, preparing the setting, implementing the plan in that setting, and finally, evaluating what happened. At that point, the change team may be ready to move on to a more extended trial at other sites, which could lead to widespread system change.

Giving a Fair Trial to a Well-Considered Solution

With a lot of relevant information on the table, the change team needs to sort through the pile, settle on the most promising alternative, and give it a try. This should be the most creative and interesting task in the process of change. However, it is easy to stumble. Too often people jump on a solution without giving enough forethought, without comparing one possibility with another, without planning, and without arranging to gauge their success when they are done.

A successful trial breaks down into five steps:

- Choose one innovation as your change project.
- Adapt the innovation to fit your situation.
- Plan the implementation.
- Put the plan into action.
- Evaluate your results so that you know what to do next.

Knowledge Base

Importance of Outside Technical Assistance at Stage 5: Try

Most of the activity identified as belonging to Stage 5: Try would be identified by Hall and Hord (2001) as moving up the level-of-use scale from II to III, that is, from "preparation" to "mechanical use": the "state at which the user focuses most effort on the short-term day-to-day use of the innovation, a stepwise attempt to master the tasks required . . . often resulting in disjointed and superficial use."

As summarized by Little (1984), the more complex and unfamiliar a proposed practice is, the more it challenges preexisting frameworks, and the more it veers from past practice, the more likely it is that educators will need help mastering it. Without such help, they will blunt or downsize innovations (Huberman & Crandall, 1983; Huberman & Miles, 1984; Loucks, 1983; Little, 1984; McLaughlin, 1990), misconstrue information and misapply techniques (Cohen & Ball, 1990), or apply new information mechanically (Loucks, 1977; Jarvis, 1987; Smylie, 1995).

Innovations relating to special education present a special challenge to the general education classroom teacher. For example, "the mainstreaming of special needs students involves new materials, a greater range of curriculum goals, and a wider variety of teaching approaches—but what it demands most is a new conceptualization of learning and teaching, one that radically broadens a teacher's definition of (professional) responsibility" (Evans, 1996, p. 65).

In their intensive and comparative analysis of innovation at 12 sites, Huberman and Miles (1984) found that timely and intensive technical assistance and training helped teachers achieve mastery. Cohen (1990) and Smylie (1995) add case evidence that such support can help resolve tensions between abstract principles and the complexity of classroom practice. This new level of comprehension, in turn, enables teachers to buy in to change, improve outcomes, and feel a sense of ownership (Crandall & Loucks, 1983; Huberman & Miles, 1984; Showers, Joyce, & Bennett, 1987).

Deal & Peterson (1999, p. 97) note that another important function that can be played only by change agents who are on-site is identifying and exploiting teachable moments, times of disruption and discontinuity when people may be open, however briefly, to new ideas and temporarily unfrozen from their daily routines.

Gersten and Dimino (2001) report on two successful interventions with elementary and middle school teachers in which special education linkers gave assistance. These initiatives were deliberately designed to take account of research on change processes such as that summarized in *Guiding Change*, Fullan (2001b), and other recent works. "We provided guidelines for determining a reasonable scope for the change effort, and factors to consider in serious implementation, such as the need for specificity and concrete guidance, the importance of establishing collegial networks, and the importance of periods of intensive and ongoing technical assistance. Within 2 years, 28 classrooms now used research-based practices that appear to be leading to growth in reading. This was done with no formal mandate from the state or district administration" (Gersten & Dimino, 2001, p. 129).

Special Education Linking Agents in Action

The Trial Stage in Hilldale County

Most of the narrative in the case study dealt with Stage 5: Try, beginning with the presentation of three alternatives to a group of teachers and their decision to select the Early Literacy Project (ELP). Once they made their selection, they essentially downsized the innovation in two respects: They chose to implement only a part of the ELP and they limited the trial to a few classrooms in only one school. Site visits were an important aspect of the case, but only the linking agent and the principal were able to participate in the out-of-state site visit even though the responsibility for implementation would rest primarily on the shoulders of teachers. A training session then became the centerpiece of the project.

An expert trainer was able to present the intervention and model the behaviors well enough for the teachers to use in their classrooms some of what they learned. At this final implementation stage, even more downsizing occurred because Morning Message became the core take-home practice for the teachers. The linking agent and the principal both monitored the progress of the project implementation and collected evaluation data on both the process and the outcomes. Word about the success spread throughout the school and to other schools. On the whole, the trial phase was well executed in Hilldale, which was the chief reason the innovation was continued after the first year and later spread to other teachers and other schools.

Choose

Even if you have done a good job of acquiring knowledge and other resources (Stage 4: Acquire), you still have a lot of work to do before an innovative idea becomes reality. First, you must assemble the collected information into a format that can be shared and discussed by members of your change team and others. Out of this social process, your objective is to choose the one innovation, out of the many possibilities, that seems to be the most promising or the most appropriate for the school setting at this time. You want to make this choosing process as open and as objective as possible. The process breaks down into four substeps: assemble and order, derive implications, generate alternatives, and conduct pretrial testing.

> **Steps in the Choosing Process**
> - Assemble and order
> - Derive implications
> - Generate alternatives
> - Conduct pretrial testing

Assemble and Order the Relevant Findings From Your Stage 4 Search. You have collected information from a number of sources. You have looked at financing issues and you have identified various people who might help you. Now you need to put all this together in a meaningful way so that the change team can compare and contrast the information.

Derive Implications. This derivation activity is not the same as acquisition. It is more a process of thinking before committing to action. It should always accompany resource acquisition, particularly when the resource information is in research reports and abstract analyses. In the derivation step, you should ask, "What does this information say about this setting and this specific problem?"

Generate Alternative Solution Ideas. What you want next is a range of possible solution ideas. Therefore, after considering the meaning of the findings, you should move into formulating action alternatives. Some of these will be suggested by the diagnosis (Stage 3: Examine), others by implications derived from the assembled knowledge base (Stage 4: Acquire). Still others may be generated by local educators working with you in brainstorming activities, and some may emerge out of a combination of these sources. You want a range of possible solution ideas, even though they may be in various stages of completeness. Having this range of possibilities puts you in a better position to make meaningful choices.

Conduct Pretrial Feasibility Testing. You now need to evaluate these alternative solution ideas according to a number of criteria. The three primary considerations in evaluation are benefit, practicability, and extendibility. Benefit simply means, How much good would it do if it worked? Practicability means, Will it really work, especially with this particular client system? Extendibility means, Will it be accepted by others and will it have staying power? By asking these questions, you should be able to reduce the number of possible solutions to one or two.

Assemble and Order the Relevant Findings

You begin Stage 5: Try by building on Stage 4: Acquire and bringing together all the findings from your search and discovery activities in Stage 3: Examine and Stage 4: Acquire. Your findings from Stage 3 should pertain to the system's needs assessments; the underlying nature of the problem or problems; relevant characteristics of the system, such as strengths and weaknesses; and the readiness for change. In Stage 3, you also identified opportunities and key persons who might help the change process as informants, as facilitators, as sanctioners, or as active participants. In Stage 4, you assembled a number of facts about possible solutions. Some are merely ideas or hoped-for outcomes offered by members of the system, reflecting their cares and concerns (Stage 1: Care). Other findings reflect the documented experience of people at other sites who are engaged in various types of change projects. Some items may come prepackaged with specific stepwise implementation strategies and materials. Some may also offer expert consultants who can fly in, drive in, or call in to explain, train, demonstrate, or help implement.

The choosing process is greatly aided by building your knowledge base and having all materials in written form, organized for comparison by various criteria. This not only will help you think and plan but also will help enormously in sharing understanding among members of the change team and subsequently among teachers and other system stakeholders. Elements of the knowledge fall into two categories: diagnostic knowledge and solution-oriented knowledge.

Diagnostic Knowledge. Major concerns of the system as a whole, perhaps listed in apparent order of intensity or numbers of people who are concerned:

- Research findings related to these types of concerns as documented in the literature
- Major features of the system relevant to this change effort
- Major stakeholders relevant to the change with an estimate of their current stance (e.g., pro or con, resistant or open)
- Strengths and assets of the system and various members, which can be brought to bear on the change effort

Solution-Oriented Knowledge
- Solution ideas from members of the client system
- Documented history of innovations and change projects already tried by this system relevant to the one under current consideration
- Documented innovations or change projects from other systems
- Research studies documenting and evaluating innovations and tried solutions related to those under consideration
- Names of experienced practitioners or experts who know about the type of change being considered
- Materials that are relevant to solutions under consideration, including packaged programs, tapes, manuals, and brochures, including data on costs, quality, and ease of use, when available

Derive Implications From the Research Knowledge Base

Most of the information derived from outside sources requires some amount of translation or reformulation. This is especially true for research reports. The standard research report is intended for communication among researchers and is not usually a good vehicle for communication from research to practice. Therefore, change agents can rarely accept a research report as written and expect it to be immediately useful and relevant for their purposes. You will want to ask, What does this mean for this particular setting and for this particular school district? This question is difficult because you have to know how to ask it; usually you need to have a good deal of practice before you can ask it well. Nevertheless, it is worth the effort.

A great deal of research is relevant and can be useful if you work hard to think through what it means in terms of the situation you are confronting. It is also worth the effort because research-based information is more likely to be valid (facts you can count on as being true) and reliable (equally true at time A and time B, situation A and situation B) than information from nonresearch sources. Research findings deserve more attention than opinions and conjectures because they are (or should be) based on systematic observation and measurement of real events.

A derivation task from research might be organized along the following lines:

- Retrieve summary statements from the research literature that seem relevant to your identified needs and concerns or to the type of solution you are thinking of trying.
- Translate some of the research jargon.
- Share with the change team and check for understanding.
- Establish relevance to your setting.
- As a group, restate the findings as implications for action in your setting.

Do not underestimate the utility of abstracts and brief summary statements of research findings as the raw material for building research-based solutions. Although many other parts of research reports (procedures, data analysis, interpretations, etc.) may sometimes stimulate your thinking about solutions, the summary is the best starting point for deriving practice implications.

Generate a Range of Solution Ideas

Ideas for solutions can come from a variety of sources. They may come from research findings as discussed above. They may also come from other systems or from commercial sources. Some solutions will be suggested more or less directly by the diagnosis or by the statement of objectives, whereas others will be suggested by the kind of resources you have available. Where good solutions are readily available from other programs and projects, it is probably wise to use them, but it is also possible and sometimes advantageous for a change team to generate its own solutions. This may not be a matter of reinventing the wheel but rather of adapting and combining ideas from various sources to produce something that is appropriate for your situation.

No real choosing is going on unless you look at more than one alternative. A range of alternatives gives users the freedom of choice and thereby the opportunity to make rational and meaningful decisions.

As you assemble this range of alternatives, practicality or feasibility need not be your first consideration. Rather, the choosing process should start as a mind-stretching experience. Fresh thinking has a liberating and energizing effect. Therefore, it is good to start with possibilities that may be unusual, a bit outside the box. Foremost in your thinking should be the questions, What would be the ideal solution? or What would do the most good? Likewise, in the early stages of the choosing process, you should not be too concerned about the details of how something works, how much it costs, and how hard it is to install and maintain. You are really looking for awareness information—information that will give a rough idea of what the innovation can do or is supposed to do. For this purpose, films, live demonstrations, field trips, and even testimonials from others who have tried it may be appropriate. At the early stages of selecting the innovation, you should not rule out unusual alternatives too quickly even if they seem to come from nonobjective sources.

Assessing Numerous Options for Innovation

The Elementary and Middle Schools Technical Assistance Center (EMSTAC) linking agent, a veteran resource coordinator and behavioral specialist, identified a need in his school for an intensive program to help students who exhibit behavioral problems in general education settings. EMSTAC helped the linking agent use research-based resources to compile information about alternative school-based programs and strategies. EMSTAC staff recommended strategies for alternative school-based programs that were empirically demonstrated to have a positive impact on student performance and behavior. The linking agent assessed the variety of strategies available to determine the best fit between the characteristics of his students and school and the features of the program. He selected facts from a variety of research-based programs and developed an alternative school-based curriculum that was best aligned with his school's needs.

Two strategies discussed in Stage 3: Examine as a part of looking at needs are particularly relevant in generating solution ideas. One is emphasizing opportunities instead of problems. As noted earlier, a focus on areas of internal strength adds a new and hopeful dimension. These opportunities sometimes suggest solution possibilities already available within the school system but not previously seen as relevant. The other Stage 3 strategy, constructing an ideal model, gives participants a chance to think through an ideal solution to their problems even if they have no immediate prospect of attaining it. The exercise is mind-stretching. It opens up new vistas and points toward the realization that solutions are at least conceivable. From conceivable you can often build a bridge to doable and from doable to doing and done.

Brainstorming is a specific technique for generating solution ideas in a small group and can lead to constructing an ideal model. There is probably no faster way to free up thinking and create bright images of potential solutions. The classic brainstorming technique involves four steps: preparing the group with background information, setting the stage, establishing and maintaining ground rules, and summarizing and synthesizing.

> **Brainstorming**
>
> - Preparing the group with background information
> - Setting the stage
> - Establishing and maintaining ground rules
> - Summarizing and synthesizing

Preparing. Before starting a brainstorming session, participants should be briefed with background information about the problem area. The briefing could take the form of written abstracts or summaries, such as research derivations and an outline of the primary needs (from Stage 3: Examine). Group members should have some shared knowledge of the basics, but they do not all have to start from the same information base. Laying groundwork is very important because even though participants in brainstorming are supposed to believe that their ideas are spontaneously generated, in actuality these ideas almost always have a foundation in knowledge they already possess. Therefore, the prior acquisition of knowledge resources (Stage 4: Acquire) is also a key precursor of good brainstorming.

Setting the Stage. To be useful, brainstorming sessions should have a specific focus, which is usually the problem or the diagnosis that has been previously determined. However, a mere statement of the problem may not be enough to trigger creative thought processes. The linking agent should set the stage by suggesting an image of some future time or set of circumstances that partially releases the participants from the reality constraints of the here and now. For example, you might ask them to think of the kind of school they would like to have in the year 2010 or 2015 or the kind of educational environment they would build if they were suddenly granted several million dollars without strings. Of course, the stage set will vary with the type of problem and should be directly relevant to the problem. The more vivid and imaginative the stage setting is, the more likely it is that the brainstorming will take a productive turn.

Establishing Ground Rules. Brainstorming shows the power of positive thinking. Brainstorming groups consciously strive to inhibit critical or negative thinking about a problem. Their most important ground rule is to engage in no criticism of ideas (your own or others) on grounds of feasibility. The only criterion is relevance to the problem or to the stage set. This kind of free-associating to solutions does not come easily; it requires practice and discipline to ward off the natural tendency to slip back into a traditional task set. Commenting on the ideas of others is allowed, but it should be in the form of piggybacking, that is, adding to a previous idea or suggesting another variation on the same theme, not criticizing or rejecting the idea.

It is also important to include a recording function as part of the ground rules. In other words, it is just as important to get it down as to get it out. You may want to appoint a recorder or to assume this task yourself so that at the conclusion of the session, a list has been generated that adequately represents the thinking of the group. This recorder function is vital and should not be slighted; the written record is the principal product and the key element in linking brainstorming to the overall problem-solving enterprise. For a small or a medium-sized group of up to about 20 people, the preferred technology is a large pad of newsprint marked in large letters with a thick marker so that all participants can see it clearly. As each page fills up, rip it off and tape it to the walls of the room in full view of all. This helps induce more piggybacking and keeps everyone mindful of the process and what it is leading to.

Summarizing and Synthesizing. Summarizing and synthesizing must also be included to make the brainstorming truly productive, but this step should be held off as long as new ideas continue to flow in. The linker or group leader plays an important role in helping members pull together their various ideas into a series of coherent solution possibilities. This fourth step reduces redundancy and makes the brainstorming product manageable. Feasibility questions and other critiques remain out of bounds until the exercise is over and its product is generated.

Brainstorming had its earliest applications in the field of advertising, a fact that may have inhibited its use by other groups. Nevertheless, it is a useful unfreezing method, which is applicable in all kinds of situations. There is no one method of brainstorming, and probably any method will have to be adapted or modified for working with particular types of groups. One good feature is that participants do not have to be experts. Groups of teachers, students, parents, or other stakeholders can be trained to conduct a productive brainstorming session with a brief orientation. It can be the turning point of a change program and is well worth trying, particularly if you feel reasonably secure in your own role as a linker.

Pretrial Feasibility Testing: Comparing and Selecting the Best

When you and your change team have several potential solutions before you, the choosing task begins in earnest. Choosing really means testing and comparing, applying criteria, eliminating some possibilities, accepting others, and modifying still others on the basis of comparative judgments. Many criteria should now come into play. The following list covers most of the important considerations: degree of benefit promised, validity and reliability of the promise, comparability of need, comparability of the developer's setting to your own, resources required for successful implementation, probable areas of resistance it will stimulate in your environment, compatibility to other innovations at your site, diffusion potential, doability, and showability.

Degree of Benefit Promised

Will this change really do a lot of good if it works? Is the promised benefit large enough to justify the effort? How many people will it help? How long will

> **Criteria for Choosing a Solution**
>
> - Degree of benefit promised
> - Validity and reliability
> - Comparability of need
> - Comparability of setting
> - Resources required
> - Probable areas of resistance
> - Compatibility to other innovations at your site
> - Diffusion potential
> - Doability
> - Showability

it help them? How much will it help them? Does it have any negative effects?

Validity and Reliability of the Promise

Will the potential solution really work, regardless of how much good it is supposed to do? What is the nature of the evidence supporting the innovation? Does it come from a credible source? Is the innovation sted by solid outcome data? Does it seem to work every time, in every setting in which it has been tried? Has it been tried in different settings?

Comparability of Need

Were the developers of this innovation trying to solve the same problems you are trying to solve? Is there a good match between the need they were meeting and the need you are trying to meet now in your situation?

Comparability of Setting

How close is the match between the developer's setting and yours? Is it practical in this setting at this time?

Resources Required

Will you be able to acquire the requisite financial, material, and human resources to make it work at your site? Some development sites that show remarkable results may have hidden advantages, such as highly educated and education-oriented parents, well-trained and highly paid teachers, and so forth. Such hidden advantages are especially likely at school sites that are proximate to universities where many developers are located.

Resistance Factors

Does any aspect of the innovation appear to contradict long-held values and assumptions of prospective users? Does it raise any red flags? Are particular people likely to be especially resistive? If so, is there any way to enlist their help or to otherwise neutralize their negative impact on acceptance? Would one selection arouse less resistance than others, either in the way it is packaged or in what it does?

Compatibility With Past and Present Innovations

Does this innovation have the look, sound, or feel of innovations that have been tried before in this setting? If so, will that familiarity make it easier or harder to adopt? Will it seem to be in conflict with other ongoing innovations?

Will it be confused with past innovations and thus be confusing to adopters? Will the failure of prior similar-looking innovations cast a pall over the new effort? If your innovation looks completely different from what people in this setting have experienced before, will this newness be seen as strangeness? Will it be seen as incompatible because "it's just not what we do here"?

Diffusibility

The diffusibility criterion asks, Will the solution (the innovation) be accepted by the school system as a whole or by a majority of its members after a trial has demonstrated its benefit and workability? The criteria previously discussed tell us a lot about diffusibility. Benefit, validity, comparability, and required resources all suggest something about the potential for diffusion. An analysis of resistance and compatibility factors tells you even more. But there are some other issues as well. Many research studies have focused on the characteristics of innovations, and they provide us with various dimensions to compare potential solutions. Here are the main factors:

Demonstrability. Can the proposed change be demonstrated easily and convincingly? Is it easy to describe and understand? Will the results of a trial be visible and persuasive?

Trialability. Can the innovation be given limited trial before the school system commits to adoption? Can it be tried a little bit at a time? Can it be tried by a few people without the whole system having to buy in at the same time?

Packaging. Is the innovation adequately packaged? Any change project in which new ideas or actions are being presented has a package. Whether or not you actually attend to packaging or are even aware of the package, it is still there. The package gives a first impression of the innovation to the potential user. It could be a black box, a total mystery revealing nothing of its true nature, or it could be, in varying degrees, revealing as well as appealing to the various senses of the beholder. In many respects, you, the change agent, may be seen as part of the package if the user receives and associates you closely with the change initiative. Ideally, an innovation should also be packaged to be both familiar and different: familiar enough to be understood but different enough to be seen as something genuinely new.

Labeling. Is the package adequately labeled? Labeling is the language side of packaging. Humans are word users first and foremost and can easily fall victim to their own unfortunate choice of words. Choosing the right word to describe this or that process for *Guiding Change* was a continual struggle. Even the words *change* and *agent* can be problematic. The word *linker* may sound strange and awkward to some ears. There is a constant tug of war between trying to be precise and descriptive on the one hand and finding acceptance and familiarity to the reader on the other. *Linkers, innovators,* and *change agents* must fight this battle of words within themselves as well as with the people with whom they are working to implement change, such as teachers, administrators, parents, and other key stakeholders. The label is especially important because it is the first word that attaches to you as you approach a new school or staff person. It comes before there is any acceptance of or familiarity with what you are talking about. Later on, you can use all sorts of words that are unfamiliar, more precise, and more informative, but at the beginning, at the labeling stage, you must choose words with great care and forethought about how they will be received.

Doability

Can a trial be done? By us? Here and now? If you are doing something for the first time, you will always experience a degree of uncertainty about whether it can be done at all or done by you or the designated innovators. This is where off-the-shelf innovations have a big advantage. It is also where old hands and self-confident hands make a big difference. Remember the first time you tried to do something new? What was the foremost question in your mind? Certainly it was not whether anyone would benefit from what you were doing, but whether it could be done at all and, more particularly, whether could it be done by you in that situation.

You want to know whether the innovation will work more or less as you expect it will. What are the potential glitches? What supporting elements are required to make it a reality? It is like the difference between reading a good play and putting the play on before a live audience.

Showability

Will a first trial of the innovation convincingly demonstrate beneficial outcomes? Before the trial, you need to think through what signs others will be looking for as evidence of effectiveness. Is the mere satisfaction of the users or audience enough? Will they be able to recognize spontaneously that the need is being met, or will you need to prepare them to look for certain signs? How long is it reasonable to wait for results to show themselves? Is one trial enough to persuade others that the change shows real and significant benefits?

All these questions should be asked before the innovations are selected. However, all questions need not be answered affirmatively. Choosing usually is a matter of compromise and trade-off among a number of advantages and disadvantages. There is no precise way of evaluating these criteria. The advantages and disadvantages will be different for different school districts in different situations and, in large part, can be determined only by the local school personnel. They know what questions are most important and least important for the people in their system.

When you are in the midst of a choosing process, and before the final commitment to one way or another, try using the foregoing factors as a checklist. Even though precision is impossible, it is important to ask these questions in some form. All too often, when you survey the remains of a school initiative after an innovation has failed, you will find that some critical feasibility question was not asked before the decision to adopt was made.

Adapt

You have now chosen one intervention, but your work is not over. Because a selected innovation will not meet all of the 10 criteria above and others that you may want to add, you may want to modify or redesign it to make it better. You may want to make improvements to increase the amount of benefit or perceived benefit, to increase workability, and to increase diffusibility. If the change team has a lot of resources (dollars, time, and staff with creativity and appropriate skills in research and development), you may be able to reshape the innovation so completely that it becomes custom-made to fit your schools and their specific problems. Usually, however, you will not have such resources, so the less adaptation you have to do, the better off you are. This is why it is so important for the linker to be a good resource gatherer who can take maximum advantage of existing innovations that are tried and true.

> ### Modifications and Adjustments Lead to Buy-In
>
> In one district, the linking agent described the general willingness to modify a program as the greatest accomplishment from his work over the past year with two elementary schools:
>
> Teachers are modifying and adapting intervention strategies to better align with their professional capabilities and the needs of their classrooms. This indicates that there is buy-in regarding the specific intervention and that personnel are willing to put forth the effort to modify the intervention in a way that makes the program usable.

Respect the Developers and Minimize Redevelopment

With substantial help from the federal government over the past 35 years, university centers and laboratories all over the United States have developed and tested a wide array of educational innovations. This great investment was made so that linkers and other change agents, and the systems on whose behalf they work, would have a range of fully developed and pretested practices, procedures, materials, and services from which to choose. Many of these development projects began in the 1960s and have gone through several generations of redevelopment and improvement to meet the needs of a wide range of users, with greater benefit and easier, less costly, and less risky implementation. Therefore, in many topic areas, the potential user may have little adaptation to do.

There are good reasons to adopt off-the-shelf innovations, whether developed by academic researchers or by private sector developers and publishers. You will probably have more assurance about what the innovation will accomplish and more security that it will not fail or disrupt the situation it was designed to help. Home-grown innovations are inherently riskier, and they require much more creative effort for success. However, in accepting the development work of others as valid for your setting and adopting these off-the-shelf innovations, you need to think carefully whether they are a good match to your situation. Ask yourself these questions:

- Is the need addressed by this innovation aligned with the need as now defined by the school system (Stage 3: Examine)?
- Are the settings and situations in which this innovation was tried and tested similar enough to this school setting? Are the students they used in their test trials comparable to the students with whom you are working? Are the teachers similarly trained and oriented? Are the administrative support systems roughly equivalent?

If the answers are no, you will know that some amount of redevelopment will be required to adapt the innovation for your setting. The change team and involved stakeholders may have to invent or reinvent one or more aspects of the innovation, thus becoming developers themselves. You may even have to create your own innovation from scratch. But before you do, make sure that you have done your resource acquisition job as well as you can (Stage 4) so that you have some assurance that you are not reinventing the wheel.

Repackage and Relabel

Your first foray into the real world of change starts with words and images—the label and the package. These are the first visible, comprehensible stimuli you will provide to the school personnel who will be implementing the new innovation and using the new strategies. If these stimuli have positive connotations for your audience, that is fine; they probably cannot hurt and they may help, provided that they do not mislead and do not lead to falsely high expectations. If the labeling and packaging are neutral, that is, "black boxes" without labels, that is also probably OK; you are not hurting yourself with most people and perhaps helping yourself with the naturally curious among them.

However, if there is no other label, then "change" is the implicit label; if the package is a black box, then you are the package. Therefore, review again what was said in Stage 2: Relate about first encounters. What you look like, what you say at the outset, and the image you cast as a person may determine the fate of your change effort regardless of its inherent value. If the label turns off your audience, there is nothing to do but to change it before you start. If the package is ugly, messy, confusing, or blurry, repackage it before you start.

Plan the Implementation

The necessity of planning may seem obvious, but busy and creative people, including most change agents, tend to underplan. Plans often go awry, and bad plans are sometimes to blame, but even a bad plan is better than no plan. Good plans share three attributes: they are written down, they are shared, and they are flexible.

Importance of a Written Plan

Any plan should be committed to paper early on and should remain in written form as it passes through modifications on its way to finality. A paper plan puts something on the table; it allows sharing among the people involved in implementation; it pinpoints problems and gaps; and it makes the commitment to action real and distinct so that the trial will not fade away into the general fog of business as usual.

Importance of a Shared Plan

A plan should be shared as widely as possible among key players and stakeholders. At the school level, these people certainly include the principal and at the district level, the superintendent and the director of special education. Sharing serves at least five purposes. First, it strengthens the relationships necessary for success (Stage 2: Relate). Second, it allows affirmation of the need (Stage 3: Evaluate). Third, it provides an opportunity to add to the resource pool of knowledge and people and often aids in getting financing (Stage 4: Acquire). Fourth, a shared plan encourages a full analysis of possible areas of resistance and difficulty. Finally, it prepares the way to extend the innovation beyond the trial site (Stage 5: Extend).

Importance of a Flexible Plan

The written plan should always be seen as partly tentative and never so sacrosanct that it cannot be changed when circumstances change and unexpected problems arise. The linking agent should also have a clear idea of what parts of the plan can be changed and what parts cannot be changed to preserve the integrity of the trial.

Components of a Good Plan

A plan must be customized to address the individual needs of the school or school district you are working with and the specific project you are working to implement. Eight elements will help guide you in developing any plan: site selection, staffing chart, approval and commitment process, training plan, materials and other resource acquisition requirements, user preparations, timetable, and budget.

Components of a Good Plan

- Site selection
- Staffing chart
- Approval and commitment process
- Training plan
- Materials and other resource acquisition requirements
- User preparations
- Timetable
- Budget

Site Selection. The reasons for selecting the trial site and the procedures followed in making the selection should be clearly stated. The trial site and the population should balance conflicting considerations, such as success potential, urgency of need, and typicality or representativeness.

Just from this short list, you can see how difficult selecting a site can be. Success is often easiest where there are the most resources and perhaps the least need, and neither success probability nor neediness is likely to coincide with typicality. Perhaps the biggest pitfall in site selection comes from ease of entry. Sites to which access is provided easily may be very atypical, yet no linkers will want to go where they are not wanted. Raising site-selection issues in the plan and then discussing them among change team members prior to action may lead to better decisions and a greater awareness of the strengths and weaknesses of various sites when results are later evaluated. Site-selection issues become particularly critical when we look ahead to Stage 6: Extend, where we are working to extend the intervention from the trial site to other sites. At that stage, both success in the trial and typicality become very important.

Staffing. Guiding Change emphasizes teamwork by suggesting a change team that comes together and stays together throughout the process. The plan should identify present and potential members together with the roles they will play and the time commitments required of them. The staffing process will be well on its way before the implementation plan is committed to paper, but seeing it in black and white solidifies the commitment and may also signal some needed shifts in responsibilities and relationships.

Clearance. For most innovations that have a schoolwide or districtwide impact, especially those within the sphere of special education that involve the interplay of general and special education teachers and students, the approval process for change can take on a bureaucratic aspect. We can see this clearly in the Hilldale case, where much time was taken up in clearing the project with the superintendent, the school board, parent groups, principals, and so forth. All these clearances have to be anticipated and planned for in advance. It is not wasted time because the approval process is a key aspect of building relationships (Stage 2: Relate), getting people on board, and educating the various stakeholders whose long-term acceptance, goodwill, and commitment are essential for long-term success. However, it is advantageous for the written plan to suggest how clearances can be combined or streamlined. The clearance list may also suggest the need for additional team members or ways to divide the clearance tasks among members.

Training. Most educational innovations require staff training. The plan should specify who gets trained by whom, when, where, and at what cost. In the Hilldale case, training was a large part of the change activity, consuming much of the time of the linker and other change agents, a lion's share of resources, and an intricate web of approvals.

Materials. What materials are needed for every student? Every teacher? Every classroom? How many of each type? Where can these materials be acquired? Is there a sufficient supply for your needs? Can they be delivered on time? What is your cost? Is copying allowed? Will you have to make some of your own? Will you need special training or familiarization in their use? Are other resources required, such as substitute teachers? Special space allocation? Audiovisual equipment? Computers?

User Preparation. Do you need to make special advance announcements of what is going to happen? Pamphlets or memos describing the innovation? Should something be distributed to teachers, students, and parents? To the local newspaper? To community leaders?

Timetable. Perhaps the most important and revealing part of the plan is the timetable. It identifies all the puzzle pieces and defines how they fit together in a logical time sequence. The written timetable is a first reality check. Is this doable? Will it fit into the school calendar? Are the staff time allotments realistic?

Budget. The budget is the first thing and the last thing that require planning. You start with a tentative budget, perhaps with a fixed limit, and then shape what you are going to do to fit more or less within those constraints. At the end of the planning process, you have to revisit the budget to see whether it all fits. You may need to go back through the plan to cut or adjust this item or that until the whole thing adds up. Now it is time to act.

Act. Whether the innovation is home-grown or off the shelf or somewhere in between, it is now time to implement the chosen innovation. As you proceed, treat your actions as an experiment: Learn as you go along, improvise as necessary, and record what you are doing. Use your plan to guide you so that you can make adjustments; do it again without repeating your mistakes and you can teach and model the same process for others.

Whenever you have the opportunity, you should plan a pilot test of an innovation before making a final selection. A pilot test will allow you to eliminate obvious bugs before committing major resources. Limited tryouts of several innovations can give preliminary data on several of the criteria listed above to help you make rational choices. Above all, the trial demonstrates the degree of the innovation's relevance and suitability to the problem at hand. Because the trial phase can also be seen as an aspect of installation and gaining acceptance, it will be discussed again in Stage 6: Extend.

> **Point of Action**
>
> - Concern has been identified.
> - Relationships have been established.
> - Dimensions of needs have been examined.
> - Resources have been acquired.
> - Action has been chosen and planned.

Accepting Risk

Any change is by its very nature risky. The larger and more significant the change is, the more risk is involved. The more innovative the change is and the greater the departure from existing practice, the riskier it becomes. What does risk mean in this context? It means, first of all, that you might fail completely or in part to achieve what you intended. It also means that you might look foolish, ill prepared, or awkward. You are exposing yourself in an uncertain situation. These are all reasons people avoid change, especially any change that seems large or ambitious. However, risk is part and parcel of the change process. The linker and any other change agent must be prepared to take risks, and they must support the trial takers in their risk taking.

You can do a few things to minimize the fear associated with taking a risk. The first is to emphasize the quasi-experimental nature of the trial; it's OK to make mistakes because you can learn from them. Another is to provide a safety net in the form of group support. This is where the change team is so important. Risk takers should not feel that they are alone in this endeavor but should have colleagues trying the same things. Risk takers should also know that a principal and other personnel are solidly behind them and will back them up. The linker's role, as clearly shown in Hilldale and other case examples, is to back up the innovator with both a flow of information and an encouraging presence while making sure that the change team remains intact.

Overcoming Inertia

The first step is always the hardest. You need to understand and appreciate the psychology of those who are holding back. Something in all of us says, "When in doubt, do nothing" or "Let someone else do it first and then let's see what happens" or "I am getting along OK now [or I am struggling already now], so why should I take on something new?" Part of the role of the linking agent is to help school personnel overcome these doubts with a gentle shove if that is what it takes. The plan and the time line help because the commitment is there. The linker is needed to keep the change process on track and moving forward.

Training

Many educational innovations involve training. It is a major feature of the Hilldale case, for example. A good training program for users in advance of the actual trial does a lot to reduce the sense of risk and to overcome inertia. Training brings together the innovating teachers, allowing them to get to know one another, share their concerns, form mutual support groups, and participate more fully in the change team. A good training program is like a good change project if it incorporates these features:

- Open discussion of needs by participants (Stage 1: Care and Stage 3: Examine)
- Opportunities for getting acquainted and sharing mutual concerns and interests (Stage 2: Relate and Stage 4: Acquire)
- Clear demonstrations by believable models of the behaviors expected
- Opportunities to safely practice new behaviors and use new materials
- Feedback on first try-outs of these new behaviors and materials
- Commitment by participants to a trial in the classroom at the first opportunity
- Commitment to record and share results of the separate trials
- Commitment by trainers to continued availability and processing of feedback

Timing

Successful trials depend on good timing. The school calendar provides natural points of entry for many innovations, especially the beginning of the school year and the midyear break. However, the linker needs to consider whether these standard times are best for a particular introduction. What else is going on that might either contribute in a synergistic way or distract and detract? The summer break always seems to be the time for teacher training. The Hilldale case illustrates that winter weather in northern states can present unanticipated problems. The installation of a new superintendent is often seen as an opportunity for reform as the new leader seeks to put his or her own stamp on the system. New leaders are also a threat to innovations that have the stamp of the previous leader.

Accepting Stumbles

Innovators need to be able to accept the inevitability of minor errors and glitches despite the best planning. However well developed the innovation is, there is still a learning curve and a degree of adaptation that must be made on the go.

Recognizing and Managing Resistance

Some amount of resistance is also inevitable and may come from any of the key stakeholders—administrators, teachers, parents, or students—who are accustomed to the old ways. It is the task of the linker or change agent to help innovators anticipate and manage such resistance.

Protecting the Trial and the Integrity of the Test

Resistance will often be expressed through attempts to modify or downgrade the innovation. Such attempts may come from higher authorities who see preserving system order as their primary task. The innovators may be similarly tempted as they run into difficulties or seek to reduce risk. It then becomes the task of the linking agent or the change agent to intervene on behalf of the innovator or the innovation to maintain the integrity of the trial. The linker will have to make a judgment call about whether a given alteration is a legitimate and appropriate adaptation or a change that undermines the intent of the trial. For example, the downsizing that took place in Hilldale with the limited adoption of Morning Message was a legitimate adaptation because it did not change the essential purpose of the change and it allowed later additions from the larger ELP package.

Connecting the Trial to the Outside: Publicity

Although the linker must protect the innovation in its trial incubation stage, trying judiciously to limit the exposure of the risk-taking innovator, it also falls to the linker to bring publicity to the change effort as it begins to show success. The more that the change team and innovating users can be formed into a social network, the easier and more automatic this spread of effect becomes. This effect is well illustrated in the Morning Message diffusion in Hilldale toward the end of the first year. Much more will be said about this diffusion process in the following chapter (Stage 6: Extend).

Evaluate

The innovator and the linker need to be able to look critically at what they are doing both during the trial and in its aftermath. A trial is meaningless without an evaluation. You need to know whether you have been successful and to what extent. If you have not been successful, you need to examine why so that you can make adjustments and do better in a second round. Evaluation is the gateway to Stage 6, which extends the innovation both to improve and continue it in its current setting and to spread the new practices to other sites that might benefit.

Two aspects of the trial change should always be evaluated. They can be summed up under the terms *process* and *outcomes*. Process refers to how the project was implemented; outcome refers to the results of those actions. Imagine the trial as a kind of experiment. In the parlance of experimental science, the process refers to the independent variables and the outcomes are the dependent variables. Ideally you need to document both sets of variables before drawing any conclusions.

> **Evaluation Data Show Success**
>
> Over the years we collected formative data on the effect of using the Balanced Literacy Initiative. We found that our students showed a 1.0 to 1.67 growth after four months of full implementation. We are now collecting summative data to assess how to improve implementation in the future.
>
> —EMSTAC linking agent

What Is the Process?

Process includes all the actions that are taken during the trial from start to finish. Thus, an evaluation of process should assess the process of choosing the innovation, the process of adapting the innovation, the process of planning, and the processes involved in taking action. Here are sample process questions in each of these areas:

- Choosing
  - Was an adequate process of choosing undertaken?
  - Did this process adequately take into account the system's needs at the time?
  - Was there adequate participation by different stakeholders in the choosing?
  - Were the alternatives fairly representative of the knowledge base?
- Adapting
  - Did any problems with the chosen innovation require adaptation?
  - Was a serious effort made to adapt the innovation?
  - Did the adaptation seriously compromise the intentions of the developers?
- Planning
  - Was there a distinct and coherent planning effort?
  - Did a written plan allow the tracking of progress in specific terms?
  - Were stakeholders involved in the planning process?

- Acting
    - Was there any problem in accepting risk or overcoming inertia?
    - Was action taken in a timely manner subsequent to planning?
    - Was there a training program prior to introduction?
    - Did the training component include any of the eight elements suggested above?
    - Was the timing of the implementation appropriate?
    - Were there stumbles in implementation? If so, were they handled well?
    - Was there significant resistance to the change?

        a. Who resisted and why?
        b. Were these concerns taken into account?
        c. Was the resistance managed well?

    - Was the integrity of the trial maintained?
    - Was there adequate publicity for the trial so that key outsiders and potential future adopters were able to keep track of the progress of the project?

How Can You Evaluate Process?

A trial change effort is not the same as a research project, so a linker cannot be expected to simultaneously be a researcher. Thus, evaluation strategies must be trimmed to suit the typical reality that you will have little time and scant resources to devote to process evaluation. Here are three simple approaches:

- Preserve documentation on what happens.
- Keep a diary.
- Use the written plan to benchmark progress.

Preserve Documentation

Most significant change efforts leave a paper trail: write-ups of proposals, interoffice memos, e-mails, outlines of presentations, clearance requests, and so on. Keep a file of such items in chronological order, starting from your earliest initiatives. Some of this material may be quantitative, such as needs assessment data, number of children in various categories of disability, budgetary allocations, number of teachers and students involved in the trial, and amounts and types of materials or other print resources used. Some of the data may be qualitative, such as discussions among various stakeholders in e-mail messages and phone conversations. These kinds of data that result as a matter of course bear direct relevance to the trial.

Keep a Diary

As a project moves forward, it is important to keep some sort of diary that records your impression of major events while they are happening. It is best if you can maintain the discipline of at least one entry a week, making more frequent entries during periods of high activity. This diary can later be reviewed as a narrative description of the project. Note in the diary weekly activities, encounters with key people, attitudes of various people toward the project at different times, the processes in choosing one innovation over others, impressions of resistance or enthusiastic embrace of project ideas, times when the project was presented especially well or poorly, and difficulties that teachers seem to be having understanding the materials or incorporating the program into their daily routine.

Use the Written Plan

It is beneficial to prepare an outline of the project from beginning to end with expected times for reaching each benchmark. Then, create a parallel plan outline to note the actual progress, including deviations from the original and some indication of why these deviations were necessary.

What Are the Outcomes?

Broadly speaking, outcomes come in three varieties: positive, null, and negative. Positive outcomes are circumstances that are attributable to the project and that improve the situation in the educational setting for someone, ideally, the students. The ultimate goal of most school change projects is to have a positive impact on the educational experience of students. This positive impact is sometimes difficult to define. Nevertheless, it is important for you, as the linking agent, to help the system recognize and value a broad spectrum of possible positive outcomes, including improved attitudes toward learning and stabilized classroom environments.

Null outcomes reflect either a lack of evidence that any change has taken place as a result of the trial or positive evidence that there are no differences between sites receiving and not receiving the trial change effort.

Negative outcomes reflect changes that are harmful or detrimental to the educational setting or to someone in it. It can be argued that any trial with a null outcome is harmful and thus a negative outcome because it represents a waste of resources, time, and energy. However, it can also be argued that the lessons learned through such an experience are beneficial to school personnel as they later work to implement other attempts at system improvements.

Program-Specific Outcomes

Every innovative program promises good results of a specific nature: improved test scores, fewer classroom disruptions, more students having access to the general education curriculum, fewer special education referrals of minority students, and many others. These expected outcomes should be fairly obvious before you even start a new program, and the more specific, observable, and quantifiable they are, the better. A well-designed and well-packaged program is likely to come with built-in outcome measures so that when you are done, you can examine the results and persuasively demonstrate the effectiveness of the innovation and the impact on others. If you choose an innovation without clearly predefined expected outcomes, it is important to establish some measurable outcomes prior to trial.

General Outcomes—Positive

For any educational innovation, the most prized positive outcomes will be in the areas of acquired and improved skills, learning abilities, and knowledge of anything valued by the culture, starting with literacy and numeracy. Special educators know well that other basics extend well beyond these intellectual items to include many social skills and proficiencies, such as the ability to work with others, to cooperate, to follow directions, to maintain an orderly work space, and so on. Indeed, one task for the special educator is to teach general educators that such outcomes are not trivial and are not to be taken for granted.

General Outcomes—Null

Null outcomes are the silent outcomes, the evidence that nothing of consequence has really changed as a result of your interventions. They can be especially elusive because there is always an ongoing stream of happenings and signs that things have happened, which are easily attributable to what you have done. As the linking agent, you want to believe, particularly if you have worked hard to do something. You may be especially reluctant to dismiss what you see as outcomes as something that would have happened anyway, regardless of your efforts.

General Outcomes—Negative

At certain times and in given situations, your interventions can actually do harm. This is particularly true if the intervention is being implemented with great adjustments that alter its integrity or if the implementation proceeds without the necessary resources or support. Even changes that have measurable benefits for one particular stakeholder may have negative outcomes for others.

Consider, for example, an innovation that supports the inclusion of students with special needs in the general education classroom. Measuring the success of the intervention is not as simple as counting the numbers of students with disabilities included in the general education classroom. Such factors as student learning (both for the students with disabilities and their nondisabled peers) and collaboration between general education and special education teachers are critical to evaluating the program's success. Thus, you would want to measure the effect of the program on both typically developing children and children with disabilities. Is the teacher-student interaction and instruction time threatened for nondisabled children? Are children with disabilities receiving all the appropriate services? As with any intervention, it is essential to evaluate the project from the perspective of all stakeholders to objectively and thoroughly determine the impact and outcomes. A positive effect for one group may result in a negative effect for another. Assessing the impact from all perspectives will ensure comprehensive evaluation.

Can You Measure Outcomes?

It is important to take an expansive view of what constitute outcomes and to keep in mind a broad range of possible outcomes, positive or negative. To stretch your thinking about outcomes, consider the effects on all the stakeholders and on the system as a whole, not just on the primary targets or beneficiaries of the change. Look for unanticipated outcomes and outcomes that affect the attitudes and motivations of different players. For example, a change that affects the social atmosphere or the self-esteem of various players may be important just for these reasons.

How can these outcomes be measured? Educators and program evaluators have several assessment techniques for just that purpose.

Standardized Tests of Knowledge, Reasoning, and Performance

For many educators, the gold standard of outcome measurement is the standardized test score. If you have them and they show something, great. But often, you do not. More often, you know that such tests are neither realistic nor fair in appraising overall student success or the quality of educational opportunity. They may even be irrelevant. It all depends on what you are trying to do. The advantages of such tests, if available and appropriate, is that they are quantitative and have great credibility up the administrative ladder as well as with parents and the community at large.

Ad Hoc Tests

Most of the time, the type of innovation chosen will directly suggest the appropriate outcomes and outcome measurements. Some of the most credible and valid measures fall into this category, particularly if they are both quantitative and behavioral. For example, a program to improve school discipline might be expected to produce fewer trips to the principal's office or fewer calls for police intervention. Among such ad hoc measures are the following:

- Behavioral changes: check-off self-report
- Behavioral changes: observers' judgments or ratings
- Behavioral changes: linker's and change team members' ratings
- Analysis of student work (e.g., grades or ratings of work samples)
- Participant self-reports
- Participant open discussion groups (focus groups)

Assumptive Outcome Assessment

Even when no easily measurable outcomes are available, it is sometimes justifiable to believe that the outcomes were positive. This is what might be called the assumptive outcome test: You did what you were supposed to do. Therefore, the results must have been what they were in other cases where they had the time and resources to do a proper evaluation. This kind of outcome measurement may not be as foolish as it first sounds; this is what physicians routinely do when they prescribe medicines that have FDA approval. Sometimes they wait around to measure the results in terms of whether the patient did or did not get better, but often the patient is not even seen for follow-up. Most trial change efforts are not supposed to be experiments in a scientific sense. Random assignment to conditions, experimental and control groups, or a set of outcome measures that meets high standards of reliability and validity is rarely available.

Akin to assumptive outcome tests are the "feels right" and "feels good" effects. The linker or key stakeholders in the change develop an impression that what happened worked well but are not able to articulate what makes them feel this way. This is the weakest form of outcome evaluation.

Extension, Copying, and Diffusion as Inferred Positive Outcomes

The next chapter of *Guiding Change* will get into what happens after the trial, how an innovation is extended into a second and third year, and how it spreads beyond the trial site. In a real sense, the extension of the innovation in any of these ways also represents a positive outcome and some proof of success for the initial trial.

Cautions on Evaluation

Although evaluating the trial is very important, you can go overboard in this direction. A few caveats are in order.

1. Do not let the evaluation process interfere with the innovation. Unless evaluation is somehow a part of what you are trying to do, the less intrusive the evaluation, the better. Do not allow the evaluation to intimidate your teachers, students, or yourself.

2. Do not pay too much attention to outliers, high or low. Even though innovations involving special education are dealing with people and circumstances that are special for a variety of reasons, you cannot expect that what you are doing is going to work for everybody. Extreme cases often swallow up the energies of the change team out of all proportion to their real importance. Recognize these as outliers and not as indications that your project has gone off track.

3. Place your change effort in the stream of all activities that are affecting your site simultaneously. A lot of parallel innovative activity will probably affect your effort in some way. It may be a positive synergistic effect—all ships rising on the same tide—but it may also be a confounding factor when you try to separate out the influence of your change trial from everything else that is going on.

Using the Results

The most important reason for an evaluation is to have some basis for what to do next. You will have several important decisions to make. The first is whether to continue, to repeat the cycle into a second and a third year. The results of your outcomes analysis will tell you whether you should go on, whereas the results of your process evaluation will tell you how to proceed, what to change, and what to add or take away. The specifics involved in these decisions are taken up in the next chapter as Stage 6: Extend. Before you move on to the next stage, you need to learn more about how to share the results with others as a way to initiate discussions.

Sharing With Your Team

Have an open discussion on what the findings mean. Discuss process findings in relation to outcome findings. Make sure that all team members understand the findings and are given a chance to offer explanations of what they think they mean and the implications for further action. Specifically, discuss what changes should be considered in the innovation for the next round, assuming that you have reached a consensus that a next round is called for. Recall the earlier choosing process and compare what you got from this effort with what was promised originally and what the other alternatives also promised.

Package the Findings

Highlight what you and your team think is important. To inform a larger audience, prepare a brief report on what you have done. This report will have many later uses but represents a minimum bid for the attention and interest of the larger community of potential users.

Share Results With a Larger Sphere of System Stakeholders

Not quite the same as the brief report for popular consumption, the presentation to other stakeholders, including people up the hierarchy of special education and general education, is a social process that requires some forethought. Again, your change team should be involved. Discuss with your team what results should be shared. Try to agree on who these stakeholders are, what emphasis should be taken with them, and which findings should be highlighted.

The trial is over. Now it is time to think about how to extend the effort in the start-up site and to other sites.

Try: Summary

A well-organized innovation trial should contain five steps in sequence. First, the major stakeholders should review the assembled knowledge resources and make a deliberate and collective choice about what appears to be the best set of actions or best program among competing alternatives. Criteria for choice should include promised benefit, validity and credibility of supporting data, compatibility with setting, and the promise of widespread applicability after trial.

The chosen innovation should be reshaped to the extent necessary to make it applicable to the intended trial setting. A flexible written plan, specifying selected site, staff, clearances, materials and training, schedule, and budget, should be developed and shared among relevant parties.

As the plan is implemented, it should be viewed as an experiment in which inertia and resistance are anticipated, risks and stumbles are accepted, and redirections of course are made while retaining the basic integrity of the innovation and the implementation plan. The trial effort should be evaluated in terms of both its process and its outcomes. Process evaluation should account for and document what happened at each step, from choosing to adapting to planning to implementing. Outcome evaluation should consider the results of standardized tests and other performance measures and include attitudinal and behavioral changes by all participants and unanticipated outcomes, both positive and negative. The change team should review the results of both types of evaluations and share them with a wider circle of stakeholders and potential future adopters. The evaluation of the trial should serve as a springboard to the next phase of the change process, which is the continuation and strengthening of the innovation in the initiating site and the extension to other sites.

Stage 6

Extend

Gaining Deeper and Wider Acceptance

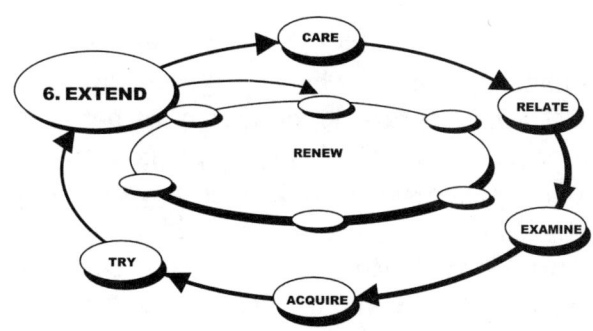

ORGANIZER QUESTIONS

- What two meanings of Extend must the linker understand?
- What are the main ways to solidify and extend changes at the trial site?
- What are effective ways to extend the trial to proximate sites?
- How do you infuse the change and the change process in the larger system?
- What are the stepping-stones of diffusion and how do they work?

Even a partially successful trial does not end the change process. One cycle is about to be completed, but other cycles are now beginning. For the trial site, that new beginning is the continuation phase, the second-year follow-through, which is the real test of whether an innovation will become part of the ongoing routine of the system. For the linker, that kind of extension is important, but equally important is the diffusion of these hard-earned innovative practices to a wider group of users: other teachers, other classrooms, even other schools.

Extending the acceptance and adoption of a new program throughout the system requires special skills and understandings that are of a different order. Here is where all that is now known about marketing and salesmanship comes into play and is a major reason the change team should include opinion leaders as well as innovators. Early adopters, those who are most eager and willing to participate in the first trial, are atypical; they are adventurers and risk takers, often somewhat on the margin of the larger system. Now the change process must go beyond these courageous few to reach the many. Many approaches are possible; some are well tested and well documented in the strong research tradition of the diffusion of innovations. This is where to turn to understand how to complete Stage 6: Extend.

During this Extend stage, the focus of effort turns to evaluating the effects of the first trial, accounting for errors and resistance encountered, making adjustments to the innovation and mode of implementation, and now extending the innovation to include new sites, new classrooms, and new facets of the program.

> **Special Education Linking Agents in Action**
>
> In April, the linking agent was invited to observe a kindergarten class at North Slope where Morning Message was being used daily as part of the morning opening exercises. The experienced kindergarten teacher gave an enthusiastic report: "I have seen tremendous gains in language skills! Since we started using Morning Message, the kids have learned how to ask questions, a concept I have had trouble teaching in the past." She expressed an interest in becoming the county Morning Message expert and coordinating teacher; she was willing to do workshops with other teachers or to model lessons.

Issues About Adoption and Diffusion

Five distinct issues should shape our thinking about extended adoption and diffusion:

Solidifying Adoption at the Trial Site (Keeping Going)

Learning what it can from a successful first trial, the trial site should commit to a second round. Only with repetition will the change begin to integrate into the teachers' behaviors and the classroom routine. More effort by the change team may be required to fully integrate the intervention into the ongoing life of the school system.

Expanding Change at the Trial Site (Going Deeper)

Although solidifying is important, keeping the innovative process *open and flexible* is equally important. A delicate balance must be maintained between these two goals. Expansion also may involve making small amendments to the intervention, adding *more innovative features* to the core, and expanding the program to more classrooms at the trial site. Most important, expanding the innovation should not be seen just in isolated quantitative terms but within the larger context of a movement toward more systemic and fundamental improvements in the local system.

Extending the Trial to Proximate Sites (Follow-On Adoption)

The first trial site is often just a subunit within the larger school system or cluster of potential users. If this is the case, an important first-order transfer is to other sites in that same cluster. In a school context, this usually means other teachers and other classrooms in that school. If the intervention is specific to students with a particular disability, the cluster comprises other teachers in the school district who work with this type of student. The first trial user can be a demonstrator and model for the others to follow. This process of extending the project has been described in diffusion research as the six-step adoption model: awareness? interest? evaluation? trial? adoption? integration? This adoption process recapitulates the trial process (Stage 5) in a streamlined, stripped-down form. However, not all follow-on users adhere to this pattern. Other adoption patterns are jumpers, fast starters, fast followers, average followers, late followers, and forced followers.

Extending Adoption to the Larger System (Diffusion I)

People accept change as members of social groups (family, neighborhood, school, community). The linker can influence widespread acceptance within a community and a school district by applying principles from diffusion research, including the six-step adoption process noted above.

Going Wider: Strategies and Tactics (Diffusion II)

Linkers who wish to see changes reach a larger audience beyond their local communities can do many things to enhance diffusion statewide and even nationally.

Solidifying Adoption at the Trial Site (Keeping Going)

At this point, you have completed Stage 5: You have successfully completed a trial. What's next? The first thing is to look carefully at what happened to determine what should be done differently next time—what should be added, smoothed out, or altered in some way so that it will work better, have greater impact, and take less time and energy. In short, you are looking forward to repeating the trial a second and a third time, gaining mastery through practice and feedback on results and gaining reassurance and comfort from the growing realization that what you have done is doable.

Lessons From the Trial Site

Implementation. The Waterford Early Reading Program, a software-based early intervention literacy program, was implemented in three pilot schools last year in Pleasant Valley School District. The linking agent worked in collaboration with administrators in the school district, the Elementary and Middle School Technical Assistance Center (EMSTAC), and local school personnel to implement the new intervention.

Evaluation. Currently the district is working through the plan that was initially developed for implementation, comparing what was intended and what actually happened throughout the process of Try. This comparison will help the linking agent and colleagues determine how both the intervention and the implementation of the intervention can be modified and adjusted to better meet the needs of school personnel using the new intervention. The linking agent is also collecting formal evaluations to provide additional information about how to increase the impact of the program in the current sites and to extend the program to new sites. Anecdotal reports from teachers and principals indicate favorable results for the students participating in the program. Supported by such feedback, the school district and the linking agent have made a commitment to a second year.

Knowledge Base

Continuation and Integration

Fullan (2001b, p. 89) states the issue clearly: "The problem of continuation is endemic to all new programs irrespective of whether they arise from external initiative or are internally developed." Many studies indicate that sustained support (usually from outsiders) is necessary to overcome barriers and to enable schools to make necessary adjustments while maintaining the integrity of the change effort (Huberman & Crandall, 1983; Loucks, 1983; Huberman & Miles, 1984; Little, 1984; McLaughlin, 1990).

Yin (1978) has proposed that proof of "routinization" of an institutional change is found in what he calls "passage completion" and "cycle survival." An instance of the former is gaining a line on the school district's line-item budget, whereas the latter is well exemplified by the school year. The validity of this formulation was borne out by Huberman and Miles (1984) in their longitudinal analysis of the relative success of 12 educational innovations (see their Table 39, p. 208).

The Concerns-Based Adoption Model (CBAM) (Hall & Hord, 1987, 2001) provides tools to "keep a finger on the pulse" of change and to collect the information needed to monitor progress, especially at the later Level-of-Use (L-o-U) stages, "routine," defined as the user of the innovation making few or no changes and having an established pattern of use (IVA); "refinement," the user of the innovation is making changes to increase outcomes (IVB); and "integration" the user of the innovation is

> making deliberate efforts to coordinate its use with others (V). This model's guidelines help readers understand the different concerns stakeholders experience as change progresses. "We would define *minimum institutionalization* as the time when all, or nearly all, members of an organization: (1) are using the innovation at L-o-U IVA or higher; (2) have resolved their self and task concerns; and (3) are using 'acceptable' configurations of the innovation. Minimum institutionalization should be the first strategic objective. Without achieving this platform, sustained use of the innovation is in jeopardy" (Hall & Hord, 2001, p. 224).
>
> The change agent can support continuation and integration in a number of ways, introducing CBAM-type measurement and reminding innovators of the need to move through Yin's passages and cycles before claiming success. Elmore (1996) suggests that a successful support strategy must "embody an explicit theory about how human beings learn to do things differently" (p. 24). Evans (1996) seems to be moving toward such a theory when he elaborates on the Lewin model by positing five "tasks of change," which can be facilitated by a change agent: "unfreezing," "moving from loss to commitment," "moving from old competence to new competence," "moving from confusion to coherence," and "moving from conflict to consensus" (p. 56). His model clearly combines psychological and social elements and moves us in the direction of diffusion research (see next Knowledge Base segment).

Learning From the First Trial

The platform for the second trial is the evaluation of the first trial. Start the Extend process with a basic question: Do the outcomes of the first trial justify a second round? Hard outcomes data may make the answer to this question easy, but most of the time you do not have an indisputable view of the real outcomes. You are left with a scattering of impressions, your own and others, and typically a mixed message. When you weigh all these outcome elements together, do you sense that there is a go for round two or not? In making the judgment on outcomes, you also have to include your view of the process. Think of what the outcomes might have been if the process had been more satisfactory—if you had had more resources, involved more or different people, done a better search, had done a better job of planning. These process questions should now be posed not as "What if?" but as "What can you do better on a second round?"

Committing to a Second Round

Having learned from the trial and knowing what must be done on a second trial, you need to test the feasibility waters once again. Are the personnel still in place? The resources? The commitments? What has changed over the year to change the nature of the task, making it easier or harder? During the trial, you have established what is sometimes called a temporary system, a mini-infrastructure of people and tasks that can get the job done. Ideally, most of this infrastructure will still be in place as you start the second round. That system gives you a strategic advantage as you go forward. If it is disrupted or dispersed, your first job will be to rebuild it.

Staying Flexible

You must always be willing and able to reassess all aspects of the change, even to include a reconsideration of the innovation choice itself. The key word is *openness*. Try to remain open to new ideas and to including new people with different viewpoints on your team.

Recycling the Major Steps of the Trial Stage as the Linker Backs Off

If you as a linker are heavily involved in the trial phase, it is now time for you to work on passing off the activity and the responsibility for implementation to others in the school system. It is important to make the intervention theirs in every sense: as something they are doing without your help, as something they own and is part of them, and as something for which they assume responsibility for continuing.

Internalizing

Adopting anything new requires providing the right kind of support until the innovation comes to be seen as "just part of the way we do things around here." A key concept is internalization, which begins at the start of any change project and grows during the implementation of the initiative in the first year; in the second year, things should run more smoothly. This process starts with the teachers' behavior and the classroom routines. The teachers know what to do and have built a strong bridge between special and general education that they can comfortably cross back and forth.

Improving Chances for Continuation

The linker's special task is to lead the school system toward self-help and responsibility for maintaining the innovation. Chances for continuance can be improved in several ways: continuing reward, practice and routinization, structural integration into the system, continuing evaluation, providing for continuing maintenance, ensuring ongoing administrative and political support, and continuing adoption capability. The linker can play a helpful role on each of these fronts.

> **Ways to Improve Likelihood of Continuance**
>
> - Continuing reward
> - Practice and routinization
> - Structural integration into the system
> - Continuing evaluation
> - Continuing maintenance
> - Ongoing administrative and political support
> - Continuing adoption

Continuing Reward. Positive reinforcement is the most important influence on human behavior. School personnel participating in the innovation must feel that there is a payoff in one way or another, and they must be able to see that the pay-off continues over time. As a linking agent, you should do all you can to make sure that the rewards are and continue to be visible. Rewards for innovation come in a number of ways. The innovation may pay off directly in improved performance, reduced costs, and saved time and labor. When these direct benefits are not immediately clear, the indirect rewards, such as the continuing encouragement and approval of others, become very important. One major reason for follow up is to provide this kind of support; the knowledge that "someone out there really cares" can be a crucial factor in promoting continued use.

Practice and Routinization: Taking the Change Inside. True adoption of an innovation does not come automatically with nominal acceptance. School personnel must become familiar with it, trying it repeatedly in the situations that are natural to them. Early trials take a lot of time and effort because change does not come easily. For a long time, teachers are likely to feel awkward and artificial even if they believe that the innovation represents a desirable and appropriate change. They must get through this period before the linker can be sure that the innovation will be accepted. Ideally, the innovation should eventually become a routine part of everyday school activity. It should become something that can be taken up and used automatically without an excessive amount of concentrated effort.

Structural Integration Into the System. Sustainable innovations become part of the way of life of the school system, embedded in everyday behavior. For this to happen, the innovation must be integrated into the existing structure. People must be given time to learn to use the new strategies and then must be given the resources to implement the program (e.g., money to buy it, run it, or maintain it). The willingness of school leaders to accommodate an innovation is probably the best index to their real attitudes toward it.

Continuing Evaluation. Some provision should be made for reinspecting and reevaluating the innovation over time. This type of activity ensures against deterioration in the quality of the innovation and provides an added incentive and reminder that the innovation is still supposed to be in operation. Evaluation need not be rigorous and detailed measurement and analysis, but it should be a self-consciously objective inspection and reappraisal, preferably performed by someone who is informed about, but not personally invested in, the innovation. Obviously, the larger the investment in the innovation and the greater its presumed impact, the more attention should be paid to reevaluation. Evaluation is one of many tasks that the linking agent should encourage others to undertake, partly because it is time-consuming but mainly because the linker may be too invested in the innovation to take an objective view. If you have expended a lot of energy in gaining acceptance for an innovation, you may not be an objective judge of its effectiveness because you will want to believe that it is being widely used in an efficient and beneficial way.

Continuing Maintenance. Regardless of the type of innovation—hardware innovations, new instructional models, or new patterns of management—breakdowns and misapplications are bound to occur after the initial installation. A maintenance system to deal with these situations is needed. Because the original linking agent cannot predict when a breakdown will occur and cannot remain on the scene indefinitely, maintenance should be a built-in function provided by someone you have trained. Without maintenance, you may get a rapid erosion of acceptance after failures begin to occur. The inability to correct errors and breakdowns rapidly breeds a distrust of the innovation, negative reactions, and rumors that the innovation will not work and will be more trouble than it is worth.

Ongoing Administrative and Political Support. Full insertion of the innovation into the ongoing life of the classroom and the school also requires support from the larger system. The principal must be behind it. The special education office must provide backup. If the intervention needs any special allocation of space, material, teacher time, or funding, these must now be provided on more than a temporary and tentative basis.

Continuing Adaptation Capability. Sophisticated acceptance and adoption require flexibility and an ability to adapt as well as adopt. Over time, the school system's and the individual user's circumstances may change. If the users can reshape the innovation to meet their changing needs, they will be more likely to continue using it effectively.

If you take care of these areas as you formulate your strategy, you are likely to succeed in stabilizing the innovation. However, complete stabilization of a particular innovation may not be desirable in the long run. Sophisticated consumers accept innovations only as long as they are more beneficial than competing innovations. Thus, stabilization should be only partial, never total. School personnel need to retain the flexibility and freedom to discontinue an innovation when something better comes along.

Expanding Change at the Trial Site

Once you have a plan, you should not be overly rigid in the way you carry it out. You must remain flexible, ever willing and able to change your plans as you gather more data on the system and its reactions to the innovation. As you proceed, you may, for example, find that the innovation is completely unacceptable to a large minority and that it divides the community, causing unhealthy stress and conflict. Such a reaction should lead you to revise the strategy of gaining acceptance; to readapt (redesign, repackage, etc.) the innovation so that it is more acceptable; or perhaps to abandon the innovation altogether in favor of one that is more acceptable to this community, addresses a more significant concern (Stage 1: Care), or diffuses more readily. To maintain a flexible posture, you should always be prepared to readapt the innovation, shift gears, and change your implementation strategy.

Readapt the Innovation

Even when you have done a very careful job of selecting and adapting the innovation prior to introducing it to the school system, you may still find that more adaptation is necessary. You should be prepared to give concessions to meet various objections so that the key elements of the change are accepted. To ensure greater understanding of the nature of the innovation, be prepared to translate the relevant information into terms that users will find more familiar, more acceptable, and more meaningful.

Shift Gears

Timing is crucial, and the system may not be where you thought it was. Therefore, be ready to shift gears—down, up, or even into reverse—in response to the extent and nature of the resistance you encounter.

Shifting Down. You may find that you have expected too much of your colleagues and that they are unable to absorb information and to adapt to the innovation as rapidly as you had planned. Your plans should be flexible. Schedules are important because they point you toward specific goals and keep the whole process moving forward, but they are not sacrosanct. Be prepared to reset projected dates for any activity and any stage at any point along the way. Never proceed to a next stage until you have trustworthy feedback that the group or key members are with you.

Shifting Up. Sometimes you may actually overanticipate resistance. When you sense that school personnel are more sophisticated or more open than anticipated, you may want to accelerate your program. Do not be too hasty about jumping ahead. Beware of silent resistance. When you end a presentation and ask, "Are there any questions?" but get no questions, it may mean that they are not really with you yet or are not fully engaged. Key opinion leaders, in particular, will often be cautious at first and will want to talk it over with trusted associates, maybe without you around. Innovators, in contrast, may be quick studies, eager to push ahead. These innovators are useful allies, but they are not the key to gaining acceptance from the larger group. Their enthusiasm can sometimes lead you astray.

Reversing Gears. The common belief that if at first you don't succeed, try, try again may not always be true in gaining acceptance for innovations. Sometimes, more pressure and more hard salesmanship will only increase the resistance. This is why your diagnosis of opposing forces is so important.

> **Evaluation Data Guides the Plan**
>
> Prospect School District was very successful in implementing a new behavior program in one of its middle schools last year. Originally, the linking agent and the change team intended to scale up and spread the program to the other middle schools in the district. However, the evaluation data collected indicated a number of adjustments that needed to be made to maximize the effectiveness of the program. Thus, it was decided that rather than expand to new classrooms, the program will target the same classrooms for more intense implementation and evaluation and training in additional techniques.
>
> Although we intended to scale up the program, the data revealed that it would be more appropriate and beneficial at this time for all currently participating teachers to delve deeper into the program, making the necessary adjustments and learning more about the program prior to spreading the intervention to new classrooms.
>
> —EMSTAC linking agent

Frequently you will be more successful in the long run if you retreat in the face of strong opposition, concentrating instead on reducing the motivation for this resistance.

Change Your Implementation Strategy

Throughout, *Guiding Change* has urged linkers to adopt an open and collaborative strategy with the key stakeholders in the school district. This posture is more likely than any other to ensure the best use of new knowledge. Collaboration works for three reasons: First, it gets the key people involved and motivated; second, it improves the quality of the adoption because the innovation is understood better; and third, it may improve the quality of the innovation itself because school personnel can make valuable contributions as they adapt it to their particular settings. An additional reason for choosing collaboration is purely ethical: It is the right way to treat other human beings. Participation is the best way to do business even when it is slower and less effective in getting you to where you want to go. To choose to be purposefully noncollaborative is to break faith with the people you intend to help; such a stance presumes that school personnel are unwilling or unable to innovate on their own initiative and must be coerced, cajoled, or tricked into acceptance. But *sometimes* collaboration just will not work. When it fails, you should consider alternatives, ranging from complete abandonment to complete deception.

Adding More Innovative Features to the Core

In many cases, such as Hilldale, the original trial will actually be of a downsized innovation or a component of a more complex and multifaceted package. An initial successful trial sets the stage for introducing more elements, which teachers in Hilldale did when they expanded from Morning Message into other features of the Early Literacy Project (ELP). The caveat is to make sure that the adopting group is ready for the additions. Is the members' comfort level with the original component high enough? Are they eager enough to go on to these expansions?

Adding More Adopters at the Trial Site

Even at the trial site, only one or two teachers may actually adopt the innovation on the first round while the others hold back, waiting to see whether the first-round trial is successful. Many of these holdouts can be encouraged to jump in on the second round, thus expanding the adopter pool at the site.

Moving Toward More Systemic and Fundamental Improvements

The originally adopted trial innovation may be the opening wedge in an expanding effort to reform the local system. In the Hilldale case study, Morning Message was one among many changes that an ambitious and forward-looking principal was making to improve the overall functioning of her school as a system for integrated learning. Any single innovation can be a door opener, and

Morning Message, with its immediate and visible classroom rewards, played that role at North Slope.

You also need to step back and look at the larger picture. Recall that you are now completing one round in a cycle, having worked through from an original concern to a defined need to a solution for that need, which you have now applied to the situation at hand. Has anything changed in this larger picture? Has the level of concern (Stage 1: Care) changed as a result of your efforts or for some other reason? Is a new need configuration now in place? Presumably you are now confronted with a new configuration of relationships as well: new leaders, new teachers, and teachers who may have changed their views.

Special educators are well aware of the unending nature of special needs. The hope for any particular innovation is that it will lead to a better way to approach improving the services and the underlying system of support. Your innovative drive has been fueled by the care that you started with. As a result of the successful trial, you are now in a better position to stimulate more caring by a larger set of people for two reasons. First, you have focused a lot of energy on a particular set of needs. Second, you have shown that something can be done about them. Your experience therefore feeds into a new round of problem solving, which involves a larger number of people at the original trial site and, potentially at least, at other proximate sites and even remote sites that become aware of what you have done.

Extending the Trial to Proximate Sites (Follow-On Adoption)

Most people adopt changes because those about them are adopting the same changes. It seems safe and reasonable to make the changes, and they have a certain sense that if they do not, they will fall behind. However, to bring people to this point—where change seems like the normal and right thing to do—a lot of other things have to take place first.

Diffusion studies, a well-established tradition of research in the social sciences, examine how the adoption of a given innovation spreads throughout a group. The findings are remarkably consistent across different fields; medicine, agriculture, and education have been the most studied. Moreover, the findings are very useful in designing approaches to the spread of innovations that you care about. Therefore, in this and the next sections, you will find brief summaries of diffusion research, first as they apply to individuals in a group and second as they apply to changing a larger system.

> **A Growing Initiative**
>
> Over the past year, the linking agent in the Springflower School District has focused implementation efforts on expanding the program in the two initial schools to include the preschool program and the other special education classes that were not included in the first year of implementation.
>
> Approximately 40% of the teachers in the two schools are involved in the initiative at this time. These teachers have started working with the remaining teachers in the schools and have begun to provide workshops on inclusion-based practices.
>
> Beyond the work in these initial sites, the linking agent is responding to a request by another school that heard about the initiative and is working with a new school site to introduce inclusion in a fourth-grade classroom.

> ## Knowledge Base
>
> ### Diffusion Research
>
> Elmore (1996) poses an interesting dilemma when he asserts that "the closer an innovation gets to the core of schooling, the less likely it is that it will influence teaching and learning on a large scale" (p. 4). The implication is that the most profound changes in education are not transportable. Even when the essential truth of this observation is accepted, however, it can also be asserted with substantial empirical support that many features of many innovations are widely spread across the entire educational system over time and become so embedded that they are no longer considered innovations and their project and program origins are long forgotten (Elmore & McLaughlin, 1988).
>
> One way to unravel the confusion about what gets transferred and what distinguishes small-scale from large-scale change is to treat each element of a complex innovation initiative as a discrete element that can be traced as it travels from person to person and group to group. This leads directly into the field of diffusion research, most ably summarized and synthesized by the rural sociologist Everett M. Rogers (1962, 1983, 1995). The originator of diffusion research within the field of education was Paul Mort (1964), who traced the diffusion of administrative innovations among school districts in New York State, starting in the 1930s. Rogers was able to point out that Mort's findings were remarkably consistent with what had been found in agriculture, medicine, third-world development, and other fields of study. Diffusion follows a predictable pattern of slow early spread among innovators until a critical mass of opinion leaders is involved. After that, the adoption curve rises sharply in an "S" pattern until 90% saturation is reached. Then it slows as the last laggards come on board. Carlson (1965) was able to replicate Mort's findings, tracing the adoption of the "new math" curriculum introduced in the late 1950s, adding sociometric data to show how opinion leaders functioned as a key element. Whereas Mort had concluded that "the average American school lags twenty-five years behind the best practice," Carlson found that modern math reached saturation in only five years. Few in education have followed this research strategy, since Carlson. Rogers, in summarizing diffusion studies in education, did not cite any work since 1965, although diffusion studies have expanded by the thousands in other fields of study.
>
> This lack of attention to diffusion studies may be somewhat misleading, however. Influenced by the successful example of the diffusion of agricultural innovations, substantially supported by the Cooperative Extension Service (Rogers, 1988), the U.S. Office of Education and later the Department of Education has sought in various ways to establish an education equivalent (e.g., the National Diffusion Network and many types of school and regional networks devoted to one or another type of change). Although many states have developed their own educational service centers, often based in counties, it is noteworthy that no federal initiative in this area has achieved institutional status.
>
> Special education may be somewhat of an exception. For some years, the Office of Special Education Programs has supported an interconnected network of regional resource centers and research facilities. The availability of this extensive technical assistance and dissemination infrastructure at the national, regional, and state levels (McInerney, Osher, & Kane, 1997) suggests that a new linker role as advocated in *Guiding Change* may be an innovation whose time has come.

How Individuals Accept Change and Adopt Innovations

In this age of the Internet and instant mass communication, it may appear that innovations can be adopted instantly. This may be true for some types of

Figure 6.1 The Six Phases of Adoption

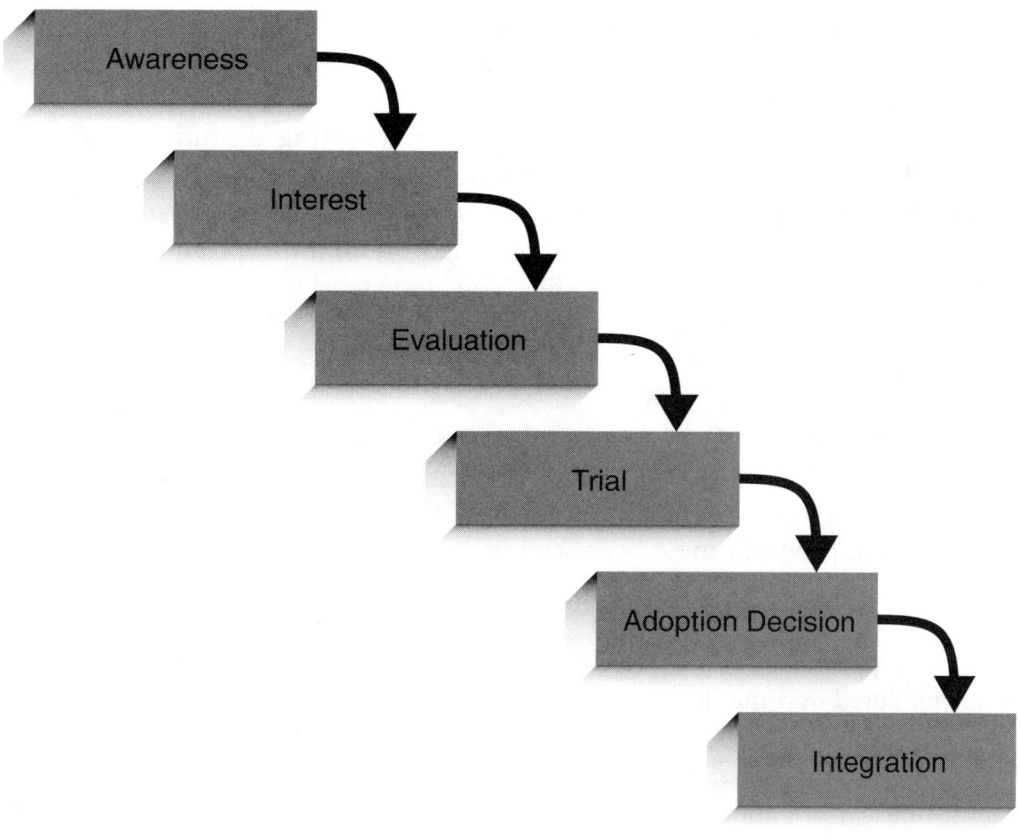

information, but as you move up the scale of information complexity and move up the scales of self-relevance and behavioral commitment, the word *adoption* takes on an entirely different meaning. This is the world that the change agent must understand and deal with.

In this world, full acceptance and adoption rarely come when an individual first learns about an innovation. The decision to adopt is a complex process that research shows usually follows a predictable pattern. Research studies of the diffusion of innovations have identified six phases, not unlike the stages of change already presented as the model for *Guiding Change,* in the process of individual adoption of an innovation, here defined as any artifact or practice that is entirely novel to the person receiving it. These steps are awareness, interest, evaluation, trial, adoption decision, and integration (Figure 6.1).

Awareness. In the awareness step, individuals are exposed to the innovation for the first time, which elicits only passive interest. Receivers need motivation to seek further information. How the innovation is presented at the beginning may well determine whether potential users are stimulated enough to move on.

Interest. The interest step is characterized by active information seeking about the innovation. Potential users have not made a judgment about whether the innovation might be suitable for their own particular circumstances. As they gather more information, the first positive or negative attitudes begin to emerge. These feelings may prompt the users to decide against adoption or motivate the users to move on to the next adoption step.

Evaluation. Before individuals can assume an accepting attitude toward the change, they need to think about the innovation in the context of their own situation. You, the change agent, together with other school personnel, have already done this thinking; you have decided on an appropriate intervention and you know why (Stage 4: Acquire). Now, to extend this wisdom to a larger circle, you will have to take new users on the same mental journey to show the legitimacy of your choices.

Trial. The initial trial of the intervention does not have to involve the entire school system. Rather, the trial should first be piloted to test the effectiveness and appropriateness of the intervention and uncover the small adjustments that will make the program most beneficial in your school setting. Once others can see the successes from the pilot test, they will more likely accept the intervention.

Adoption Decision. At the adoption decision step, the results of the trial are weighed and considered and the decision is made to adopt (or reject) the innovation.

Integration. Even when a favorable decision is made, true adoption will not happen until the innovation is routinely used. It must be integrated into the day-to-day working life of the teacher, the administrator, or other users.

Matching Change Agent Activities to Adoption Steps

A linker can organize presentations and support activities to facilitate each of these six steps: awareness ? stimulate, interest ? inform, evaluation ? demonstrate, trial ? train, adoption decision ? help, and integration ? support. In dealing with school personnel, try to coordinate your activities with what you know will be the adoption steps of potential users. Try to understand where they are in the sequence at any given time. Think through these six steps so that you can be with potential adopters, not ahead or behind. As you proceed, be prepared to go back as individual adopters slip back and to keep up as other adopters jump ahead. Figure 6.2 illustrates the relationship that should be maintained between the school personnel's process and the linker's activities.

Awareness ? Stimulate. At the beginning of your contact with potential users, your primary objective should be simple exposure—exposure to the concern, to the need for change, and to the availability of one or more change alternatives. You want to make sure that they hear and see and that they get an idea of what the innovation is all about. The image should be clear and positive. Most of all, you want to instill curiosity, a motivation to seek more information. There needs to be something in this initial message that will turn them on. Therefore, it should be brief, interesting, easy to understand, and rewarding in some way.

Figure 6.2   Coordinating Linker Activity to Support Adoption

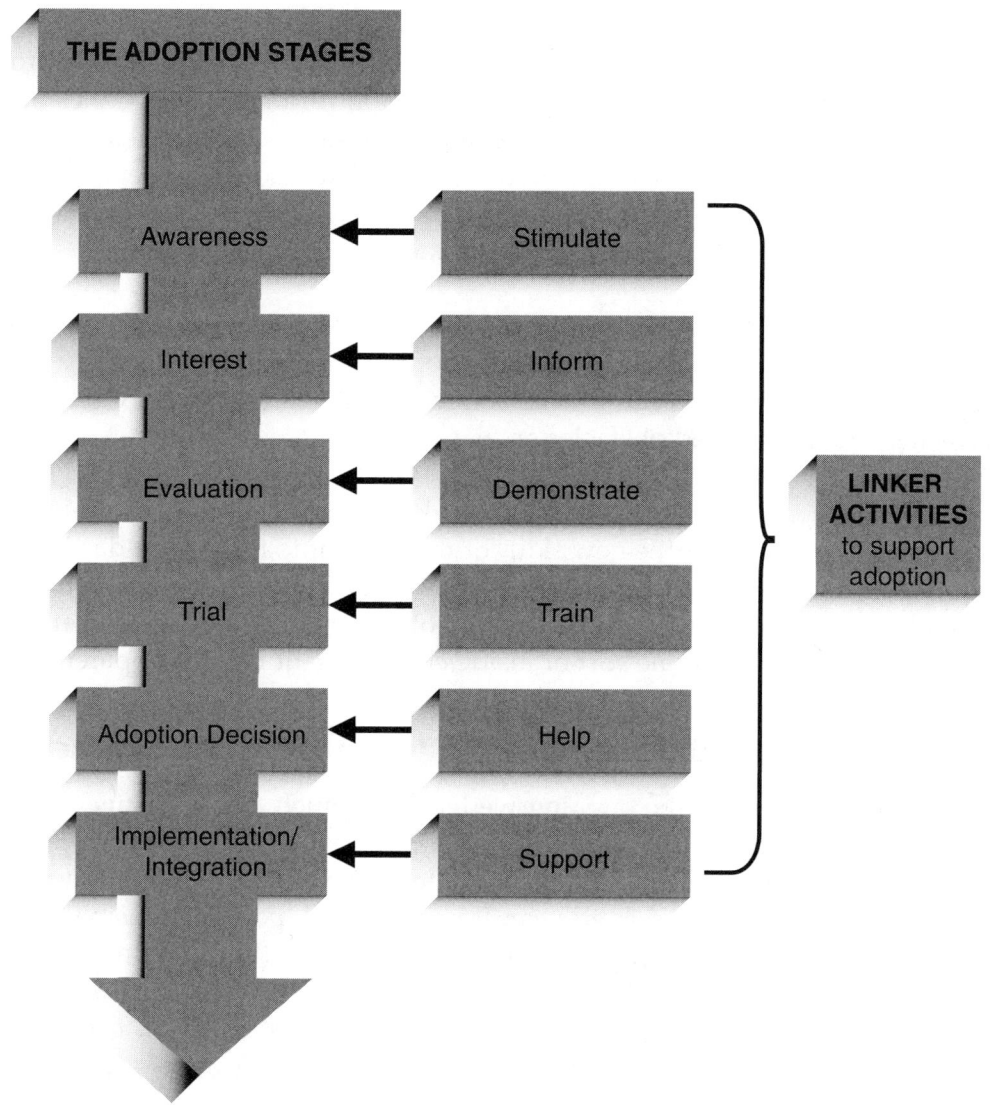

Interest ? Inform. During the interest step, expect and encourage individuals to come to you for facts and to become actively involved in the search for information. If they are really interested, they will also seek information from any other source available, most commonly from their associates in the school system. Promote group discussion not only to satisfy the need for information but also to air doubts and mold positive attitudes about the innovation. Group discussion can be used to support individual risk taking.

Evaluation ? Demonstrate. As potential adopters begin to make their mental trial, they will continue to seek information. Take this opportunity to provide information that will enable them to envision the innovation being applied to their own situation. An aid to this type of communication is a demonstration in the home environment under natural conditions. If they see for themselves how it actually works in practice, they will be more inclined to accept the intervention and want to implement it in their own setting.

Trial ? Train. As users commit to trial, they will need additional support from you, including some type of training to help them fulfill their new roles or to carry out these new activities. The possibility of failure is very real; they need maximum support and encouragement. You should also help users evaluate their own experience as they make the trial; results may not be apparent or appreciated unless you can point out what they are.

Adoption Decision? Help. After trial, potential adopters are in a position to adopt or reject the innovation, but a decision to adopt is not the end of the story. Help them adjust to the new situation and be ready to provide your services when problems and unexpected obstacles arise.

Integration ? Support. After adoption, the linking agent can do many things to nurture the integration of the new skills or materials into the day-to-day behavior of the adopting system. Practice sessions, reminders in newsletters, and brief follow-up questionnaires on frequency of use and usefulness are useful. At this point, the need for some sort of inside change agent is most apparent.

Using the First Trial to Launch Wider Diffusion and Greater Impact

The first trial can be the opening wedge for a much larger change process affecting more people in more significant ways. What they observed happening at the trial site during the first cycle is going to be the central exhibit for new trials at different sites in the second year. It is the model, perhaps sensibly modified, to be followed, the demonstration that proves that they can do it, in their place, with their resources. Therefore, it is important when moving on to diffusion within the system to use what you can from the first site trial. Take a hard look at the evaluation of that first trial and work from there.

Packaging the Trial Evaluation for a Larger Audience. On the basis of the evaluation of the trial, the linker should prepare a pamphlet or a brief lecture, possibly including snippets of audio- or videotape and samples of materials or student work. The presentation should have three sections. First, describe the innovation, its developers, the supporting research and theory, and the expected outcomes. Second, summarize the outcomes in whatever form you were able to collect them. Third, review the process, explaining how the innovation was implemented, who was involved, who was brought in from the outside, what difficulties were encountered, and how it could be implemented at other sites.

Sharing and Discussing the Results. The linker should take every opportunity to informally discuss what happened with colleagues. At the appropriate moment, set up a meeting to make your presentation. Try to get people to come who represent different levels of the system in both special and general education. A brief presentation at a regular staff meeting is often a good start. Move from that to a more extended presentation when you sense that the interest level is reasonably high.

Allowing Visits and Observation. Seeing is believing. Nothing is more convincing to an interested potential adopter than observing a new practice in person, especially if it is done well and has good consequences that are apparent in the reactions and new behaviors of students. Yet many innovators resist direct observation, sometimes for good reason: The observation could backfire if the examples go badly, which may happen for reasons having nothing to do with the true worth of the innovation. The optimal situation is a system that has a tradition of openness. Its members feel comfortable observing one another, giving and receiving honest feedback and asking questions to create a constructive dialogue aimed at better performance overall.

Recruiting Trial Site Pioneers as Linkers and Change Agents. A successful trial site can be a gold mine for new linkers and change agents. A convinced and successful adopter will have the spark to light the engine of diffusion. You can sense, for example, that the North Slope principal in the Hilldale case, having received statewide recognition for this and other innovative efforts, is ready for a larger stage and a wider sphere of influence among fellow principals and others. The seeds of the innovation will travel with her wherever she goes.

Transforming the Trial Change Team Into a Diffusion Change Team. A real change team that develops at the initial trial site can often become the core for a new team that expands the innovation to other sites within the system.

Applying the Six-Step Adoption Process Model to the Trial as an Innovation. The first trial should be viewed from the perspective of the six-step adoption process described above. As suggested in Figure 6.1, specific activities should be planned to bring potential new users to each stage of *awareness, interest, evaluation, trial, adoption decision*, and, finally, *integration*.

Recapitulating the Trial Process. Each new adoption is also a trial for the new would-be adopter. Therefore, you need to view each new adoption as potentially involving a cyclical change process analogous to that of the original trial site. For each new potential adopter, therefore, you need to raise once again the questions of Care, Relate, Examine, and Acquire as well as the steps within the new Trial, but with a difference. The process of adoption at these new sites should be greatly streamlined and accelerated. The pace will depend on the persuasiveness of the original trial and the ability of the new adopters to identify fully with the old adopters, trusting them and the authenticity of the process.

Extending Adoption to the Larger System

People accept change as members of social groups (family, neighborhood, school, community). The linker can influence widespread acceptance by applying principles from diffusion research.

How Groups Accept Change and Innovation

Diffusion research indicates that information about innovations is spread primarily through social relationships, both formal and informal. The world is made up of many vast and multiply connected networks. A person's position in these networks is the best indicator of when and whether that person is likely to adopt an innovation.

Common Things and Key People. A group can be defined as a number of people who have some things in common: common backgrounds, common interests, common circumstances, common values, common problems, common needs. Any one of these commonalties can work as either a barrier against change or a pathway toward change. A major reason for people to organize into groups is to conserve and protect what they have. On the one hand, social institutions are established to preserve the old ways and to keep new ways out, thus maintaining the status quo. On the other hand, all social organizations must also allow some new elements to enter. However, when entry is permitted, changes are supposed to be acceptable, which usually means what the group is accustomed to. The network structure of the social system acts as a filter. In trying to secure acceptance by the system as a whole, a linker first has to understand who plays what kind of role in this filtering process.

It is important to track the relative influences of different players. Some of these influences are from official power (the designated leaders), some are purely ideational (outside experts and miscellaneous media, such as professional journals and newsletters, newspaper articles, pamphlets, and perhaps audio- and videotapes and broadcasts), and some are primarily social (opinion leader and social contacts). The earliest adopters tend to be more oriented to outside sources. Later adopters are subjected to the full force of influence from a variety of sources, official, intellectual, and social. This convergence of forces brings about a systemwide conversion to the new practice.

Three types of people play a significant part in generating such group acceptance. These are the *innovators*, the *leaders*, and the *resisters*. To understand who they are and how they work, social scientists have studied their characteristics extensively.

The Innovators. Innovators tend to be intelligent and risk-taking; they travel a lot, they read a lot, they depend on outside sources of information, and they are usually receptive to influence by outside change agents. They also tend to be marginal to their home communities. They may be viewed as oddballs or mavericks, and they do not usually have a great deal of direct power or influence. Hence, they can be both an asset and a liability to the change agent. These people will be committed to a new idea and willing to stand up and be counted even though they risk the scorn and ridicule of others. Usually, the first inside members of inside-outside change agent teams can be recruited from this group.

The Leaders. Many studies of how groups accept innovations have singled out and identified one social role: the opinion leader. Opinion leaders are found in any community and are the key to the growth of any movement. Study after study has shown that certain influential people are held in high esteem by the great majority of their peers. They tend to have control of the wealth and power of society. Although they are usually not the first to try out new ideas, these opinion leaders always have a finger on the public pulse, simultaneously listening to both the innovators and the resisters so that they can better size up a developing situation. They watch the innovator to see how the idea works, and they watch the resister to test the social risks of adopting the idea. Indeed, in many cases, they are eager to observe these changes because their continuing status rests on their ability to judge innovations. They want to be the champions of the *innovation whose time has come*. Therefore, they adopt changes when they become popularly feasible but before they are fully accepted by the majority.

Leadership of any kind—formal, informal, administrative, or elective—has critical strategic importance in a change program. The school superintendent, the principal, and the esteemed senior teacher will all hold a great deal of opinion leadership on a wide range of innovations. Some act as legitimators, making the majority feel that it is OK to try something new without an ax falling. Others serve as facilitators, approving and rewarding the innovators and encouraging others to follow their example, getting clearance, providing funds and release time, and generally making it easier to be an innovator. Still others are gatekeepers, opening up or closing off access to needed resources, funds, outside consultants, training courses, and so on. The gatekeeper is often not the top person in an organization and may have a specific function, such as business manager, training director, or even the boss's secretary.

The Resisters. Many social systems also have members who assume the active role of resisters or critics of innovation. They are the defenders of the current system. Although these people are conservative in a strictly logical sense, they may wear all kinds of labels, from radical and liberal to reactionary. Resisters have successfully prevented or slowed down such diverse innovations as the fluoridation of community water supplies, urban renewal, atomic power plants, legal abortion, the integration of neighborhoods, and the preservation of the environment. From the diversity of the examples listed above it is evident that innovation resisters do not all march under the same banner. Ideologically, they are a mixed group, yet they tend to function in the same way. As self-appointed preservers of the current system and social order, they play a big part, and often a useful part, in society by resisting intrusions from alien influences; they are the antibodies in the social bloodstream.

How the Linker Can Gain Group Acceptance

The linker can use knowledge about the group to plan and carry out an effective strategy for gaining group acceptance, but to plan a strategy, you must first have the knowledge, which means once again making a diagnostic analysis of the key stakeholders as a social system.

Identifying the Forces For and Against the Innovation. Stage 3: Examine described a diagnostic process in which the linker and key persons collaboratively define needs and objectives. If you and your partners in the change process have worked through Stage 3: Examine, Stage 4: Acquire, and Stage 5: Try, you now have a tried and tested innovation. Now the change task becomes winning support from a larger circle. To start this process, you need to address two questions:

- What are the key common things shared by system members?
- Who are the most important key people in the system?

Draw up a rating form that you can use to identify and compare the forces that are acting for and against the desired change. To analyze the common things, make two columns on a sheet of paper, one marked "forces probably favoring this innovation" and the other marked "forces probably opposing this innovation." Under these headings, list the special characteristics of this particular group that might affect acceptance, such as commonly held values and beliefs, characteristic modes of thought and behavior, shared circumstances, common needs, and commonly perceived group objectives. Once you have identified a number of such characteristics, rank-order them in terms of relative importance and the relative ease with which they could be altered. This list will provide some good guidelines for an action program to improve the chances of acceptance.

From the previous examination and analysis of the school or school system (Stage 3: Examine), draw up a list of innovators, leaders, and resisters. Some of the innovators will already be working as inside members of the change team. Others will have been vocal in their support. Still others will be identified with one or another of the characteristics listed under "forces favoring." Check the innovators list and examine how they rate on the degree to which they understand the innovation, the extent to which they are truly representative of the client system as a whole, the amount of influence (opinion leadership) they have with other system members, and the extent of their contact and influence with the formal and informal leadership of the system.

Take an inventory of the leadership. Who are the formal leaders and gatekeepers for this type of innovation? Who are the informal leaders? The example-setters? The facilitators? The legitimizers? Rate the leaders on such dimensions as their attitude toward both innovators and resisters, their visibility, their relationship to one another, and their ability to lead.

Resisters may be identified by their previous outspokenness against this or other innovations or by their expressed objections to the innovation. They may also personify some of the characteristics on the "forces against" list. It is important, however, to identify resisters before they become vocal and committed to oppose this particular innovation. Resisters, like innovators, should be judged for their relative influence. If you can find any way to get potential resisters working for the innovation, *do it!*

Using the Key People as Stepping-Stones. A number of social scientists have described innovation diffusion as a two-step process. In the first step, outside information about the innovation reaches the opinion leaders. In the second step, the opinion leaders pass on the information to their followers by word or example. This formula sounds elegantly simple but will work only if two conditions are present in the system. First, the opinion leaders must be innovators or innovation-minded. Second, these leaders must have good follower connections throughout the system. As a change agent, you usually cannot count on either of these conditions, and it would be dangerous to assume them. However, this basic concept of steps can be used effectively if you can synthesize all the information from your analysis of the key people and key roles in the system. An adequate strategy may have to include not one but four stepping-stones to gain group acceptance.

- *Stone 1.* Introduce the innovation to a core group of innovators. Get them to try it out, to become sophisticated in its use, and to demonstrate its use to others.
- *Stone 2.* Begin to work with concerned citizens who are potential resisters. Answer their questions. Show them that the innovation does not violate established values. If you get no cooperation from resisters and if they are already vocal and mobilized, at least do what you can to protect the innovators and to make the innovation less vulnerable. Have well-reasoned answers to legitimate questions. Such safeguards will not silence all detractors but may limit their ability to turn the rest of the community against the innovation and against you as its advocate.
- *Stone 3.* Bring the innovation to the attention of the leaders. Allow them to observe innovators in action and to sound out reactions of potential resisters.
- *Stone 4.* Allow the leaders to lead the way to the rest of the system. Get them to make a public commitment. Organize them into supporting committees.

Always Keeping the Individual in Mind. In following any strategy to gain group acceptance, do not forget the individual. Each person has his or her own step-by-step process of moving toward acceptance. Thus, while working on evaluation or trial with innovators, you may need to be working on awareness and interest with leaders. A good program should be planned to give individuals the kind of information they are ready for at a given time.

Winning Over the System. When the stepping-stone process is plotted graphically as the number of adoptions within the system over time, you can begin to see why the social relations within the system are so important. When opinion leadership combines with a media push and a persuasive demonstration, the number of adopters escalates rapidly until a solid majority is on board. The process slows down as the most resistant and least change-oriented members gradually follow. Figure 6.3 illustrates this adoption curve in an idealized form.

The diffusion of an innovation begins with the acceptance of the idea by a few key members of a community. From there on, it begins to spread more rapidly, usually through word-of-mouth contacts between friends, neighbors, and relatives. This person-to-person process is very effective. Once it has started and clusters of people who accept the idea are talking it up, there may

Figure 6.3 The Adoption Curve

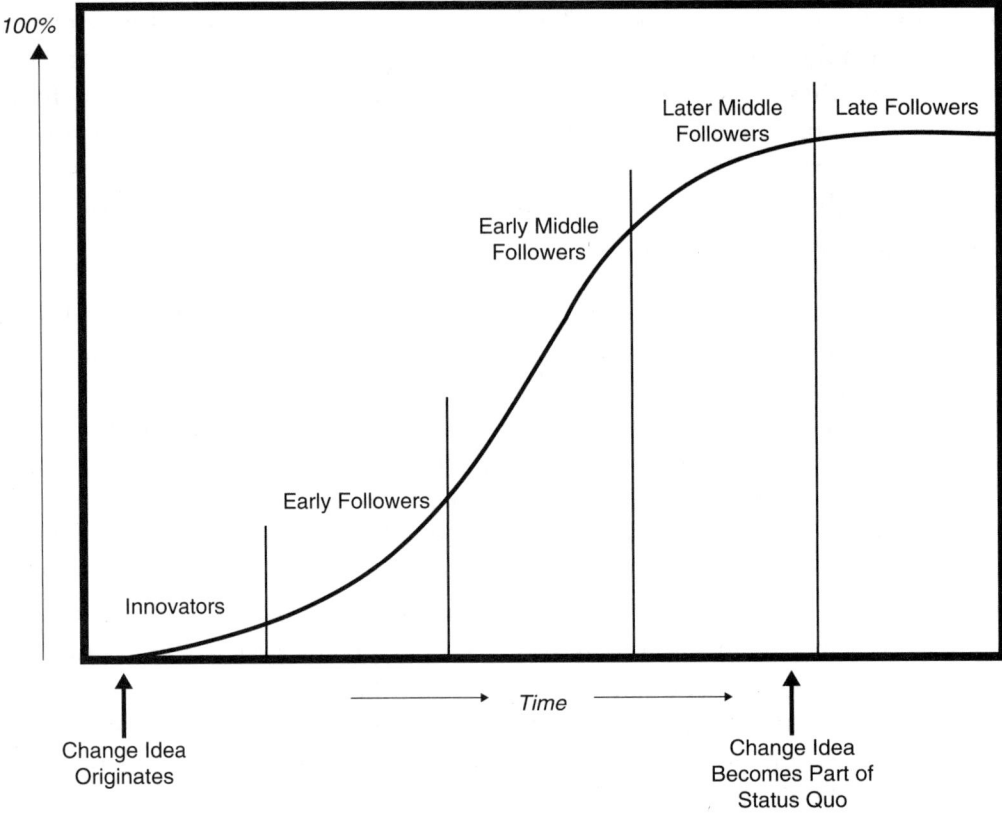

be no stopping it. As momentum gathers, a chain reaction may be generated from the critical mass of early adopters in influential roles. The rate of acceptance undergoes a rapid upswing until a majority has been won over.

Variations of the Adoption Curve

Only the luckiest innovations show an adoption curve like that in the figure. Most fail on the launching pad, not even getting past the first successful trial. Of those that succeed, a great number are unique in that they are customized to the circumstances and inspiration of the innovator at one time and in one place. They go no further despite the energy invested by the innovator and the innovator's judgment of success.

Innovations that go beyond the first trial show a tremendous variation in the rate at which diffusion extends through a system. Some diffuse to a few other sites in the second or third year and then fade out or merge with others in the ongoing stream of school activity. Others succeed at diffusion only after a very slow uptake at one or two other sites and a gradual accretion of individual adoptions over some years. This flat curve is more likely to appear in highly decentralized systems that have no widely recognized collegial opinion leaders and an uninterested official administrative leadership.

> **Special Education Linking Agents in Action**
>
> The Hilldale case study fits the pattern of a steep adoption curve to some extent, particularly the highly innovative North Slope School:
>
> At the first faculty meeting in the fall, the linking agent addressed the North Slope staff and thanked them for their participation in the summer training. She offered to serve as a support person and to facilitate communication with Troy as questions might arise during the year. She also offered to be available to model and coach Morning Message (MM). Within a few days, the linker had received several requests to model MM. Each time she entered the building, someone else approached her about coming to his or her classroom. Teachers in grades 3, 4, and 5 were most eager to learn how to facilitate a Morning Message lesson.

In contrast, some steep adoption curves suggest simultaneous adoptions across the system. This can happen where the system is highly integrated with well-recognized and innovative opinion leaders and a supportive and interventionist administration. Steep adoption curves are most easily achieved where a great deal of preparatory work has been done and where all key stakeholders have already achieved a real consensus.

Sometimes administrators deceive themselves about the nature of innovation adoption, imagining that they can dictate change as a one-step process that follows the administrator's solo adoption decision. Educators are a more resistant lot than the model implies. Real change requires a long prelude of demonstration, persuasion, discussion, and practice, regardless of the administrative mandate that provides the authorization. This is particularly true in special education where administrative mandates often initiate change activity, overriding unspoken resistance and resentment. Genuine change lags considerably behind the edict, waiting for a certain level of consensus that something must be done to develop. The one-step administrative edict model of innovation is mostly an illusion.

Competition, Coexistence, and Market Dominance

As in every other sector of American society, innovations in education are continually competing with one another for attention and acceptance. The models of adoption for one innovation also apply to any other, such that the adopter is faced with choices at every turn, choices that are made more difficult by the clamor of conflicting claims and counterclaims. Purveyors of change all believe their own innovation is the best one. This is particularly true for commercial vendors, but it is also partly true of all innovation developers. They are all engaged in a continuing battle for priority and even dominance, a kind of Darwinian struggle in which only the fittest survive. The wise educator, school, school system, or linking agent knows the marketplace and shops carefully, comparing claims and prices and observing how other consumers are making out.

Characteristics of Winners in the Innovation Marketplace

Many factors account for the success of one innovation over another or for the relative steepness of the adoption curve of one versus another. Most factors are social; they relate to the configuration of the social network and the attitudes and values of the members of the social system. However, a number of important factors pertain to the innovation itself. Most prominent among these are simplicity, observability, visibility of reward, and similarity to past innovations.

Simplicity. Simple innovations require minimal effort and no risk on the part of adopters. Unfortunately, most educational innovations, apart from pencil and paper, are not in this category. Complex and multifaceted innovation packages often diffuse more rapidly when they can be broken into simple elements or when certain simple elements can be showcased, as in the Morning Message of the ELP, which diffused rapidly in the Hilldale case.

> **Seeing Is Believing**
>
> They were able to visit three schools...and see classrooms where ELP strategies were being successfully used. ...They were very enthusiastic about returning to North Slope to share what they had seen. They were particularly impressed with the written language aspects of ELP.

Observability. Seeing is believing. Any innovation that can be demonstrated easily to a number of potential adopters has a diffusion advantage, but the tradition of closed classroom doors makes observability difficult in education. Demonstrations by skilled professional trainers at inservice meetings are less persuasive than seeing colleagues actually perform the new practices in their own classrooms.

Visibility of Reward. Adoption is hastened if the adopter can see good results coming quickly and obviously. Such results need not be just student test scores. Merely the fact that something is fun and easy to do and arouses student interest or improves student attitudes and classroom discipline may be enough to get an early trial adoption.

Similarity to Past Innovations. The ideal innovation looks new in certain important respects but very familiar in most others. Incremental change is more easily accepted than dramatic change. An innovation that requires too many new behaviors and seems strange invites skepticism and resistance.

Adopters Who Do Not Fit the Pattern

Not all adopters fall into the categories of innovator, leader, and resister. In addition, you will probably be faced with fast starters, jumpers, emergency responders, and forced adopters.

Fast Starters. A few potential adopters are always ahead of the curve, eager to take on a new project in part because it is new and in part because they are constantly on the lookout for anything that will improve their practice. These people are avid readers of the research literature and have a good sense of what is out there. They are self-starters, self-teachers, quick studies, and sharp observers. For the linker, such people are a blessing because they can form the nucleus of a new change team.

Jumpers. Another type, which the linker should be more wary of, are the jumpers. They want to adopt something because it is new or hot but without thinking through what is really needed or what will really work in their situation. Jumpers tend to bounce from one innovation to another, never completely examining the full potential of any innovation and the way it could meet the needs of their school or school system.

Emergency Responders. Some people want to adopt an innovation quickly in response to their sense of urgency but without thinking through what they really need or what they are capable of doing. These emergency responders are ineffective unless they are just lucky and happen on the solution that is appropriate for their setting.

Forced Adopters. Sometimes practitioners adopt an innovation only because they feel pressured to do so by superiors or state requirements. Such forced adoptions can come about even when the adopters reject the change in concept and principle and view it as fundamentally unworkable and inappropriate. In the difficult interface between special and general education, you may find many of these so-called adoptions unless you have carefully laid the groundwork through relationship building, conducting participative needs assessment, and choosing solutions that span the general-special education divide.

The Interaction of Development and Diffusion

The research-based development of new practices and programs to enhance special education has been going on for many years and will continue for years to come. The result is a continual flow of improvements into the marketplace, each new improvement competing with, and sometimes replacing, what has come before. Special education linkers have the prime task of keeping ahead of this curve, sorting out innovations that are simply relabeled and repackaged from the true innovations, and determining which alternatives have a sound research basis and have emerged from a well-conceived and extensive developmental effort.

Promising innovations tend to be transformed through many developmental cycles until they take on many of the characteristics of winners discussed above. Thus, development may result in accelerated adoption curves. They may be so transformed that they become new and begin new curves.

Going Wider: Strategies and Tactics (The Second Stage of Diffusion)

Communication has four elements: the messenger, the message, the medium, and the receiver. If you get the right message across to the right people in the right way, acceptance will follow. Medium refers to how you communicate an idea and can come in many forms: written and oral presentations, video and film, demonstrations, person-to-person contacts, group discussions, conferences and workshops, and electronic media.

Written and Oral Presentations

Written and oral presentations can be useful for providing awareness, but only if the message is brief and to the point. Opinion leaders tend to be media-oriented; some will read about the innovation in the local newspaper and may even go to a school meeting to hear a lecture. This kind of exposure may create awareness *and* interest, but it may also create awareness *and* resistance if the message is not carefully composed. A major difficulty with written communication is the fact that the linking agent has no control over the conditions of exposure. Words can be torn from context and meanings can be distorted with no assurance that the receiver hears the essence of the message.

Video and Film

The drawbacks of traditional written and oral message forms have led to a trend toward carefully packaged audio-visual presentations, of which the TV commercial is perhaps the most notorious. Such presentations are primarily effective in creating awareness and perhaps interest. At their worst, video presentations are simply lectures on tape. The medium is used most effectively when visual effects are created to make the message more attractive. Videos work best when time, money, and creative energy are invested in the production. Most linking agents will not have the resources to make their own films, but the developers of the intervention may have interesting and lively videos that introduce the innovation to the key personnel in the school system. It is always wise to *preview* these tapes to make sure that production quality is adequate before you risk exposure to a large or important audience. Some videos are also useful for getting a group to start thinking about needs. It could also be beneficial to create a special videotape of the setting to illustrate areas of need. In any case, video should almost always be used in conjunction with group discussion and as a prelude and stimulus to group interaction involving the problem or the situation.

Demonstrations

Sometimes it is possible to put on live demonstrations of the innovation for potential adopters or to take potential adopters to other settings where the innovation has already been implemented. This approach can be effective for building interest and for pretrial evaluation, but as a technique, it should be handled carefully. Two conditions must apply before a demonstration is advisable. First, the setting and the conditions must appear to be natural and similar to those prevailing in the school or school system. Second, the change agent must know that the demonstration will work and will clearly illustrate the positive features of the innovation. A demonstration that fails can be a disaster for a change project.

Person-to-Person Contacts

It is important for the linker to make personal contacts with leaders, opinion leaders, potential resisters, and other key people. Such contacts have several advantages over the one-way approaches discussed above. First, these people can provide feedback on the reactions of school staff and students, including some idea of the kinds of resistance that you are likely to encounter and that the change team must plan to overcome. Second, building a relationship through personal contact is helpful in increasing the reality of the innovation. It forces key stakeholders to seriously think about the change project. It also gives them an opportunity to express feelings of doubt and difficulty and to talk about their own needs in personal terms.

Personal contact with the linker is probably most vital when the potential adopter is about to make a trial. The presence of the linker is required to legitimize and reinforce the decision to try, to provide needed information and help in the trial itself, and to applaud and otherwise reward the trial effort, once made. This last point is especially important when the results of the innovation trial effort are not immediately visible.

However, person-to-person contact is a slow and costly method if you plan to reach each and every member of a large system. Therefore, it is sometimes necessary to restrict these personal contacts to key people. Wherever possible, you should try to multiply yourself by training and encouraging insiders to take on the direct contact task. Additionally, personal contacts from insiders are probably more effective for legitimizing innovation, especially if these insiders are opinion leaders. Such contacts can help reduce resistance by getting the innovation around the "NIH syndrome" (not invented here). Resisters to change commonly invoke NIH on the grounds that they are unique, their situation is unique, and their needs, concerns, and problems are unique. Therefore, no solution ideas developed elsewhere have any relevance and can be rejected out of hand. Because uniqueness can always be claimed with a certain amount of validity for any situation, the NIH cry has a certain ring of legitimacy, but it shuts down innovative thinking.

Group Discussion

Group discussion serves many of the same functions as person-to-person contact but reaches more people. Groups also have special advantages:

- They increase the feeling of safety and the willingness to take risks.
- They move individual users toward a commitment to try the innovation.
- They legitimize feelings of doubt about the innovation and about the ability to try it out. Once legitimized, the doubts and fears can be addressed through frank discussion and considered in a more rational light. Reasonable doubts must be addressed.
- They give the school system an opportunity to move toward a consensus.
- They create a sense of participation in the decision to adopt.

Conferences, Workshops, and Training Events

When complex innovations are under consideration, you will usually need to arrange conferences or workshops that involve key members of the school system. These meetings can be used for holding diagnostic sessions (Stage 2);

identifying relevant resources (Stage 3); brainstorming and choosing alternative solutions (Stage 4); facilitating individual awareness, interest, and evaluation; and providing a relatively safe environment to practice new skills, try out the innovation, and mobilize social forces (leaders, opinion leaders) on behalf of the change (Stage 5).

The design and management of such meetings is an art, not a science, and it deserves a handbook of its own. An ideal conference should be an enjoyable experience for all participants. It should also help participants learn new ideas and skills and identify problems and solutions. Participants should diffuse the knowledge they gain at the conference to all key stakeholders and undertake subsequent self-practice and further inquiry. Effective conferences generate an atmosphere that fosters interaction among the various stakeholder groups, which results in increased networking and collaborative development of new ideas. Such conferences also stimulate other people to initiate similar meetings. Here are some general points that you should keep in mind and some of the outcomes that conference planners should strive for.

Who Should Attend? At least some probable opinion leaders should be included. Other attendees should represent a cross section of prospective users and reflect prevailing attitudes and concerns, but there should not be so many that genuine participation by each attendee is restricted.

Where Should It Be Held? Off-site meetings are usually preferable because they separate attendees from their daily routines. A large square table gives each participant equal space and a view of the other participants, which maximizes informal give-and-take discussion.

When Should It Occur? The typical inservice session is held between school sessions to avoid interfering with the ongoing flow of classroom life. Nothing is inherently wrong with this, except that the more remote the training experience is from this flow, the more difficult it is to make the mental connection between the new ideas and behaviors and the everyday life of the teacher. Ideally, innovations should be introduced as close as possible to expected trial implementation so that what is learned can be put into practice before it has gone stale.

Publicity. Any training event that is integral to a change effort must be actively promoted beforehand in whatever media are appropriate for the intended participants. Preferably, such publicity is multichanneled and includes announcements at staff meetings, e-mail, flyers, memos, and inserts in routine staff newsletters and bulletins. Publicity continues to be important after the event to reinforce the memories of participants and to alert the system that something new may be entering its professional world.

Materials. Any training event should be accompanied by materials, including background reading, workbooks, and take-home, reusable items.

Process. Training sessions should be sequenced to allow a full exploration of the change that is proposed and full simulated transit through the seven stages of the change process. Each session should be designed to allow all participating members to engage in interactive discussion and to express concern about the various roles and interests.

The New World of Electronic Media

By the time this book is in your hands, a majority of the people with whom you need to relate as a linker will be reachable through cyberspace. The Internet is the truly big innovation of our time, and its many uses continue to expand at a mind-numbing rate. This avalanche of change has had many consequences, most still unknown. However, one general consequence is known: The Internet affects all types of communication strategies, and its penetration into personal and professional lives will continue to grow. Electronic communication in its many forms—e-mail, Web sites, listservs—has become an essential part of any diffusion strategy.

Orchestrating a Multimedia Program

One medium may be just right for one particular audience at one point in time, but this does not constitute a total program for gaining the acceptance of the school system as a whole. A complete program requires several media approaches to reach various groups with the kinds of messages they are ready to hear. Planning such a program involves four principal considerations:

- *Types of people you wish to reach.* What kinds of media are they accustomed to and what kinds will they respond to? As more and more people come online and use more and more Internet resources, this configuration will probably change. Your strategy will have to change with it.

- *Appropriate media for stage of individual acceptance.* Calibrate your media to the likely stage that the majority of your audience has reached.

- *Appropriate media to reach different key individuals.* Innovators, designated leaders, and opinion leaders may be oriented to different media.

- *Redundancy at every stage.* Never assume that anybody gets the message the first time or that everybody gets it by the second or third time. Review the essential message with your prospective users again and again by employing the same and different media.

Extend: Summary

Stage 6: Extend refers to two related processes: first, extending the life of the change and firming up use at the original adopting site; second, extending the change activity to other sites, to those that are proximate and aware of what has been going on and, later, to those that are more remote to the system as a whole. After obtaining a commitment to a second round, the linker works toward integrating what has been learned while adding more innovative features to the core and more adopters at the trial site.

In extending the change to proximate sites, the linker should use the six steps that a new adopter must go through: awareness, interest, evaluation, trial, adoption decision, and integration. The original adopters have already gone through these steps. Now the challenge is to lead adjoining and remote sites through them. A packaged version of the original trial evaluation becomes an invaluable aid at this point. It allows a wider sharing of what happened, what was needed to make it work, what aspects are most important to imitate, and what to avoid.

In extending adoption to the larger system, the linker must understand who the key players in that system are: the innovators, the opinion leaders, and the resisters. Such knowledge can lead to a stepping-stone strategy, connecting in a systematic and sequenced manner to each of these key players and hence to the system as a whole.

As the linker seeks wider and wider acceptance, a variety of media need to be orchestrated to produce impact. These include written and oral presentations, video, live demonstrations, group discussions, and workshops. Electronic media such as e-mail, Web sites, and listservs are also becoming mandatory features of any diffusion strategy.

Stage 7

Renew

Encouraging Ongoing Change

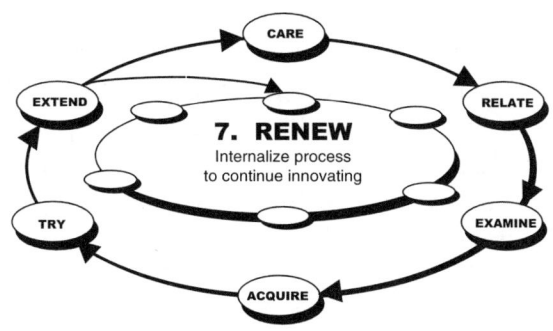

ORGANIZER QUESTIONS

- What are four signs that a system has truly absorbed an innovation?
- What does "improve the process" mean and how can this be done after the first cycle of change has been completed?
- What are the various ways to keep a change process fresh?
- What is a self-renewing system?
- What is involved in installing a change-specializing subsystem?

Change is a process that never really ends. Having proceeded through the six stages from Care to Extend, you should now have a deeper appreciation of the complexity and difficulty of first developing a change project and then implementing it in a way that gains widespread acceptance. Changing a system from scratch is a messy, costly, and inefficient business. Thus, it is important for the linker to view each project as building on the last in a process sense so that with each cycle, the system builds a greater openness, readiness, and capacity for accepting other changes. Eventually the system will accept changes of greater scope and impact, thus transforming the system and its members into a functioning change team. This last stage is not so much a stage as a restart. Once a successful change has been demonstrated, how do you instill the motivation and the understandings to create a continuing process within the system? How do you sustain commitment? How do you keep the changes fresh and relevant? This is the road to renewal.

You have succeeded in implementing a new practice and you have seen the practice spread throughout the system and, perhaps, on to other systems. But your work is not done because change should be ongoing. After your initial success, you need to take another look at what the system is doing and where it is. The process should start again with a new look at what the system cares about now. The concern pot is always boiling, and new concerns rise to the top, driving you once again through these same stages, now focused on another area or perhaps a reformulation of the original problem now seen in a different light. This time, however, the linker and the system should both be a little wiser, having come to understand more about how change works.

What can be done to internalize this learning so that change becomes a continual process internal to the system as a whole? This is the process of renewal. Stage 7: Renew is both an ending and a new beginning with a new set of considerations. The goal has expanded from implementing specific reforms to reforming the system as a whole, building on what has been done with a particular innovation in Stages 1 through 6.

Special Education Linking Agents in Action

Take, for example, the case of the Hilldale County Schools. Diffusion did take place and the literacy innovation spilled over from special education to general education classrooms, from students with one kind of disability to students with different disabilities. You can begin to see how a well-designed and coordinated innovation, led by a team with a mission to improve the reading and writing opportunities for children with special needs, can have a strong impact on general education instruction.

By the second and third year of implementing an intervention, people are more comfortable with the changes they have instituted and begin to add back in more elements from the original package. The initial adoption of a single component, Morning Message, was a wedge to open the door for the Early Literacy Project (ELP) program as a whole and a more comprehensive and far-reaching change in classroom practice. As the Hilldale County Schools linking agent moves on to work with middle school populations, it is clear that she has worked through the steps in the process of change, which she can apply to new settings and other interventions. Likewise, we expect that Catherine Snow, the principal at North Slope School, will start using her newly developed change teams to look at other ways in which her school can be improved.

How Do Systems Absorb Changes?

The first project in and of itself is a kind of system, what you might call a temporary system, surviving on the margins of the larger system. In the Hilldale case study, the linking agent's successful experience using the ELP in one school encouraged her to extend the innovation to other schools and to make presentations with the principal and teachers using the ELP strategies on "The North Slope Story." The initial trial site was transformed into a demonstrator site for the entire district and became the focus of a diffusion effort that will have significant impact.

As a system, albeit temporary, the project has at least four distinct properties: an authority, usually very circumscribed, providing temporary legitimacy; a right to proceed with a change activity; a set of resources or resource commitments; a set of roles with designated incumbents representing activities or functions required to complete change tasks; and an integrative plan that explains how resources, roles, and activities go together to produce a desired outcome within the larger system context.

When the individual project ends, all these elements are threatened with extinction. If the project is generally deemed a failure, they may actually become extinct. But any interested parties who believe that the project should be continued or that something should be saved from this first effort will begin to direct their energies toward reconstituting these elements, first for a second round, then for subsequent rounds, and eventually, perhaps, for an ongoing process internal to the larger system and, in every sense, inseparable from the larger system. Full transfer of an innovation, if it happens at all, happens only gradually through a series of developments that could also be called stages. These stages recapitulate the stages of acceptance of innovations described throughout *Guiding Change*.

The three-stage Lewin model (unfreezing, moving, and refreezing), discussed in Stage 1: Care, is worth reviewing here. If the first trial has been successful and is widely recognized as such, the system has been unfrozen to this extent. It has also been moved to the extent that real change has been experienced throughout the system (success with Stage 6: Extend by spreading the practice throughout the larger system). However, it has certainly not been refrozen, which is the first task under renewal. Refreezing signifies that the innovation has achieved permanent status in terms of the four elements mentioned above: authority, resources, roles, and integrative plan. In other words, there have to be

- An ongoing authority or sanction to change
- Credible commitments to provide resources on a continuing basis
- An acceptance by the larger system of the new linking agent roles
- An acceptance of the schema of interconnections that helps define the change subsystem and its relationship to the larger system

The change process as it was enacted in Hilldale and explained in the case study provides a strong example of a system's progress through the three stages of the Lewin model.

Improve the Process

"Improving the process" can mean various things:

- Include more participants
- Work on tougher problems that affect more people more deeply
- Complete the cycle more quickly and at less cost
- Achieve outcomes more certainly with more benefits for more people

Look at what was accomplished in the first round with a critical eye and then take steps to improve the process in future rounds. Evaluate what has been done, taking a retrospective look at the various steps along the way; redesign; and reach out to more members of the system.

Retrospection

Take another long hard look at the evaluation of the trial and whatever additional evaluation you were able to make of the extension effort (Stage 6: Extend). Look back at what happened and consider the implications. The stages of *Guiding Change* make up a useful framework for retrospection. For each stage, ask the following questions:

- How much effort was devoted to this stage? Was this enough or too much?
- Was this stage handled well? If not, what could have made it better?
- Would more planning or a better plan have led to more success?

Jot down your reflections. Ask others who participated in various aspects of the project to do the same. Then set aside a time to go over the notes and discuss them with others.

Redesign of the Process

Your retrospective analysis positions you to redesign the change process. Redesign may involve imposing more structure, streamlining, developing skills, or adding resources.

Imposing More Structure. Redesign may simply be a matter of making the process more coherent and orderly. The first time around you may have gone with the flow or done what seemed possible and practical as you went along without much forward planning and without consciously organizing your effort into stages. This is fine: The good linking agent is a realist and a pragmatist, always practicing the art of the possible. However, the redesign is an opportunity to become more organized. Thus, you may want to add steps that were ignored during the first round or expand steps that were slighted.

Streamlining. At the other extreme, you may decide that you have been too orderly, following a lock-step scheme that sometimes got in your way. The linking agent certainly has to be opportunistic and pragmatic; a plan that is too tight or too detailed can be counterproductive. The desire to streamline the process and make everything more efficient may tempt the linking agent to cut certain people or groups out of the process. This can be dangerous if people then feel that they have been left out. Thus, as you go about streamlining, make sure that you stay connected to all the people who were involved in the first round unless it is clear that they want to remove themselves from the process. Further, if someone really does want out, as part of your retrospective you should find out why they want to separate themselves.

Developing Skills. The first-round evaluation should consider whether you or key members of your team have the requisite skills in different areas (e.g., making a diagnosis, relating to others, acquiring new knowledge). How can you strengthen weak skill areas or bring in new team members who have such skills?

Adding Resources. No change project ever has enough resources to do the job completely right. Given fiscal realities, can you add to your resources on the second round? Can more people be encouraged to volunteer their time? Are special funds or grants available if the project is tilted in a certain way?

More Inclusive Outreach

Of all the things that you might do to make the second round more successful than the first, including more people has to be at the top of the list. Change is a people process: informing people, getting people better connected to each other, getting people concerned and committed to change, and getting them to work toward a common goal. Much of your first-round activity involved getting to know the system and getting acquainted with its members, especially the key movers and shakers.

Spotting the Key Persons and Groups. By the second round you should have a better idea of who the key people are: innovators, opinion leaders, resisters, and other key stakeholders. Some of them may have been involved in the first or second rounds, but many others probably were not. You may begin to realize who many of them are only as you attempt to extend the innovation. Now is the time to bring them on board.

Creating Special Events to Bring People In. The most obvious way to start widening the circle is to involve

---

The Importance of Getting People to Relate to the Need for Change: Obtaining Buy-In From Teachers

After he went through the Elementary and Middle School Technical Assistance Center (EMSTAC) Linking Agent Training Seminar, the linking agent from a district in Pennsylvania used what he learned about the importance of establishing positive relationships with key people in the district to implement a reading program in elementary school classrooms. He achieved buy-in from teachers with a three-step strategy: He arranged for presenters to share reading programs during a faculty meeting; he arranged for teachers to observe reading programs in surrounding school districts; and he asked the teachers to vote for the program that they wanted to implement.

more people in the redesign effort, starting with the retrospective. Consider the need to have special time set aside and special events to bring this off. These events could include a review conference at which opinions and observations are elicited, perhaps employing some of the brainstorming rules (discussed under Stage 4: Acquire). The size and format of this meeting should be tailored to the scope of the anticipated second-round activity.

Using Media to Increase the Sense of Inclusiveness Across Groups. To include more people, you must extend the lines of communication; you must use media familiar to the people you want to reach and suitable to the purpose. At least four considerations are relevant here: the size of the group you want to reach, the geographic dispersion and cultural diversity of this group, the types of media these groups are tuned in to, and the appropriateness of such media for conveying the types of messages you want to convey.

The frontline media for local outreach are newsletters and newspapers that serve a particular audience, such as a school newspaper or an administrative newsletter. If everybody reads it, that is where you want to place stories on what you have done and that is where you want to solicit interest and recruit new adherents.

Some mass media exposure may also be appropriate in the form of announcements or general interest features. Even though they are aimed at the general population, such items may spark special interest and even action among innovators. General interest messages can be prepared for audio and video formats, which makes them available for radio and television broadcasts and also for training and other targeted efforts. In reaching out to a more inclusive set of supporters within the system, remember three important rules of communication:

- Never rely on only one medium to get the message across.
- Never rely on only one message or one type of message.
- Never rely on a message delivered at only one time and in one place.

Keep the Change Fresh

It is important to maintain the vitality of the change effort, to sustain and increase the energy investments of the key players, and to preserve the sense that something new and important is happening. You can do this in a number of ways: bringing in new blood, being sensitive to and responsive to changes in the local environment, being continually open to redefining the boundaries of the system, being continually open to redefining the nature of the concern, being on the alert for new resources and knowledge sources, and being constantly ready to reshape and repackage the innovation.

Bring In New Blood

When you include more people in the process, you increase the likelihood that a new set of actors will be involved in the second and subsequent rounds.

This is to the good, provided enough first-round players are still around to maintain continuity of learning.

Respond to Changes in the Local Environment

Times have changed since you first arrived on the scene. Some key roles have been filled by different people. There may have been political, economic, or social changes unrelated to what you are doing that have improved or worsened the atmosphere and people's willingness to take risks.

Be Open to Redefining the Social Unit to Whom You Are Linking

Your initial conception of whom you were helping may have been too limited. The social boundaries of any system in need are always somewhat arbitrary. You tend to limit system boundaries to the set of people you can realistically deal with at a given point in time. With experience, you come to recognize that initial social unit as something embedded in something larger. How much of that larger system you now choose to include in your redefined system is also arbitrary, but the decision is important because it defines the limits and dimensions of the change effort. Redefining the system is always an enlightening exercise and is one way to keep the change fresh.

Be Open to Redefining the Nature of the Concern

Replay Stage 1: Care. Reconsider what the true concerns of this redefined system are. Are the levels of concern the same as they were in your prior analysis? Are the priorities different? Does redefining the system change the nature and levels of concern?

Be on the Alert for New Resources and Knowledge Sources

As you worked through the stages of change in the first project, you probably became aware of many resources that you were not using. Which of these resources could you now apply to an expanded and renewed change effort?

> **Helping East Dover *Try* New Learning Strategy Interventions and *Renew* and *Extend* Its Balanced Literacy Programs**
>
> The East Dover School District began working with EMSTAC in June 1999. The initial intervention involved a balanced literacy program for third-grade students in resource rooms. This program then expanded from 9 to 18 classrooms. The intervention is now in the Renew and Extend stages. This year, the district is also implementing the Kansas University SIMS Learning Strategy program to help support a districtwide process of inclusion. They are training both special education and general education teachers, with the goals of reducing the number of children assigned to resource rooms and serving them more effectively in the general education classroom. This intervention is now in the Try stage.
>
> The district relied on EMSTAC primarily for research about effective reading practices and inclusion, for contacts with possible consultants, and for support in designing an evaluation for the balanced literacy intervention. The linking agent became a local expert in the process of becoming a change agent and made several presentations on this topic in conjunction with EMSTAC.

Be Ready to Reshape and Repackage the Innovation

If your second-round effort involves continuing in the same direction as the first effort and building directly on what you have already done, don't be locked in to presenting the innovation in the same way. Redefine what you are trying to do so that the effort will have more appeal to particular stakeholders.

Knowledge Base

How to Reach the Renewal Stage

Hall and Hord (2001, p. 82) reserve the term *renewal* for the top level (VI) on their Levels-of-Use scale, describing this as a "state in which the user re-evaluates the quality of use, seeks major modifications or alternatives to achieve increased impact, examines new developments in the field, and explores new goals for self and the system." Only 2.5% of their database of studies reached this level.

In Fullan's latest formulation (2001a, p. 44), "leading in a culture of change means creating a culture (not just a structure) of change. It does not mean adopting innovations, one after another; it does mean producing the capacity to seek, critically assess, and selectively incorporate new ideas and practices—all the time, inside the organization as well as outside it." Fullan (2001b, p. 196) also urges outside education consultants to "focus on capacity-building: the school/district must go beyond these first steps (of adopting a particular change) toward greater capacity to engage in actions that generate internal commitment for continuous improvement."

Hall and Hord and Fullan point to contrasting approaches to reaching renewal goals. The former (closer to the approach taken in *Guiding Change*) is project based and implies that the renewal edifice can be built brick by brick, each new change building on the integrated residue of its predecessor. In contrast, Fullan appears to suggest that wholesale change is the way to get there, guided by system leadership.

Special educators may sometimes find themselves in positions of schoolwide leadership where they can add special needs concerns to the mix of a wholesale reform, but this will be the exception, not the rule. Hence, the piecemeal incremental approach of *Guiding Change* or the program-focused orientation of the Concerns-Based Adoption Model (CBAM) are arguably more applicable and immediately useful for special educators. Perhaps the wisest counsel on renewal comes from Lieberman (2001), herself a veteran of decades of change agentry and collaborative research on change: "Successful change agents recognize that their ultimate goal is to work themselves out of a job by facilitating the growth of leadership in the groups that they have organized or led" (p. 161).

Create a Self-Renewal Capacity

This chapter contains an implicit message: School personnel can and should learn to conduct change projects for themselves. You, as the starting linking agent, should be able to teach them how or at least show them the way. This is the key to self-renewal. A self-renewing school or school system has four features: a positive attitude toward innovation in general, an internal subsystem with a specific change-advancement mission, an active inclination to seek external resources, and a perspective on the future as something to plan for.

A Positive Attitude Toward Innovation

Many successfully adopted innovations seem to fade and disappear over time because the systems that adopted those innovations failed to fully incorporate the innovative norms and attitudes that are fundamental to innovative behavior. Consider the history of the school or school system that you have been working with. Are the personnel typically on the forefront of new developments in special education? Do they seem to look forward to change as a potential improvement rather than as a threat?

If you answer these questions in the negative, the major issue becomes how you can instill an innovative attitude. Three ways are possible: Make the positive results as visible as possible, provide many secondary rewards (praise, financial aid, recognition of achievement) to those who take the risk to innovate, and help the innovators become more influential and assume more leadership.

A Change Function Internal to the Host System

Not until after World War II did a number of large corporations decide that they should have their own research departments to conduct advanced planning and design new products. These social units, which were assigned to work on innovations as a full-time job, were the first internal change agencies. Through the 1960s and 1970s, this idea caught on across many types of organizations, including school districts, so that research departments became an accepted part of many systems. Unfortunately, such entities were rarely given either the mandate or the resources to experiment extensively with change or innovation projects. As budgets were tightened, these units had more and more restricted missions. Nevertheless, where vestiges of such institutions remain, you have the possibility of developing or recreating internal change agencies. Such entities can then become home bases for continuing change and system self-renewal activities. A subsystem for innovation should incorporate features such as full-time linking agents who understand the innovation process and the capacity and mandate to train all staff in the skills of linking agentry.

Inclination to Seek External Resources

Innovativeness is much more than a passive receptivity to new ideas. Self-renewing systems are habitually aggressive in seeking out new solutions. They have an active faith that outside resources will be useful and a willingness to walk the extra mile to get them. Rural sociologists discovered a long time ago that innovative farmers took more trips to town. They were more "cosmopolite," willing and able to go outside their immediate environment. The same is true for special educators. If they have a habit of visiting other systems, attending all sorts of meetings and training programs, they will keep coming home like Marco Polo, bringing all kinds of new ideas and new products to their colleagues.

You can promote an external orientation in several ways. Encourage and facilitate travel and outside visiting. Get school personnel used to the idea that visiting and conferencing are legitimate and enjoyable activities. Set up site visits and demonstrations away from home. What they learn about the specific innovation may be less important in the long run than the fact that they got out of their rut and began looking at the rest of the world.

A Positive View of the Future

A self-renewing system believes in progress. It believes that things can be better in the future, especially if you plan carefully and conscientiously and develop a capacity to forecast community needs and desires 5 and 10 years hence. It also means setting aside time and resources to think about the future and to draw up tentative programs to meet future needs. (See again brainstorming in Stage 4.) This sort of planning is not simply an intellectual exercise or a pleasant escape into science fiction. On the contrary, a perspective on the future helps put the present in focus and may suggest things that you can do today that you would not have thought of in more time-bound contexts.

From Item Change to System Change

Most of *Guiding Change* has discussed change as if it were a discrete phenomenon, an activity or a set of behaviors that can be added to a classroom or a school or a school system to make it work better or achieve more. This is a useful way to look at change, especially at the beginning, because it isolates specific steps and stages and lays down rules of behavior that will guide the linking agent through clear benchmarks and on to a definable point of success. It is also likely that merely by adding discrete innovations to a system you are marginally improving the system as a whole. Yet there will come a time when you should turn your attention away from these specific innovative projects and toward the goal of changing the system as a whole in more fundamental ways. This is a more radical goal and perhaps a more dangerous one, but *Guiding Change* must in the end address these larger issues of system change.

What Are System Changes?

Guiding Change has addressed the how of change more than the what. It assumes that the change itself is something desirable, preferably something of proven value according to many criteria, something that will demonstrably and assuredly help people in tangible ways. But now, as you address the question of fundamental system change, you need to come back to the question of what is really better for a complex social system. The question is too big to be answered here in any completeness, but a few highly qualified indicators can be suggested. Systems can be seen as changing for the better as they grow larger, become

> **What Are System Changes?**
> - Growing larger
> - Becoming more integrated
> - Becoming more differentiated
> - Providing more rewards
> - Becoming more effective as innovators and problem solvers

more integrated, become more differentiated, provide more rewards, and become more effective as innovators and problem solvers.

Growing Larger. The ability to grow and to keep growing is an important criterion of positive system change. Growth may simply mean increasing the size of a system, but positive growth signifies something further—serving more people, employing more people, providing more products and services. It may also mean becoming more inclusive, including more people in decision making and other activities. Growth, in itself, is not always good. Some types of growth are dysfunctional. You have to ask what represents *positive* growth. Some things can always be added or expanded to make the system better.

Becoming More Integrated. Becoming more internally connected is another aspect of positive change that has been stressed throughout *Guiding Change*. The more linkages there are among members of the system, units of the system, people performing different functions, people at higher and lower levels of the structure, and so on, the stronger the system will be and the better able to carry out its mission. Thus, connectedness is probably an *a priori* good for any system.

Becoming More Differentiated. The other side of the integration coin is differentiation. In the animal kingdom, there is no question that the higher species are far more differentiated; that is, different sets of cells specialize their functions to a much higher degree. The same is true of organizations: The more specialized their roles and subunits are, the more new functions they can perform. However, the division of labor can also lead to more problems. Thus, greater differentiation without equal or greater integration can be a disaster. Creating a new unit, even a change unit, has distinct costs; it requires new links of communication, changes in rules and procedures—in a word, integration.

Providing More Rewards. Systems exist to provide "goods" in the broadest sense of that word. These goods can be thought of as incentives or rewards for the people who are providing inputs to the system, who are members of the system, or who are receiving outputs from the system. Rewards in these three categories may be different, but they are all important. On the input side are investors and suppliers. The ability of the system to take in more supplies, whether they are students or books or other materials, benefits someone in the larger community. If the school is able to inspire more investment of time and money and support from parents and others, this, too, is a positive system change. Within the system itself, if more members can be gainfully employed, if members are more satisfied with their work, and if the work environment leads to higher productivity and a higher quality of life for members, these are all countable and significant goods as well. Finally, on the output side, if the system produces graduates who are more highly skilled, more knowledgeable, better able to earn incomes, better able and more willing to contribute to society as citizens, better able to be good parents, better able even to enjoy life for themselves and to fulfill their lives in a well-rounded way, these are all important goods on the output side.

Becoming More Effective Innovators and Problem Solvers. Finally, you should list as an important positive outcome the ability of the system to function better as an innovator and problem solver. Effective systems should always be innovative, trying to find ways to perform more functions and perform them better, while striving to solve the problems that are always there, both within the system and within the larger world of which it is a part. This, too, is an *a priori* good, and it is this good toward which *Guiding Change* is especially directed.

Taking On the Most Fundamental Concerns of a System

System change happens when the people involved in a system get down to dealing with the most fundamental concerns that they have, both individually and collectively. Yet it is exceptionally difficult to get people to really take a serious look at what is wrong with the status quo for at least four reasons. First, the fundamental concerns are generally large; to many, they may seem overwhelming. Second, these concerns are often characterized as intractable, ingrained, and not subject to change almost by definition. Third, trying to deal with these fundamental concerns probably involves displacing vested interests. Fourth, because they are fundamental concerns, it is often hard to be honest about them and to admit failure in handling them, especially failure to create an atmosphere of trust where honest and frank give-and-take can take place.

To get to these fundamental concerns, the linking agent may have to make elaborate preparations. For example, you may have to build trust through successful encounters about smaller issues, smaller projects, innovations with less impact. You may also have to wait for special windows of opportunity, times when the system is shaken by some set of crises so that a new configuration of people and relations has come into being. You may also have to marshal substantial resources and get solid commitments of support from key power brokers.

Even with all this groundwork in place, it may also be necessary sometimes to campaign for the change on a grand scale. This may require considerable resources, vocal support from key informants and opinion leaders, and much planning and preparation. For example, it will probably be necessary to organize high-visibility events that propel the system toward introspection. It will also be necessary to repeatedly advertise the need for change and to do so using many channels and many types of spokespersons.

Redoing the Organizational Chart

All systems have a structure and all systems can be charted to show relationships, both formal and informal, among people and elements. Some relationships are hierarchical and based on power, whereas others are merely associative and communicative. Some are functional lock-ins, such as the need to perform one task before another—to acquire resources before production and to produce before distribution, for example. Some of that structure may be revealed in the formal organizational chart. If there isn't one, any insider should be able to draw one from their mental chart. Sometimes an organizational chart is described as not real or not important. If you are faced with this assertion, ask what the real organizational chart is or in what ways reality diverges from the chart as given. Sometimes there are both a formal organizational chart and an informal, unofficial, and unwritten chart. Again, it is important to know how and where the two converge and diverge.

A redo of either the formal or the informal chart represents a systemic change, that is, a change in the basic structure of the system that cannot be undertaken lightly. Any such change is likely to imply a redistribution of power, some losing, others gaining, some being dealt in for the first time, others feeling that they are being pushed aside. This is why such changes have to be carefully prepared in advance with plenty of participation within and across levels. If you are seeking a place on the chart, as suggested in the previous section, then you too represent a systemic change with all the threat and disruption that this might imply for others. If you are not on the chart, or if you are on the chart but are not clearly connected to anybody, you may not really exist for the system. It is an important clue to where you stand. New projects, new teams, and new people doing new things are necessarily marginal to the organization. They exist in parentheses on the chart and are connected to other entities by dotted lines if at all. System change requires that those dotted lines solidify.

Redoing Budgets

The budget is the hardest subsystem to crack. There is always that distinction between soft money and hard money. Soft money is soft in two ways. First, the system leadership did not have to struggle to get it (even though the linking agent and his or her collaborators fought mightily for it). The leadership may see it as just falling into their laps, without significant effort on their part and with little commitment to fund the change with hard money later. There may even be the added bonus of an overhead allowance that goes into their general operating fund. Second, some money is also soft because it is almost always temporary; it is there to support the temporary system of the project until that project has run its course of one, two, or, at the most, three years. Thus, the project can be housed in temporary space and staffed by temporary people. In some cases, the funds intended for the temporary system of the change project are even vulnerable to looting by a revenue-starved system, which can assign project staff to other duties, appoint token staff who really do nothing for the project, and otherwise divert funds to subsidize traditional system activities.

Getting a place on the permanent budget, or changing the way the permanent budget is allocated, represents a substantial step toward lasting change and is one of the greatest challenges for any linking agent. This real budget is the one that represents the hard money—what is basic to the survival of the system, what must be saved from year to year. Items that are recognized and given line-item status in this budget are truly integrated and accepted within the larger system. The real budget is what the leadership and the local taxpayers will continue to support even in the direst fiscal emergencies. No system really changes significantly if the allocations in its real budget do not change.

A certain logic suggests that true positive change should be more possible in times of stress and financial stringency. The argument goes that a budget crunch forces the system to rethink its priorities (getting to more fundamental concerns) and the way it goes about its business (redoing its organizational chart). Unfortunately, experience generally shows the contrary. When things get tight, people understandably defend their turf and their livelihood with bitter tenacity. Those that have been with a system the longest and are most invested in the status quo will fight the hardest to save what they have. Further, they will be in the strongest position to do so. Shrinking resources tend to set up zero-sum games when any change is perceived, correctly or not, as "you win, I lose." Sometimes this is the reality, but the linking agent should always be looking for "win-win" or non-zero-sum games in which the change benefits all, or at least some, without threatening others.

Changing the Rules

Finally, real system change means changing the way the system works and what it is striving to achieve. Every system has a charter, sometimes written, sometimes implied, but real, nevertheless. The charter states what you are here for, why you are working together, your values, and your basic operating philosophy. It is a useful exercise for any organization to reexamine its charter once in a while to consider how the real charter of today deviates from the written charter of the past. This organizational self-reexamination is not something to be taken lightly. It is costly and usually requires outside help from linking agents specializing in organization development.

Knowledge Base

Wholesale Reform Strategies

Several approaches to wholesale change have been tried in education over the past three decades, most with mixed success as summarized concisely by Sashkin and Egermeier (1993).

One approach to system renewal is organization development (OD). OD originally evolved out of social psychology as a tool for improving business performance through enhanced interpersonal relations. For many years it has also been applied to educational organizations as well (see Fullan, Miles, & Taylor, 1981) with somewhat mixed results. OD consultants focus on improving relationships within the organization coupled with feedback on performance and problem solving based on feedback and honest confrontation of differences. The new social environment thus created is supposed to resemble Fullan's "culture of change." One such program, Onward to Excellence (OTE), was developed for schools by the Northwest Regional Educational Laboratory (NWREL). It involves establishing faculty-administrator teams who are trained to collect and analyze school data and solve problems in a step-by-step manner somewhat similar to that advocated in *Guiding Change*. Butler (1989) reports that several hundred schools participated over a period of five years, producing long-term positive outcomes even including standardized student test score increments.

> The most widely publicized approach to wholesale school change is probably the effective schools movement inspired originally by the work of Edmonds (1979). Components of an effective school include a safe climate for learning, high teacher expectations for their students, emphasis on basic skills and time-on-task, clear instructional objectives, and strong leadership from the principal (Sashkin & Egermeier, 1993, p. 7). However, a comprehensive review by Bossert (1985) of program implementations in elementary schools concluded that "there is no single formula for combining these ingredients." Reviewing the data from secondary schools, Corcoran (1985) concluded that effectiveness results not from any particular combination of elements but from the creation of a "culture of achievement" out of a mix of norms, rules, rituals, values, technology, and curricular elements.
>
> The American Institutes of Research (1999) has put together a compendium of research on 24 models of schoolwide reform including those mentioned above, finding that only 3 could give strong evidence of positive effects on student outcomes over time, although 11 others showed some promise. Ten programs had minimal effects. What should be noted here, however, is that none of these programs puts much emphasis on special needs students or the changes in the support culture that are required to serve them. Yet there is a clear and continuing mandate to put special education solidly in the mix. Schoolwide reform models are incomplete if they do not make room for special needs and the support system elements that they require.

Installing the Change Function

The school district personnel and specific teachers in the school must now be prepared for continued and renewed implementation of the change project. Increased commitment is needed in terms of both time and financial resources to ensure greater success and integration of the new initiative. The following steps are essential to ensuring the institutionalization of these new practices: regenerating the authority and acquiring long-term legitimacy, recommitting the resources, solidifying new roles, reconfiguring and integrating, and orchestrating the process.

Necessary Steps for Installing Change

- Regenerating the authority; acquiring long-term legitimacy
- Recommitting the resources
- Solidifying new roles
- Reconfiguring and integrating
- Orchestrating the process

Regenerating the Authority and Acquiring Long-Term Legitimacy

Authority for change can come from many sources. Mandates of all sorts have been popular with politicians in the past 20 years because of the belief that change—or the appearance of change—can be brought about without public expenditure. Such mandates often work, at least as catalysts for change, but they have many drawbacks, including heightened resistance to change. No linking agent wants to be seen as the police officer or even as the agent of a policing authority. If that authority is seen as relatively remote and unable to enforce its mandates, the foot in the door provided by that authority may be nearly useless, especially when it comes to the second round. Thus, one important task in moving toward renewal is to localize the authority basis of the change activity by gaining support from the local school board, the superintendent, principals, and teachers.

Move away from mandates as the basis of legitimacy as soon as possible. You want to go from mandates to voluntary acceptance and from acceptance to commitment and the embrace of specific changes and the change process in general. *Guiding Change* has spent considerable time discussing consensus building: reaching out, including more people, letting more people participate in decisions. The reason you have to spend so much time and effort on such things is that you need to broaden and strengthen the authority basis for the change activity, starting with the invitation to be in the school system in the first place and going on to the point at which the school system has embraced a self-renewing capacity.

Recommitting the Resources

Real change requires resource commitment, first from some temporary source perhaps but eventually from dependable, continuing, and usually local sources. Resources mean money, certainly, but also people, space, and time. All these items have a calculable price tag even if they are donated, and there will always be some resistance to providing them.

The way resources are viewed for short-term versus long-term commitments differs greatly. The shorter the commitment, the easier the resources are to come by; the longer the commitment, the tougher the acquisition is going to be. Innovation—doing anything new—requires untethered, uncommitted resources. Consider the various ways in which such resources might come into being.

- Resources could be donated from outside the school system, from a private foundation, a government, or even an individual. Such resources tend to be small; the donor typically has a short-term interest, requires the activity supported to be clearly new and innovative, and sometimes has an ulterior motive. Thus, these resources are most suitable for new start-ups—especially those with high visibility—rather than for second-generation efforts or attempts to transfer or install the change process as such. The ulterior motive is usually to demonstrate a principle or an ideology and to set an example for others to follow (seed money for the pilot project). If the external resources consist of money from a government source, there are likely to be all kinds of strings attached, including a requirement that the project show success and some promise that it can be continued without more government resources.

- Resources could be donated or volunteered by individuals or organizations within the community. Some of the same strictures apply to local support. These supporters want to have a quick impact that reflects well on themselves. They want to contribute to something that is new and something that will later be picked up by others. There is a crucial difference, however, between local donated resources and remote external resources: The local donors care about you because you are part of them and their world (see Stage 1: Care) and they will continue to be there and to care after the initial effort is over and done with.

- Resources could be provided from the budget of the system. This is the toughest source of resources for innovation, especially for school districts, which are perennially pressed to tighten their budgets and to earmark all funds for the most necessary expenditures. Nevertheless, the school budget is the only place where the resources are going to come for anything that is going to last in the long run. The funds for reform start with the school budget because they will have to end there; if they start in the budget, there is a clearer system commitment from the beginning.

How do you get resources for change from the tight budgets typically found in school districts across the country? A number of ways are possible. First, you can look to underused resources, such as space that is vacant part of the day. Other resources may also potentially have dual uses. Most role and function definitions in a system have some amount of vagueness or looseness that may allow an innovative activity to slip in. Mandates from an outside authority may compel the local school system to do "something" in a particular area that can then be interpreted as fitting the innovative project. Even if there are no official mandates, there can be implied mandates, concerns that are so obvious or so pressing that the school system leadership feels bound to shake loose some resources. All systems have some small amount of their resources set aside for general purposes or to meet unexpected situations. Such resources may be very limited, but they are available, nevertheless. Gaining access to such resources represents a major challenge to the linking agent and to the supporters of the change.

Getting on board the regular budget requires overcoming many barriers. The system's accountants and auditors may act as financial gatekeepers. The political leadership always hates to ask for new taxes to pay for anything. The administrators do not want to cut anything to make way for something new unless they see a clear advantage not just for student learning but for themselves and their situation. Generally, they do not want to do anything that will make trouble with the unions.

Changing the system always generates a cost. When you ask permission to play around with something new with a little money from somewhere else, the system sees minimal threat. But the more you ask for a share of the system's own ongoing resources, the more you threaten the system as it is. Yet you must do this sooner or later.

Solidifying New Roles

Any new subsystem such as a change project, however temporary, sets up new roles and new expectations that the larger, older system must relate to. At first, these new ways of relating can be extremely awkward and uncomfortable. There will be a tendency to deny the existence of the new subsystem, to continue to act as if everybody is doing what they were doing before. Signs of this may manifest as people not showing up for meetings, failing to put out announcements or insert agenda items into meetings, using the wrong names, giving out wrong or misleading information about the new activity, and so forth. The change team is thus always struggling to set these "mistakes" right, reminding people of who they are and what they are trying to do.

In the first cycle of change activity, such forms of resistance, although annoying, may seem relatively trivial, but after the first cycle and as you move toward the development of an internalized change function role, definitions, designations, duties, and reciprocal expectations need to be clarified and accepted by an ever-widening circle of actors in the parent system. This means writing down what the roles and arrangements are, discussing them with key actors in the parent system, and getting consensus on labels and designations and their meanings. An important part is deciding where something belongs: what department it goes in; who reports to whom; what offices or other spaces they occupy; and when and how they get reviewed.

Labels. Labels can be very important. Be careful not to pick labels that confuse what you are trying to do with some other type of activity. Be careful not to pick labels that might be red flags to one or another constituency. The term *linking agent* implies a less intrusive approach but will also be subject to misinterpretation and might even be a red flag to some.

Training. Training can also be an important part of the role solidification process. Training for role holders gives them images of what they are supposed to be and an opportunity to practice new role behaviors in a protected environment. Designated linking agents and other specialists supporting an innovative effort need specific training in the process of change. Training of some sort is also desirable for other members of the system who will have significant relationships with the new change unit.

Reconfiguring and Integrating

The new change unit is like a new wing on a house. There has to be a blueprint for how it fits into the larger structure. Where and how it connects must be clearly shown, and then these connections have to be authorized and agreed to. Next, the new relationships have to be tried out and redesigned and then practiced and practiced. Innumerable connections, both formal and informal, have to be made and then strengthened before the new unit is truly an integral part of the old system. This takes time. It also takes repeated efforts and a persistent will on the part of those who want to make the change. Many types of actions represent this solidification of status and integration into the system. Here is a partial list.

- *Standing Committees (Versus Ad Hoc Committees).* The original change effort may have been sanctioned or monitored by an ad hoc committee. As this group continues to meet, the question will arise about whether it should receive permanent status. Any move to extend the life of this group will support the integration of the innovation into the system.

- *Annualized Activities.* Anniversaries are extremely important in the integration of the new elements of a system. Each succeeding anniversary represents an achievement and a shift from temporary toward permanent status.

- *New Responsibilities Defined in Writing and Shared.* As new roles and functions become clarified, they get written down, shared, and amended, perhaps to make them conform with what the larger system wants and can tolerate.

- *New Connections and Lines of Communication and Authority.* Any new connections that can be made between elements representing the change effort and elements belonging to the host system are positive steps toward integration. Such connections could be of many types: shared or adjacent quarters, conversations, exchange of greetings, interoffice visits, e-mail exchanges, and so on. The more frequent and the more routine these connections become, the more de facto integration there will be.

- *New Units, New Offices.* Any sustained innovative effort needs a home, a place to call its own, a place where it can build its identity, strengthening its internal connections and planning and preparing for each and every new attempt to move the larger system. Sooner or later this means that the project must become a unit or office and that this unit must be recognized by the larger system for what it is. While the unit gets its special place to facilitate greater internal connectedness within the team, it must also build multiple connections to key units and elements of the larger system.

Orchestrating the Process

When all is said and done, you have to wonder just how much influence an individual linking agent can have on this overall process. The answer is probably not a great deal unless you, the linking agent, are highly placed in the system to begin with. Even then you can be swiftly overtaken by events and circumstances quite beyond your control. A vision of what the total process ought to look like is, nevertheless, helpful even when it seems to be spinning out of control. It allows you to guide the process to the extent that you can, intervening at strategic points when opportunities arise and knowing, perhaps, when to stand back.

A flow to the affairs of all organizations allows for some types of innovation at some times and none whatsoever at other times. For example, there will always be times when school budgets are the primary concern of school boards and administrators, who ask everyone to tighten belts, cut costs, cut staff, cut orders, and so on. As long as these times of stringency last, it will be difficult to put forward any significant change efforts except those dealing specifically with budget cutting. Even such economy innovations are difficult to bring off because people are all busy defending what they have. How often have you heard that "the last hired is the first fired"? This principle of fiscal stringency applies to anything and is the enemy of all efforts to extend and renew the change process.

Fiscal stringency campaigns have a life cycle of their own, however; they wax and wane. When they are on the wane, change efforts have an opportunity to reassert themselves once more. Thus, the linking agent must be able to feel the pulse of the larger system, always on the lookout for the right moment, sensing the changing levels of tension among members and the ups and downs of levels of concern for issues related to the change process. In other words, the linking agent needs a good sense of timing. The effective linking agent is a pragmatist, practicing the art of the possible while keeping the longer-range goals of change in view. The linking agent must be able to identify the "magic moments" when forward movement and acceptance of new ways of doing things are possible. The other side of this coin is being able to play the waiting game in the sometimes long periods between these magic moments. Know when and where to place your bets, when to act and not to act.

Terminating and Moving On

A linking agent can make a career out of one innovation or one school or school district. For such a linking agent, disengagement is not an issue. However, for many others who choose a career as a linking agent, the day of disengagement will come. Think about the consequences of disengagement and preserve a system well in advance of your last day. The two questions that should concern you most are When? and How?

When Do You Begin to Disengage?

Begin to think about disengagement when you start to observe signs that the system is internalizing the innovation or, preferably, that a self-renewal capacity is present. Three basic conditions allow withdrawal on happy and honorable terms: good evidence (1) that the originally diagnosed problem is on its way to solution, (2) that the innovation has been accepted by the leadership and is beginning to diffuse among other system members, and (3) that a capacity for self-renewal is emerging. Which of these three criteria you choose will depend on your own objectives. Conditions 1 and 2 are more limited than 3, but you may not be able to wait for 3 to develop if you have competing demands and obligations from other school systems or parts of the same school system. It may take experience and clinical insight to sense the moment when your system is ready to step out on its own.

How Do You Disengage?

Because of the need for follow-up and continuing aid in adaptation, disengagement should be gradual. Do not leave the system personnel without fully thinking through with them how they will carry on without you. Discussions and specific commitments to continued work should be part of this closing phase. You should also be sensitive to psychological problems that surround any act of disengagement. Remember that you have worked to create a strong relationship in which there has been some degree of mutual dependency. If you have done your job right, you now have many good friends throughout the organization. These people will be reluctant to see you go, and you will be reluctant to leave on this account alone. Talk to them about the necessity of termination and discuss how they will carry on.

Complete termination, however, is neither necessary nor advisable in many situations. Even after you have departed, you should be available for emergency help and scheduled annual reunions. These continuing friendships are important rewards and among the great satisfactions of playing the role of a linking agent. When linking agents have succeeded in gaining acceptance, they may be inclined to think that their job is done and that it is up to the people they have helped and worked with to take over the task of long-term maintenance. This assumption is reasonable; the responsibility of the linking agent must end somewhere. Your time and energy are not unlimited, and other schools and school districts with problems are waiting for your help.

Renew: Summary

Stage 7 could be called the introduction to the advanced course in change agentry. Not precisely a stage, it is both an end point and a new beginning with a whole new series of stages all rolled into one. Most systems absorb change reluctantly, and the conditions for long-term inclusion are hard to meet: authorization, commitment of people and resources for the long term, and acceptance that is widely shared among system members. As the initial cycle is completed, it is time to take a retrospective look at what has happened and then to design additional cycles that improve the process, include more participants, work on tougher problems, and achieve more substantial benefits. To keep the innovative process fresh, you may need to bring in new blood, redefine the problem and the need, set new boundaries, and be on the alert for new resources and opportunities.

The concept of system self-renewal goes a step beyond by suggesting that organizations can welcome change on a more permanent basis while still retaining their essential integrity. Self-renewing systems have a generally positive attitude toward innovations and innovating, an external orientation, and a positive view of the future; they are also likely to include a special subsystem with the mission of innovation search, acquisition, and management. This kind of subsystem is where linkers and other types of change agents can find a home base and where change teams can be organized and nurtured. However, no change manual is complete without considering the problems related to the act of disengagement, the final termination of the relationship, should this become necessary or desirable.

Summary and Synthesis

Guiding Change is intended to introduce special educators to the change process. We have taken a model of planned change that has been developed in many other contexts—business, government, agriculture, and general education—and applied it to the special circumstances of special educators. After receiving training on the seven stages, a number of special educators across the United States have applied the model as they introduced a wide variety of innovations mostly at the school and school district levels. They were not always successful, but their shared experience provides evidence that the model is helpful and works well as a guide and a process-focusing tool for special educator change agents. One detailed example appears at the beginning of *Guiding Change*. The Hilldale case illustrates, first of all, how complex and difficult the change process really is and also how applying the model substantially helped an experienced special educator and saw her through to a successful conclusion with positive changes that affected many schools in her district.

The compression of the entire process into seven stages is a somewhat arbitrary simplification. In the real world, no process is likely to come out so cleanly, but that is not the point. We have proposed the seven stages as a way to organize your thinking about a great many issues. We could easily describe 10 or 20 stages, but the resulting schema would be too complex, especially for an ever-shifting real-life, real-time situation. Even though we have simplified the change venture into seven stages, it may still appear daunting to those who are just starting out. *Guiding Change* is really just a starter course for special educators on how to initiate and manage changes in educational systems, changes within the special domain of special education, and changes in the way the world of special education meshes with the larger world of education in general.

Each Stage Is Also a Dimension of the Change Puzzle

Each stage represents a cluster of ideas that go together. There is also a compelling logic behind aligning the stages in the sequence presented. The first and paramount consideration in any change effort is the type and level of concern that drives the action. This is called Stage 1: Care, which leads directly to the question, Who cares? This "who" on closer examination turns out to be a complicated set of issues about the nature of the social system in which the change is to take place, the leadership, the different roles, and the connections among them, all of which can be summed up by the word *relate*. An important part of Stage 2: Relate is the formation of the first rudimentary change team, the small group of people who will work most closely with the change agent to move the effort forward. Having defined the system and selected the first team, you should return to the question of care and need in a more complex and analytical way. The full range of system needs is examined, causal factors are considered, and priorities are rated, thus the name Stage 3: Examine.

The needs assessment sets the stage for action, but the first action should be a comprehensive search for and acquisition of appropriate resources that we need when we start a new project. This includes funds and people but also, very significantly, ideas about what to do. These ideas should be drawn from near and far with a priority on models of practice that have been tested and shown to be effective in settings similar to ours. All these search activities fall under the heading of Stage 4: Acquire. Now, with resources assembled, you are ready to undertake the first trial of the change project. Stage 5: Try includes selecting a preferred alternative, the plan of implementation, the actual tryout, and its evaluation. In some respects, the first trial represents a full cycle of change, but it should never be viewed as the end of the road. The outcomes of a trial always lead somewhere. A failed trial should lead to a restart of the process with a revised plan or the trial of an alternative from the resource pool. A successful or even partially successful trial should lead to both a continuation of the activity with appropriate revisions at the trial site and its spread, or diffusion, to other sites—Stage 6: Extend.

The last stage, Stage 7: Renew, is really an extension of the Extend stage, suggesting that what has been learned through the six previous stages should now be incorporated and integrated into the system as a continuing change capacity. Thus, it encompasses the recapitulation of the change process but now considers other concerns and involves other sites within the system until all members are change-oriented and proactive in the pursuit of self- and system improvement.

How the Stages Relate

Where the formulation above may be misleading is in the sequencing aspect. Although the logic of the sequence is sound, it is also true that each stage is a dimension that deserves continued consideration throughout the process, regardless of the primary stage you are immersed in at a particular moment. In the midst of building relationships with key system stakeholders (Stage 2: Relate), the linker may well be besieged with diverse concerns that do not line up well with the original Stage 1: Care issue. For example, the initiating concern may be to improve the inclusion of certain students with special needs. The principal of the school, however, may be more concerned with discipline and stability in the classroom environment; the special education teacher may be concerned about preserving her special role with the students. These two concerns from two important stakeholders may run counter to the change agent's initial concern. Nevertheless, we need to factor them into the equation not only as we build relationships but also when we further assess and prioritize the needs (Stage 3: Examine) and seek resources (Stage 4: Acquire). As the change team moves on into the busy mix of activities in Stage 5: Try, it is easy to lose track of the originating Stage 1: Care issue.

The cross-cutting aspect of each dimension is even more obvious at Stage 2: Relate. Relationships are important at every stage, starting at the very beginning. The salient care issue is articulated by some person who identifies with some group. As he or she makes first contact with a change agent, a relationship is formed. As progress is made through each stage, more and more relationships are initiated, and existing relationships are strengthened. Even the last stage, Stage 7: Renew, depends on the relationships that have built up within the system to form the core of the continuing change team. Guiding change in special education also requires negotiating relationships between special educators and general educators at every stage and at every level.

Examining and reassessing needs are also processes that require attention at more than one time. A preliminary diagnosis is made at the Care stage and is somewhat revised with each new relationship. Everybody has a personal idea about what the real problems are. A clear prioritization of needs may be the useful product of Stage 3: Examine, which sets the project on a clear course. However, the knowledge acquisition that then follows may bring to light new opportunities and concerns, which may require revamping those priorities.

A far-reaching and aggressive Stage 4: Acquire effort may uncover a number of facts and suggest a number of opportunities that were not in the original thinking of the change team. These knowledge sources may suggest that the original care issue was somewhat misplaced or that energies might be more profitably focused on another concern. They may also suggest that certain additional persons should be included as participants or change team members (Relate). Some degree of resource acquisition should be going on throughout the change process. Resource acquisition issues apply to Care, to the needs assessment (Examine), to the diffusion phase (Extend), and even to Renew. For example, as a successful trial nears completion, the change team should be looking for alternative ways to publicize and disseminate its findings and to demonstrate to others how it managed various implementation issues. The team may want to make inquiries both locally and through the Internet about how similar projects handled similar issues. Beyond that is an enormous research literature on marketing and diffusing innovations, which might prove useful. The change team can then develop its own plan to extend the innovation to other sites, adapting information from these sources.

When it comes to renewal, change agents can draw from a rich literature, particularly from recent decades, that documents where wholesale school and school district–level reform has been attempted, sometimes successfully (e.g., the effective schools movement of the 1980s). An important question for a special education linker to ask in reviewing this literature is whether total system reform efforts really leave adequate room for special needs children.

Diffusion issues, which *Guiding Change* discusses under Stage 6: Extend, should also be of concern from the very beginning of a project. Because any given change project starting from scratch is likely to be difficult and expensive, you should always ask how many people are likely to benefit in the long run. A project that is readily demonstrated and has wide potential applicability throughout the system is more likely to deserve this maximum effort. For example, special education innovations that also bring significant benefits to all students or all classrooms clearly have a diffusion advantage over those whose usefulness and applicability are relevant only to special education.

In summary, it should be understood that regardless of their status as sequential stages, these seven clusters of change process issues apply in a multitude of ways throughout a particular change project, even though a change agent focuses on a particular stage at a particular time.

Each Stage Suggests a Special Type of Change Agent

Each of the seven stages also represents an area in which a particular type of change agent might flourish. You cannot be all things to all people, and in a very real sense, fully guiding or managing all the change stages is an all-things-to-all-people sort of job. A specific set of knowledge, skills, and reward value attaches to each stage. Because each stage is important, someone who can help a system through even one stage is moving the whole process forward. It is important to have some idea of who you are and what role you are best suited to perform within the larger process. Then you can think about how to stretch your skills or add to your knowledge and training so that you can work effectively in additional stage areas. You can also consider whom you can recruit to your change team to fill in those areas where you are weak.

The Advocate-Catalyst: Focus on Caring. People who initiate change from a strong advocacy position can rightfully be considered change agents. Special education has many such people, often parents of children with particular kinds of disabilities. These advocates focus on caring not as a deliberate strategy but rather because they feel deeply about a particular issue. Either they personally feel injured, exploited, oppressed, or ignored, or they are deeply committed to and identify with some subgroup that they believe is in such a state. Specific solutions are often advocated as remedies—African American studies, community control, special classes, the abolition of special classes, and so forth. These solutions may later become the focus of the change effort, but not necessarily. These people are catalysts for change. They energize the process. They get things going in the first place.

Even though caring is their focus, catalytic agents can greatly increase their effectiveness by attending to the other stages. Probably the hardest task for the catalyst is to see these situations from the point of view of the existing system leadership (sometimes referred to as "the establishment"). To understand a point of view is not to accept it, but such understanding helps the catalyst know when and how to be an effective influencer. Catalyst change agents need this understanding because sooner or later, they will need to confront those leaders and either overcome their resistance or win their support.

The Social Process Consultant: Focus on Relating. The most extensive research literature on change deals with issues of relating: how to organize more effectively, how to lead, how to build consensus, and how to connect and coordinate the members of a social system around common goals. Organization development, or OD, is an approach that maintains that a socially healthy system automatically works on solving its major problems, is sensitive to the needs of all its members, and seeks out and applies appropriate solutions without the aid of outside specialists. From its initial focus on improving the performance of business organizations, OD has now moved widely into all kinds of social organizations, including schools and school districts. As a result, many change agents are available, for a price, to help educators at all levels deal with system improvement in a manner that is essentially content-free. That is, they focus not on a particular need area but more broadly on how to make people relate better to one another and act more effectively as a single system. They are social process change agents.

Pure process helping of this type, although always needed in some sense, can be a tough sell when educators are faced with specific and serious problems. This is especially true in special education, where the needs of a subgroup are confronting and competing with the needs of the larger system. However, the relating skills of social process change agents are important even for advocate-catalysts so that they can cultivate indigenous leadership among those to be served. Beyond advocacy, movement toward change requires an organizer and a promoter of togetherness, someone who can infuse a feeling of common identity and purpose.

The System Diagnostician: Focus on Examine. Special education has been a field of concentrated research inquiry for many decades. As a result, many academics and others have a good diagnostic understanding of students with special needs and of the teachers and systems that serve them. They know what the problems are in a descriptive sense even if they cannot fix them. They, too, can be consultant specialists who conduct needs assessments and point out areas that need improvement. Such assistance can certainly play an important part in an overall change strategy. Pinpointing needs sometimes can stir action, particularly when the idea is also conveyed that solutions can be found. Thus, diagnostic activity is probably going to be more effective if it is linked to a productive search for solutions.

The Resource Linker: Focus on Acquiring Resources. There can be an important place in the flow of a change project for someone who just does the connecting, someone who knows where to go to get things, knows how to do searches, knows how and where to find support in the form of funds, people, and knowledge. Such a person may not have a direct stake in the project, may not necessarily share the care, and may not even be involved in the trying or extending stages. Yet such a person may be able to provide guidance or direction on all these things through the simple ability to connect. This person could be called the linker, but only in the narrowest sense. As you saw in the case study, a special education linking agent can play a much more proactive part, becoming seriously involved in each of the stages. It is this expanded notion of a linker that is highlighted in *Guiding Change*.

The Solution Giver: Focus on the Trial. Perhaps the most common type of change agent is the solution giver, someone who is committed to a particular solution or program or set of materials or innovative project. This person may have developed the program or may have received specialized training to demonstrate how it works and how it can be implemented. At a certain point in the change process, such people are needed. The important question is, When? If a particular solution giver is introduced too soon, alternatives may be foreclosed prematurely. It is especially important for the system and the change team to have a good fix on the problem (Stage 3: Examine) and to have explored and arrayed a number of resources before jumping to a particular solution.

The Diffusion Specialist: Focus on Extend. It is standard practice in business organizations to have a marketing department and a sales staff. In educational settings, such functions are more likely to be assumed informally. Nevertheless, major education publishers and materials developers do have marketing departments that serve the same function. It is worth noting that during the 1970s and 1980s, the U.S. Department of Education supported a nationwide network for diffusing educational innovations in which developer-demonstrators played a major role. These were successful project teams that were given additional resources to disseminate their innovations and help users with implementation. There is no question that diffusing successful innovations requires special skills, some of which are discussed in Stage 6: Extend.

The System Change Consultant: Focus on Renew. A popular view in the 1980s was that effective schools had certain gross characteristics that could be emulated by other schools to improve overall performance. Thus, by changing leadership styles and focusing on instruction, clear goals, high expectations, performance reviews, and other changes at a systemic level, wholesale positive change could be generated. Change agents involved at this level have gone several steps beyond the social process consultant identified with Stage 2: Relate. They are more proactive and clearly more involved in other stages.

Guiding Change does not feature this change agent role for a number of reasons. First, this role assumes that the change agent will be in a position of great power with respect to the system leadership. Although certain legislative mandates and laws give special educators a kind of clout within the educational system that they would not otherwise have, it is not likely that they would be called on to lead a change effort of this scope. Second, wholesale school change based on externally generated ideal models is contradictory to the care-based, bottom-up orientation of problem solving advocated here. Third, it is unreasonable to expect any change agent to have the omniscience seemingly required by such a role.

The Linking Agent as a Synthesis of Change Roles and Functions. Of the many possible ways to configure change agents, the most valuable and broadly useful is the concept of linker or linking agent. This is the central proposition of *Guiding*

Change. This person is not merely a connector to resources but is someone who uses an understanding of all seven stages to guide the process—connecting people to other people, building change teams, helping prioritize needs, pointing the way to acquiring resources, and helping an expanded change team navigate through trial and extension to renewal.

The primary mission of the special education linker is to help special educators become effective resource linkers for themselves. The linker change agent should also be able to show special educators at all levels the resources they have within themselves and among their own group. Ultimately, special educators are best served by a network of two-way contacts, which includes other special educators and a variety of resource persons, groups, and institutions. Effective problem solving and self-renewal over time require multiple exchanges with inside and outside resource persons, each representing special knowledge, skills, or services relevant to different needs at different times. The linker therefore is not simply a one-time joiner but a network builder. The linker's efforts at one point on one problem may seem like a small contribution in itself, but each new link adds to a growing user capacity for reaching out and pulling in relevant knowledge and relevant others to work collaboratively on problems.

Thinking as a linker and not as a doer also helps the change agent avoid the superperson trap. It is nice to have the skill to do something on your own, but it is nearly impossible for one person to possess the full range of skills that go into a successful change effort. The linker may have some of these skills, but the emphasis is on finding others inside or outside the system who either have these skills or can be trained to have them. The linker understands not only that teamwork is necessary but also that change teams should include members with skills or strengths that reflect each of the seven stages.

The linker's manifesto thus follows the seven stages. It is not enough to care. You need to share the care. It is not enough to build relationships with stakeholders. You must build change-oriented relationships among the stakeholders. It is not enough to assess the needs or to decide on your own what is needed. You must teach the stakeholders how to take a hard look for themselves at what they need. It is not enough to make a wide-ranging search for knowledge and other resources. You must help, guide, and support the stakeholders as they go about their search. It is not for you to decide what to try but to help them through a process of deciding what alternatives are best and then help them implement their decision. It is not your job, as linker, to process the results of a successful trial but rather to guide the system leaders toward extending and diffusing the successful elements. Finally, it is not up to you, the linker, to ensure renewal but rather to point the way to the system leader and other stakeholders, encouraging them to establish the ongoing arrangements that lead to a renewal capacity.

Three Concepts Cut Across All Stages: Openness, Connection, and Structure

Three major themes cut across all seven stages and represent another way of summarizing what is most important in managing any planned change activity.

These themes also apply to the linker change agent, to the change team, to the people who authorize and supervise the change, and to the people who will be most affected by it. For the linker, this set of three ideas constitutes a short-form guide to day-to-day change-directed behavior, always in the forefront of thought and action. These guiding principles are openness, connection, and structure.

Openness. Change will not happen without a lot of openness. That is easy to say but much harder to practice. Back at the beginning of *Guiding Change*, we talked about Kurt Lewin's concept of unfreezing, which means opening up the system so that new ideas, new people, new arrangements, new relations, new ways of doing things can flow in. At the same time, the change agent has to be open to what the system is saying about itself. If it is saying, "Sorry, we're not open," you may have to respect that stance. Or maybe you have to find the particular areas or the particular modes of approach that will not give that answer. The dual challenge for the change agent is to find the people within the system who are open and to be open to what they have to say.

Even when the system provides an opening, a great many openness issues remain. You and they need to be prepared to consider a range of concerns (openness on the Care dimension) and to explore the real and imagined needs of many stakeholders (openness on the Examine dimension). In this process, you and your emergent change team will need to be open to including a widening circle of players (openness on the Relate dimension). Once you have your priorities in place, you will need to be open to a wide array of potential resources, including research knowledge and innovative practice models from near and far (openness on the Acquire dimension). You must make sure that the decision to begin Stage 6: Try is truly based on a consideration of alternatives. You must also be sure that in proceeding to implementation, you are taking full account of the concerns (see Hall, 1974; Hall & Hord, 1987) of those who will be directly responsible for implementation.

If you and your team achieve some degree of success, you will have the additional responsibility of follow through so that the change continues and spreads to other sites within the system and perhaps to other systems. Is the system open to such an expansion? Is the change agent open to considering the various ways that expansion might be accomplished (openness on the Extend dimension)? Finally, the change agent should be considering how to make the system more broadly open to change. Is it enough that a particular change in a particular site was successful? Is it possible to draw from the lesson of success a new attitude toward innovating?

Connection. The second overriding principle is connection. You started with understanding the importance of making a good connection between the change agent and key members of the system. Then you need to focus on connecting people to their real concerns and to one another around their concerns. The next task for the change team is to connect together the pieces of the need puzzle so that the diagnostic picture makes sense as a whole and so that priorities for action line up in a meaningful order (connection on the Examine dimension). Stage 4: Acquire is all about connecting: connecting people to resources, connecting resources to needs, connecting one type of resource to another to create a more powerful and relevant innovation. Implementation involves connecting concepts and plans to the reality of action.

After a successful trial, extension and diffusion will not happen unless the trial is connected to the larger system, and renewal will not happen unless key system members make a connection between the specific change and the larger possibilities of change, using this success as a springboard to a larger and longer change process within the system.

Structure. A third crucial element that must run through every successful change effort is structure or structuring. With all the openness at your disposal, you still must bring coherence out of chaos. At the very beginning, out of all the cares and concerns expressed, a focal concern must emerge. Then, the change agent must select from the many members of the system who have a legitimate stake in the outcome, giving full consideration to the existing system structure, determining who is likely to be most relevant and helpful, and building a coherent and cohesive change team.

Likewise, the change team should take a structured approach to the examination of needs, defining needs in clear terms and using well-reasoned criteria to establish priorities. Similarly, the acquisition of resources should proceed in an organized and logical way with some attempt to be comprehensive.

Stage 5: Try emphasizes the importance of both planning and evaluation by presenting a feedback loop from the results of evaluation to the revision of plans. Another structured and time-projected plan should be in the works for continuing and extending beyond the trial and for later integrating the new activities into the ongoing system. At the end of the road, the change agent should be working toward the evolution of a permanent internal structure to support this and other change efforts.

Your Own Role, Your Team, and Your Strategy

A change agent in top form might be able to contribute in a large way at every stage of the problem-solving process, even working to build internal capacities for continued self-renewing problem solving within the system. Perhaps all change agents should strive for this ideal, but most will concentrate their efforts at one stage or another, depending on their comfort with their own skill mix and their perception of the demands of the situation. An important strategic choice for the change agent is whether to intervene directly or indirectly. In the most indirect form, the change agent is a friendly observer, fully aware of the process but intervening primarily by posing questions so that the members of the system feel that they are the primary decision makers at every stage. More active process helping might include suggesting key issues, sources, and solution ideas.

Defining Your Own Role

It is in the very nature of special education that teachers and others who work in this field are frequently cast in the role of change agent, whether they intend it or not. The bottom-line intent of this field is to intervene in the lives of students and the routines of general education to bring about serious and lasting changes. Anyone in special education can be a change agent. The main requirements are a desire to bring about change and the energy and time to invest in making it happen. In defining your own role, keep these points in mind.

- The different change agent roles are not mutually exclusive. Some people can be catalysts, diagnosticians, solution givers, process helpers, and linkers all at the same time. Further, knowing how to be effective in one role will help you be more effective in the others.
- You can be an effective change agent as either an insider or an outsider. Sometimes outsiders see things more objectively, and they are usually freer to work in a variety of ways with different members of the system, but insiders can be effective in different ways. As an insider, you are more familiar with the system; you feel its problems more deeply. You are also a familiar face and a known quantity, which may be good or bad depending on what your image has been up to now inside the system. Being seen as a partisan for one particular faction or cause will help you with that faction and the advocates of that cause but will tend to undermine your ability to be a bridge, a unifier, or a helper across the full array of stakeholders.
- The inside-outside dimension should have special resonance for special educators vis-à-vis other educators. A special educator who is trying to induce changes in general education classrooms may be cast as an outsider even though he or she is very much an insider to other special educators. Showing empathy with the concerns of the general classroom teacher should help bridge the gap.
- Sometimes it helps to be in a formal position of authority as leader or supervisor to bring about change in a group. The leader is the most important gatekeeper to change, the person who sets the tone, opens the doors, and provides psychological and material support. An effective leader is a good change agent in a formal sense, but a staff person can be equally effective and sometimes can provide the kind of help-without-threat that is difficult to get from a superior.
- You can be an effective change agent working from above or below. It is much harder to work from below and to bring about change when you do not have formal power, but it can be done. The linker in the Hilldale case study started out with very little formal power. She became effective because she understood the process, projected a nonthreatening image, chose appropriate points of leverage, and followed through.

Assembling the Change Team

From the moment you enter the scene as a linker, you should be thinking "team." As you gradually assemble your team, you should be thinking of ways to expand the team by broadening the skill mix and the representation reach. The three main considerations are inside-outside status, process skill areas, and content expertise for the problem or innovation.

Inside-Outside Status. The good change team ought to include outsiders (to give perspective and access to external resources), insiders (to provide system connections, institutional memory, credibility, and caring), and boundary spanners (to provide intersystem linkage and team cohesion).

Process Skill Areas. The stages of *Guiding Change* correspond to the set of skills that a change agent ideally should have. The linker needs to ask which among these skill areas are most relevant, most urgently needed, or most lacking in the situation at hand and for the problem area that has been defined.

Content Expertise for the Problem or Innovation. It is always good to be an expert, to know the content area backward and forward, but it is the lot of linker change agents to work at times far outside their sphere of technical competence. You may enter the situation with one sort of thing in mind, but a truly open process of discovery, of eliciting system concerns and honestly analyzing needs, will often lead in unanticipated directions. Content expertise is undeniably important both to establish credibility as a problem solver and often just to get the job done and do it well. But there is a caveat: It is not the linker but the system that is ultimately responsible for the innovation. Success should not hinge on the specific content expertise of a particular change agent.

Developing Strategies

A sequel to *Guiding Change* could be written to help potential linkers select the most appropriate strategies for dealing with different circumstances and different types of systems. Here are a few ideas.

Alternative Strategic Choice by System Condition. It would be good if all systems welcomed change, had adequate resources, and worked together as a real system, but most systems do not present these attributes and many are not even functioning as truly integrated "systems" with shared goals. Consider four entry situations: frozen systems, systems in internal conflict, systems in disarray, and systems with very low internal capacity. What are some of the strategic options the change agent should consider?

Strategies for Frozen Systems. Some systems resist the very idea of changing because they either are self-satisfied or believe that any boat-rocking activity might sink them. In Kurt Lewin's term, these systems are "frozen." Thus, the first change agent task is to unfreeze them at least enough to get some semblance of a change process started. Here are four ideas on how to start the thaw.

- *Promoting inside advocacy.* Almost always, some people inside the system will be aware of serious needs and concerns and of who "feels the pain." These people want change and may be willing to speak out if you give them the right kind of encouragement and a little push. The linker should identify these change-oriented insiders and find ways to reenergize their efforts.

- *Linking the system to stimulating outsiders.* It may be possible to recruit outside expert consultants to give talks that stimulate thinking and arouse a significant level of caring among a handful of insiders. These motivated insiders then become passionate internal advocates who can begin the unfreezing process.
- *Reflecting negative self-images back to the system members.* A mirror is sometimes needed to show people how they really look. There are many ways to get people to look in the mirror to see themselves, metaphorically speaking. Certain change agents are skilled at holding up mirrors and documenting and sharing their observations of system deficiencies in ways that challenge and create discomfort without threat.
- *Evoking images of future potential and desired goals.* Sometimes it is better to accent the positive, to create images of what might be. This might be called the "Music Man" strategy, as in the Broadway musical. The Music Man changes a smug, self-satisfied community by giving its citizens some images of what they might be. Inspired by the images, they do things they had never done before and probably thought they were not capable of doing. The point is that people do not automatically think about positive futures. Someone new from the outside may be needed to conjure up images of potential. Then the members should be encouraged to build their own images of a positive future (e.g., What do we want our school to look like in five years?). The new images create a dissonance between the current state and the projected future state as members go on to ask, How do we get there from here? What do we need to do first?

Strategies for Systems in Conflict. Some systems may be engaged in such internal strife over one concern that all other issues, needs, and concerns are left unattended. In effect, these systems are frozen in conflict, usually between two power groups—teachers versus administrators, teachers and administrators versus parent groups, teachers versus school boards. There is an understandable temptation to leave such systems alone, to wait until conflicts are somehow resolved or at least brought down to a simmering level. However, the change agent may not have the luxury of avoidance. Moreover, some conflicts may present some opportunities. The change agent has at least four strategic approaches for dealing with systems in conflict.

- *Appeal to superordinate values, concerns, and goals.* The most idealistic strategy is to get people to start defining their long-term goals in ways that are inclusive rather than exclusive. If you go high enough on the ladder of abstraction, all people have similar goals, values, and concerns.
- *Introduce conflict resolution as the primary change objective.* Systems embroiled in internal conflict are not functioning very well as systems. The first concern in this situation is integration: connecting members from opposing sides, forming new internal linkages, setting joint goals, dividing labor in new ways that are mutually beneficial, and above all, getting members to see themselves as parts of a larger system that will function much better if everyone works together.
- *Mobilize the energy of conflict in the service of positive change.* One major difference between systems that are merely frozen in the status quo and systems

in conflict is that in the latter, energy for action is manifest. In theory, if part of this energy could be turned to good purpose, some kinds of positive change might happen. For example, it is easy to get people to talk, to come to a few meetings, to work at achieving shared goals even though these are initially in the service of the conflict. Then the talk can be diverted away from conflict and toward objectives that everybody wants to achieve.

- *Create improbable linkages.* Change agents can sometimes start positive change in systems in conflict by connecting key parties, that is, by electing members of warring parties. The people, the major representatives of opposing groups, are chosen because they have a certain openness or reasonableness. Perhaps they are getting battle weary. Perhaps they see gaining personal advantage within their own group by taking a new position.

Strategies for Systems in Disarray. Some systems may be characterized by weak connections, little awareness of shared goals, and few functioning cooperative endeavors. In these cases, the first task of the change agent is to create what is not there even at the most rudimentary level. For such nonsystems, clearly the first change target is Relate: bringing people together, having them identify common goals and common interests, and helping them develop temporary systems that may later evolve into enduring structures for working together.

Strategies for Low-Capacity, Resource-Poor Systems. People and systems that already have abundant resources are in a good position to be creative, to take risks, and to have their risks pay off in good results. The change agent has to think of how to work most effectively with systems that are in great need but are poorly endowed. A lot can be done, particularly within a larger culture that has substantial resources. Four strategic levers are worth considering.

- *Identify hidden treasures.* Most systems are not adequately aware of the real resources that they already have. The time and work of people are great resources of even the poorest systems. Major people resources are often ignored, for example, the students in a school, parents, and retirees in the community who want to be useful.
- *Build connections.* Building new connections, the linker's central goal, costs little but creates access to a whole universe of resources, ideas, technology, and experts. Connections also increase the opportunities for pooling resources across poor systems or between poor and not-so-poor systems.
- *Network to similar systems.* Many good examples of school and school district networking to promote innovation are available. It is generally true that higher-capacity and resource-rich systems are more likely to engage in networking, but this need not be true. Informal and formal networking can take place with minimal resources if existing channels of communication are used to the fullest and networking opportunities are aggressively sought and exploited.
- *Set realistic but significant goals.* With limited capacity and resources, how far should you reach? It is detrimental to progress to set ambitious goals and then fail to reach them. Thus, the emphasis should be on setting goals that are achievable and putting together an action plan that will work with the

resources at hand. This does not mean setting goals that are trivial just to go through the motions; it means setting goals that are meaningful and challenging within realistic limits, things the members will have to work hard to accomplish and will be proud to have done.

Linkers and Other Change Agents in the Larger Context

Leaders can also be change agents, and change agents can assume leadership roles, but leadership and change agentry are not the same.

Leaders Versus Change Agents. Much has been written about leadership and change as if the primary role of the leader is to be a change agent. This is partly true and partly not true. A good leader is conservative in the literal sense of preserving the established system in its recent state. Leaders are charged with maintenance; they make sure that everything keeps working and that everybody keeps doing what they are supposed to do. The leader is also the chief protector, who ensures that the system is not attacked from without or undermined from within.

In addition to preserving the status quo, a good leader must embrace change. Human social systems are constantly subject to change pressures. Leaders have to be arbiters of which pressures are good, which are bad, which should be welcomed as positive enhancements to the system, and which are threats to be suppressed or repelled. All of this suggests that the wise leader is ambivalent about change, embracing it at times and putting the lid on it at other times.

It is certainly possible to add another layer to all these responsibilities by also anointing the leader as the change-agent-in-chief. This appears to be the intent of much recent writing (e.g., Fullan, 2001a; Kotter & Cohen, 2002). *Guiding Change,* however, makes no assumptions about a change agent's status as leader. Some leaders are change agents and some change agents are leaders, but there is no necessary connection between the two. The prescriptions in this book should be useful to anyone who is involved in a change activity. That person could be a school superintendent or a principal or a director of special education, but such status is not required. In fact, it can sometimes be counterproductive because leaders have so many demands placed on them and because part of their role is to defend the system against many kinds of changes.

Another troublesome aspect of anointing leaders as change agents is the rather mixed record of innovation imposed from above. Ideally, successful innovation should combine elements of top-down and bottom-up influences. When innovation is seen as coming primarily from above, the lower-level people who will be responsible for implementation tend to feel that their own real concerns are not being adequately addressed. They have no sense of ownership. As a result, implementation is limited and perfunctory. Change agents who are not so clearly identified with the leadership do not have this taint.

Natural Linkers Versus Designated Linkers. Every field has a few good natural linkers, people who seem to have a good feel for how to connect people to resources and help use those resources to steer a path to positive outcomes. *Guiding Change* is based partly on the experiences of such people, but it is also based partly on the experiences of special educators who took on the role as part of an experimental project. The linker in the Hilldale case study was one such person. However, many other designated linkers have been trained in the seven-stage CREATER model. They have also successfully pursued innovative projects in many different settings, at different levels, in different regions of the country.

Change Agents Who Want to Block a Change

You are concerned about a major innovation activity that is going on in your school. What can you do about it? *Guiding Change* provides you with a series of points on which you can challenge the would-be innovators. Do they really have the serious concerns of children and teachers in mind? Have they related to all the people who should be involved in the decision? Have they adequately assessed and prioritized needs and implementation issues? Have they made an adequate effort to get all the information they should be looking at, inside and outside the system? The latest research? The best-demonstrated and most relevant practices? Have they considered alternatives? Have they planned adequately? Have they considered long-term consequences and the potential for spreading to other sites? These are all possible project stoppers, especially if they expose major weaknesses and arouse the concerns of significant stakeholders.

Guiding Change should be useful to any educator at any level with respect to understanding, coping with, managing, or even blocking a change activity.

Special Education Needs Linkers

If our society is serious about the goal of leaving no child behind, and if we are someday going to provide optimal learning environments for all learners, the systems we have created for teaching and learning will have to undergo major changes. Nowhere is this need more obvious than in special education. Yet we know that change is a complex process that will not work very well unless it is guided by people who understand the change process at many levels. Change agents of all types are needed: catalysts, solution givers, and process helpers. But most of all, we need a new cadre of linkers, people who understand and can provide help on the full range of elements that contribute to a successful effort. Where will we find these people?

Many special educators at all levels should be promising candidates to fill the linker role. Many of them are long accustomed to being advocates for children and for changing the circumstances under which children with special needs are educated. Undoubtedly they have at some time challenged the established order in the classroom, the school, or the district. Most have a core area of expertise, which gives them special legitimacy and a point of entry into the affairs of schooling in general.

The linker project that inspired this book has shown the way. It is now time for this model of change to spread. No one needs permission to assume this role. No one will ever be forced to take it on. But it is badly needed. Every school district in the country should be home to at least one special education linker who can energize a bottom-up change process as strong as the top-down efforts that are forced by state and federal mandates.

A Final Message

To those special educators who have now read this book and believe that they have absorbed its essential message, please realize that *Guiding Change* was not written as just an intellectual exercise. It is intended for use in real-life encounters by people who want a better world. All of us have opportunities in our daily lives to become change agents at least part of the time in small ways or large. You can start anywhere. You can define your role narrowly or broadly. You can focus on one CREATER stage or on all seven. You can work with any system at any level on any sort of problem or concern. The point is to start, to make the effort to move your educational world forward.

You can use this book in whatever way you wish, but if you begin to use it as a guide to your own change efforts, you can be secure in the realization that you are standing on the shoulders of many who have gone before you. You have at your fingertips a body of knowledge based on the success and fail experiences of many change agents in education and other fields. *Guiding Change* is one distillation of that experience. Follow the wisdom gleaned from these pages to shape your own future either as a linker or as another kind of change agent. It should help you work more effectively, achieve better results over a longer time, and avoid the most common mistakes of the past.

Please begin.

References

American Institutes of Research. (1999). *An educators' guide to schoolwide reform.* Washington, DC: Author.

Argyris, C. (2000). *Flawed advice and the management trap.* New York: Oxford University Press.

Ball, D. L. (1995). Blurring the boundaries of research and practice. *Remedial and Special Education, 16*(6), 354–363.

Berman, P., & McLaughlin, M. W. (1975–1978). *Federal programs supporting educational change, 1-10.* Santa Monica, CA: RAND.

Borko, H., & Putnam, R. T. (1995). Expanding a teacher's knowledge base: A cognitive psychological perspective on professional development. In T. R. Guskey & M. Huberman (Eds.), *Professional development in education: New paradigms and practices.* New York: Teachers College Press.

Bossert, S. T. (1985). Effective elementary schools. In R. M. J. Kyle (Ed.), *Reaching for excellence.* Washington, DC: U.S. Government Printing Office.

Butler, J. (1989). *Success for all students.* Portland, OR: Northwest Regional Educational Laboratory.

Carlson, R. O. (1965). *Adoption of educational innovations.* Eugene: University of Oregon, Center for the Advanced Study of Educational Administration.

Carnine, D. (1995). Becoming a better consumer of research. *The School Administrator, 6*(62), 10–16.

Carnine, D. W. (1997). Bridging the research-to-practice gap. *Exceptional Children, 63*(4).

Carnine, D. W., & Gersten, R. (1985). The logistics of educational change. In J. Osborn, P. T. Wilson, & R. C. Anderson (Eds.), *Research base for literacy.* Boston: D. C. Heath.

Cohen, D. K. (1990). A revolution in one classroom: The case of Mrs. Oublier. *Educational Evaluation and Policy Analysis, 12*(3), 311–329.

Cohen, D. K., & Ball, D. L. (1990). Relations between policy and practice: A commentary. *Educational Evaluation and Policy Analysis, 12*(3), 249–256.

Cook, B. G., Gerber, M. M., & Semmel, M. I. (1997). Are effective school reforms effective for all students? The implications of joint outcome production for school reform. *Exceptionality, 7*(2), 77–95.

Corcoran, T. B. (1985). Effective secondary schools. In R. M. J. Kyle (Ed.), *Reaching for excellence.* Washington, DC: U.S. Government Printing Office.

Corwin, R. G., & Dentler, R. A. (1984). *Structural barriers to dissemination.* Unpublished paper, National Institute of Education.

Cox, P. L., & Havelock, R. (1982). External facilitators and their role in the improvement of practice (A study of dissemination efforts supporting school improvement). Andover, MA: The Network.

Crandall, D. P., & Loucks, S. (1983). *People, politics, and practices: Examining the chain of school improvement.* Andover, MA: The Network.

Datnow, A., & Stringfield, S. (2000). Working together for reliable school reform. *Journal of Education for Students Placed at Risk, 5*(1 & 2), 183–204.

Deal, T. E., & Peterson, K. D. (1999). *Shaping school culture.* San Francisco: Jossey-Bass.

Deno, S. L. (1989). Problem solving and special education services: A fundamental and direct relationship. In M. Shinn (Ed.), *Curriculum-based measurement: Assessing special children.* New York: Guilford Press.

Edmonds, R. R. (1979). Some schools work and more can. *Social Policy, 9,* 32.

Elmore, R. F. (1996). Getting to scale with good educational practice. *Harvard Educational Review, 66,* 1–26.

Elmore, R. F., & McLaughlin, M. W. (1988). *Steady work: Policy, practice, and the reform of American education.* Santa Monica, CA: Rand.

Engelmann, S. (1992). *War against the schools' academic child abuse.* Portland, OR: Halcyon.

Evans, R. (1996). *The human side of school change.* San Francisco: Jossey-Bass.

Fink, E., & Resnick, L. (1999). *Developing principals as instructional leaders.* Unpublished paper. High performance learning communities project, Learning R&D Center, University of Pittsburgh (cited in Fullan, 2001a).

Fuhrman, S. H. (1992). *Uniting producers and consumers: Challenges in creating and utilizing educational research and development.* Paper presented at the International Seminar on Educational Research and Development, Washington, DC.

Fullan, M. G. (1982). *The meaning of educational change.* New York: Teachers College Press.

Fullan, M. G. (2001a). *Leading in a culture of change.* San Francisco: Jossey-Bass.

Fullan, M. G. (2001b). *The new meaning of educational change* (3rd ed.). New York: Teachers College Press.

Fullan, M. G., & Miles, M. B. (1992). Getting reform right: What works and what doesn't. *Phi Delta Kappan, 73*(10), 774–782.

Fullan, M. G., Miles, M. B., & Taylor, G. (1981). *Organization development in schools: The state of the art.* Washington, DC: U.S. Department of Education.

Gersten, R. (1990). Enemies—real and imagined: Implications of "Teachers' Thinking about Instruction" for collaboration between special and general education. *Remedial and Special Education, 11*(6), 50–53.

Gersten, R., Carnine, D., & Woodward, J. (1987). Direct instruction research: The third decade. *Remedial and Special Education, 8*(6), 48–56.

Gersten, R., & Dimino, J. (2001). The realities of translating research into classroom practice. *Learning Disabilities Research & Practice, 16*(2), 120–130.

Goldenberg, C., & Galimore, R. (1991). Local knowledge, research knowledge, and educational change: A case study of early Spanish reading improvements. *Educational Researcher, 20*(8), 2–14.

Goodlad, J. I. (1984). *A place called school: Prospects for the future.* New York: McGraw-Hill.

Grose, K. (2001). Partners in school innovation: An unusual approach to change facilitation. In F. O. Rust & H. Freidus (Eds.), *Guiding school change: The role and work of change agents.* New York: Teachers College Press.

Gross, N., Giacquinta, J. B., & Bernstein, M. (1971). *Implementing organizational innovation: A sociological analysis of planned change.* New York: Basic Books.

Hall, G. E. (1974). *The concerns-based adoption model: A developmental conceptualization of the adoption process within educational institutions* (ED 111 791). Austin: University of Texas, R&D Center for Teacher Education.

Hall, G. E., & Hord, S. M. (1987). *Change in schools: Facilitating the process.* Albany: State University of New York Press.

Hall, G. E., & Hord, S. M. (2001). *Implementing change: Patterns, principles, and potholes.* Boston: Allyn & Bacon.

Hamilton, J., Dailey, D., Mesmer, E., Ritter, S., Shami, M., Nishi, L., McInerney, M., Gerver, M., Corwin, H., & Bauman, W. (2002). *Elementary and Middle Schools Technical Assistance Center: Final evaluation report and adjustments.* Washington, DC: American Institutes for Research.

Hargreaves, A. (1996). Transforming knowledge: Blurring the boundaries between research, policy, and practice. *Educational Evaluation and Policy Analysis, 18*(2), 105–122.

Harris, S. L., Eiseman, J. W., Harris, R. C., Crandall, D. P. & Doyle, J. A. (1979). *Preparing for dissemination: A study of technical assistance for developer-demonstrator projects in the NDN*. Andover, MA: The Network.

Hatch, T. (2000). *What happens when multiple improvement initiatives collide*. Menlo Park, CA: Carnegie Foundation for the Advancement of Teaching.

Havelock, R. G. (1970). *A guide to innovation in education*. Ann Arbor: University of Michigan, Institute for Social Research.

Havelock, R. G., & Huberman, A. M. (1978). *Solving educational problems: The theory and reality of innovation in developing countries*. New York: Praeger.

Havelock, R. G., with Zlotolow, S. (1995). *The change agent's guide* (2nd ed.). Englewood Cliffs, NJ: Educational Technology Publications.

Hood, P. D. (1975). *Similarities and differences among and between producers, diffusers, and consumers of research: The need for communication*. Paper prepared for discussion at the Special Interest Group on Research Utilization at the annual meeting of the American Educational Research Association, Washington, DC.

House, E. R. (1981). Three perspectives on innovation: Technological, political, and cultural. In R. Lehming & M. Kane (Eds.), *Improving schools: Using what we know* (pp. 42–114). Beverly Hills, CA: Sage Publications.

Huberman, A. M. (1983). Recipes for busy kitchens: A situational analysis of routine knowledge use in schools. *Knowledge: Creation, Diffusion, Utilization, 4*(4), 478–510.

Huberman, A. M. (1995). Professional careers and professional development: Some intersections. In T. R. Guskey & A. M. Huberman (Eds.), *Professional development in education: New paradigms and practices*. New York: Teachers College Press.

Huberman, A. M., & Crandall, D. (1983). *Implications for action: A study of dissemination efforts supporting school improvement*. Andover, MA: The Network.

Huberman, A. M., & Miles, M. B. (1984). *Innovation up close: How school improvement works*. New York: Plenum.

Jarvis, P. (1987). *Adult learning in social context*. London: Croom Helm.

Kane, M. B., & Kocher, A. T. (1980). *The dissemination and use of educational R&D in the United States: An analysis of recent federal attempts to improve educational practice*. Paper presented at the conference on the Political Realization of Social Science Knowledge and Research: Toward New Scenarios, Vienna, Austria.

Kaufman, M., Schiller, E., Birman, B., & Coutinho, M. (1993). A federal perspective on improving practices, programs, and policies in special education. *Evaluation and Program Planning, 16,* 263–269.

Kennedy, M. M. (1991). Following through on follow-through. In E. A. Ramp & C. S. Pederson (Eds.), *Follow-through: Program and policy issues*. Washington, DC: U.S. Department of Education, Office of Education Research and Improvement.

Kotter, J. P. (1996). *Leading change*. Boston: Harvard Business School Press.

Kotter, J. P., & Cohen, D. S. (2002). *The heart of change: Real-life stories of how people change their organizations*. Boston: Harvard Business School Press.

Lee, G., & Barnett, B. (1994). Using reflective questioning to promote collaborative dialog. *Journal of Staff Development, 15*(1), 16–21.

Lewin, K. (1951). *Field theory in social science*. New York: Harper.

Lieberman, A. (2001). The professional lives of change agents: What they do and what they know. In F. O. Rust & H. Freidus (Eds.), *Guiding school change: The role and work of change agents* (pp. 155–162). New York: Teachers College Press.

Lippitt, R. O., Watson, J., & Westley, B. (1958). *The dynamics of planned change*. New York: Harcourt, Brace.

Little, J. W. (1982). Norms of collegiality and experimentation: Workplace conditions of school success. *American Educational Research Journal, 19,* 325–340.

Little, J. W. (1984). Seductive images and organizational realities in professional development. *Teachers College Record, 86*(1), 85–101.

Little, J. W. (1993). Teachers' professional development in a climate of educational reform. *Educational Evaluation and Policy Analysis, 15*(2), 129–151.

Loucks, S. F. (1977). *Levels of use of the innovation: The conceptualization and measurement of a variable useful for assessing innovation implementation by individuals.* Paper presented at the annual meeting of the American Educational Research Association, New York.

Loucks, S. F. (1983). *Defining fidelity: A cross-study analysis.* Paper presented at the annual meeting of the American Educational Research Association, New York.

Loucks-Horsley, S., & Roody, D. S. (1990). Using what is known about change to inform the regular education initiative. *Remedial and Special Education, 11*(3), 51–56.

Louis, K. S., Kell, D. G., Dentler, R. A., Corwin, R. G., & Herriott, R. E. (1984). *Exchanging ideas: The communication and use of knowledge in educational settings.* Washington, DC: National Institute of Education.

Louis, K. S., & Miles, M. B. (1990). *Improving the urban high school: What works and why.* New York: Teachers College Press.

Louis, K. S., & Rosenblum, S. (1981). *Linking R&D with schools: A program and its implications for dissemination and school improvement policy.* Washington, DC: U.S. Department of Education, Office of Education Research and Improvement.

Malouf, D. B., & Schiller, E. P. (1995). Practice and research in special education. *Exceptional Children, 61*(5), 414–424.

Marris, P. (1975). *Loss and change.* New York: Pantheon Books.

McDermott, R. P. (1993). The acquisition of a child by a learning disability. In S. Chaiklin & J. Lave (Eds.), *Understanding practice: Perspectives on activity and content.* New York: Cambridge University Press.

McInerney, M., Osher, D., & Kane, M. (1997). *Improving the availability and use of technology for children with disabilities.* Washington, DC: Chesapeake Institute.

McLaughlin, M. J., & Warren, S. H. (1992). *Issues and options in restructuring schools and special education programs.* College Park, MD: Center for Policy Options in Special Education.

McLaughlin, M. W. (1990). The Rand Study ten years later: Macro perspectives and micro realities. *Educational Researcher,* 11–16.

McLaughlin, M. W., & Talbert, J. E. (1992). *Social constructions of students: Challenges to policy coherence.* Paper presented at the symposium Bringing Together Diverse Perspectives on the Context of Secondary School Teaching conducted at the annual meeting of the American Educational Research Association, Washington, DC.

Miles, M. B. (1981). Mapping the common properties of schools. In R. Lehming & M. Kane (Eds.), *Improving schools: Using what we know* (pp. 42–114). Beverly Hills, CA: Sage.

Mishler, E. (1979). Meaning in context: Is there any other kind? *Harvard Educational Review, 49,* 1–18.

Mort, P. R. (1953). Educational adaptability. *The School Executive, 71,* 1–23.

Mort, P. R. (1964). Studies in educational innovation from the Institute of Administrative Research. In M. B. Miles (Ed.), *Innovation in education.* New York: Teachers College Press.

Osher, D., & Kane, M. (1993). Diversity and the challenge of improving educational outcomes: The case of students with serious emotional disturbance. In C. R. Ellie & N. N. Singh (Eds.), *Children and adolescents with emotional and behavioral disorders: Proceedings of the 3rd annual Virginia Beach conference.* Richmond, VA: Commonwealth Institute for Child and Family Studies.

Pellegrini, A. D., & Horvat, M. (1995). A developmental contextualist critique of attention deficit hyperactivity disorder. *Educational Researcher, 24*(1), 13–20.

Reigeluth, C., & Garfinkle, R. (1994). *Systemic change in education.* Englewood Cliffs, NJ: Educational Technology Publications. (ED 367 055)

Richardson, V. (1990). Significant and worthwhile change in teaching practice. *Educational Researcher, 19*(7), 10–18.

Rogers, C. R. (1951). *Client-centered therapy.* Boston: Houghton Mifflin.

Rogers, C. R. (1969). The characteristics of a helping relationship. In W. G. Bennis, K. D. Benne, & R. Chin (Eds.), *The planning of change* (2nd ed.). New York: Holt, Rinehart & Winston.

Rogers, E. M. (1962). *Diffusion of innovations.* New York: The Free Press.
Rogers, E. M. (1983). *Diffusion of innovations* (3rd ed.). New York: The Free Press.
Rogers, E. M. (1988). The intellectual foundation and history of the agricultural extension model. *Knowledge, 9,* 492–510.
Rogers, E. M. (1995). *Diffusion of innovations* (4th ed.). New York: The Free Press.
Rust, F. O., & Freidus, H. (2001). *Guiding school change: The role and work of change agents.* New York: Teachers College Press.
Sarason, S. B. (1982). *The culture of the school and the problem of change* (Rev. ed.). Boston: Allyn & Bacon.
Sashkin, M., & Egermeier, J. (1993). *School change models and processes: A review and synthesis of research and practice.* Washington, DC: U.S. Department of Education, Office of Educational Research and Improvement, Programs for the Improvement of Practice.
Showers, B., Joyce, B., & Bennett, B. (1987). Synthesis of research on staff development: A framework for future study and a state-of-the-art analysis. *Educational Leadership, 45*(3), 77–87.
Sieber, S. D. (1981). Knowledge utilization in public education: Incentives and disincentives. In R. Lehming & M. Kane (Eds.), *Improving schools: Using what we know* (pp. 42–114). Beverly Hills, CA: Sage.
Sieber, S. D., Louis, K. S., & Metzger, L. (1972). *The use of educational knowledge: Evaluation of the pilot state dissemination program* (Vols. 1 & 2). (ED 065–739–740). New York: Columbia University, Bureau of Applied Social Research.
Skirtic, T. M. (1991). Students with special education needs: Artifacts of the traditional curriculum. In M. Ainscow (Ed.), *Effective schools for all.* London: David Fulton.
Slavin, R. E. (1989). PET and the pendulum: Faddism in education and how to stop it. *Phi Delta Kappan, 70*(10), 752–758.
Smylie, M. A. (1995). Teacher learning in the workplace: Implications for school reform. In T. R. Guskey & A. M. Huberman (Eds.), *Professional development in education: New paradigms and practices.* New York: Teachers College Press.
Talbert, J. E., & McLaughlin, M. W. (1994). Teacher professionalism in local school contexts. *American Journal of Education, 102,* 123–153.
Turnbull, B. J. (1981). *Federal linkage alternatives: Types of help provided for school improvement by dissemination and technical assistance system.* Washington, DC: Educational Policy Development Center.
Turnbull, B. J. (1984). *Connecting dissemination with school improvement.* Washington, DC: National Institute of Education.
Turnbull, B. J. (1991). *Research knowledge and school improvement: Can this marriage be saved?* Paper prepared for the National Academy of Sciences/National Research Council Committee on the Federal Role in Education. Washington, DC: Policy Studies Associates.
Tyack, D., & Cuban, L. (1995). *Tinkering toward utopia: A century of public school reform.* Cambridge, MA: Harvard University Press.
U.S. Department of Education, Office of Special Education Programs. (1995). Research in the Education of Individuals with Disabilities of the Individuals with Disabilities Education Act. Washington, DC: Author.
Wagner, M., Blackorby, J., Cameto, R., Hebbeler, K., & Newman, L. (1993). *The transition experiences of young people with disabilities.* Menlo Park, CA: SRI International.
Yin, R. K., with Quick, S. K., Bateman, P. M., & Marks, E. L. (1978). *Changing urban bureaucracies: How new practices become routinized.* Santa Monica, CA: Rand.

Index

ACIE (Atlantic Coalition for Inclusive Education). *See* Case example, special education linking agent
Acquire stage, seeking and finding resources, xxix*fig.*, xxx, xxxiv
   case example, 109
   implementation costs, 131
   interstage connectedness, 195–198
   knowledge theory of change
      decision and implementation preparation, 99–100
      need side search, 98
      research *vs.* practice gap, 97–98
      resource tools, 100–101
      solution side search, 98–99
      specific problem and solution, 101–104
   linker's role, 78, 199–200
   materials acquisition
      alternative materials comparison, 105–106
      electronic resources, 106–110
      learning more about, 111–112
      material development levels, 104–105
      permanent capacity for, 111
   organizer questions, 77
   people theory of change, 86–87
      communication focus, 87
      expert information services, 93–95
      Internet search for people resources, 96–97
      limitations of, 95–96
      modelers of change, 92–93
      people as experts, 93–95
      process of change, 92–93
      using experts wisely, 95
   people theory of change, project leaders
      candidate questions, 91–92
      ideal candidate attributes, 88, 90
      recruitment strategy, 90–91
      the stand-outs, 88
      talent pool, 87
   programs and practices, 77–78
   project leader attributes of, 88
   in renewal stage, 179–180, 181, 188–189
   summary regarding, 112–113
   time, money, energy costs to acquire, 78
   See also Knowledge theory of change; Materials acquisition; Money theory of change; People theory of change; Summary and synthesis
Action, point of, 131
Action research, xv–xvi
Ad hoc testing, 138
Adaptation capability, 150
Adequacy rating dimension, 71
Adoption of innovation, adoption curve, 164*fig.*
   variations of, 164–165
      adopters, non-standard, 166–167
      case example, 165
      competition, coexistence, market dominance, 165
      development and diffusion interaction, 167
      innovator characteristics, 165–166
      observability, 166
      similarity to past innovations, 166
      simplicity, 166
      visibility of reward, 166
Adoption of innovation, phases of, 154–155, 155*fig.*

adoption decision, 156, 157
Adoption Process Model, 159
awareness, 155, 156
change agent activities linked to, 156–158, 156fig.
evaluation, 156, 157–158
integration, 156, 157
interest, 155–156, 157
trial, 157
Adoption of innovation, to larger system, 145, 159
accepting change and innovation, 160–161
common things, key people, 160
gaining group acceptance, 161–164
group acceptance strategies
adoption curve, 164fig.
adoption curve, variations of, 164–167
pro and con forces identification, 161–162
use key people as stepping stones, 162–153
win over the system, 163–164
innovators, 160
leaders, 160–161
resisters, 161
Adoption Process Model, 159
Advocacy, advocacy groups, xxi, 13–14, 198
American Institutes for Research, xiv, 84, 187
Analytic phase, of diagnostic process, 49–50, 54
adopt linking posture, 56–57
beware of obvious, 55
case example, 58
collaborate on diagnostic process, 56
identify opportunities, 56
rate data, prioritize real problems, 55
respect the obvious, 55
rethink and rework diagnosis, 57–58
search for underlying causes, 57
systemic analysis
change activity as temporary system, 65
communication environment, 64–65
diagnostician change agent, 199
goal achievement structure, 64
goal analysis, 63–64
research regarding, 65
rewards system, 65
system goals, 64
Argyris, C., 9
ASIG (Atlantic State Improvement Grant), CS 19
Assumptive outcome assessment, 138–139
Atlantic Coalition for Inclusive Education (ACIE). *See* Case example, special education linking agent
Atlantic State Improvement Grant (ASIG), CS 19

Ball, D. L., 63, 116
Barnett, B., 71
Bauman, W., xxiii, xxxiv, 9, 25
Bennett, B., 63, 117
Berman, P., 25, 29
Bernstein, M., 52
Blackorby, J., xxiii
Blind disability, xiii
Borko, H., 63
Bossert, S. T., 187
Brainstorming process
establish ground rules, 122–123
preparation, 122
in renewal stage, 181
set the stage, 122
summarize, synthesize, 123
Butler, J., 186

C-R-E-A-T-E-R process check list, xxviii, xxxiv
for project leader attributes, 88, 90
unfreeze-move-refreeze change model and, 4, 175
Cameto, R., xxiii
Care stage, establishing need for action, xxviii–xxix, xxixfig., xxxiv, 10fig.
advocate-catalyst change agent, 198
case example, 2–3, 9
Concerns-Based Adoption Model (CBAM), 8
discipline, alternative approaches to, 9, 22
do's and don'ts of, 16
helping instinct, xxvii
in-trouble indicators, 5–6
concerns all over the lot, 7, 9
concerns are intense, 8

concerns aren't what they seem, 7–8
personnel not engaged, 6–7
system is frozen, 6
system not leveling with outsiders, 7
trouble bubbling under the surface, 7
when everything seems fine, 6–7
inside forces, 10, 10*fig.*
educators inside school system, 11
families of students, 11
lack of synchronization, 11
parent and student advocates, 11
teachers or administrators, 11
unforeseen inside events, 11
interstage connectedness, 195–198
linking agent roles, 15
loss, anxiety, struggle, 8–9
making it worthwhile, 2–3
organizer questions, 1
outside forces, 10, 10*fig.*
federal laws and mandates, 13
inside-outside linking agent meetings, 12
linking agent role, skills, 12, 13
local community, 12–13
national advocates, groups, 13–14
new technologies, 14
popular culture and mass media, 14
unforeseen outside events, 14–15
project leader attributes of, 88
research regarding, 8–9
responsibility issues, 15–16
shared meaning, 8–9
special education linking agents example, 2–3
summary regarding, 17
superficial acceptance, false consensus, 9
too much caring, 2
unfreeze-move-refreeze change model, 3–5, 175
case example of, 4–5
permeable *vs.* unpermeable barriers, 4
stability barriers, 3
value issues, 15–16
See also Summary and synthesis
Carlson, R. O., 154
Carnine, D. W., xxiii, 100
Case example
of acquire stage, 109
of assessing innovations options, 121
of care stage, 2–3, 9
of change gone wrong, xxiv–xxvii
change agent as people-resource linker, xxxii
change agent as process helper, xxxii
change agent as solution giver, xxxii
of diffusion, 153
of discipline, alternative approaches to, 9, 22
of examine stage, 50–51, 68
of extend stage, 144
of innovation options assessment, 121
of modifications and adjustments, 127
of relate stage, 21, 22, 23, 33–34
of renewal stage, 174
of trial stage, 117
of try stage, 121, 127, 179
See also Case example, special education linking agent (chronological); Case example, special education linking agent (labeling exercise)
Case example, special education linking agent (chronological)
care stage
general education history, CS 2
special education history, CS 2
relate stage
establishing linking agent role, CS 2–CS 3
site selection, CS 2–CS 3
insider and outsider change team, CS 4–CS 5, 33–34
establishing external linkages, CS 6–CS 7
circle of participation expansion, CS 8–CS 9
implementation planning, CS 9
external and internal linkages strengthening, CS 9–CS 10
examine stage
establishing need for change, CS 4–CS 5
acquire stage
technical assistance liaison, CS 5
organizing a field trip, CS 7
try stage, 117, 121
initial response rejection, CS 5
finding the match, CS 6
planning the intervention, CS 6

bureaucratic hurdles, CS 6
shaping the message, CS 7–CS 8
try, CS 9
in-class demonstration and
    implementation, CS 10
more evaluation data, CS 13
second-year evaluation, CS 14
extend stage
    spreading process, CS 10
    spread to special education
        populations, CS 10–CS 11
    external linking and feedback,
        CS 11–CS 12
    planning continues, CS 12
    implementation solidification,
        CS 12–CS 13
    training event 2, CS 13–CS 14
    innovation reshaping, CS 14–CS 15
    evaluation platform strengthening,
        CS 15–CS 16
    diffusion extension, CS 16–CS 17
lessons learned
    change, resistance to, CS 23
    change, in spite of resistance,
        CS 23–CS 24
    building relationships equals
        success, CS 24
    systemic examination of needs,
        CS 24–CS 25
    innovation downsizing, rebuilding,
        CS 25
    demonstration, importance of, CS 25
    effects, spreading of, CS 25–CS 26
    innovation extension and
        strengthening, CS 21
    linking agent lessons, CS 21
setting, CS 2
theory *vs.* reality, CS 1
See also Case example, special
    education linking agent
    (labeling exercise)
Case example, special education linking
    agent (labeling exercise)
    resources acquisition, for new trial,
        CS 18–CS 19
    building new sense of caring, CS 19
    SIM model, training, CS 20
    resources acquisition, follow up, CS 20
    budget crisis, CS 21
    weakened response, CS 21
    linker role conflict, CS 21–CS 22
    frustrations, CS 22
    SIM model, awareness and interest
        extension, CS 22–CS 23
Catalyst linking agent role, xxxi, 7
    advocate-catalyst change agent, 198
    by experts, 93, 94
CBAM (Concerns-Based Adoption
    Model), 8, 146–147, 180
Center to Identify and Meet Technical
    Assistance Needs of Elementary and
    Middle Schools, xxiii
Centrality rating dimension, 71
Change agent
    advocate as, xxi
    assembling change team, 204
        content expertise, 205
        inside-outside status, 205
        process skill areas, 205
    content expert, xxi
    helping instinct in, xxvii
    importance of, xxxiii–xxxiv
    moral purpose concept, 8
    process consultant, helper, xxi–xxii
    role definition, 203–204
    who block change, 209
    See also Change process; Inside linking
        agent; Money theory of change;
        Outside linking agent; People
        theory of change; Summary and
        synthesis
Change process, xxiv
    action research validation, xv–xvi
    case example, xxiv–xxvii
    change agent role
        as catalyst, xxxi, 7
        as people-resource linker,
            xxxii–xxxiii
        as process helper, xxxii
        as solution giver, xxxii
    change as a content, xxiv
    checklist for, xxxiv
    connection theme, 202–203
    cycle of change, stages, xxviii,
        xxix*fig.*, xxxi
        acquire, xxx
        care, xxviii–xxiv
        examine, xxx
        extend, xxx
        relate, xxix–xxx
        renew, xxx
        try, xxx

definitions, xxvii
openness theme, 202
positive change, xxvii
as process of renewal, 173–174
research regarding, xxxi
in special education, xxiii
step-wise model of problem
 solving, xxxi
strategies, by system condition, 205
strategies, for frozen systems
 future potential, desired goals, 206
 inside advocacy, 205
 negative self-image reflection, 206
 outside stimulation, 206
strategies, for resource-poor systems
 build connections, 207
 identify hidden treasures, 207
 network to similar systems, 207
 realistic, significant goals, 207–208
strategies, for systems in conflict
 create improbable linkages, 207
 mobilize energy toward positive
  change, 206–207
 resolution as primary objective, 206
 superordinate values, concerns
  and goals, 206
strategies, for systems in disarray, 207
structure theme, 203
termination of, 192–193
See also Acquire stage, seeking and
 finding resources; Care stage,
 establishing need for action; Case
 example, special education
 linking agent; Examine stage,
 understanding the problem;
 Extend stage, gaining acceptance;
 Money theory of change; People
 theory of change; Relate stage,
 building a relationship; Renew
 stage, encouraging change;
 Summary and synthesis; Try
 stage, moving from knowledge
 to action
Client system, xxvii
Cohen, D. S., xxxi, 116, 117
Collaboration
 in data collection process, 56
 as knowledge resource, 101
 in problem identification, 56
 systematic diagnostic program, 70
 in trial expansion, 152

Collaborative Strategic Reading, CS 5
Communication skills
 communication environment, 64–65
 confrontation of differences, 45
 feedback solicitation and, 6–7
 of innovation expansion, 145, 167
  conferences, workshops, training
   events, 169–171
  demonstrations, 168
  electronic media, 171
  group discussion, 169
  multimedia program, 171, 178
  person-to-person contacts, 168–169
  video and film, 168
  written and oral presentations, 168
 listen, reflect, inquire, 67
 in people theory of change, 87
 in renewal stage, 191
 responsiveness, 42–43
 system analysis of, 64
Community, social environment
 linking agent relationship with,
  34–36, 35*fig.*
 outside linking forces, 12–13
Concerns-Based Adoption Model
 (CBAM), 8, 146–147, 180
Continuation
 adaptation capability, 150
 evaluation, 149
 factors of, 146
  administrative and political
   support, 150
  continuing evaluation, 149
  continuing maintenance, 149–150
  continuing reward, 148–149
  practice and routinization, 149
  structural integration, 149
 maintenance, 149–150
 research regarding, 146–147
 reward, 148–149
Cook, B. G., xxiii
Cooperative Extension Service, 154
Corcoran, T. B., 187
Corwin, H., xxiii, xxxiv, 9, 25, 63, 99
Corwin, R. G., xxxiii
Counselor. *See* School counselor
Cox, P. L., xxxiii
Crandall, D. P., xxxiii, 25, 99, 116, 117, 146
Cuban, L., 52, 63
Cycle survival of institutional
 change, 146

Dailey, D., xxiii, xxxiv, 9, 25
Data collection phase, of diagnostic
    process
  assemble data, 54
  lay out taxonomy, 53
  think system, 54
Data collection process, of diagnostic
    process
  case example, 68
  collaborative, systematic diagnostic
    program, 70
  diagnostic monitoring, 70–71
  group interviews, 68
  high-profile approach, 69–71
  key system informants, 67
  low-profile approach, 66–69
  observe, 68–69
  outside diagnostic research team, 70
  problem vocalizer technique, 66–67
  research regarding, 71
  self-diagnostic workshop, 70
  system outputs measurement, 69–70
Datnow, A., 51
Deaf disability, xiii
Deal, T. E., 9, 52, 71, 117
den Heyer, Isabel, xvii
Dentler, R. A., xxxiii, 63, 99
Department of Education, U.S., xxiii,
    31, 111
  diffusion programs, 154
  Internet resources of
    National Institute on Disability and
      Rehabilitation, 107
    Office of Special Education
      Programs, 107
    Rehabilitation Services
      Administration, 107
Deshler, Don, lii
Destructive confrontation, 73–74
Diagnostic knowledge, 119
Diagnostic tools. *See under* Examine
    stage, understanding the problem
Diffusion, diffusibility, 164*fig.*
  adoption of innovation, adoption
    curve variations, 164–165
    adopters, non-standard, 166–167
    case example, 165
    competition, coexistence, market
      dominance, 165
    development and diffusion
      interaction, 167
    innovator characteristics, 165–166
    observability, 166
    similarity to past innovations, 166
    simplicity, 166
    visibility of reward, 166
  adoption of innovation, phases of
    Adoption Process Model, 159
    recapitulating trial process, 159
    recruitment, 159
    sharing, discussing results, 158–159
    visits and observation, 159
  adoption of innovation, to larger
    system, 145, 159
    accepting change and innovation,
      160–161
    common things, key people, 160
    gaining group acceptance, 161–164
    innovators, 160
    leaders, 160–161
    resisters, 161
  case example of, 153
  demonstrability, 125
  diffusion change team, 159
  doability, 125
  extending adoption to larger
    system, 145
  going wider strategies and tactics, 145
  group acceptance strategies
    adoption curve, 164*fig.*
    adoption curve, variations of,
      164–167
    individual focus, 163
    pro and con forces identification,
      161–162
    use key people as stepping stones,
      162–153
    win over the system, 163–164
  innovation expansion strategies,
      145, 167
    conferences, workshops, training
      events, 169–171
    demonstrations, 168
    electronic media, 171
    group discussion, 169
    multimedia program, 171
    person-to-person contacts, 168–169
    video and film, 168
    written and oral presentations, 168
  labeling, 125–126
  packaging, 125, 158
  publicity, 133

showability, 125
small *vs.* large-scale change, 154
trialability, 125
See also Adoption of innovation, phases of; Adoption of innovation, to larger system
Dimino, J., 117
Discipline, alternative approaches to, 9, 22
Documentation, 135
Downing, Joyce Anderson, xvii
Doyle, J. A., 25

E-mail electronic resource, 110
Early literacy program. *See* Case example, special education linking agent
Early Literacy Project (ELP), CS 5–CS 17
Edmonds, R. R., 187
Education
  content issues, 59–60
  process issues, 59
  system issues, 60–61
  See also Department of Education, U.S.; Special education
Education for All Handicapped Children's Act, xiii, 8, 11
  See also Public Law 94–142
Education system. *See* School system
Educational Resources Information Center (ERIC), 103, 106–107
Effective schools movement, 187
Egermeier, J., xxxiii, 100, 186, 187
Eiseman, J. W., 25
Electronic resources. *See* Internet resources
Elementary and Middle Schools Technical Assistance Center (EMSTAC), xiv, CS 2–CS 3
  discipline, alternative approaches to, 9, 22
  funding from, 84
  Internet tool used by, 14
  list serves, 109
  Web site, 106
  See also Case example, special education linking agent
Elmore, R. F., 147, 154
ELP (Early Literacy Project), CS 5–CS 17
EMSTAC (Elementary and Middle Schools Technical Assistance Center), xiv, CS 2–CS 3
  funding from, 84
  Internet tool used by, 14
  list serves, 109
  Web site, 106
  See also Case example, special education linking agent
Englert, Carol Sue, CS 5–CS 6
Entry phase, of diagnostic process, 52–53
ERIC (Educational Resources Information Center), 103, 106–107
Evaluation
  case example, 146
  cautions regarding, 139
  by experts, 94–95
  of innovation trial, 103–104, 134
  of on-going trial, 149, 151, 156, 157–158
  of outcomes
    negative outcomes, 137
    null outcomes, 137
    positive outcomes, 137, 139
    program-specific outcomes, 136–137
  outcomes, measurement of
    ad hoc tests, 138
    assumptive outcome assessment, 138–139
    extension, copying, diffusion, 139
    standardized tests, 138
  of process
    keep a diary, 135–136
    preserve documentation, 135
    use written plan, 136
    team sharing of, 140
    using the results, 139–140
Evans, R., 116, 147
Examine stage, understanding the problem, xxix*fig.*, xxx, xxxiv
  analytic phase, 49–50, 54
    adopt linking posture, 56–57
    beware of obvious, 55
    case example, 58
    collaborate on diagnostic process, 56
    identify opportunities, 56
    rate data, prioritize real problems, 55
    respect the obvious, 55
    rethink and rework diagnosis, 57–58
    search for underlying causes, 57

case example, 50–51, 68
data collection phase
   assemble data, 54
   lay out taxonomy, 53
   think system, 54
data collection process
   case example, 68
   collaborative, systematic diagnostic program, 70
   diagnostic monitoring, 70–71
   group interviews, 68
   high-profile approach, 69–71
   key system informants, 67
   low-profile approach, 66–69
   observe, 68–69
   outside diagnostic research team, 70
   problem vocalizer technique, 66–67
   research regarding, 71
   self-diagnostic workshop, 70
   system outputs measurement, 69–70
diagnosis integration, 72–73
   limitations of, 73–74
diagnosis process, 49–50
   entry phase, 52
   initial conclusion, 52
   medical diagnosis analogy, 51
   problem from solution separation, 53
   quick fix, 53
diagnostic inventory, 57–63
   case management, 60–61
   definition of the domain, 58–60
   education content issues, 58–59
   education process issues, 59
   education system issues, 59–60
   equalization of opportunity, 61–62
   generation education curriculum, 62
   special education infrastructure, 63
   student classification and identification, 60
diagnostic matrix/checklist, 72
importance of, 51–52
interstage connectedness, 195–198
organizer questions, 49
problem identification, 50–52
   case example, 50–51
project leader attributes of, 88
research regarding, 51–52, 63, 65
set of rating dimensions
   adequacy, 71
   centrality, 71
   resource magnetism, 72
   system motivation, 71
summary regarding, 74–75
systemic analysis, 63–64
   communication environment, 64–65
   diagnostician change agent, 199
   goal achievement structure, 64
   research regarding, 65
   rewards system, 65
   system goals, 64
See also Summary and synthesis
Experts and expert information services
   acquiring and using wisely, 95
   as knowledge source, 93–94
   as legitimizer, 94
   as motivator and catalyst, 93
   as motivator-inspirational leader, 94
   as process and outcome evaluator, 94–95
   as process specialist, 93
   as role model and demonstrator, 94
Extend stage, gaining acceptance, xxix*fig.*, xxxiv
   adoption curve, 164–165, 164*fig.*
      competition, coexistence, market dominance, 165
      development and diffusion interaction, 167
      emergency responders, 167
      fast starters, 166
      forced adopters, 167
      jumpers, 166
      winner characteristics, 165–166
   adoption to larger system, 145, 159
      accepting change and innovation, 160–161
      common things, key people, 160
      gaining group acceptance, 161–164
      innovators, 160
      leaders, 160–161
      resisters, 161
   caring *vs.* understanding, xxx
   case example, 144
   diffusion specialist change agent, 200
   going wider strategies, tactics, 145, 167
      conferences, workshops, training events, 169–171
      demonstrations, 168

electronic media, 171
group discussion, 169
multimedia program, 171
person-to-person contacts, 168–169
video and film, 168
written and oral presentations, 168
interstage connectedness, 195–198
organizer questions, 141
project leader attributes, 88
proximate site expansion, 145
   adopting change, change agent activities, 156–158, 157*fig.*
   adopting change, phases of, 154–156, 155*fig.*
   diffusion research, 154
   growing initiative, 153
   wider diffusion, greater impact, 158–159
summary regarding, 171–172
trial site expanding change, 145
   adopters, 152
   features, 152
   evaluation data, 151
   implementation strategy changes, 152
   improvements focus, 152–153
   readapt innovation, 150–151
   shifting gears, 151–152
trial site solidification, 144
   administrative and political support, 150
   case example, 146
   continuation factors, 146, 148–150
   continuing adaptation capability, 150
   continuing evaluation, 149
   continuing maintenance, 149–150
   continuing reward, 148–149
   evaluation, 146
   first trial lessons, 147
   flexibility, 148, 151–152
   implementation, 146
   internalizing, 148
   practice and routinization, 149
   research regarding, 146–147
   second trial, 147–148
   structural integration, 149
See also Adoption of innovation, adoption curve; Adoption of innovation, phases of; Adoption of innovation, to larger system; Diffusion, diffusibility; Summary and synthesis

Familiarity, of linking agent, 42
Feasibility testing criteria, 118
   comparability of need, 124
   comparability of setting, 124
   compatibility, 124–125
   degree of benefit, 123–124
   diffusibility
      demonstrability, 125
      doability, 125
      labeling, 125–126
      packaging, 125
      showability, 125
      trialability, 125
   resistance factors, 124
   resources required, 124
   validity and reliability, 124
Fink, E., 29
Freidus, H., xxxiv
Friendliness, of linking agent, 41–42
Fuchs, Doug, CS 5
Fuchs, Lynn, CS 5
Fuhrman, S. H., 99
Fullan, M. G., xxxi, xxxiii, 8, 9, 25, 29, 99, 146, 180, 186

Galimore, R., 25
Garfinkle, R., 65
Gatekeepers, 22, 25, 39
General education teacher, as linking agent, 26–27, 26*fig.*
Gerber, M. M., xxiii
Gersten, R., 100, 117
Gerver, M., xxiii, xxxiv, 9, 25
Giacquinta, J. B., 52
Goldenberg, C., 25
Goodlad, J. I., xxiii
Grose, K., xxxiv, 41, 71
Gross, N., 52
Group interviews data collection method, 68
Guiding Change (Havelock and Hamilton)
   educator use of, xiv–xv
   functions of, xxiv–xxvii
   graduate student use of, xv–xvi
   instructor use of, xiv–xv
   as process change agent, xxi–xxii

Hall, G. E., xxxiii, 8, 41, 146, 147, 180, 116–117
Hamilton, J., xxiii, xxxiv, 9, 25
Hamilton, James, xix–xx
Hard money. *See* Money theory of change
Hargreaves, A., 63
Harris, R. C., 25
Harris, S. L., 25
Harwood, Pamela, xvii
Hatch, T., 9
Havelock, Ronald, xix, xxxiii, 25, 65
  change process research, xxxi
  See also Case example, special education linking agent (chronological)
Hebbeler, K., xxiii
Herriott, R. E., xxxiii, 63, 99
Hilldale County school district, xxxvi–xxxvii, 2–3
  See also Case example, special education linking agent
Holingsead, Candice, xvii
Hord, S. M., xxxiii, 8, 14y, 41, 116, 146, 180
Horvat, M., xxiii
Huberman, A. M., xxxiii, 8, 25, 41, 63, 65, 116, 117, 146

IDEA (Individuals with Disabilities Education Act), xiii, xxiii, 60, 61
  funding for, 80
  Part D programs, 13, 80
Individualized education programs (IEPs), 61
Individuals with Disabilities Education Act (IDEA), xiii, xxiii, 60, 61
  funding for, 80
  Part D programs, 13, 80
Innovation. *See* Adoption of innovation, phases of
Inside linking agent
  building a relationship
    inside advantages, 39
    inside disadvantages, 39–40
    inside-outside team, 34, 41
    outside advantages, 40
    outside disadvantages, 40–41
  in change process, 10, 10*fig.*
    educators inside school system, 11
    families of students, 11
    lack of synchronization, 11
    parent and student advocates, 11
    teachers or administrators, 11
    unforeseen inside events, 11
Inside-outside team
  experts and expert information services
    as knowledge source, 93–94
    as legitimizer, 94
    materials acquisition, 111
    as motivator and catalyst, 93
    as motivator-inspirational leader, 94
    as process and outcome evaluator, 94–95
    as process specialist, 93
    as role model and demonstrator, 94
  leadership potential, 90
  outside technical assistance, 116–117
  relationship building, 34, 41, 47
  systematic diagnostic program, 70
Integration, research regarding, 146–147
Internet resources, 14
  communication using, 171
  EMSTAC, 106
  for funding, 86
  people resource search, 96–97
  U.S. Department of Education
    National Institute on Disability and Rehabilitation, 107
    Office of Special Education Programs, 107
    Rehabilitation Services Administration, 107
  use of, 107–108
    e-mail, 110
    knowing when to stop, 109
    listservs, 109–110
    presearch, mid-search conferencing, 108
    printing and copying, 108
    sharing search experience, 108–109

Jarvis, P., 116
Joyce, B., 63, 117

Kane, M., 25, 154
Kane, M. B., 25
Kell, D. G., xxxiii, 63, 99
Kennedy, M. M., 25
Knowledge
  brainstorming and, 122, 123, 181
  diagnostic knowledge, 119

knowledge-linking change agent
concept, xxiii
from research base, 120
solution-oriented knowledge, 119
See also Knowledge theory of change
Knowledge base box concept, xxiii
Knowledge theory of change
knowledge acquisition strategies
decision and implementation, 99
external sources, 99–100
need search, 98
solution search, 98–99
stages of, 99
knowledge defined, 97
research regarding, 97, 99–100
research *vs.* practice, 97–98
resource tools
building awareness, 100
information systems, 101
maintaining awareness, 100
periodicals and mass media, 100–101
personal acquaintance network, 101
specific problem and solution
contact knowledgeable person, 102
observe innovation in operation, 102
obtain evaluation framework, 103–104
obtain evaluative data, 102–103
obtain innovation on trial, 103
obtain written source overview, 101–102
See also Materials acquisition
Kocher, A. T., 25
Kotter, J. P., xxxi

Labeling, 125, 128, 190
Leadership components, xxxi
Least Restrictive Environment/Neighborhood Inclusion Project, CS 2
Lee, G., 71
Legitimization, by experts, 94
Lewin, Kurt, xxxi, 4, 175
Lieberman, A., 180
Linking agent in change process
case study, 2–3, 4–5
vs. change agents, 208
concept explained, xxiii
vs. designated linkers, 208–209
in diagnostic process, 56–57
discipline, alternative approaches to, 9–10, 22
Guiding Change function of, xxiv
Hilldale County example, 2–3
importance of, xxxiii–CS 2
in-trouble indicators, 5–6, 5–9
concerns all over the lot, 7
concerns are intense, 8
concerns aren't what they seem, 7–8
personnel not engaged, 6–7
system is frozen, 6
system not leveling with outsiders, 7
trouble bubbling under the surface, 7
when everything seems fine, 6–7
inside forces, xxiii, 10, 10*fig.*
educators inside school system, 11
families of students, 11
lack of synchronization, 11
parent and student advocates, 11
problems faced, 11
teachers or administrators, 11
unforeseen inside events, 11
outside forces, xxiii, 10, 10*fig.*
federal laws and mandates, 13
inside-outside linking agent meetings, 12
linking agent role, skills, 12, 13, 14, 15
local community, 12–13
national advocates, groups, 13–14
new technologies, 14
popular culture and mass media, 14
unforeseen outside events, 14–15
process, xxi–xxii
synthesis of change roles, functions, 200–201
value issues in helping, 15–16
See also Care stage, establishing need for action; Case example, special education linking agent; Change agent; Change process; Relate stage, building a relationship; Summary and synthesis
Lippitt, R. O., xxxi
List serve electronic resources, 109–110
Listening skills, 67
Literacy program. *See* Case example, special education linking agent
Little, J. W., 25, 63, 116, 146

Llewellyn, C. Val, CS 1–CS 26
   See also Case example, special education linking agent
Local pride concept, 21
Loucks, S., xxxiii, 99, 116, 117, 146
Loucks-Horsley, S., 100
Louis, K. S., xxxiii, xxxiv, 63, 99, 100

Malouf, D. B., xxiii
Mariage, Troy, xl–xli
Marris, P., 9
Mass media factors, 14
   care stage, 14
   defusion, 171
   knowledge theory of change, 100–101
   renew stage, 178
Materials acquisition
   comparing alternative materials, 105–106
   costs regarding, 104, 105
   electronic resources
      e-mail, 110
      get others involved, 108
      knowing when to stop, 109
      listservs, 109–110
      presearch, midsearch conferencing, 108
      printing, copying, 108
      sharing Web searches, 108–109
      U.S. Department of Education, web sites, 106–107
      where, when to start, 106
   helping a system learn about, 111–112
   materials development levels, 104
      good ideas, 105
      production models, 105
      prototypes, 105
      validated models, 105
   in renewal stage, 179–180
   self-renewal capacity, 111
McDermott, R. P., xxiii
McInerney, M., xiii–xvi, xvii, xxiii, xxxiv, 9, 25, 154
McLaughlin, M. J., xxiii, 29
McLaughlin, M. W., xxiii, xxxiii, 25, 52, 63, 99, 116, 146, 154
Mental retardation, xiii
Mesmer, E., xxiii, xxxiv, 9, 25
Metropolitan Schools Study Council (Mort), 79
Metzger, L., xxxiv

Miles, M. B., xxxiii, 8, 41, 63, 99, 100, 116, 117, 146, 186
Minimum institutionalization, 147
MM (Morning Message) writing improvement method, CS 8–CS 17
Money theory of change, 78–79
   administrator support for funding, 81
   educational systems as economic entities
      federal funding, 79–80
      tax base funds source, 79
   hard money, 80–81
      innovations using, 81
      in renew stage, 185–186, 188–189
   limitations of, 80
   linker's role, 85–86
   Metropolitan Schools Study Council, 79
   money plus ideas focus, 79
   nonmonetary resources, 80
   smart *vs.* dumb money, 80
   soft money
      innovations using, 81–82
      pump priming, long run failure, 83–84
      pump priming, short run success, 82–83
      in renew stage, 185–186, 188–189
      smart money acquisition strategies, 84–85
      sustainability issue, 81
      uses for, 81–82
   See also Pump priming funding philosophy
Morning Message (MM) writing improvement method, CS 8–CS 17
Mort, Paul, 79, 154

National Defense Education Act, 19, 58, 106
National Diffusion Network (NDN), 31
National Institute on Disability and Rehabilitation Research (NIDRR), 107
NDN (National Diffusion Network), 31
Needs identification, 54
   prioritization, 55
   in special education, 63
   within system, xiii, CS 24–CS 25
Newman, L., xxiii

NIDRR (National Institute on Disability and Rehabilitation Research), 107
Nishi, L., xxiii, xxxiv, 9, 25
Nondirective counseling, xxi

OD (organization development), 186
Office of Special Education and Rehabilitative Services (OSERS), 107
Office of Special Education Programs (OSEP)
    Elementary and Middle Schools Technical Assistance Center, xiv
    funding from, 84
    national infrastructure focus, xiv
    Special Education Technical Assistance and Dissemination Network, xiv
    Web site of, 107
Onward to Excellence (OTE) social environment program, 186
Organization development (OD), 186
OSEP. *See* Office of Special Education Programs
OSERS (Office of Special Education and Rehabilitative Services), 107
Osher, D., 25, 154
Outside linking agent, CS 5
    building a relationship, 39
        inside-outside team, 34, 41
        outside advantages, 40
        outside disadvantages, 40–41
    in change process
        outside forces, xxiii, 10, 10*fig.*
        federal laws and mandates, 13
        inside-outside linking agent meetings, 12
        linking agent role, skills, 12, 13, 14, 15
        local community, 12–13
        national advocates, groups, 13–14
        new technologies, 14
        popular culture and mass media, 14
        roles of, 12
        skills, 13
        unforeseen outside events, 14–15
    inside-outside linking agent meetings, 12
    insider and outsider change team, CS 4–CS 5, 33–34
    reflective questioning, 71
    See also Inside-outside team

Packaging, 125, 128, 158, 180
PALS (Peer Assisted Learning Strategies), CS 5
Partners in School Innovation program (San Francisco, CA), xxxiv
Passage completion of institutional change, 146
Peer Assisted Learning Strategies (PALS), CS 5
Pellegrini, A. D., xxiii
People theory of change
    communication focus, 87
    expert information services, 93–95
    Internet search for people resources, 96–97
    limitations of, 95–96
    modelers of change and process of change, 92–93
    people as experts
        acquiring and using wisely, 95
        as knowledge source, 93–94
        as legitimizer, 94
        as motivator and catalyst, 93
        as motivator-inspirational leader, 94
        as process and outcome evaluator, 94–95
        as process specialist, 93
        as role model and demonstrator, 94
    people as resource focus, 86–87
    project leaders
        ideal candidate attributes, 88, 89–90*table*, 90
        questions asked by candidate, 91–92
        recruitment strategy, 90–91
        the stand-outs, 88
        talent pool, 87
    team approach to, 91
    using experts wisely, 95
Personal value context, 15–16
Peterson, K. D., 9, 52, 71, 117
Plan components
    act, 131
    budget, 131
    clearance, 130
    materials, 130
    site selection, 129–130
    staffing, 130
    timetable, 131
    training, 130
    user preparation, 130–131

Point of action, 131
Popular culture factors, 14
Positive reinforcement, 148–149
Power
    being used as a pawn, 45
    equal distribution of, 44–45
    of linking agent, 38, 39
Power of positive thinking, 122
POWER (plan, organize, write, edit, and rewrite) writing improvement method, CS 8–CS 17
Principal. *See* School principal
Problem vocalizer, 66
Process change linking agent, xxi–xxii
Process consultant or helper, xxi
Production model development level, 105
Prototype materials development level, 105
Public Law 94–142, xiii, xxiii, 11, 60
    reauthorization of, 13
    special education services, 61
Public Law 105–17, xiii, xxiii
Pump priming funding philosophy
    linking agent's role, 83
        broaden conception of resources, 86
        change team preparation, 85
        identify financial outside resources, 85
        in-system funding sources identification, 85
        Internet funding search, 86
        sort out money issues, 85
    long run failure
        demonstration failure, 83
        hard money budget inflexibility, 83
        plan and gain commitment failure, 83–84
    project failure, 83
    short run success, 82–83
    smart money acquisition strategies
        build awareness of money sources, 83
        involve hard money gatekeepers, 85
        match need to known resource pools, 83
        parade proposal, 85
        shape need into a proposal, 83
    soft *vs.* hard money, 82, 185–186
Putnam, R. T., 63

Recruitment, of project leaders, 90–91
Reedy, Kristin, xvii
Reflective questioning, 71
Rehabilitation Services Administration (RSA), 107
Reigeluth, C., 65
Relate stage, building a relationship, xxix*fig.*, xxxiv
    assessment tools, 47
    case example, 21, 22, 23, 33–34
    change team, xxix–xxx, 20
    danger signals, 20, 45–47
    ideal relationship, 47
        confrontation of differences, 45
        openness, 43
        power equality, 44–45
        realistic expectations, 43–44
        reciprocity, 43
        relevant parties, involvement of, 45
        reward expectations, 44
        structure, 44
        threat minimization, 45
    initial encounters, management of, 47
        familiarity, 42
        friendliness, 41–42
        responsiveness, 42–43
        rewardingness, 42
    inside *vs.* outside linking agent
        inside advantages, 39
        inside disadvantages, 39–40
        inside-outside team, 34, 41, 47
        outside advantages, 40
        outside disadvantages, 40–41
        social process consultant change agent, 199
    interstage connectedness, 195–198
    linker configurations
        change team members, 34
        community, social environment, 34–36, 35*fig.*
        district level special education office, 29–30, 30*fig.*
        general education teacher, 26–27, 26*fig.*
        other levels, other places, 30–31, 31*fig.*, 32*fig.*
        school counselor, 28–29
        school principal, 29
        special education teacher, 27–28, 28*fig.*

university-based linkers, 31–34
organizer questions, 19
primary group members, 20–21
    gatekeepers, 22, 25
    group leaders, 21–22
    group norms, 21
    influential members, 22
    key stakeholders, 22
    power centers, 23
project leader attributes of, 88
relationship stages, 36–37
    no prior relationship, 37
    redefining an existing relationship, 38–39, 179
    reestablishing a good relationship, 37–38
    reestablishing an uncertain relationship, 38
research regarding, 25
school district as social network, 20, 22–25, 24–25*fig.*
summary regarding, 47–48
tasks of, 18
See also Summary and synthesis
Relationships. *See* Relate stage, building a relationship
Renew stage, encouraging change, xxix*fig.*, xxx, xxxiv
    case example, 173, 174, 179
    change function installation
        annual activities, 190
        authority and legitimacy, 187–188
        connections, communication, authority, 191
        labels, 190
        process orchestration, 191–192
        reconfiguration and integration, 190–191
        resources, 188–189
        responsibilities, 191
        roles, 189–190
        standing committees, 190
        training, 190
        units, offices, 191
    change process explained, 173–174
    improving the process
        adding resources, 177
        buy-in from teachers, 177
        creating special events, 177–178
        developing skills, 177
        imposing more structure, 176
        intragroup inclusiveness, 178
        key persons and groups, 177
        more inclusive outreach, 177–178
        retrospection, 176
        streamlining, 176–177
        using media, 178
    interstage connectedness, 195–198
    keeping change fresh
        bring in new blood, 178–179
        nature of the concern redefinition, 179
        new resources and knowledge sources, 179–180
        reshape and repackage, 180
        respond to local environment changes, 179
        social unit redefinition, 179
    organizer question, 173
    project leader attributes of, 88, 90
    research regarding, 180, 186
    self-renewal capacity, 180
        change function internal to host system, 181
        external resources search, 181–182
        positive attitude, 181, 182
    summary regarding, 193
    system change consultant, 200
    system change features, 182–183
        budget changes, 185–186
        fundamental concerns, 184
        growing larger, 183
        more differentiation, 183
        more innovation, problem solving, 184
        more integration, 183
        more rewards, 183
        organization development, 186
        organizational chart changes, 184–185
        reform strategies, 186–187
        research regarding, 186
        rule changes, 186
    systems absorb changes, 175
    termination and moving on strategies, 192–193
    timing, 192
    See also Summary and synthesis
Resnick, L., 29

Resource magnetism rating dimension, 72
Resources
   access to, xxiv
   implementation costs, 131
   linking agent assigned, 38, 199–200
   in renew stage, 185–186, 188–189
   See also Acquire stage, seeking and finding resources
Responsiveness, of linking agent, 42–43
Rewards system
   adoption curve, 166
   in building a relationship, 42, 44
   in extend stage, 148–149
   for goal achievement, 65
   in renew stage, 183
   in systemic analysis, 65
Risk of change, 131–132
Ritter, S., xxiii, xxxiv, 9, 25
Rogers, Carl, xxi, 71
Rogers, E. M., 154
Roody, D. S., 100
Rosenblum, S., xxxiii, 100
Routinization of institutional change, 146, 149
RSA (Rehabilitation Services Administration), 107
Rust, F. O., xxxiv

Sarason, S. B., 52, 63
Sashkin, M., xxxiii, 100, 186, 187
Schiller, E. P., xxiii
School counselor, as linking agent, 28–29
School district, 20
School personnel, 20
School principal, as linking agent, 29
School system, 20, 54
   analysis of, 63–64
      change activity as temporary system, 65
      communication environment, 64–65
      goal achievement structure, 64
      rewards system, 65
      system goals, 64
   collaboration, 56
   data collection process
      case example, 68
      collaborative, systematic diagnostic program, 70
      diagnostic monitoring, 70–71
      group interviews, 68
      high-profile approach, 69–71
      key system informants, 67
      low-profile approach, 66–69
      observe, 68–69
      outside diagnostic research team, 70
      problem vocalizer technique, 66–67
      self-diagnostic workshop, 70
      system outputs measurement, 69–70
   as economic entity, 79–80
   educational system issues, 59–60
   educative content issues, 58–59
   educative process issues, 59
   strengths identification in, 56
Self-renewal capacity, 111
Semmel, M. I, xxiii
Shami, M., xxiii, xxxiv, 9, 25
Showers, B., 63, 117
Sieber, S. D., xxxiv, 63
SIM (Strategic Instruction Model), CS 19–CS 23
Site selection issues, 129–130
Skirtic, T. M., xxiii
Smylie, M. A., 116, 117
Social setting of reform, xxiv
Social skills training, elementary and middle school, 9
Social system, school as, 20, 54
Soft money. *See* Money theory of change
Solution-oriented knowledge, 119
Special education
   case management, 60–61
   change process focus in, xiv–xv, xxiii
   diffusion programs, 154
   equalization of opportunity, xiii 61–62
   federal funding, 79–80
   federal support for change in, xiv
   general education curriculum access, 62
   historical perspective on, xiii
   individual needs focus, xiii
   individualized education programs, 61
   infrastructure of, 63
   knowledge *vs.* practice gap, xxiii
   money sources for, 84
   research *vs.* practice gap, 97–98
   resistance factors, 63
   student classification, identification for, 60
   as a system, xxvii

team approach to, 91
technology innovation, xxii
trial stage case example, 117
See also Special education teacher;
    Summary and synthesis
Special education teacher, as linking
    agent, 27–28, 28*fig.*
Special Education Technical Assistance
    and Dissemination Network, xiv
Staffing, 130
Stakeholders, 22
    evaluation results, sharing with, 140
    outcomes
        measurement of, 138–139
        positive/negative, 137
    resistance from, 133
Standardized tests, 138
Strategic Instruction Model (SIM),
    CS 19–CS 22
Stringfield, S., 51
Summary and synthesis
    change agent per stage
        acquire stage, resource linker,
            199–200
        caring stage, advocate-catalyst, 198
        examine stage, system
            diagnostician, 199
        extend stage, diffusion specialist, 200
        relate stage, social process
            consultant, 199
        renew stage, system change
            consultant, 200
        roles and functions synthesis, 200–201
        trial stage, solution giver, 200
    change agents blocking change, 209
    change process complexity, 195
    change team assembly, 204
        content expertise, 205
        inside-outside status, 205
        process skill areas, 205
    intrastage connections, 201–202
        connection, 202–203
        openness, 202
        structure, 203
    linkers in larger context
        vs. change agents, 208
        vs. designated linkers, 208–209
        importance of, 209–210
    role definition, 203–204
    stage detail summary, 195–196
    stages interrelating, 196–198

strategy development
    for frozen systems, 205–207
    for low-capacity systems, 207
    for resource-poor systems, 207–208
    system condition focus, 205
    for systems in disarray, 207
System
    analysis of
        change activity as temporary
            system, 65
        communication environment, 64–65
        goal achievement structure, 64
        goal identification, 63–64
        rewards system, 65
        system goals, 64
    client system, xxvii
    data collection process
        case example, 68
        collaborative, systematic diagnostic
            program, 70
        diagnostic monitoring, 70–71
        group interviews, 68
        high-profile approach, 69–71
        key system informants, 67
        low-profile approach, 66–69
        observe, 68–69
        outside diagnostic research team, 70
        problem vocalizer technique, 66–67
        self-diagnostic workshop, 70
        system outputs measurement, 69–70
    defined, xxvii
    diagnostic inventory of, 57–63
        case management, 60–61
        domain definition, 58–60
        education content issues, 58–59
        education process issues, 59
        education system issues, 59–60
        equalization of opportunity, 61–62
        generation education curriculum, 62
        special education infrastructure, 63
        student classification and
            identification, 60
    as economic entity, 79–80
    examination of needs, CS 24–CS 25,
        54, 55
    school as social system, 54
    special education as, xxvii
    strengths identification in, 56
    system openness concept, 4
System motivation rating
    dimension, 71

Talbert, J. E., xxiii, 52, 63
Taxonomy
   as classification system, 53
   needs assessment, 54, 55
Taylor, G., 186
Team approach, to special education, 91
Technology
   in special education, xxii
Timetable of implementation, 131
Training, 25, 130
   case example, CS 13–CS 14, CS 20
   communication skills, 169–171
   during implementation, 130, 132
   in renew stage, 190
   social skills, 9
Trial. *See* Try stage, moving from knowledge to action
Trivialization, in assessment, 63
Try stage, moving from knowledge to action, xxix*fig.*, xxx, xxxiv, 118
   adapt the innovation, 126–127
      minimize redevelopment, 127–128
      repackage, relabel, 128
   alternative solutions, 118, 120–122
      assessing options, 121
      brainstorming, 122
      case example, 121
      establishing ground rules, 122–123
      preparing, 122
      setting the stage, 122
      summarizing, synthesizing, 123
   case example, 117, 121, 127, 179
   derive implications, 118, 120
   emphasize opportunities, 121
   ideal model focus, 121
   interstage connectedness, 195–198
   organizer questions, 115
   outcomes
      negative outcomes, 136, 137
      null outcomes, 136, 137
      positive outcomes, 136, 137
      program-specific outcomes, 136–137
   outcomes, measurement of
      ad hoc tests, 138
      assumptive outcome assessment, 138–139
      extension, copying, diffusion, 139
      standardized tests, 138
   outside technical assistance, 116–117
   plan the implementation
      accepting risk, 131–132
      accepting stumbles, 133
      flexible plan, 129
      good plan components, 129–131
      managing resistance, 133
      overcoming inertia, 132
      publicity, 133
      shared plan, 129
      test integrity, 133
      timing, 132–133
      training, 132
      written plan, 128–129
   pretrial feasibility testing criteria, 118
      comparability of need, 124
      comparability of setting, 124
      compatibility, 124–125
      degree of benefit, 123–124
      diffusibility, 125–126
      resistance factors, 124
      resources required, 124
      validity and reliability, 124
   project leader attributes of, 88
   research regarding, 116–117
   results, evaluation of, 134–135
      cautions regarding, 139
      keep a diary, 135–136
      preserve documentation, 135
      written plan, 136
   results, use of, 139–140
      package the findings, 140
      team sharing, 140
   search stage findings, 118
      diagnostic knowledge, 119
      solution-oriented knowledge, 119
   solution giver change agent, 200
   summary regarding, 140–141
   trial experiment, 116–118
   See also Summary and synthesis
Turnbull, B. J., xxxiii, 100
Tyack, D., 52, 63

Underlying causes, search for, 57
United Nations teacher-training projects, 25
University-based linking agents, 31–34
User preparation, 130–131

Validated model development level, 105
Value context, of change, 15–16
Vaugh, Sharon, CS 5

Wagner, M., xxiii
Warren, S. H., xxiii
Waterford Early Reading Program, 146
Watson, J., xxxi
Web. *See* Internet resources

Westley, B., xxxi
Woodward, J., 100
World Wide Web. *See* Internet resources

Yin, R. K., 146

The Corwin Press logo—a raven striding across an open book—represents the union of courage and learning. Corwin Press is committed to improving education for all learners by publishing books and other professional development resources for those serving the field of K–12 education. By providing practical, hands-on materials, Corwin Press continues to carry out the promise of its motto: **"Helping Educators Do Their Work Better."**